THE NOVEL

The Novel

Language and Narrative from Cervantes to Calvino

André Brink

NEW YORK UNIVERSITY PRESS
Washington Square, New York

© André Brink 1998

First published in the U.S.A. in 1998 by
NEW YORK UNIVERSITY PRESS
Washington Square
New York, N.Y. 10003

This book is printed on paper suitable for recycling and
made from fully managed and sustained forest sources.

CIP data available from the Library of Congress
ISBN 0–8147–1330–0

Printed in Malaysia

Literature is, and cannot be anything but, a kind of extension and application of certain properties of language

– Paul Valéry

Literature knows [. . .] that in writing one cannot say anything extraneous to writing, or express any truth that is not a truth having to do with the art of writing

– Italo Calvino

Contents

Introduction:
Languages of the Novel

1

The Age of Realism, in many ways the last great affirmation of the Enlightenment with its impressively self-confident faith in reason and in reason's access to the real, drew to an end as the nineteenth century began to spill into the twentieth. In a turmoil of uncertainty prefiguring Eliot's later wry conviction that 'human kind / Cannot bear very much reality', Modernism was born. A remarkable revolution swept through all the arts. The faith in representation, which for so long had shaped Western culture, was wavering; and, in Santayana's famous phrase, mankind started dreaming in a different key.

In the arts this new key was determined by a widespread discovery – or, in some cases, rediscovery – of the medium as the message. From Cézanne onwards, painting turns its back on a long tradition of 'truth to nature' as it begins to focus on the materiality of paint on canvas. The theatre renounces its earlier attempts to create the perfect illusion and in the plays of Pirandello and his contemporaries embraces the space of the stage as stage (which to Shakespeare would have been nothing new). In Stravinsky, and even more so in Schönberg, music is no longer to be enjoyed simply as a melodic system but turns its attention to the very processes which *produce* melody.

And so it is only to be expected that literature, too, begins to foreground its own medium, language, first in the poetry of Mallarmé and Rimbaud, and the fiction of Flaubert and Henry James. Soon, from the ranks of early Modernists, amplified by that time by what Kundera (1988:63) calls the 'polyhistoricism' of Broch and the conjuring acts of memory performed by Proust, rose the definitive figure of James Joyce. As McGee (1988:2) phrases it, 'At every phase in the development of recent literary theory, Joyce appears as an example and an authentic symptom of his and our historical moment.'

Starting with the early dissolution and reassembling of sentence structures to accompany the emotional ebb and flow in *A Portrait of the Artist as a Young Man*, moving with dizzying virtuosity through

1

the ever-changing languagescapes in *Ulysses*, Joyce finally pushes language to an extreme in *Finnegan's Wake*, perhaps the single greatest narrative monument of the twentieth century, comparable to Picasso's achievement in *Les Demoiselles d'Avignon* or *Guernica*. As MacCabe, a pivotal critic in Joyce criticism, so convincingly demonstrated, Joyce's writing radically changes the entire relationship between text and reader, moving from one of passive consumption to active engagement and transformation. Reading becomes 'an active appropriation of the material of language' (MacCabe 1978:11). In opposition to the nineteenth-century manipulation of 'metalanguage' by Eliot and others, (that is, an authorial language through which the many languages of different characters in the text are ultimately controlled in order to guide the reader in establishing what is real or true and what not),[1] Joyce offers no correctives, no final truths, and forces the reader to become actively involved in the free play of language through the various discourses of the novel. Even if, as McGee and many others have since indicated, MacCabe underestimates the functions of interpretation, his watershed reading of Joyce firmly established the primacy of language *as* language in the Modernist (and later the Postmodernist) novel. In many respects the whole of the Postmodernist novel – from Beckett to Nabokov, from Robbe-Grillet to Márquez, from Calvino to Barth, from Pynchon to Kundera – may be said to be spinoffs from *Ulysses* and *Finnegan's Wake*. This is particularly important in the sense that '*Ulysses* and *Finnegan's Wake* are concerned *not with representing experience through language but with experiencing language through a destruction of representation*' (MacCabe 1978:4, my emphasis).

Not that one should underestimate the 'story' level in these two novels: there are magnificent narrative impulses throughout both of them, and purely in terms of an old-fashioned 'plot' they are among the richest texts in the genre. But ultimately all these various stories collapse, like old stars into a Black Hole, within the language in which they are told. Language becomes its own greatest story. In *Ulysses*, among so many other things, 'the story of language' is told in the hospital chapter, where the reader witnesses, and is drawn into, the evolution of the English language from Anglo-Saxon to American jazz-speak; and in *Finnegan's Wake* the whole history of Ireland, telescoped into that of a hod-carrier, assumes the form of language. This must be understood quite literally: the text does not 'tell the story in language' but *transforms the story into language*. Language becomes the condition of story.

At the same time these novels are amazingly dense *intertexts*, subsuming within them something of the history of the novel as a genre – reaching back across the centuries to the epics of Homer and the sagas of Iceland and the myths and folktales of Ireland; but also, and very specifically, to Joyce's predecessors in English fiction and drama. In the process the two novels prepare the soil for a further flowering of texts that will draw on *them*. Writing produces more writing, stories prompt more stories, and each of these erupts in versions of the other.

This becomes the hallmark of the Postmodernist novel during the closing decades of the twentieth century, a development so spectacular, so widespread, and so charged with diverse energies that it brought in its wake a frenzy of critical and theoretical activity and an increasing polarisation of *aficionados* and detractors. But whatever the merits and demerits of the phenomenon (and it is prudent to remind oneself that the label 'Postmodernism' has been, since its inception, no more than an umbrella term for a staggering variety of forms, styles, experiments and manifestations),[2] there is one crucial aspect on which there appears to be consensus: the foregrounding of *language* – language as language, language in its implication with narrative.

This preoccupation concerns what Lodge (1966) reads as the 'language of fiction', but also goes far beyond it: it involves, paradoxically, both the celebration and the radical subversion of language. It is a celebration in its often over-the-top demonstration of the spectacular properties of language; and simultaneously a subversion in the way in which, increasingly, language spectacularises its own opacities, and attempts to erase itself in the process of writing. Looking back from the end of the twentieth century, it seems inevitable that the great adventure of Modernism and Postmodernism in the novel should eventually produce the kind of text exemplified by Salvador Elizondo's *The Graphographer*, a passage from which serves as epigraph to Mario Vargas Llosa's *Aunt Julia and the Scriptwriter* (1983):

I write. I write that I am writing. Mentally I see myself writing that I am writing and I can also see myself seeing that I am writing. I remember writing and also seeing myself writing. And I see myself remembering that I see myself writing and I

remember seeing myself remembering that I was writing and I
write seeing myself write that I remember having seen myself
write that I saw myself writing that I was writing and that I was
writing that I was writing that I was writing. I can also imagine
myself writing that I had already written that I would imagine
myself writing that I had written that I was imagining myself
writing that I see myself writing that I am writing.

There are many philosophical aspects of this passage that invite
comment – not least of which would be an insight illustrated by a
child's description of remembering quoted in a recent psychological study (Loftus & Ketcham 1994:38): 'My memory is the thing I
forget with.' But for the moment our concern is with the focus on
language as, itself, a narrative activity.

But what does this mean for our reading of the novel? And is this
really as new as it sounds?

                                    2

Our response may borrow from the experience of painters and
their public in the second half of the nineteenth century when the
rise of photography caused great turmoil in the field of art: there
were painters who renounced their *métier* because photography
appeared to have taken over what many artists, for a very long
time, had come to regard as the prerogative of *their* art: the faithful
visual representation of nature (or of history; or of dreams, or
whatever). But there were others to whom the experience was
truly liberating, as they discovered – or rediscovered – that the
primary business of painting had *never* been visual representation
as such but, instead, the exploitation of all the possibilities available in the process of bringing paint and canvas together. From the
passionate immersion of the Impressionists in the here-and-now of
the fleeting instant which they attempted to translate into brush-
strokes and daubs of paint, arose the acknowledgement that even
in the most 'realistic' periods of painting the artist's true vocation
had always been the processes of interaction with his/her material.
Retrospectively this was acknowledged to have been as true of
Corot as of Rembrandt, as true of Jan Steen as of Bosch, as true,
in fact, of Leonardo as of Zeuxis (whose painting of grapes, it is
said, was so true to life that birds came to peck at it).

This does not imply that these artists as individuals were necessarily conscious of it: but *painting* was aware of it, as it pursued the never-ending dialogue between pigments of different kinds on surfaces of different kinds. The final confirmation of the discovery, if confirmation was still required, came with the shock provided by Mondrian, Malevitch and Kandinsky in their 'abstract art' – which was arguably the most 'concrete' form of painting the world had seen up to that point, confronting the viewer with the unmediated reality of paint as paint, the whole of paint, and nothing but paint.

And it is my argument that the same may be said of language and the novel. It is in narrative language, I believe, that one should look for the key to the full experience of engaging with the genre. 'It is the world of words', says Lacan (1977:65), 'which creates the world of things.' One is reminded of Magritte's famous painting of a pipe bearing the title *Ceci n'est pas une pipe – This is not a pipe*, which is, of course, strictly true: what we have before us is not a pipe but a painting of a pipe. This can be confirmed, in the domain of literature, by any reader who takes up a book to make the simple and basic, but immensely significant, discovery that there are no people or houses or trees or dogs between the pages, but only words, words, words.

Of course this holds for any literary artefact from any period, not just for the novel; but it makes sense to acknowledge, in narrative, the radical shift brought about by the invention of printing. As Bakhtin, among others, argued, the displacement of the epic poet's voice by the written narrative of the novelist, also meant that the reader, previously a listener, entered into a completely different relationship with language – and with narrative. *Here* lie, already, the roots of what Joyce rediscovered at the beginning of the twentieth century. This, it seems to me, provides the key to what may justifiably be called the novel experience.[3]

Language, as Bakhtin also notes (in Shukman 1983:94), remained the 'raw material' of the narrator, but because of the uniqueness of the signifying system embodied in language (unlike 'a piece of clay [which] on its own *has no meaning*': Bakhtin: loc. cit.), the interaction between *what* was said and *how* it was said, between medium and message, between what was traditionally and artificially separated as form and content, was altered decisively. More than had ever been the case in oral/aural literature, language in the novel became important, not as 'the embodiment of some kind of cultural essence, but the use of language in a particular place and time'

(Ashcroft et al. 1989:71–2). And the significance of language lies in the perception that it exists 'neither before the fact nor after the fact but in the fact [...] It provides some terms and not others with which to talk about the world' (ibid.:44). Even more radically, language in the novel did not only tell a story, but reflected on itself in the act of telling.

If this is true of those great fanfares and fun-fairs of novels written by Rabelais, Cervantes or Sterne, finally to erupt in Joyce and his successors, it is my argument that this is *no less true* of the most 'classical' or 'traditional' or 'realistic' of novels, whether by Defoe, or Marivaux, or Jane Austen, or Stendhal, or Manzoni, or Zola.

3

The question is whether there has ever been anything like 'the' traditional or classical novel. I tend to share Bakhtin's belief that for a genre in an unceasing process of *becoming*, there *is* no singular Great Tradition, no Ideal Form, no Definitive Shape. Or, if tradition there be, it may just as well be approached, as Kundera does with such panache in *The Art of the Novel* and *Testaments Betrayed*, as a series of texts rich in invention, humour and imaginative eruption, a legacy of 'testaments' to which authors like Gombrowicz, Broch and Musil restored the novel of the twentieth century.

Yet I differ most emphatically from Kundera when he argues that this is the only 'real' or 'true' history of the novel and that those early testaments were 'betrayed' by the Realism of the eight-eenth and nineteenth centuries. Not only did the older testaments persist in Sterne and Diderot and de Sade, in Kleist and Emily Brontë and much of Dostoevsky, but Realism itself opened up whole new landscapes to be explored by the novel in its inherence in language. Joyce is not only the heir of Sterne but also of Defoe and Fielding. Inasmuch as Realism came to be perceived as the 'only' Great Tradition of the novel, of course it had a pernicious influence. But it seems unfair to blame the *novel* for the restricted vision of a *critical* tradition endorsed by Ian Watt.

I should make it very clear from the outset that I am not propos-ing, in this book, to offer a new or 'alternative' History of the Novel (although much may be said for such a project). My argument is quite simply that what has so persistently been regarded as the prerogative of the Modernist and Postmodernist novel (and of a few rare predecessors), namely an exploitation of the storytelling properties of language, *has in fact been a characteristic of the novel since its inception.*[4] It informs the great, 'obvious' texts (of which *Ulysses* must remain the prime example), but also the most 'conventional' ones, from Madame de Lafayette to George Eliot, or from Fielding to Trollope, or from Fanny Burney to Anthony Powell. And by the time language began to flaunt itself, through more and more spectacular devices, as the primary business of the novel in Modernism and Postmodernism, it is my contention that it had by then already established a remarkable tradition of proving just that, if in less obtrusive ways.

But in order to illuminate this claim it is necessary to start with as simple and basic a view of language as possible.

4

Two small boys strike up a quarrel which turns into a fight. Their mother intervenes and demands to know what has happened. In the way we all, ceaselessly, transform our lives into language, into story, they offer her their versions of the event. Language *as* story, as invention, as accusation or excuse, as explanation or justification, as alibi or apology or attack. Each of the boys, knowing that his backside depends on it, does his utmost to persuade the mother; to persuade himself. Which version will she believe? Everything depends on that. And, given the framework of a patriarchal culture, how will she report the event to her husband when he comes home that evening? Pursuing it even further, if, at work the following day, he finds an occasion to tell an anecdote which might assert his authority, or ingratiate him with his superiors, or simply smooth over a boring or embarrassing situation, into what new narrative territory will his language take him, his wife, and his sons? Into what new territories are *we* (as readers, as observers, as participants) being enticed?

From the moment the event was first reported – or even more precisely, from the moment it had first been verbalised in order to be made reportable – it has existed exclusively in terms of language. This is the origin of history; it is also the origin of narrative.

It may be said that what we have dealt with so far essentially involves speech acts, as described *inter alia* by Austin (1962) or

Searle (1969 and 1974). In the process of communication, each of these acts involves a threefold process: it is a *locution*, which is the fact of utterance; it is an *illocution*, which denotes the act performed *in* saying something (this concerns the difference between a simple statement, a question, an exclamation, a warning, a threat, or whatever); it is also a *perlocution*, in which the anticipated or presumed result of the locution determines its interpretation. In schematic form, this is vested in the triangular relationship between speaker, speech and listener – or, in terms of the familiar model described by Jakobson (1960:350–77), sender, message and receiver.[5] Within this relationship, the locution is perceived only in its own terms, isolated from any specific context or situation (something which is literally unthinkable), while the illocution involves the relationship between the speaker and the speech, and the perlocution the full and complex relationship between all three of the impulses comprised in the act.

The starting point of the exercise is the conception of language as an act of communication: after all, 'Language, when it *means*, is somebody talking to somebody else, even when that someone else is one's own inner addressee', as Michael Holquist points out in his introduction to Bakhtin's seminal essays on the novel (Bakhtin 1981:xxi).

Now to be useful in the description of language in fiction, this notion of speech as an act has to be modified and complicated, in order for us to accept the locution or utterance (the 'facts' of the story) as 'real' while acknowledging the illocution as make-believe, that is as 'fiction'.[6] Or, in David Lodge's simpler terminology (1990:96), we must approach the literary text, 'not [as] a real speech act but an imitation of a speech act'. And, even more so in the case of a highly complex form of narrative like a novel, 'what is commonly called a "message" is in fact a *text* whose content is a multilevelled *discourse*' (Eco 1979:57).

I do not propose to follow the processes involved in this cluster of theories through all their intricate meanderings; all I need at this stage to borrow from it is the notion of narrative itself as an act (or the imitation or imagining of an act): an act of language – taking due note of Derrida's concept of language, not as 'speech' but as *writing*, as *écriture*.[7] Of course, speech acts are involved every time characters in a novel enter into a dialogic situation (whether they actually converse or interact in other ways), but the important consideration is that the narrative as a whole may itself be read as an extension and complication of such acts in its constantly shifting position somewhere between the narrator and the reader. In the transaction between narrator and reader, as Barthes so succinctly demonstrates in *S/Z* (1975:89), an act of *exchange* is involved: 'One narrates in order to obtain by exchanging; and it is this exchange that is represented in the narrative itself: narrative is both product and production, merchandise and commerce, a stake and the bearer of that stake.'

This does not mean that language and narrative are necessarily the same thing. Yet they are more than merely 'analogous'. In some respects language may be regarded as a *form* of narrative; but it would be just as admissible to see narrative as a form of language. As Lacan said of language and the unconscious, one may say of language and narrative that the one is shaped like the other. More specifically tuned in to our present purpose, it may be said that *language has a propensity for narrative.*

5

A host of theorists have been assiduously exploring the links between language and narrative. In *The Poetics of Prose* Todorov examines language as a *model* for narrative, and syntax for narrative grammar, bearing in mind the distinction between 'mediatized' and 'immediate' language (Todorov 1977:27). This is in line with the way in which Searle and other Speech Act theorists like Ohmann (1971), Fish (1976) or Pratt (1977) have bridged the gap. Todorov takes as his starting point the coincidence of parts of speech in grammar with specific narrative functions: nouns provide a model for one's reading of characters; predicates illuminate the concept of plot; in the same way narrative parallels are found for adjectives and verbs. From here, Todorov proceeds to the secondary categories of grammar, 'which are the properties of these parts: for instance, voice, aspects, mood, tense, and so forth' (Todorov 1977:113). And beyond the level of propositions, Todorov discusses the possible relations between such propositions – relations of time, of logic, or of space.

His conclusion is of particular relevance to the present discussion: 'Ultimately, language can be understood only if we learn to think of its essential manifestation – literature. The converse is also true: to combine a noun and a verb is to take the first step toward

narrative. In a sense, what the writer does, is to read language'
(ibid.:119).

The exploration of such links between narrative and grammar
have resulted in a whole school of 'narrative grammar' within
narratology (for example Gerald Prince: 1982). In studies like
Roger Fowler's *Linguistics and the Novel* (1977), aspects of such
parallels are pursued further, for instance the correspondence
between 'deep' and 'surface structure' proposed by Chomsky's
transformational-generative grammar; and the kind of distinction
narrative structuralists made between 'story' and 'plot' or, in Form-
alist parlance, between *fabula* and *sjuzet* (that is, roughly, between
the story as it can be assembled or deduced from the narrative as a
whole, and its specific emplotment within that narrative, where
chronology may be disturbed, points of view shifted, narrative
situations varied, and so on).

The details of each of these contributions to the debate need not
detain us: what matters is the persistent concern of philosophers
and theorists of language and literature to link the two processes.
The relationship is summarised most imaginatively by Barthes
(1975:127): 'The sentence is a *nature* whose function – or scope –
is to justify the culture of the narrative.'

6

These perceptions come to a head in the remarkable developments
in language theory in the twentieth century that accompany the
radical shift in fiction-writing we have already noted. And in order
to appreciate more amply the functioning of narrative language in
the novel it would be illuminating to look briefly of some of these
modern turns. They were signposted, initially, by Heidegger, Saussure and Wittgenstein, and subsequently pursued by (among several others) a quartet of French thinkers from various disciplines:
Michel Foucault, Jacques Lacan, Roland Barthes and Jacques Derrida. Judging from the expanding library of studies on their writings, one could wander almost interminably through the labyrinth
of forking paths they have charted. But for our present purpose it is
not necessary to garner more than a few salient points from their
writings.

In one way or another all these thinkers challenge the tradition
stigmatised by Derrida as logocentrism, prevalent in Western

thinking from Plato onwards, and based on a notion of essence, of a primordial Word which speaks the world into being ('And God said, Let there be light: and there was light'). In this view, the meaning embedded in language is prepackaged, and its dependability is guaranteed by two givens: the authority and the presence of the speaker. In the dawn of civilisation it was expressed in the animistic belief that every natural object, whether tree or rock or spring or mountain, literally encapsulated its 'meaning' in the form of a god or sprite or nymph or other supernatural being believed to inhabit it.

Heidegger still remains quite close to such a vision of language, on which much of his concept of Being depends; but at the same time he destabilises the received wisdom by introducing a separation between word and world:

> When we go to the well, when we go through the woods, we are always already going through the word 'well', through the word 'woods', even if we do not speak the words and do not think of anything relating to language. (Heidegger 1971:52)[8]

With Ferdinand de Saussure we cross the threshold into the domain of language as part of a social and cultural contract by approaching it, not as a metaphysical truth but as a system of signs. This system definitively replaced all earlier beliefs in *essences* in language with the notion of *difference*: when a signifier and a signified are fused in a sign, a process which is characterised, at least at the time when it occurs, by pure randomness, 'their most precise characteristic is in being what the others are not' (Saussure 1959:117). These signs, as we all know by now, do not function by virtue of the 'presence' of a meaning trapped in them, but merely the absence of other meanings: *cat* 'means' 'cat' only because in a given linguistic situation it is *not* a hat or a mat, or a plucked green chicken.

Wittgenstein extends these indications of a shift in our perception of language to the quite radical view that reality itself, and our whole experience of it, is shaped and determined by the language in which we conceive it. It is summarised in perhaps the most famous statement of his *Tractatus*: 'That the world is *my* world, shows itself in the fact that the limits of the language [...] mean the limits of *my* world' (Wittgenstein 1983:151). In such a view the traditional notion of 'referentiality' falls away entirely: language can no longer refer to something 'out there' but, at most, only to language itself.

Roland Barthes will figure prominently in many of the discussions to follow in this study. Suffice it to say at this stage that his notorious statement about 'the death of the author' (Barthes 1988) was another celebration of the demise of authority and presence in our reading of the text; while his inventive explorations of the orgasmic pleasures, the *jouissance*, of the text (in *The Pleasure of the Text*, 1976, *A Lover's Discourse*, 1979, and elsewhere) highlight both the physicality of language and its primacy in human experience, to the extent that experience becomes *equated* with language (Barthes 1975). For Barthes, meaning is never stable or given, but exists only as 'flickers' and possibilities (see for example Barthes 1975:19).

The most radical innovator, and of pervasive importance for the discussions to follow, has undoubtedly been Jacques Derrida. In his view of the endless intertextuality of our world an extreme in the twentieth century's perception of language is reached. One of the most widely known (and most misquoted) lines in his *oeuvre* must be: '*There is nothing outside of the text* [there is no outside-text; *il n'y a pas de hors-texte*]' (Derrida 1976:158). And in *Writing and Difference* he phrases it most emphatically:

> Everything that is exterior in relation to the book, everything that is negative as concerns the book, is produced *within the book*. The exit from the book, the other and the threshold, are all articulated *within the book*. The other and the threshold can only be written, can only affirm themselves in writing. One emerges from the book only within the book. (Derrida 1978:76)

What we encounter in Derrida is the exuberant subversion of a logocentric world, replacing the authority, the presence and the hierarchies of speech with the absences and *traces*[9] of writing (*écriture*): floating signifiers within a boundless process of dissemination, pointing towards endlessly displaced, deferred and different meanings. These are the attributes of continuous supplementation,[10] for which Derrida has coined the term *différance*. In language he perceives an absence of finality in meaning: there is, at most, an iterability (discussed with great flair in *Limited Inc.*[11]) – a world not only decentred and deconstructed, but permanently *sous rature*, that is, under provisional erasure, a palimpsest in which earlier or alternative meanings are never completely obliterated.

These deep-seated suspicions about language also permeate, in quite different ways, the thinking of Lacan and Foucault. In Lacan the marker of unreliability in language is its inherent 'otherness', the fact that it is by definition the language of *others*, primarily of the oppressive Father and his Symbolic Order[12] – a language always already used and shopsoiled in the mouths of others. It reverberates with Rimbaud's famous utterance: '*Je est un autre* – I is another.' 'The subject', argues Lacan (1991b:244), 'is separated from the Others [...] by the wall of language. In other words, language is as much there to found us in the Other as to drastically prevent us from understanding him.' Elsewhere he specifies that 'this Other [...] is distinguished as the locus of Speech' (Lacan 1977:305).

For Foucault, too, a point of departure is the awareness that 'the relation of the sign to its content is not guaranteed by the order of things in themselves' (Foucault 1977:63). From there, he undertakes some of his most stimulating enquiries into language as an historical phenomenon and as part of the power strategies involved in being human: that is, in negotiating ourselves and our Others. In him, as in Derrida, what remains in the final analysis is language itself. Because language *is* the human text. Taken to an extreme, Foucault arrives at a view of literature consonant with the passage from Elizondo quoted above: he sees it as

a manifestation of a language which has no other law than that of affirming – in opposition to all other forms of discourse – its own precipitous existence and so there is nothing for it to do but to curve back in a perpetual return upon itself [...] [I]t addresses itself to itself as a writing subjectivity, or seeks to reapprehend the essence of all literature in the movement that brought it into being; and thus all its threads converge upon the finest of points – singular, instantaneous, and yet absolutely universal – upon the single act of writing (ibid.:300)

In short, writing, having freed itself from the old imperatives of expression or representation, becomes 'an interplay of signs arranged less according to its signified content than according to the very nature of the signifier' (Foucault 1984:102).

To place it in a slightly different context: Hofstadter (1980:30) quotes a Zen koan concerning two monks arguing about a flag fluttering in the wind. The first insists that the flag is moving, the other that it is the wind. Finally a patriarch arrives and says, 'Not the wind, not the flag; mind is moving.' In our reading of novels the conclusive remark would be, 'Not the flag, not the wind; language is moving.'

7

It is time to proceed to another aspect of the argument: the acknowledgement that we perceive ourselves, our lives, as narrative, as *story*, a perception that derives, among other things, from our discovery of a language-shaped world, that is, a world shaped 'like' language, a world shaped 'by' or 'through' language – and most pertinently by and through language ordered as narrative.

It is sobering to reflect, for instance, on how much of 'the world' exists in our experience *already* mediated by language. As Bakhtin formulated it (1981:338):

> In real life people talk most of all about what others talk about – they transmit, recall, weigh, and pass judgement on other people's words, opinions, assertions, information [...] At every step one meets a 'quotation' or a 'reference' to something that a particular person said, a reference to 'people say' or 'everyone says', to the words of the person one is talking with, or to one's own previous words, to a newspaper, an official decree, a document, a book and so forth.

But even if it is not already second-hand by the time we receive it, our very perception of the so-called 'real' depends on language: language imposes on us the need to perceive, interpellate and interpret the 'real' (that is, whatever, in any given context, is regarded consensually as 'real') in a way language can handle, with a grammar it can make intelligible to us, and preferably to others as well. Our perception of 'story', as of 'language', and our perception of life (birth – growth – death; beginning – middle – end), form such a close weave that it would be futile to try and disentangle what is, essentially, a chicken-and-egg situation. If narration is defined more and more, as Ray (1990:11) indicates, to include 'the fundamental ordering activity of consciousness, as it makes sense out of the world and asserts its identity', its coincidence with language becomes even more obvious. 'We cannot take a step in life or literature without using an image', says Barbara Hardy (1975:4):

> It is hard to take more than one step without narrating. Before we sleep each night we tell to ourselves what we may also have told others, the story of the past day [...] We begin the day by narrating to ourselves and probably to others our expectations, plans, desires, fantasies and intentions [...] The stories of our days and the stories in our days are joined in that autobiography we are all engaged in making or remaking.

Cognitive psychology has taken due note of this, and from Bakhtin's concepts a theory of a 'dialogic self' has developed, to the point that psychologists like Sarbin and Bruner talk about 'the narrative nature of the human psyche' (quoted in Hermans et al. 1992:27). Following Vico's idea of a creative force through which 'humans can alter the physical world and make history' (p. 24), and Vaihinger's elaboration of the notion of *as if* as a starting point of the individual's interaction with the world, these theorists posit narration as a principle of cognitive existence: 'Narration is not only evident in the example of walking along a path, but is the main characteristic of all human activities' (p. 26). And as du Preez (1991:198) formulates it, 'You become [...] more and more of a character in the story of your own life.'

8

It is in the novel, more acutely than in any other genre, Bakhtin argues, that we are confronted with 'the major and crucial fates of literature and language' (1981:8), and more than any other writer he has influenced my perception of the many languages at work in the novel. Among the three 'basic characteristics' Bakhtin identifies in the novel, the very first is 'its stylistic three-dimensionality, which is linked with *the multi-languaged consciousness, realized in the novel*' (ibid.:11, my emphasis). His concept of languages in the novel is not quite identical, however, with my use of the term. Bakhtin has in mind the actual plurality of language forms activated in any novel: 'territorial dialects, social and professional dialects and jargons, literary language, generic languages within literary language, epochs in language and so forth' (p. 12) – whereas in this study my own focus is the *notion* or *concept* of language as a system, as a phenomenon, as a practice, as a process. Inevitably, such a reading must take note of the 'contemporary reality with its diversity of speech and voice' (p. 25), and I accept that what I shall term the 'language' of any given novel consists, actually, of a great plurality and diversity of components and styles. But my premise is not so much the materiality of the languages at work in a text as *the way in which a particular view and concept of language is demonstrated implicitly or explicitly in the text*. As I hope to show in these pages, we encounter language conceived of as translation in the *Don Quixote*, language as a web of social deceit in *La Princesse de Clèves*, language as a gender trap in *Moll Flanders*, as dialogic tension in *Jacques the Fatalist and His Master*; in *Emma* it becomes a parlour game played to exorcise the darker forces of society; in *Madame Bovary* it functions as scandal, in *Middlemarch* as a system of quotations – and all of this long before the rise of Postmodernism, with which this kind of linguistic consciousness has come to be most specifically associated.

Acknowledging the differences of definition between Bakhtin's approach and mine, I subscribe to Bakhtin's belief that 'the language of a novel is the system of its "languages"' (1981:262); and I find particularly useful his important notion of the *heteroglossia* that characterises language: that is, the perception that 'every concrete utterance of a speaking subject serves as a point where centrifugal as well as centripetal forces are brought to bear' (p. 272). The result is an experience of strangeness within language: Bakhtin speaks of 'another's utterance in a language that is itself "other" to the author as well' (p. 303). There is, in short, an awareness of 'other-languagedness' at work in the novel (p. 294).

The recognition of the dialogic nature of language once again converges with my own argument in this study when Bakhtin explains that,

> all languages of heteroglossia, whatever the principle underlying them and making each unique, *are specific points of view on the world, forms for conceptualising the world in words, specific world views, each characterized by its own objects, meanings and values.* (p. 292, my emphasis)

Where Bakhtin comes closest to my own approach in this study, is in his discussion of specific authors and novels, as for instance when he discusses Rabelais's 'philosophy of the word', which to him is 'a philosophy expressed not so much in direct utterances as in stylistic practice' (pp. 309–10).

9

By pursuing my hypothesis about the inherence of language in the novel, and of narrative in language, I shall be attempting something both ambitious and very simple: to illustrate that the self-consciousness of language/narrative in the Postmodernist novel goes back to the very beginning of the novel as we have come to know it; but also that the nature of this consciousness, and the means through which it is expressed, is unique to each novel. Such an approach, like any other, can of course be valid only if it succeeds in opening up new perspectives on the texts concerned. It does not presume to supplant other perspectives and practices: at best, it may suggest that among innumerable other ways of approaching and exploring a narrative text, *a novel's implicit or explicit demonstration of a theory, a philosophy, a view or notion of language, may open up new dimensions to the reader's enjoyment of the text.*

If such an approach merely repeats other readings of the novels under scrutiny, there can be no special room for it. But if it does uncover meanings not (yet) arrived at by other points of entry into a given text, it would have justified itself.

The procedure runs roughly parallel to William Ray's project in his splendid and illuminating *Story and History* (1990), 'to seek a theory of narration and the novel within the stories the novels themselves tell about narration' (Ray 1990:vii). If Ray is interested in the '"narrativation" of reality' (ibid.:6), my focus is the narrativation of language, and vice versa. In his focus on the way in which social reality in the eighteenth century helped to fashion the novel which, in turn, helped to fashion reality, Ray inevitably dwells on questions that often overlap with my own; and in several respects, as will become clear as my enquiry unfolds, I am indebted to him. But my field of enquiry is both narrower and more diffuse than his, and in the end, prompted by different considerations, moves in a wholly different direction. A crucial difference in

approach is that Ray provides a meticulous and incisive exploration of the novel in a specific period, the eighteenth century,
whereas my enquiry ranges more widely and – deliberately –
much more randomly.

This derives, at least in part, from an urge to test my hypothesis
in encounters with as great a diversity of texts as was feasible
within the physical limits of this book. More often than not I shall
examine directly the relationship between language and narrative;
but to avoid monotony, the focus in some chapters may shift
towards more tangential aspects of the problematic, allowing me
to stalk the texts in more various ways.

10

Why have I focused on the novel? Most of the observations I have
made in the course of developing the argument above, concern, to
start with, language as such, and proceed from there to language in
its relation to narrative. But they would be true of narrative in its
numerous forms, from short stories to the narratives of history and
perhaps even to newspaper reports. The choice of the novel is to a
large extent prompted, quite frankly, by personal preference. But
another consideration has also been the abiding popularity of the
novel as a genre (in spite of regular announcements of its death),
and its prodigious propensity for renewing itself. Also, and importantly, the scope of the novel – its range and density, its complexities on every conceivable level – and consequently, the compass of
its involvement with language, is such that it lends itself most
felicitously to an enterprise of this kind. Any short story also
engages with language: but the novel has to *sustain* this engagement, and complicate and amplify and vary and interrogate and
reinvent it at every turn, for a considerable duration. As a result,
what one comes up with after immersing oneself in a novel, may
perhaps more compellingly display the possible gains (and also the
cost) of the enterprise.

It is important to repeat that I am in no way attempting an
alternative history of the novel. Neither is there any grand system
underlying my choice of specific novels. Once the notion had
occurred to me, it became a game with its own seductive processes
– the consequence of a wish to revisit a number of novels acknowledged as 'milestones' along the road of fiction, from the early

seventeenth century to the late twentieth century, and chosen from my personal favourites.

Any serious reader of literature, asked to name English novels prior to Postmodernism in which language is spectacularly foregrounded, would probably come up with Sterne and Joyce first of all, followed by James and Woolf and others: but the very obviousness of these choices have eliminated them from my list (not without much soul-searching). There was no perversity in this decision: but the very nature of the enquiry suggested that it might be more productive to explore novels where the centrality of language was, at least at first sight, less discernible.[13] I only wish I had more space to examine at great length more novels from the nineteenth century, most particularly those which go by the dubious name of Realism, but I trust the readings from Austen, Flaubert and Eliot will serve as pointers towards rereadings of Dickens and Thackeray, Meredith and Hardy, Balzac and Zola, George Sand and the Brontës and others. In not a single one of their texts does language dissolve into the legendary transparency of a picture window through which the reader's gaze can wander, unchallenged, across the landscape of the story beyond: on the contrary, in each of them, in one way or another, the self-awareness of the medium presents the reader with startling new discoveries and challenges.

In the texts from the twentieth century, as many critics have already pointed out, language features more explicitly and even spectacularly than in any of their predecessors: but by this time, I hope, it will be clear that what has for so long been regarded as the distinguishing feature of Modernism and even more especially of Postmodernism, merely confirms a long and adventurous development spanning the centuries. And it is not by any means a linear process, because, as I shall try to indicate, Postmodernism is – among so many other things – a snake swallowing its own tale, as it returns, playfully, ironically, and with lighthearted seriousness, to what once appeared to be its age of innocence.

In our time, even pleasure has become an academic concern, but however academic my own approach may be, I hope that something of the sheer pleasure of the novel experience will be conveyed by the chapters that follow.

1

The Wrong Side of the Tapestry

Miguel de Cervantes: *Don Quixote de la Mancha*

1

In the opening chapter of the *Don Quixote*, as one of the most enduring adventures of literature is about to begin, the hidalgo of the story, 'verging on fifty, of tough constitution, lean-bodied, thin-faced, a great early riser and a lover of hunting' (p. 31),[1] is depicted within the double space of his world: the drab reality of his house ('His habitual diet consisted of a stew, more beef than mutton, of hash most nights, boiled bones on Saturdays, lentils on Fridays, and a young pigeon as a Sunday treat': p. 31), and his library, which consists for the most part of books on knight-errantry. This library has almost literally replaced the hidalgo's real world: he has sold most of his property in order to buy the books. So irrelevant is the reality of the place he lives in that the narrator does not even deign to divulge the name of his Manchegan village; and of the man himself we are informed only that 'they say that his surname was Quixada or Quesada' (p. 31). The only names in this chapter – with the sole exception of the village barber's – that are assigned with any certainty to individuals are those of the knights, heroes and giants of the hidalgo's books. And the main action of the opening situation is constituted by processes of naming, of his horse, his lady, and himself. As an unmistakable extension of these processes we are told of his attempt to make a helmet, fashioning a visor from pieces of pasteboard. When a single sword-blow demolishes in a moment what has taken him a week to make, he patiently sets about reconstructing the visor and this time, 'not caring to make another trial of it, he accepted it as a fine jointed headpiece and put it into commission' (pp. 33–4). This act of faith, on which all his future adventures, encounters and ordeals will be predicated, is synonymous with his choice of worthy names: for Rocinante, Dulcinea, Don Quixote de la Mancha. In each case the name is more than a mask for a paltry reality: what really happens is that in each case the name transforms what *is* into what *may be*. It is the condition of what the world, and generations of readers, will come to call his 'madness'. And having set the stage for himself, Don Quixote can now take the decisive step, riding, as it were, out of his home and into language.

2

The full implications of this step unfold very gradually throughout the progress of the narrative, to reach a moment of emblematic truth in Don Quixote's arrival, near the end of his travels, in Barcelona, where he visits a printing press (Part II Chapter lxii). As Robert Alter says in a fine essay, 'Mirror of Knighthood, World of Mirrors': 'At such a moment we can hardly forget that Don Quixote himself is no more than the product of the very process he observes, a congeries of words set up in type, run off as proof, corrected and rerun, bound in pages, and sold at so many reales a copy' (in Alter 1978:4–5).

The visit culminates in the hidalgo's discovery of the proofs of a book called 'the *Second part of the Ingenious Gentleman Don Quixote de la Mancha*, composed by someone or other, native of Tordesillas' (p. 878). Don Quixote, experiencing at the time the events written up in the 'real' Part II (which we as readers are holding in our hands at the same time), is confronted with a fake version of himself. Yet his 'real' Part II could not have existed had his Part I not been published in 1605, ten years earlier, and disseminated throughout Spain and the rest of Europe. A few days before the visit to the printing press, in fact, Don Quixote was riding on a mule through the streets of Barcelona bearing on his back a parchment on which someone had written in large letters, '*This is Don Quixote de la Mancha*' (p. 870). It would seem that reality and language can no longer be disentangled; each requires the other. Ceci n'est pas une pipe.

And yet the overlap is not complete: there is both a lack and an excess in language as presented by the *Don Quixote*. The nature of this lack and this excess, that is, the quality of language which makes the *Don Quixote* possible as narrative, as a novel, is illustrated in many scenes preceding the visit to the printer. One example occurs in II:iv (repeated in II:xxvii) where an error is pointed out in the 'original' account of Sancho's riding on his ass after the encounter with the galley slaves (I:xxiii). Sancho's response is significant: 'I don't know how to answer that [...] All I can say is that perhaps the history-writer was wrong, or it may have been an error of the printer's' (p. 493). Once their history has been written up, that is, sanctioned and canonised in language, there is always the possibility that the written account (not only in plagiarised or invented versions by other authors, *but in the 'authorised version' itself*) may be wrong – a condition which Diderot will place under new scrutiny a century and a half later. In this way, the writer's and printer's authority is subverted long before the travellers reach Barcelona.

3

In the scene at the printer's the problem is approached from another, highly illuminating, angle: the whole discussion of the printing process, from its technicalities to its economy, is informed by an extensive discussion of the phenomenon of translation and the urge towards 'proper equivalents'.

The hidalgo himself voices his doubts about the fidelity, and the credibility, of translation: 'It seems to me that translating from one tongue into another [...] is like viewing Flemish tapestries from the wrong side; for although you see the pictures, they are covered with threads which obscure them so that the smoothness and gloss of the fabric are lost' (p. 877).

This remark, linking as it does language and imaging, as well as the notions of original and copy, reality and representation/illusion/fake, acquires its full significance only if one bears in mind that the whole of the *Don Quixote* is presented to the reader as a Spanish translation from an original document in Arabic.

The reader is first explicitly alerted to the presence of at least one other author at work in the narrative (that is, alongside or behind the Miguel de Cervantes Saavedra who identified himself in the Prologue as the 'father' or 'step-father' of Don Quixote) by the interruption of the encounter with the Basque (I:viii–ix):

The unfortunate thing is that the author of this history left the battle in suspense at this critical point, with the excuse that he could find no more records of Don Quixote's exploits than those related here. It is true that the second author of this work would not believe that such a curious history could have been consigned to oblivion [...] This caused me great annoyance. (p. 74)

Only then are we given the background to the present text; and it comes as a surprise, to say the least, after an early disparaging reference to the Prophet as an inventor of tall tales in I:v, to learn that the story, written in Arabic on 'some parchments and old papers' (p. 76), was allegedly bought by the second author from a young pedlar in Toledo. Deducing from a note in the margin on Dulcinea del Toboso that it must be a version of the already well-known story of Don Quixote, the author pays fifty pounds of raisins and three bushels of wheat to have the manuscript translated. It is the transcription of this translation the reader is now allegedly confronted with.

It is important for the reader's relationship with the narrative that at the outset we are informed that Don Quixote's companion is called both Panza and Zancas 'at different times in the history'. As Alter (1978:9) points out, this never happens in the narrative we are offered, so we must conclude that either this information is erroneous, or the new author has taken it upon himself to revise the manuscript in the retelling; either way, the version now in the hands of the reader – written by a Moor, translated into Spanish, commented upon in the margins, revised and retold by a Spaniard – is not to be trusted. We are reminded quite explicitly that to Spanish Christians of the sixteenth and seventeenth centuries the Arabs were first and foremost a 'nation [of] ready liars' (p. 78); and, as I have already indicated, we are cautioned several times about the unreliability of translation as such. But this is what 'written language' *means* in the *Don Quixote* – hence the narrator's (or the narrators') preoccupation, throughout the narration, with the dual – and shaky – nature of his/their story. And this consciousness, one should bear in mind, is superimposed on Cervantes's seventeenth-century reader who would, as a matter of course, *already* have been steeped in the old Spanish narrative tradition of *era y non era*: 'Once upon a time there was and there wasn't ...' (a tradition derived, most significantly, from an even more ancient *Arabic* narrative formula: *kan ya makan*).

As González points out, translation involves a crucial concern of Cervantes's entire relationship with his predecessors:

Cervantes's parody of the romances of chivalry went so far as to include something that was a topic of every chivalric romance: the claim that the text was a translation into Spanish from a manuscript found far away and written in a foreign, sometimes archaic, language (favourite languages included English, German, Arabic, Hungarian, Phrygian, as well as Greek and Latin). (González 1987:79. n.24)

In fact, González argues that, 'translation is at the very heart of the novel as a genre, and [...] it is one of the key defining characteristics of that most undefinable of genres' (ibid.:65). We shall return to this in the chapter on Márquez.

The significance of the strategy invariably lies in the way in which it subverts all notions of presence and authority in the text before the reader. 'The materiality of a word cannot be translated or carried over into another language. Materiality is precisely that which translation relinquished. To relinquish materiality: such is the driving force of translation' (Derrida 1978:210).

4

But translation is merely one among several strategies employed by Cervantes to interrogate the credibility of his own text. To make sure that the reader remains conscious of the unreliability of language, the end of Part I of the *Don Quixote* restores us to an awareness of the textuality of the text by offering the reader a clutch of verses: 'These were such verses as could be deciphered. The rest, as the characters were worm-eaten, were entrusted to a university scholar to guess out their meaning' (p. 461); and Part II opens with a pertinent reminder of Cide Hamete Benengeli's role as 'original' author (p. 471). Such references become more and more frequent in the course of the third journey.

In the prelude to the encounter with the lions (II:xvii), the narrator interrupts himself to comment:

And here it is to be noted that when the author of our true history came to this passage he exclaimed and cried: 'O brave and incomparably courageous Don Quixote de la Mancha! True mirror of all valiant knights in the world! Thou new and second Don Manuel de Leon – honour and glory of Spanish knights! In what words shall I recount this most fearful exploit, or with what arguments make it credible to future ages? [...] Let your deeds themselves praise you, valorous Manchegan, for here I leave them in all their glory, lacking words to extol them'. (p. 575)

Even *before* Don Quixote confronts the lion in what turns out to be a most *un*heroic encounter, he is already *written into victory*, and into history, by Cide Hamete Benengeli. And it is almost inevitable that after the incident the hidalgo should change his identity and his image – which coincides with his 'reality' – by changing his name to 'The Knight of the Lions', fulfilling what Cide Hamete had written beforehand in his apostrophe to 'thou new and second Don Manuel de Leon'.

A number of chapters later the original author is himself apostrophised:

In very truth, all who enjoy stories like this should show their gratitude to Cide Hamete, its first author, for his meticulousness in recording its minutest details [...] O most renowned author! O fortunate Don Quixote! O famous Dulcinea! O droll Sancho Panza! May you live, jointly and separately, for infinite ages, to the delight and general amusement of mankind! (p. 721)

At times Cide Hamete even acts as commentator in his own margin, expressing doubts about his *own* veracity:

The translator of this great history from the original written by its first author, Cide Hamete Benengeli, says that when he reached the chapter relating the adventure of Montesinos' cave he found written in the margin in the hand of this same Hamete these words: 'I cannot persuade myself that all that is written in the previous chapter literally happened to the valorous Don Quixote [...] But I cannot possibly suppose that Don Quixote, who was the most truthful gentleman and noblest knight of his age, could be lying [...] So if this adventure seems apocryphal, it is not I that am to blame, for I write it down without affirming its truth or falsehood. You, judicious reader, must judge for yourself, for I cannot and should not do more.' (p. 624)

An even more revealing passage occurs at the opening of II:xliv:

> They say that in the real original of this history it states that
> when Cide Hamete came to write this chapter his interpreter did
> not translate it as it was written [...] So, being confined and
> enclosed within the narrow limits of the story [...] he begs that
> his pains shall not be under-valued, and that he shall be praised
> not for what he writes, but for what he has refrained from
> writing. (pp. 745–6)

Here the very silences and interstices in the writing are activated.

The same happens to the distances between the different narratorial voices, through which the concept of 'translation' is charged
with dramatic force. In II:xliv both Moor and Christian worlds
(indicative of two different 'realities') are brought into play by
Cide Hamete's observation that, 'Moor though I am, I know very
well by the commerce I have had with Christians that holiness lies
in charity, humility, faith, obedience and poverty' (p. 750).

At one point a chapter opens in Moorish way with a threefold
invocation of Allah (p. 514) – but not long afterwards a much more
convoluted opening to a chapter illuminates the intricacies of the
relationship:

> Cide Hamete, the chronicler of this great history, introduces the
> present chapter with these words: '*I swear as a Catholic Christian*',
> on which his translator observes that Cide Hamete's swearing as
> a Catholic Christian, he being a Moor, as he doubtless was,
> meant only that as a Catholic Christian, when he swears, swears,
> or should swear the truth, and observe it in all he says, so he
> would tell the truth, as if he had sworn like a Christian Catholic,
> in writing of Don Quixote. (p. 646)

What this self-conscious use of narrative language – that is, of
language as always and already translated by others – achieves
is, above all, the impression of reality as existing *at a remove*. In the
remarkable confrontation with the Squire of the Wood (II:xii–xv)
the most the strange knight can say about the Don Quixote he
encounters is that 'you are as like to that knight I conquered as
one egg is to another' (p. 556); after the fight, Don Quixote unmasks
the knight to look at him: 'He saw, our history relates, the very
face, the very physiognomy, the very image, the very picture of the
bachelor Samson Carrasco' (p. 558) – *and for that very reason Don
Quixote does not believe what he sees.* Images and perceptions are as

suspect as translations: in fact, they function in the narrative exactly as translation functions in the act of narration.

5

The traditional view of Don Quixote and his relationship with Sancho Panza concerns the dichotomy between reality and unreality (where the latter may be illusion, or fantasy, or imagination, or dream); between reason and unreason; ultimately between madness and sanity. In Part I this is demonstrated, with spectacular effect, in every scene where Don Quixote's imaginings appear to be shipwrecked on the ridges of mundane or cruel reality: the giants are windmills, the Saracen armies a flock of sheep, the castle a lowly inn.

This pattern of binary thinking is particularly evident in Auerbach's famous mimetic approach based on the phenomenon of 'representations of everyday life in which that life is treated seriously, in terms of its human and social problems and even its tragic complications' (Auerbach 1974:342): the 'everyday' is not defined more closely and is interpreted on a 'common sense' basis. Auerbach's fine but overly rigorous approach examines mainly the way in which Don Quixote's *idée fixe* leads him constantly to avoid both despair and a return to sanity. Or as Close (1990:17) so neatly phrases it, 'The historical world is bent to the laws of the fictitious one.'

'This solution', says Auerbach (1974:340), 'appears each time the exterior situation establishes itself as in insuperable contrast to the illusion.' Reality, in other words, is rather simplistically seen as purely 'exterior'; and the realism of the text, for Auerbach, resides in 'a vigorous capacity for the vivid visualization of very different people in very varied situations, for the vivid realization and expression of what thoughts enter their minds, what emotions fill their hearts, and what words come to their lips' (p. 354). In other words, the 'sensory' is the key to Cervantes's realism. 'In the resulting clashes between Don Quixote and reality no situation ever results which puts in question that reality's right to be what it is. It is always right and he wrong; and after a bit of amusing confusing it flows calmly on, untouched' (p. 345). What an emasculated and impoverished reading, both of the text and of 'reality'!

At the very least, one should acknowledge, not only an increasing *interaction* between the different levels of reality, but a more and more subtle *inherence* of each in the other. The whole of Part II is incomparably more complex, and more subtle than the – apparently – stark oppositions of Part I. Of particular importance is the remarkably sophisticated sequence in the Duke's palace in Part II, where 'reality' itself is transformed by the play-acting of the nobility.

In this long sequence, where the Duke and his household persistently 'play up to' the hidalgo's madness by offering him an experience of the fantastic, that is, when the world (reality) begins to resemble Don Quixote's representations of it, the very logic that allowed such a representation in the first place must do away with it. As the world of reality appears to become more and more mad, so the madman appears to become increasingly sane. Phrased differently, Don Quixote is mad when he accepts the reality of his representation (as in the case of the windmills or the sheep perceived in Part I as giants or Saracens); but he may be seen as becoming sane when his representation becomes a reality. Within what During (1992:34) terms 'an imperialism of seeming' Don Quixote exposes ever receding dimensions of meaning.

The juxtaposition of two episodes from Part II illustrates this in a particularly dramatic fashion. From the descent into the 'enchanted solitudes' of the cave of Montesinos (II:xxii – xxiii) Don Quixote returns with a tale that taxes all belief: although Sancho judiciously and loyally asserts that, 'I don't believe that my master's lying' (p. 621), he does suggest that the hidalgo must have been bewitched down there. After the imagined ride, blindfolded, on the back of the magic horse Clavileño (II:xli),[2] Sancho is the one who returns with a fabulous tale of his view of the earth no bigger than a grain of mustard seed' (p. 733), while Don Quixote quietly comments: 'Sancho, if you want me to believe what you saw in the sky, I wish you to accept my account of what I saw in the Cave of Montesinos. I say no more' (p. 735).

A significant clue is provided when, near the end of the story, Don Quixote acknowledges an inn *as* an inn, and the narrator explains: 'I say that it was an inn because Don Quixote called it one, contrary to his usual habit of calling inns castles' (p. 848). This does not so much convey the suggestion that Don Quixote has changed as that reality is *still* constituted, as it has been throughout the narrative, by 'saying' it, that is, in and through *an act of lan-*

guage. This discovery sends the reader back to Part I with a heightened awareness of the complexities and subtleties below the surface of apparently simple contrasts and binarities. If anything, one
finds oneself in what Alter (1978:6) calls a state of 'ontological
vertigo'.

The key to this crucial perception lies in the acknowledgement of
the *Don Quixote* as a fictional exploration of Erasmus's concept of
'folly', and of the dawning, after the blind faith of the Middle Ages,
of a new Age of Doubt. This is an insight offered by Carlos Fuentes
in what must be one of the greatest essays on the *Don Quixote*,
'Cervantes, or the Critique of Reading' (in Fuentes 1990).
Approaching the novel as one of the first signs of 'a modern
divorce between words and things' (ibid.:51), Fuentes elaborates
on this break as one between 'analogy' and 'differentiation': our
modern challenge lies in 'how to accept the diversity and mutation
of the world, while retaining the mind's power for analogy and
unity, so that this changing world shall not become meaningless'
(p. 49).

Fuentes quotes Trilling: 'All prose fiction is a variation on the
theme of *Don Quixote* [...] *the problem of appearance and reality*'
(p. 50). And this is linked to Erasmus, and to 'the duality of
truth, the illusion of appearances, and the praise of folly' (p. 52).
We are reminded of Erasmus's words, 'The reality of things [...]
depends solely on opinion. Everything in life is so diverse, so
opposed, so obscure, that we cannot be assured of any truth' (p.
52; see Erasmus 1971, Chapter 45). Reason can only see itself as
reason 'through the eyes of an ironical madness: not its opposite
but its critical complement' (Fuentes 1990:53). The medieval person
believed, the new human being *doubts*. Fuentes's key phrase is: *All is
possible, but all is in doubt*: 'Even as they are won, these new realities
are doubted by the critical spirit, since the critical spirit founded
them' (p. 55); and in Cervantes, indeed, doubt is the very key to,
and the condition of, reality. And doubt, we should add, is the
condition of language – most particularly when language itself,
viewed as 'translation', as 'the words of others', becomes necessarily suspect. Where, in all this, lies sanity, and where madness?

Part II of the novel drives home the problem in a particularly
striking manner, in the syncopation of sequences featuring Sancho
on his 'island', and Don Quixote in the ducal palace. As even the
'sane' characters (the Duke and his household) indulge more and
more dizzyingly in play-acting, all sense of reality becomes

blurred. In the midst of this increasingly precarious world, an extremely poignant incident occurs in II:xliv and II:xlvi where Don Quixote discovers a ladder in his green stockings, an 'irreparable disaster' which he finds incomparably more disconcerting than the encounters with the seemingly amorous Altisidora and the cats and bells which accompany the discovery. Is this an extreme of madness – or of sanity? Surely, by this time we cannot be confident about either.

6

Let us therefore try a different approach. What we term 'reality', it should be clear to the twentieth-century reader, is no more than a historically and culturally determined *construct*, a system of received, and accepted, ideas of how we believe the world to be: it is based on *perception*, or what Erasmus termed 'opinions' – but perception already presupposes interpretation and imaging, in other words, translation.

In the Middle Ages, the material world was regarded as merely the adumbration of divine truth: angels and devils were more 'real' than tree or stone. With the Renaissance and the rise of humanism, reality is removed from the hand of God and allowed an independent, and substantive, existence. In other words, reality comes to be perceived as a duality: the world, and the human being, objectivity and subjectivity (which coincides with the notion of 'nature' as autonomous object, and 'personality' as autonomous subject). In the Age of Reason this will debouch in the Cartesian division between *res cogitans* and *res extensa*: the human being is *personal*, the 'world' a collection of objects. Hence the very concept of realism arises from the belief that the objective world can be perceived, known and described.

Only after Kant was the impossibility of knowing the *Ding an Sich* acknowledged, and a dichotomy of *being* and *seeming* established. Yet Cervantes, the Spaniard, is, like Shakespeare, the Elizabethan, not only fully a man of his time but much larger than his time: he knows the tradition of *Era y non era / kan ya makan*, which is borne out, as we have seen, by the narratorial situation of the *Don Quixote*. The narrative may set out to be a critique of chivalric romance and, by the same token, of the pre-Erasmian medieval world-view: Don Quixote, who denies the 'real' in favour of his illusion, is a fool and a madman, and explicitly portrayed as such. But the greatness of the text resides in the way in which it develops into a critique of the real itself. Cervantes, as Marthe Robert points out (1980), does not simply debunk chivalric romance as he has come to know it in the *Amadis* tradition, but also *revives* it. By the time he writes the *Don Quixote*, *Amadis* has been out of fashion for at least thirty years. It is, however, a revival in an entirely different key, which will embrace, among many other things, all the accounts about the discovery of the New World by the conquistadores (see Peter Hulme's brilliant study *Colonial Encounters*: 1986).

The key to the 'problem' of the *Don Quixote* is that it does not simply set up fiction *in opposition* to reality: *both* sides of the equation are products of language. If the Don's 'madness' is the consequence of overindulging in the reading of chivalric romances, the 'sanity' of the world is constituted just as much by linguistic strategies: Cide Hamete Benengeli and his world are determined by the texts of Islam just as much as the Spanish world of Cervantes's time is filtered through the texts of Roman Catholicism, the accounts of the conquistadores, the accumulation of songs and narratives contributed by whomever Don Quixote and Sancho Panza encounter on their travels, in inns or taverns, in remote mountain ranges or by the wayside, on the Manchegan plains, in the castle of the Duke, in Sancho's 'island' or wherever. Sancho himself, traditionally regarded as the representative of sanity and reality in opposition to the Don's madness, is constructed, as a character of fiction, from a treasure-house of received wisdom, folklore, idioms, proverbs, quotations – the whole massive layer of what Barthes terms the 'cultural code' of a narrative text (1975:20, 206). It is revealing that when Sancho enters his 'island', he is also met by the reality of writing: the inscription on the painting which announces, in Nostradamus fashion, his arrival on that very day. Just as much as the hidalgo's reality is predetermined by chivalric romance, Sancho's is here revealed to be the consequence of what, in Diderot's terminology, has already been written up on the Great Scroll.

To argue, as Auerbach and many others have done so persistently over the years, that the Don's madness is constantly offset against, and in fact defeated by, the 'real world' is to misread the extent to which the entire narrative world of the *Don Quixote* is a construct of language: language experienced as *translation*, as *alien*, as *the language of others*. On p 611 Don Quixote reminds Sancho Panza, 'That question and answer are not yours, Sancho [. . .] You have heard them from somebody.' This becomes *everybody's* problem in the text. And within this general context, the Don's own language (that is, the language of his 'madness', of his dreams and illusions and 'aberrations'), presents no less consistency, no less *sense* than that of Sancho, or the priest, or the barber, or the innkeeper, or the Yanguesan muleteers, or the Duke, or the deceitful Altisidora.

'Madness fascinates because it is knowledge', says Foucault (1985:21) and in this respect Marthe Robert would be wide off the mark in arguing that 'whichever way we look at it, one thing is certain and that is that it cannot be diagnosed as an anomaly or virtue currently found among human beings – it is unprecedented and wholly improbable [... it] sets [Don Quixote] beyond every locatable moral or spiritual attitude, at the extreme limit of what is human' (1980:115). On the contrary, as Foucault claims, 'at the secret heart of madness [...] we discover, finally, the hidden perfection of a language [...] Language is the first and last structure of madness' (1985:95–100).

Foucault spells it out: 'The ultimate language of madness is that of reason, but the language of reason enveloped in the prestige of the image, limited to the locus of appearance which the image defines' (ibid.:95). Hence, in the *Don Quixote*, the intimate association between the way in which the Don visualises (and, to coin a word, visionarises) the grammar of chivalric romance in its transposition, its translation, to the all-encompassing 'discourse' (again Foucault's word: ibid.: 99) of what from the outside looks like madness. Inside, we are reminded by Don Quixote himself upon his return from the Cave of Montesinos, resides 'the coherent argument I held with myself' (p. 615). 'Language is the first and last structure of madness, its constituent form; on language are based all the cycles in which madness articulates its nature' (Foucault 1985:100). Language itself opens into both 'real' *and* 'imaginary' worlds, and makes not only Don Quixote, but Sancho Panza, possible. Through the manipulation of this double-edged language, Riley (1962:64) perceptively remarks, the hidalgo 'is trying to live literature and be not only the hero of his own story but also, in so far as he can control events, its author'.

7

It may be revealing to examine how the Don reacts to extreme physical manifestations of the 'real world' (granted that, by now, we have to take that world with a grain of salt). Even from the surface of the narrative it is clear that this 'real world' often poses challenges to Don Quixote – in the form of *hunger* (for example after the encounter with the shepherds in I:xviii or at the end of the puppet show, II:xxvi); of *sex* (as in the attempted seductions by Maritornes in I:xvi or Altisidora in II:lxix); or, most often, of *pain*. To what extent do such experiences impose, at the very least, an awareness of the limits of the body, and consequently a discovery or acknowledgement of the 'real' world?

At a very early stage of his errantry, beaten up by the muleteers (I:iv-v), Don Quixote's solution, significantly, is 'to think of some passage in his books' (p. 52); he even manages to think himself fortunate, 'for it seemed to him that this was a disaster peculiar to knights errant'; and when the pain suffered in the encounter is so bad that he cannot even stay on the donkey, he finds a remedy in 'stories' (p. 54). At the same time he offers the most glorious affirmation of his identity in the whole novel: 'I know who I am [...] and I know, too, that I am capable of being not only the characters I have named, but all the Twelve Peers of France' (p. 54).

In the language of madness, as defined by Foucault, narrative actually bestows on Don Quixote a *greater* sense of reality. This happens even when he acknowledges physical suffering: after the encounter with the windmills (I:viii) he reminds Sancho that, 'if I do not complain of the pain, it is because a knight errant is not allowed to complain of any wounds, even though his entrails may be dropping out through them' (p. 69); and following the beating by the monk's servants (I:x), he admits his sorry state: 'Observe, brother Sancho, that this adventure and others of its kind are not adventures of isles but of cross-roads, from which nothing is to be gained but a broken head and the loss of an ear' (p. 81): but immediately afterwards he dispels the agony by finding his customary solace in tales of chivalry. When Sancho persists, the hidalgo comes up with the remedy of the magic balsam, itself a manifestation of chivalric discourse – and while the balsam nearly kills Sancho it strangely cures his master.

In a particularly eloquent defence of this 'language', the Don pleads the cause of his state:

'I only want to argue from my own sufferings that it is most certainly a more painful and belaboured one, hungrier and thirstier, more miserable, ragged and lousy; for there is no doubt that knights errant of old suffered much ill-usage in the course of their lives.' (p. 98)

In other words, there is neither denial of, nor escape from, the reality of suffering, but an *acceptance* of it – *because it is part of the fictifying career he has chosen*. He comes as close to 'reality' here as in the remarkable encounter with the lion (II:xvii) where he demonstrates not just foolhardiness but remarkable courage in challenging a predator which he *knows to be a lion*.

In I:xv begins one of the most horrendous sequences of physical suffering in the whole story. During the sojourn at the inn mistaken for a castle, following the bruising encounter with the Yanguesans, Don Quixote is so much in pain that he cannot sleep; yet this prompts the escape into a new fantasy (one of the only instances where hallucination may be ascribed to the delirium of pain); when Maritornes comes to his bed in error, he turns down the offer, among other reasons because he is too 'bruised and battered' (p. 123). As his pain persists, he turns to the remedy of his magic balsam, but is interrupted and subjected to further blows. After taking the potion he is reported to feel 'recovered and well', but only a few pages later he is still too bruised even to dismount to help Sancho who is being tossed in the blanket: so the balsam's effect may well have been illusory, or at least merely temporary. Very soon afterwards, the Don is again beaten up severely by the shepherds, but when he turns to Sancho for assistance the squire responds by vomiting in his master's face – to which the hidalgo quietly resigns himself: 'All these squalls which greet us are signs that the weather will soon clear and things go well for us' (p. 140). At least, for once, Don Quixote admits that he can now do with some bread and fish heads, and that such food would be preferable 'to all the herbs in Dioscorides' herbal'. Yet even in this agony (apart from all his wounds he has lost a number of teeth), he accepts pain as part of the rewards of chivalry.

I have dwelt on this sequence at some length for various reasons. The most obvious is that it illustrates the purely relative nature of 'reality': its worst excesses can so readily be neutralised, almost without exception, not so much by a retreat into fantasy (or into language) as by reducing the events themselves to narrative invention. The violence perpetrated on Don Quixote is so excessive, the cumulative effect so outrageous, that by no stretch of the imagination can it still be called 'realistic'. A contemporary equivalent would be a cartoon in the *Tom and Jerry* mould where, in the course of a single episode, Tom would be beaten, dismembered, flattened, pulverised, liquidised many times, coming back for more after every catastrophe. As Alter (1978:9) puts it, in a slightly different context, 'Internal consistency is quietly substituted for verisimilitude, though not so quietly that we do not reflect for a moment on the substitution.'[3]

In reply to Nabokov's notorious criticism of the *Don Quixote* as 'one of the most bitter and barbarous [books] ever penned', Kundera (1995:60–1) pertinently points out that,

> We are not in the world of Zola, where some cruel act, described precisely and in detail, becomes the accurate document of a social reality; with Cervantes, we are in a world created by the magic spells of the storyteller who invents, who exaggerates, who is carried away by his fantasies, his excesses.[4]

This is why, for an understanding of the 'real' in Cervantes's text, we should look more at present-day cartoons than at nineteenth-century novels. But Don Quixote, of course, goes far beyond *Tom and Jerry* in the suspension of disbelief, as a single instance should demonstrate. In II:xliv, after the hidalgo has been painfully suspended from a window by his arm, he is finally released: his reaction is to mount Rocinante, couch his lance, and charge at the very people who have just saved him. This is no simple repetition of the previous clashes between madness and sanity, or two levels of reality: it is an act designed to transform the (intensely real) suffering of a moment before into 'enchantment'; and the narration of the event is a ludic demonstration of the bewitching properties of *language*.

Minutes later, confronted with the inn-keeper who is being beaten up, he refrains from intervening, on the grounds that a knight should not interfere in the quarrels of squires. Coming from the man who in II:xvii will not hesitate to challenge a lion in his cage, this cannot simply be dismissed, as the women of the inn do, as 'cowardice': it is a much more complicated manifestation of the dizzying interaction of the various kinds of reality that erupt from language. As in the case of Hamlet, we are left unable to distinguish between feigned madness and the real thing, reality and its masks, reality and its many Others – *because they are all dependent on language*. Have we not been warned before, as early as I:xvii, not to trust all facile opposites? In that chapter, in the wake of all the confusion created by Don Quixote's 'mistaking' the inn for a castle, the hidalgo, with perfect equanimity, admits that the inn may merely have *appeared* to be a castle: yet even so he shrewdly refuses to pay for his lodging, as knights are not supposed to sink so low.

8

A crucial problem in one's evaluation of the complexity of play in which all notions of reality and fiction in the *Don Quixote* are ensnared, lies in the question: Where does the critic position himself/herself in relation to 'madness': within madness, or within reason? If it is the latter, which cannot but be the case, how can one evaluate madness except by branding it as 'reason's Other'? The text anticipates the question. From the point of view of the cluster of narrators themselves, Don Quixote is undoubtedly mad: but the narrator is thoroughly, and persistently, discredited (or at least subverted and interrogated) by the narrative situation as such, which reveals Cide Hamete Benengeli's account as, *at the very least, unreliable.* If Cervantes wishes to discredit the tradition of chivalric romance,[5] he has to place himself *outside* that tradition, and outside madness, within the domain of reason and of 'the real': but by using a questionable narrator, he interrogates *his own* position. And he allows Don Quixote to speak, in a Foucauldian language, from *within* madness, increasingly lending a beguiling validity to madness – precisely by avoiding a glib opposition between sanity and insanity. Neither has substance of its own, each is constantly produced and defined by the other. In the twentieth century, Lacan has noted that madness is an *effect* of sanity. Consequently, Don Quixote does not necessarily offer the, or even an, 'alternative' to sanity, but he does undermine the total authority (and the authoriality) of the real. And that validity resides in the concept of *story*, based on the convention of *Era y non era.* In the *Don Quixote*, through the strategies of language-as-translation, *everything* (that is, both the traditionally 'real' and the traditionally 'imagined') is presented as story.

9

At every halt on the journey (that is, at every point of rest or equilibrium in the narrative, as 'journey' and 'narrative' signify each other) where Don Quixote and Sancho Panza meet new characters, the outcome of their interaction is almost invariably storytelling. But these characters do not only *tell* stories, they turn themselves into stories. 'Every man is the child of his own works', says Don Quixote on p. 48 – and 'works' might just as well have been 'words'. The whole of the Spain they traverse is translated into a weave of story.

A particularly telling encounter (in every sense of the word) occurs in I:xxii when Don Quixote and Sancho meet a chaingang of galley-slaves. The scene is preceded, significantly, by the episode in which the hidalgo dons a barber's brass basin in the belief that it is the enchanted golden helmet of the wizard Mambrino; and he is still wearing the basin on his head when he confronts the prisoners' guards. This not only provokes the reaction one might expect from the guards, but also 'loads' the reader's approach to reality in the scene that ensues. In the guards' case, their reaction is prompted by the fact that they read the basin as part of a sign-system different from Don Quixote's: 'Put that basin straight on your head, and don't go about looking for a cat with three legs', the sergeant reprimands him (p. 178). Our own approach, on the other hand, is informed by a knowledge of *both* the sign-systems involved.

The episode opens with a metaphoric view of the chain-gang: they seem 'like beads on a great chain' (p. 171). This image, like the hidalgo's helmet, immediately complicates the singleminded reality of the scene. Don Quixote is offered the guards' version of the history, but insists on questioning each prisoner separately: an affirmation of the notion of *subjective* reality. It is reinforced when one of the slaves talks about the situation in which a man's life depends on his own version of events, rather than on 'witnesses and proofs': and of course Don Quixote concurs. He, too, constantly acts against the grain of truth.

In these conversations, each character's more or less elaborate self-invention is accompanied by a thumbnail sketch that puts the story in a different perspective. One is described as 'a musician and a singer' (p. 172) – which is translated into 'confessing on the rack'; another intimates that he has been sentenced to five years on the galleys 'because I was short of ten ducats' (p. 173) and it is left to the visitors to figure out what he has really done. Each story becomes a metaphoric intervention, a version of reality told with the purpose of designating the real *in other words*, that is, finding a new language to represent reality – which is what the whole novel is about.

In another respect the scene becomes a *mise-en-abyme* of the novel as a whole: that is, from the way in which the prisoners transform themselves into story and their biographies into fiction, it is clear that *language determines reality*. To the rascal Gines de Pasamonte (alias Ginesillo de Parapilla), who will return in Part II of the narrative, *living* his life is in fact identical to *writing* it – and so the writing can only finish when the life ends. The reader can only fully evaluate the submerged meanings of the scene when in a sequence of later chapters (I:xxxix-xliv) the captive tells his story: it purports to be a *'true* tale', yet follows the traditional pattern of a fairytale (the father who divides his estate among three sons), and in the course of his story he refers to 'a Spanish soldier, called something de Saavedra', who was in a battle with him (p. 355). 'That Saavedra should appear in the narrative of a fictional character invented by Saavedra', says Alter (1978:17), 'is the author's way of affirming his absolute proprietorship over the fictional world he has created.' I should suggest the opposite: having allowed 'his' story to be filtered through a cluster of other narrators, each as disreputable as the rest, he subverts his own authoriality so thoroughly as to anticipate Barthes's notion of the 'death of the author'.

Once again that 'internal consistency' of which Alter (ibid.:9) spoke elsewhere is more important than any attempt at verisimilitude. One is reminded of another story told by Cervantes, about two students who toured through Italy, entertaining the inhabitants of each village on the town square with the story of their participation in the Battle of Lepanto; but in one village they ran into trouble when an old veteran of that battle confronted them publicly with convincing proof that they had made it all up. They were promptly strung up on the gallows, but just before they could be hanged they begged from the local duke the favour of being allowed to hear the authentic story of the Battle of Lepanto told by the veteran himself. The old man needed little persuasion; but his version – the 'true' version – was so boring and pedestrian in its presentation that the populace promptly demanded that the students be freed and the veteran hanged in their stead. To their everlasting honour it must be said that they interceded for the old soldier's life, and in the end all three were spared; but the essential point had been made: the quality of a story lies in its telling, not its veracity.

What remains, in the *Don Quixote* as a whole, and in each story invented by fictional characters within it, is not an *author* but just narrative – or again, as Barthes would have it, *text* – that is, stories that tell themselves and their inventors into being, through the act of language.

This becomes even more spectacularly evident when the narration is presented as *theatre*. Auerbach (1974:351) was one of the first critics to argue that the complicated play of 'disguises and histrionics' in the story turns reality into 'a perpetual stage without ever ceasing to be reality' (one may disagree with the last part of the statement). Nowhere is this more in evidence than in the famous puppet scene mounted by none other than the erstwhile galley-slave Gines de Pasamonte, alias Ginesillo de Parapilla, now known as Master Peter (II:xxxvi). This triple disguise is replicated in the narrative situation where the Second Author narrates what the translator has made of Cide Hamete Benengeli's 'original' – and this is, significantly, the occasion where the garrulous Moor is reported to have sworn 'as a Catholic Christian'.

Like the *Don Quixote* as a whole, the puppet-master's story is based on chivalric romance, involving the rescue of a damsel in distress, none less than the daughter of Charlemagne, the beauteous Melisendra, from the clutches of an evil Moor, by the noble knight Sir Gaiferos, her husband. Whenever in the course of the performance a 'point' is made about reality, it is also subverted. At the crucial moment, just as the lovers are fleeing from the palace of the Moor, Don Quixote interrupts the play because he finds the ringing of bells improbable (Moors, he insists, would have used kettle-drums). But immediately afterwards he enters so fully into the reality of a performance he has just accused of being improbable, that he 'kills' the puppets. When challenged, he falls back on the explanation of 'magic' and on 'seeming'. Then, suddenly, the mundane realities of hunger and supper intervene to restore him to the 'sane' world, yet the next moment he denies that the puppet he destroyed is Melisendra. And after having paid compensation for the wrecked puppets, he wants to know whether Melisendra and Sir Gaiferos are safely back in France.

It is revealing that Foucault (1985:189) should also have recourse to the theatre in his discussion of madness: the theatrical performance, he argues, provokes 'a crisis which marks the point at which illusion, turned back upon itself, will open to the dazzlement of truth' – or, formulated at greater length:

The fulfilment of delirium's non-being in being is able to suppress it as non-being itself; and this by the pure mechanism of its internal contradiction – a mechanism that is both a play on words and a play of illusion, games of language and of the image; the delirium, in effect, is suppressed as non-being since it becomes a perceived form of being; but since the being of delirium is entirely in its non-being, it is suppressed as delirium. And its confirmation in theatrical fantasy restores it to a truth which, by holding it captive in reality, drives it out of reality itself, and makes it disappear in the non-delirious discourse of reason. (Foucault 1985:191)

In short, the *Don Quixote* 'calls into question the status of fictions and of itself as a fiction' (Alter 1978:15).

10

The supreme example in the *Don Quixote* of the status of fiction, and consequently of the language which is the condition of that fiction, is the role of Dulcinea del Toboso. Don Quixote, as many commentators have pointed out over the centuries, *knows* that Dulcinea is his own invention, 'yet [is] deadly serious about his unswerving devotion to the ideal fiction he has made for himself' (Alter 1978.:25); but more important than this restatement of the novel's most obvious tension is the fact that this *fiction* largely determines what happens to Don Quixote in 'reality'.

In the opening chapter, casting around for a lady to whom he can dedicate his exploits as knight errant, the hidalgo remembers one Aldonza Lorenzo, 'a very good-looking farm girl, whom he had been taken with at one time, although she is supposed not to have known it or had proof it it' (p. 35). From this tenuous root in 'reality' grows the Dulcinea del Toboso of the hidalgo's fantasies: and the driving force behind her conception is the 'musical' and 'strange' sound of her *name*. As in so many other instances in the novel, the action of *naming* determines reality – but far from representing an essentialist or Adamic concept of language as theorists like Thiher (1984) would ascribe to linguistic theory prior to the twentieth century, the referentiality of the name 'Dulcinea del Toboso' is fortuitous. If there is any reality attached to it, it comes after the fact, not before.

I suppose it may be argued that the name does contain an essence – an essence distilled from all the ladies of chivalric romance. But this does not bring one very far, as the signification attributed to it would remain so vague as to remain almost meaningless. Which is why it seems to me more promising to approach 'Dulcinea del Toboso', at the outset, as a near-empty signifier, constructed almost exclusively around its own sound qualities and its as yet unrealised possibilities. If it is to function as a signifier it will have to be filled in during the course of the narrative.

Initially, even the suspect grain of reality there may be in the name (that is, its reference to the 'very good-looking' Aldonza Lorenzo) is subverted in the famous chapter where we first learn about the 'original' manuscript of the *Don Quixote*. Because what first attracts the attention of 'our' author is a note in the margin; and this is translated, extempore, by the young vendor as follows: 'They say that Dulcinea del Toboso, so often mentioned in this history, was the best hand at salting port of any woman in all La Mancha' (p. 76). This, rather than beauty, appears to be her claim to fame.[6]

Soon afterwards comes the encounter with the Basque, narrated – significantly – in the form of a commentary on a *picture* of the event. The outcome of the episode is that Don Quixote sends his first victim to El Toboso to be dealt with according to the lady's pleasure. Then follows the terse observation: 'The terrified and distressed ladies [the Basque's companions] did not consider what Don Quixote required nor ask who Dulcinea was, but promised him that the squire should carry out the knight's command' (p. 79). The signifier remains open.

There is a hint of progress when Don Quixote, pressed by some travellers on their way to a funeral, provides a remarkably detailed description of his inamorata:

'[H]er name is Dulcinea; her country El Toboso, a village in La Mancha; her degree at least that of Princess, for she is my Queen and mistress; her beauty superhuman, for in her are realized all the impossible and chimerical attributes of beauty which poets give to their ladies; that her hair is gold; her forehead the Elysian fields; her eyebrows rainbows; her eyes suns; her cheeks roses; her lips coral; her teeth pearls; her neck alabaster; her breast marble; her hands ivory; she is as white as snow; and those parts which modesty has veiled from human sight are such, I think and believe, that discreet reflection can extol them, but make no comparison.' (p. 100)

But even a cursory examination will reveal that this is no 'description' – except, indeed, in the form of a catalogue borrowed from the 'impossible and chimerical attributes of beauty which poets give to their ladies'. In the most literal sense her body here 'is a citation: of the "already-written"' (Barthes 1975:33). And Don Quixote confirms the process through which she has been constructed when her degree of Princess is derived, not from her station in life or in society, but from the fact that she is his mistress.[7] Her whole existence is vested in him, and his interlocutor acknowledges this: 'For she would count herself fortunate to have all the world know that she is loved and served by such a knight as your worship appears to be' (loc. cit.). But, of course, by this time *his* whole existence, his *raison d'être*, his very sense of reality, is predicated on *her*!

The Don skirts very closely past the possibility of reality and identity when her existence as a sexual being is broached, but at the last moment 'those parts which modesty has veiled from human eyes' are assigned to what 'I think and believe' – an evocation of the same act of faith which initially led the hidalgo to accept the cardboard visor of his helmet without testing it a second time.

A significant inversion is added to the image constructed in front of the reader's eyes when Dulcinea's lineage is described, not in terms of her *ancestry*, but in terms of her possible *descendants*: it is 'a lineage which [...] may yet give noble birth to the most illustrious families of future ages' (p. 101).

Dulcinea again features prominently in I:xxv when for her sake Don Quixote indulges in a spell of penance in the mountains.[8] While he knows very well that Dulcinea cannot read or write, he sends her a love letter: in this scene, in other words, Dulcinea is restored to the peasant girl who first served as her model; and at one point Don Quixote even reverts to the use of her original name:

'I am quite satisfied [...] to imagine and believe that the good Aldonza Lorenzo is lovely and virtuous; her family does not matter a bit, for no one will inquire into that for the purpose of investing her with any order and, for my part, I think of her as the greatest princess in the world.' (p. 210)

When Sancho returns from the mission to the lady, and mischievously offers his master a most unflattering version of Dulcinea's appearance, winnowing wheat, Quixote immediately 'translates' the account into flattering terms, even when the descriptions become unbearably coarse (pp. 268–70). If Don Quixote has any suspicion of treachery (because Sancho has returned much sooner than expected) he readily finds a magical explanation:

'You must have gone and returned through the air [...] From which I conclude that the sage necromancer, who is my friend and looks after my affairs [...] must have assisted you on your journey without your knowing it.' (p. 270)

This is, indeed, *play* in the fullest sense of the word, that is, in the dialogic awareness of an event (specifically an event in language) as *both* real and unreal, mad and sane.

On several other occasions Dulcinea plays a key role as marker of the relationship between reality and unreality, madness and sanity, notably in the descent into the cave of Montesinos (II:xxiii), where during the three days of his visit (that is, 'a little more than an hour' in 'real' time: p 620) Don Quixote allegedly meets his lady. She appears remarkably similar to the peasant girl he and Sancho met in II:x and whom Sancho pretended at the time to identify as Dulcinea, persuading his master that her peasant appearance was the result of the knight's enchantment. Upon hearing the Don's report, Sancho bursts out laughing, 'for knowing as he did the truth about Dulcinea's pretended enchantment, and that he had been her enchanter and the inventor of the story, he finally realized [...] that his master was out of his mind' (pp. 621–2): another demonstration of the power of language in constituting the 'real'. In the hidalgo's account of the encounter, Montesinos suggested that Dulcinea was no match for the magician's own lady, whereupon Don Quixote neatly solved the whole problem by deciding that 'the peerless Dulcinea is who she is, and the lady Doña Belerma is who she is, and was – and there let it rest' (p. 619). The move towards Dulcinea's independent existence is particularly significant in the light of what is yet to come.

In this episode, as in the previous one referred to, one has to bear in mind the extent to which, as Alter (1978) phrases it, much of the Don's story is shaped by his 'acute consciousness of "the sage who is to write the history" of his exploits, for it is only through the writing down that he can be sure he has become as real as Amadís [...] Don Quixote, a bookish man, actually wants to become a book' (pp. 8–9).

What we read as a narrated text (twice-narrated, thrice-narrated, *ad infinitum*), exists for Don Quixote, caught *in* that text, as a story *still to be told*; and his own function lies in the *tellability* of his tale, in what Derrida would term the *iterability* of his language.[9]

But tellability and iterability in the hidalgo's story-to-be-told do not exist, as it were, in a state of total futurity: they are determined, precisely, by the fact that they *have* been told before – in the chivalric romances to which he wishes so passionately to be restored. In the end Don Quixote must return to the 'subtle immensity of writings' (Barthes 1975:122) that has spoken him into existence.

11

The decisive event in this process, and also the culmination of the Dulcinea theme in the novel, is one of the sublime moments in Western literature. It is the last encounter with the Bachelor Samson Carrasco, masquerading as the Knight of the White Moon: defeated in the skirmish, Don Quixote is bound by the terms of their pact to acknowledge that his adversary's mistress is superior to Dulcinea del Toboso:

> Then, battered and stunned, without lifting his vizor Don Quixote proclaimed in a low and feeble voice, as if he were speaking from inside a tomb: 'Dulcinea del Toboso is the most beautiful woman in the world, and I am the most unfortunate knight on earth; nor is it just that my weakness should discredit that truth. Drive your lance home, knight, and rid me of life, since you have robbed me of honour'. (p. 890)

Eighteen years before Galileo, this is Don Quixote's *Eppur si muove*. It is also a profoundly liberating experience: by announcing Dulcinea's status as the most beautiful mistress in the world, irrespective of whether he abjures her or not, he grants her an autonomous existence, releasing her from all dependence on *his* faith and *his* imagination. But by the same token he can now no longer be dependent on *her* – and if he relinquishes the lady who has provided the ultimate justification for all his exploits, there is, quite literally, no sense in continuing to live. And so, irrespective of what the Bachelor or the code of chivalry requires of him, Don Quixote hereby condemns *himself* to death. Which indeed follows soon afterwards.

On his deathbed, entreated by the Bachelor Samson Carrasco to 'cease your idle tales', the hidalgo replies: 'Tales? [...] Up to now they have been only too real, to my cost. But, with Heaven's aid, my death shall turn them to my profit' (p. 936). This is followed by his ultimate recourse to the translative powers of language, as he makes his final confession and dictates his testament. The last codicil of the testament entreats his heirs to track down the disreputable author of the false *Second Part of the Exploits of Don Quixote de la Mancha* in order to beg of him, 'with the greatest earnestness, to forgive the occasion I unwittingly gave him of publishing so many gross absurdities as are therein written; for I quit this life with an uneasy conscience at having given him an excuse for writing them' (p. 938).

He dies with a proverb on his lips: '*Señores* [...] *vamonos poco a poco, pues ya en los nidos de antaño no hay pájaros hogaño*' (Cervantes 1958:455): 'Let us go gently, gentlemen [...] for there are no birds this year in last year's nests' (p. 938). And he leaves the final word to the alleged 'original' author of the text, who is also an invention of the text, Cide Hamete Benengeli: '*Para mí sola nació Don Quijote, y yo para él; él supo obrar, y yo escribir*' (Cervantes 1958:457): 'For me alone Don Quixote was born and I for him. His was the power of action, mine of writing' (p. 940). With these words he is folded back into his own text, subsumed into his own speech.

The word has the final word.

Era y non era. Kan ya makan.

2

Courtly Love, Private Anguish

Madame de Lafayette: *La Princesse de Clèves*

1

It is difficult to imagine a divide more dramatic than that between the *Don Quixote* and what has widely become known as 'the first French novel', Madame de Lafayette's remarkable little gem, *La Princesse de Clèves*, first published in 1678. It still glows with dark brilliance among the many other early attempts of the new genre of the novel to define itself in opposition to a long tradition of more or less outrageous romance. Still caught in many respects in the severe prescriptions of propriety and restraint of French classicism and very much the product of the century that produced Racine and Corneille, it lacks both the wild inventiveness of the *Don Quixote* and the exuberance with which authors like Defoe, only a few decades later, could bring to their representations of the life of the lower classes.

La Princesse de Clèves is steeped in the glamour and intrigue of court life; and apart from the occasional glimpse of a footman being sent on an errand, there is hardly a hint in the text of any society beyond that of the court and the aristocracy surrounding King Henry II of France (1494–1549). If this novel has affinities with anything that happened in the genre beforehand, it is, intriguingly, with the *erotica pathemata* , or 'tales of erotic suffering', of the late Greek period. Most pertinent among these is the *Chaereas and Callirhoë*, an early Romeo and Juliet story written by the legal secretary Chariton some time between 100 bc and 150 ad. This narrative, like Madame de Lafayette's, 'might be summarised in three words: psychology, rhetoric, history' (Hägg 1983:16). Rhetoric is described as 'deliberations of various kinds, where the participants eloquently present their arguments' (p. 16). The importance of history is defined by the remark, 'It seems as if he wished to legitimize the novel as literature through its historical framework and historiographic form' (p. 16). Psychology resides in 'his interest in the human mind. The "inner process", the sorrow and happiness of the characters, their hopes and fears, not least their irresolution in difficult situations involving choice' (p. 16). And Heiserman (1980:86) illuminates another point of comparison by describing the *Chaereas and Callirhoë* as 'the story of a woman whose fated Aphrodisian beauty conflicts with her ethos, her characteristic desire to be faithful to societal and familial ideals'. For all these parallels, however, Chariton's tale ultimately relies much more than Madame de Lafayette's on external adventure.

Even more intriguing than the link with the past, is the way in which Madame de Lafayette, in what Alter (1989:186) calls 'the beautifully precise vagueness of the language', appears to pave the way to the future, to something Derrida achieves in a text like *Limited, Inc.* (1977), in which he demonstrates with great clarity and precision that it is *impossible* for language to be clear and precise.

2

La Princesse de Clèves opens with an image of the court of Henry II a century before the novel was written – not only of its inimitable 'splendour and refinement' (p. 23),[1] but particularly of its proliferation of factions and intrigue, its 'ordered turbulence' (p. 34).[2] Each of the powerful personages at the court has a following; each is enmeshed in a network of intrigue, of private feuds, relationships and affairs – all the more insidious because the protocol and the codes of court life forbid that anything comes into the open: 'all these currents were hidden and there was no sign of concern' (p. 136).

To survive in this environment one has to make powerful friends, mainly through alliances based on sexual promise or play. Long before the feminist slogan *The private is the political* was coined, Madame de Lafayette demonstrated the implication of the personal in the public, of love and power in an 'atmosphere of intrigue and confidentiality' (p. 108).[3] On the surface, most noticeably on the surface of *language*, politeness, propriety, refinement, wit, and rhetorical brilliance determine all aspects of social intercourse; below that surface, everything seethes with deceit. A man like Sancerre may have three or four mistresses – one of them none less than the reigning Queen herself – each of them necessary for the power-struggles in which he is involved; so each must be kept secret from the others. And not even the reader knows for sure whether he actually has sexual relations with all or any of them: the very word *amant*[4] leaves the reader in the dark; and given its context, that is exactly as it should be. Everything in the novel is predicated on Mme de Chartres's early warning to her daughter: 'If you judge appearances in this place [...] you will often be deceived, because what appears to be the case hardly ever is' (p. 46).

It is this teeming world of beautiful people jostling for positions of power and ruled by draconian, if wholly unwritten, codes and laws of behaviour, which determines the plot, itself so deceptively simple in outline: the beautiful, unspoilt sixteen-year-old heroine,[5] a niece of the powerful family of the Vidame de Chartres, is brought to court by her mother for the sake of social advancement. Several of the most powerful men in the realm fall in love with her, but most are eliminated by reasons of state; and eventually she marries the somewhat colourless but thoroughly devoted Prince de Clèves. Almost immediately afterwards she meets the dashing courtier and notorious ladies' man, the Duc de Nemours (who at the opening of the novel is set to become a suitor of Queen Elizabeth of England), and both fall head over heels in love. But the Princesse is resolute not to become part of her deceitful environment, while her suitor, for once truly and wholly in love, is so shaken by the experience that he, too, departs from all the accepted codes of behaviour in order to be true to this exceptional young woman. (One is wryly reminded of what the Marquis de Sade was to write a century later, in *Justine*: '*Dans une société totalement vicieuse, la vertu ne servirait à rien* [In a wholly vicious society there would be no sense in virtue]'.) The course of their love – during which they only have three meetings in private – is determined by her resolve to remain faithful to her husband, while Nemours has to restrain his passion in order to be worthy of his love. Eventually the wretched Prince de Clèves dies of a fever brought on by his outrageous jealousy (he has sent a spy to follow Nemours when the latter travels to the estate where the Princesse has been left alone; and although the Duc did no more than gaze at his love, the Prince cannot believe that nothing untoward has happened). At last the Princesse is free to marry the man she loves; but in a scene of beautifully controlled dialogue she turns him down. The reason she advances is that his love has been conditional all along upon the obstacles between them; once married, she argues, he will revert to his old habits and take new mistresses, which will kill the very love for which both have sacrificed so much. But behind this argument lies a deeper consciousness: her need to regain her independence of mind, and to reclaim the individual language that has been her emblem and which has become compromised by her involvement in court society. When she retires to a convent, it does not only place a distance between her and the world but becomes a retreat, as I hope to demonstrate, beyond the reach of language.

The integrity of their narrative is surrounded – and invaded – by the innumerable intrigues surrounding them. The text offers, in particular, four further stories of various lengths, which amplify and complicate theirs: the story of the long-standing affair between the King and Madame de Valentinois, which prejudices almost all the other relationships at the court (pp. 45–9); the story of the faithless Madame de Tournon who manipulates three different lovers to secure the best position for herself before she suffers what the text seems to present as a well-merited death for an offending female (pp. 61–70); the story of Henry VIII of England and Anne Boleyn (pp. 80–2); and, at great length, the story of the Vidame's own *erotica pathemata* (pp. 86–104).

This last story impinges in a particular way on the triangular relationship of the Princesse, her husband and her suitor, and as it is revealing of the kind of intrigue that characterises this world it merits a closer look. It breaks the surface of court society when an unsigned love letter falls from the Vidame's pocket during a game of tennis. But there is some confusion as to whose pocket it fell from, and it is handed to the Queen's daughter-in-law, the Dauphine (later Mary, Queen of Scots), with the news that it belonged to the Duc de Nemours. The Dauphine hands it to the Princesse de Clèves to try and identify the handwriting. She is, of course, overcome by horror at the idea that her own suitor, who has always protested the exclusivity of his passion for her, should secretly have another mistress.

In the meantime the Vidame has discovered the loss of his letter and turns to his closest friend, the Duc de Nemours, for help. He has reason to be frantic, as he has been amorously involved with several ladies at the same time, one of whom is Queen Catherine de Médicis, who will be furious if she should learn that her most trusted lover has been having other affairs on the sly after he has sworn his faith to her:

> 'If the Queen sees that letter, she will know that I deceived her and that, almost at the same time as I was deceiving her with Mme de Thémines, I was deceiving Mme de Thémines with another: imagine the idea that this will give her of me and whether she can ever trust me on my word.' (p. 100)

The Queen knows that the letter has been handed to the Dauphine; and what the Vidame now requests of Nemours is that *he* should retrieve the letter and confirm that he is the one who lost it. To add to the Vidame's anxiety, there is a real possibility that the Dauphine may show the letter to another close friend, Mme de Martigues, who is the third woman in the Vidame's web.

Upon being told that the Dauphine already believes it is Nemours's letter, he is profoundly shocked, anticipating how such a report, at a court where nothing is ever kept secret for long, will affect the Princesse. But he is persuaded when the Vidame hands him a note from one Mme d'Amboise, a friend of the luckless Mme de Thémines, requesting the Vidame to return the letter to the desperate writer: Nemours is given permission to show this note to the Princesse (whose role in Nemours's life no-one suspects), in order to exonerate him in her eyes.

The plot thickens when Nemours uses this as a pretext to pay a late-night visit to the Princesse to enlist her aid in retrieving the letter from the Dauphine. The Princesse prudently refuses to receive him, but her husband, more readily persuaded of the gravity of the affair, leads the Duc to his wife's bedroom, where he leaves them alone to resolve the matter. This is only the second time the two meet in private and it is a scene charged with great emotion. Once the Princesse is convinced by Mme d'Amboise's note that Nemours really had nothing to do with the lost letter, she is eager to help solve the problem.

This becomes more precarious when, the next morning, the Dauphine demands her letter back, as the Queen herself has by now heard about it and, suspecting the Vidame's involvement, wants to read it. Unable to tell the Queen that the letter has been passed on to the Princesse (who may be compromised because the Vidame is her uncle and a family plot may be suspected), the Dauphine has played for time. To escape from the

quandary, the Princesse explains that she had shown the letter t
her husband, who gave it back to Nemours. The Dauphine
flabbergasted: 'It is your fault for giving him the letter: ther
not a woman in the world except you who confides all that she
knows to her husband' (p. 107).

The only solution is for the Princesse to write, from memory, a
forged version of the letter to be passed on to the Queen; this
forgery, which takes most of the day, allows the two lovers to
spend more time together than ever before, or after, in their lives.
In the end the Queen is not fooled by the forgery after all; but the
main result is that she suspects the Dauphine herself of complicity.
'This idea so greatly fuelled her hatred for the Dauphine that she
never forgave her, but persecuted her until she had driven her out
of France' (p. 109). Having lost all faith in the Vidame too, she ends
the relationship of confidence with him and embarks on a long
process of revenge which will eventually, we are told, lead to his
final ruin a year after the present story has ended.

For the Princesse the story of the letter marks a moment of
terrible insight: into the unsuspected jealousy she is forced to
acknowledge in herself; into the extreme of passion of which she
discovers herself to be capable; and, most significantly, into the
possibility of betrayal which lurks even in the noblest relationship.
Nemours has been proved innocent, for now. But for the first time
she has to accommodate the possibility of betrayal, somewhere in
the future; and eventually this will be the driving force behind her
final renunciation of the relationship. The event has demonstrated
what the intrigues which define life at court really amount to, and
what they are capable of.

What concerns us at the moment, is that all the deceit and all the
misrepresentations which constitute this particular intrigue, are
based on the use and misuse of *language*, and that the whole whirl-
pool of events centres around a *letter*, the most visible and tangible
evidence of language in action in this closed world.

3

'Artifice and dissimulation' (p. 70) is the phrase with which the
estimable Prince de Clèves brands the intrigues Mme de Tournon
resorts to in order to cope with the attentions of her three lovers;
and this is a fair description of the dissimulation and the disguise

of feelings which characterise the use of language throughout the text.

The tendency of language to dissimulate and deceive is conveyed in a wide variety of ways – whether it is the Queen who hides her jealousy of the Duchesse de Valentinois in order to maintain her own hold on the King (pp. 23, 98); or the Cardinal de Lorraine who chides the Chevalier de Guise for professing his love of Mlle de Chartres, 'though without telling him the true reason for his disapproval' (p. 25); or the admirable Mme de Chartres herself, who constantly encourages her daughter to be frank, yet prefers not to divulge the means Mme de Valentinois as a fourteen-year-old girl used to obtain a pardon for her father from the previous King; or the Prince who, upon discovering that a portrait of the Princesse has disappeared, feigns to speak to her 'in jest' when he is really deadly serious, saying 'to his wife (though in tones that showed he did not believe it) that she must have a secret lover' (p. 84);[6] or the famous – anonymous – love letter discussed above, in which Mme de Thémines announces her decision to renounce her feelings for the Vidame:

> 'I thought that, if there was one thing that might revive your feeling for me, it was to show you that my own feelings had changed; but to do so by pretending to hide the fact from you, as if I did not have the strength to admit it [...] I was sustained by the pleasure of using deception towards you as you had towards me.' (p. 90)

Particularly relevant, too, are the attempts by the Duc de Nemours, in his first meeting with the Princesse without others present, to convey to her his love by speaking in roundabout and general terms: '[T]he real test is not to give way to the pleasure of being with them; it lies in avoiding them, for fear of revealing to others, and almost to themselves, the feeling that we have for them' (pp. 74–5).

One of the most brilliantly contrived scenes in the novel takes place in the Dauphine's bedroom, some time after the Duc de Nemours had stealthily crept into a closet in a pavilion on the Prince de Clèves's estate, where he happened to eavesdrop on a crucial conversation: the Princesse's confession to her husband (without mentioning any names) that there is a man who is in love with her and that, although she is resolved to remain faithful to the Prince, she would prefer to remove herself from the court lest her own feelings be tempted too far.[7] Overcome by this first direct evidence that the Princesse is as much in love with him as he with her, Nemours confides in his best friend, the Vidame – pretending, typically, that he is talking about something that has happened to a friend of his. The Vidame is not fooled by the ruse. Although he is sworn to secrecy, the inevitable happens and the news is spread about the court: the only part of the story to remain concealed is the name of the woman involved. In due course the Dauphine also learns about it, and being herself one of the keenest gossips in the court, she summons the Princesse to her bedroom to share with her the juicy titbit about the mysterious love affair of the Duc de Nemours with some unknown woman who had the temerity to tell her husband about it.

Naturally, the Princesse is horrified to learn that the most intimate conversation of her life has become common knowledge (even though nobody knows as yet that she is the woman concerned). At this moment – a *coup de théâtre* if ever there was one – the Duc de Nemours himself arrives and is invited into the bedroom (which in the eighteenth century was often used for private but perfectly proper visits). 'Here is the man himself', announces the Dauphine, 'and I mean to ask him about it' (p. 125).

Then follows the scene handled with such consummate narrative skill. After his initial bewilderment at being confronted with the news that his best friend, the Vidame, has betrayed his confidence, Nemours eloquently sticks to his version of the story, namely that it refers to one of his friends, not to himself. At the same time he must try to allay the Princesse's suspicions. But even more importantly, he wishes to convey to her, without daring to reveal anything directly, what he really feels. In a novel constructed, as a whole, around the deviousness and deceit demonstrated by the strategies and mechanisms of language, this is indeed a scene of incomparable subtlety:

'The Vidame cannot say that it concerns me [says the Duc de Nemours], since I told him the opposite. I might claim to be a man in love; but as for being a man loved, I do not think, madame, that this is a thing you can attribute to me [...] I was concerned, madame [...] for my friend's interests and because he might justifiably reproach me with having repeated a secret that is dearer to him than life itself. Even so, he confided no more than a part of the story to me, and did not name the person whom he loves. I only know that he is the man most in love and most to be pitied in the world.' (p. 126)

As for the report of the lady's confession to her husband, he says, 'I am almost inclined to agree with Mme de Clèves that this story cannot be true' (p. 127). To which she promptly replies,

'Indeed, I think it cannot be [...] And, even if it were so, how could anyone have spoken about it? It is hardly likely that a woman who was capable of such an extraordinary action, should be weak enough to talk about it; and it is impossible that her husband would mention it, either, or he would be a husband very undeserving of the trust she had shown him.' (p. 127)

As in Derrida's *Limited Inc*, language triumphs in its very demonstration of its own deceit. By using the stratagems of concealment and obfuscation, both the man and the woman implicated in the affair manage to escape from the scene, unscathed by the damage language can cause. But there is a final twist to it: at the end of the conversation the King and his retinue also arrive, and as the Princesse tries to escape in the throng, 'she tripped on the train of her dress and stumbled: she used this as an excuse to escape from a place where she did not feel she had the strength to stay, and returned home' (p. 128). Ultimately this – literal – Freudian slip trips her, as a comment on the deviousness of the language in the entire preceding scene.

An important key to this functioning of language in *La Princesse de Clèves* is an incident often overlooked in the web of intrigue woven by the narrative: soon after the Prince has told his wife the story of Mme de Tournon and her three lovers, there is a gathering at the court where the King and Queen discuss horoscopes and predictions. 'The Queen had great faith in them [...] Others argued that, in the vast number of predictions made, the few that proved to be true merely demonstrated that it was only an effect of chance' (p. 77). The King goes even further: 'I have been told so many things that are false or implausible that I have become convinced nothing certain can be known' (p. 77); and as an example of preposterously false predictions he tells the assembly about an astrologer who forecast that the King would be killed in a duel. The Duc de Nemours promptly takes the cue to assert that, 'I am the person in the world who should trust it the least' (p. 78) and in the Princesse's ear he whispers that, 'It has been foretold that I shall be made happy through the favours of the person in the world for whom I shall have the most overwhelming and respectful passion.' This ingenuous attempt to turn the conversation to his own advantage by using language to say the opposite of what he hopes for, is marred by a more disingenuous twist: 'It is for you to judge, madam, whether I should believe in predictions.'

Even then the scene is not over: challenged by the Dauphine to repeat what he has whispered to the Princesse, he immediately offers a new version, which subverts in front of the reader's eyes any pretence in language to speak the truth: 'I was remarking, madame, that it was foretold me I should attain a much greater fortune than I could ever have dared aspire to' (p. 78). Only a few changes in the wording, and a completely new meaning emerges.

The full implications of the scene only come to light much later, when the King is indeed killed in a duelling accident (p. 136). This prompts the reader, not only to return to the original discussion on horoscopes, but to reconsider Nemours's turn of phrase; in a very real sense the whole linguistic structure of the narrative is thereby placed at risk.

But it also prompts a conclusion which is of the utmost importance if one compares *La Princesse de Clèves* with other, later, novels: for Madame de la Fayette *language is not inherently treacherous*, its unreliability stems from the perception that it is so often used to lie and dissimulate that one can never be quite sure what it is supposed to mean in any given situation. More pertinently, the predicament caused by the web of treachery spun by language at the court is that if anyone within that enmeshed society *does* speak the truth – which is precisely the force that drives the Princesse – *it cannot be believed*, because everybody has become too thoroughly conditioned by language-as-dissimulation to recognise the truth when it is spoken. Nowhere is this demonstrated so poignantly as in the scenes where the Princesse confesses her total innocence to her husband, which he is simply unable to accept at face value.[8]

4

One consequence, borne out by the rest of the novel, is that, in a world where everything is manipulated by language and turned into 'stories', and where the norm of language is deceit, one has to turn to other sign-systems if one wishes to glean the truth. This 'other language', this alternative to language, is usually visual – a perception which underlies the extensive code of seeing, observing, gazing, in the text: since language cannot be trusted, the characters have to be on the constant lookout for other signs which can communicate what cannot be spoken. Sometimes the code functions in a quite spectacular way, as in the scene where Nemours looks on while the Princesse has her portrait painted (pp. 83–4). It gives the Duc the opportunity to steal another miniature which the painter has temporarily removed from its box (p. 85); she, in turn, sees him doing so, but pretends not to. More often than not the signs are less obtrusive: expressions, small gestures, smiles, frowns, and above all, blushes.

Unfortunately these signs can also be misread. Quite tellingly, the Prince de Clèves reveals his mistrustful nature even before Mlle de Chartres accepts his offer of marriage. When he expresses his doubt about her affections, she protests, 'You can surely not doubt [...] that I feel joy when I see you; and I blush so often when I do so, that you cannot doubt, either, that the sight of you disturbs me.' To which he ungracefully replies, 'I am not deceived by your blushes [...] They derive from feelings of modesty, not from those of the heart' (p. 40). And this is the problem of sign-systems designed to function as alternatives to language: since they can be decoded in various ways, they tend to become just as misleading as language.

The most elaborate use of a sign-system as an alternative to language occurs in what has become, for critics through the ages, the most famous scene of the novel. The setting is once again the pavilion in the forest on the estate of the Prince de Clèves, where the Princesse has withdrawn in the absence of both her husband and the Duc de Nemours on a journey with the King. It adds to the complexity of the episode to bear in mind that the Prince left his wife after yet another scene of great emotional upheaval between them, in which language is represented in its greatest confusion: 'I adore you, I hate you, I offend you, I beg your forgiveness; I am filled with wonder and admiration for you, and with shame at these feelings. In brief, there is no longer tranquillity or reason in me' (p. 144).[9] When Nemours learns that she has gone to Coulommiers, he finds a pretext to absent himself from the King's company in the hope of contriving to meet her alone. But the Prince de Clèves overhears the conversation between Nemours and his sister,

Mme de Martigues, in which this plan is hatched and sends his own gentleman in pursuit to spy on Nemours.

When Nemours arrives on the estate in the dead of night, he finds the Princesse in the pavilion tying ribbons in his colours around an old malacca cane of his which she has acquired under false pretences from his sister. The implications are too obvious to be missed (even if this was written more than two centuries before Freud). The eloquence of this 'other language', in a context where speech has been ruled out by the rules of society and the Princesse's own strict moral code, lends the scene a persuasive power that speaks more strongly than anything else the Duc de Nemours (or the reader) could have observed. But this is not yet the end. It is as if the scene is propelled by an urge to turn its scrutiny upon itself, an urge towards a metacommentary: having finished her play with the cane, the Princesse turns her gaze to a painting (or, more specifically, a *copy* of a painting) she has acquired for the pavilion, and which features, in the company of the King and his court, the Duc de Nemours. What happens here is a remarkable telescopic scene of observers observed: the reader sees the Prince 'observing', as it were, from a distance, the spy looking at the Duc de Nemours looking at the Princesse looking at the copy of a portrait of himself. William Ray (1990), among others, has commented on this scene in a particularly illuminating way, if in the context of a slightly different argument:

> The privacy of this expression is doubly ironized, for not only is Nemours observing this rite of adoration from a hiding spot behind the hedge, but he himself is being observed by a spy sent by the Prince. When the latter hears the man's vague report that the duc spent the night in the estate, he suspects the worst and dies of a broken heart. Thus even the Princesse's most radically enclosed gesture of self-expression is overseen, appropriated, and reinterpreted by others. (pp. 37–8; see also pp. 41–2)

I do not entirely agree with this argument and shall soon return to it; but for the moment our focus is on the process (and on the need) of finding an alternative sign-system to language – and the dangers of misinterpretation implicit in it. At the same time, precisely because it is *not* language, this scene highlights once again the problem with all such systems, *including* language: the inability to control meaning; and the precarious nature of the communication involved. The ultimate object of the whole process of gazing is the picture: the copy of an image of the real man (who is in the scene too, but unobserved by her). It is fake; it is a delusion, an imitation, a deceit – and its presence blinds the observer to whatever the scene may contain of reality (the real Duc).

5

Within this general framework the workings of language need to be looked at more precisely. Because not everybody in the narrative handles (or is allowed to handle) language in the same way; nor does language treat *them* all the same. In the narrowly structured patriarchy of the French court, the rules of conduct have been laid down by men; and it is men who control language. In a society where huge official receptions are arranged by noblemen merely 'to show off the ladies of the court' (p. 12), a husband is in absolute control of his wife's freedom of movement and of speech. Even a doting husband like the Prince de Clèves decides from one moment to the next 'what conduct he should prescribe for her' (p. 130); and disturbed by 'his violent and uneasy passion for her' (p. 41), his power over her acquires frightening overtones of violence. All the more reason for language to resort to subterfuge and dissimulation.

Men are indeed free to speak their true feelings: as soon as the Prince falls in love, he 'could not speak of anything else' (p. 31); and all the other suitors vying for the favours of Mlle de Chartres become 'unrestrained in their praise' (p. 32); and like the rest, when the Duc de Guise is smitten by her, he promptly 'declared his intentions and his passion' (p. 39). Jealous of the Duc de Nemours, he 'could not restrain himself from telling her that M. de Nemours was fortunate to have first made her acquaintance' (p. 44). Even when the King, as a young man, became his own father's rival in love, 'nothing could force him [...] to disguise what he felt' (p. 47). But it goes far beyond 'a natural tendency to tell all that one knows to the person one loves' (p. 123): it is the urge to *dominate* that woman through the power of language; and then to trap her in a web of language woven by public dissemination.[10] (It is in this respect that Ray (1990:35–41) is particularly perceptive.) And it is no accident that on more than one occasion a passionate discussion between the Prince de Clèves and his wife is ended by his stalking out of the room without allowing her an opportunity to reply (pp. 131, 144). It is the same male urge which drives Nemours constantly to contrive situations in which he can see the Princesse without being seen in return: the male gaze and the male use of language fulfil the same function in the power-play of patriarchy.

Women, on the other hand, are expected to remain silent and never to speak their feelings (except, in the strictest confidence, to a close relative, friend or ally.[11] The only women who do speak their minds at times are those in positions of power (the Queen, the Queen mother, the King's mistress, the Dauphine), because in these positions they function as honorary males. This is a rule of propriety the Princesse observes from the outset, not so much because it is imposed by court society, as from the example of her mother:

Mme de Chartres [...] often described love to her daughter, showing her all its attractions, the more easily to persuade her of its dangers; she told her of men's lack of sincerity; and of the domestic misfortunes occasioned by liaisons. (p. 30)

This is why she responds to the Prince's early complaint that she does not demonstrate much love during their engagement, by explaining that, 'I do not think propriety permits me to go any further than I do' (p. 40); and why, after the first dance with Nemours has turned her head with the discovery of new possibilities of emotional experience, the most she can do is to go 'into her mother's room to tell her about it; and she praised M. de Nemours with a particular tone that gave Mme de Chartres the same idea that had occurred to the Duc de Guise' (p. 44). Later, when her feelings for Nemours are crystallised into love, 'she was less disposed to tell her mother her mind [...]: without exactly deciding to conceal anything, she said nothing' (p. 51). And when she learns about her suitor's 'business with England' (that is, the plans to marry Elizabeth) 'the same feeling that made her curious obliged her to hide her curiosity' (pp. 79–80).

During the first half of the novel, whether through natural reticence, the lessons of her mother, or her exposure to court life, the Princesse strictly obeys the rules of language applied to society's views on female propriety. But much of the fascination of the narrative resides in the way in which she comes to break all those rules. It begins when, following the disclosure of Mme de Thémines's letter to the Vidame, she intimates more about her

feelings to Nemours than is 'proper' in her circumstances (p. 105);
the next step is her confession to the Prince. And after the death of
her husband she takes the extraordinary step of openly telling
Nemours about her love (pp. 164–8). This episode, in which language, as it were, catches up with itself by reinscribing its earlier
blanks and silences, becomes even more significant as it follows a
brief but highly charged scene in a garden outside the city, where
she goes to be alone, only to discover Nemours 'lying on one of the
benches, deeply wrapped in thought' (p. 161). It is an exact reversal
of the pavilion scene where he directed his gaze at her in an
unguarded moment: at last she can *return* the male gaze. At the
same time, through the services of Mme de Martigues, she discovers the window in the Vidame's apartment from where
Nemours had taken to looking out in the hope of seeing her, and
by staring back at this observation post, she neutralises it and rises
to the male challenge (p. 160). So it comes as no surprise that
immediately afterwards she finds the courage to confront Nemours
openly: the gaze is translated into language, and no code of propriety can contain her any more. What makes it even more significant, as I have indicated earlier, is that she expresses her desire
to have this private encounter publicised by reporting it to the
Vidame, that notorious gossip (p. 170).

These scenes prepare her for her final withdrawal into a convent:
it is not an act of renunciation, or an admission of defeat. And it is
more than an 'oblique' proposal of 'private representation [...] as
an alternative to social reality' and 'a perfect demonstration [...]'
that objective knowledge is favored at the expense of internal
knowledge' as Ray (1990:41, 49) argues. On the contrary, I see it
as a bold step to reclaim her independence, by once more – or at
last – taking charge of her own life. This can only be done by
wholly turning away from the corroded and corrosive court language which has so contaminated her. Withdrawing into a convent
means a decisive renunciation of *language* – that language which
her experience at the court has made suspect and destructive. What
she requires from, and affirms in, this act of withdrawal is a
combination of *absence* and *distance* – precisely those attributes of
language Derrida will explore so eloquently in the late twentieth
century. It may be a sad comment on her world that a woman's
only valid response to male language should reside in silence,[12]
just as Cordelia's silence damned her in Lear's eyes. But this is not
the ultimate statement of the novel: the *narration* does not end with

the *story*. The Princesse de Clèves opts out of language, *but the narrator tells her story*. The use of language by the narrator corrects its abuses in the narrated world.

6

One of the reasons why *La Princesse de Clèves* has impressed readers over the centuries is the remarkable subtlety and precision with which language conveys the most refined nuances of the inner emotional experience of the main characters. Often this happens in the form of interior monologue, as in the long passage, worthy of a young Werther, reflecting the turmoil in the mind of the Duc de Nemours after witnessing the revealing scene in the pavilion (p. 151). Even when such a chaos of feelings is registered in reported speech, the twentieth-century reader may be amazed by the ability of a seventeenth-century pen to record so finely so many shades of emotion. The same is true, among numerous other examples, of a passage which would not have been amiss in Racine's *Andromache*, '*brûlé de plus de feux que je n'en allumai*': it captures the Princesse's anguish when she first, mistakenly, suspects Nemours of infidelity:

All she could see was that M. de Nemours did not love her as she had believed, but that he loved other women and was deceiving them as he was her. What a thing that was to see and know for a person of her temperament, passionately in love, who had just displayed her feelings[13] to a man whom she judged unworthy, and to another whom she had scorned for love of him! There could be no sharper or more bitter anguish than she felt, and it seemed to her that the acuteness of the pain derived from what had occurred during the day and that, if M. de Nemours had not had any reason to believe that she loved him, she would not have been troubled by his loving someone else [...] It seemed to her that the writer of the letter showed intelligence and character, and deserved to be loved; she admired her willpower, which she judged superior to her own, and envied the strength of mind that had enabled the woman to hide her feelings from M. de Nemours. From the end of the letter, she saw that the writer believed herself to be loved; and the idea occurred to her that the discretion the prince had shown, and which she had found so touching, was perhaps merely because of his love for this other, whom he did not want to displease. (p. 90)

– and this is a mere extract from a passage that continues for much longer.

During her first meeting alone with Nemours the Princesse is in such a state of emotional confusion, subject to the most conflicting impulses, that the narrator's powers of reportage are taxed to the utmost:

> It occurred to her that she ought to reply and not to endure it. It occurred to her also that she should not understand or give any sign that she applied what he said to herself. She felt she should speak and thought she should say nothing. (p. 75)

Language which demonstrates itself to be so finely tuned to the expression of such fluctuations of emotion stands in striking contrast to the processes of covering up and deceit we encounter in the speech of the characters.

But does this mean that language in *La Princesse de Clèves* is, after all, reliable? Not at all. The narrator employs a wide number of strategies to ensure that readers, even when they are deeply moved by this language, should nevertheless remain alert to the fact that even the delicate capturing of scenes, relations and emotions cannot altogether dispel the narrator's own caution (if not distrust) about the instrument she is handling with such finesse. The first signal to the reader *not* to accept uncritically whatever is narrated, is embedded in one of the most noticeable characteristics of the narrative, its tendency towards exaggeration and superlatives. In the very first sentence of the novel we learn that, 'At no time in France were splendour and refinement so brilliantly displayed as in the last years of the reign of Henry II [...] never has any court possessed so many lovely women and admirably handsome men' (p. 23). The Duc de Nemours is described as incomparable, 'nature's masterpiece' (p. 25), the Maréchal de Saint-André as displaying 'the greatest liberality ever seen in a private individual' (p. 27), the Dauphine's mother as 'a perfect beauty' (p. 38), while of the Princesse it is said that 'there was never anyone who possessed so much natural candour' (p. 41). On practically every page of the novel such superlatives abound; and surely their proliferation must warn the reader to apply some caution to the reliability of such persistent overstatement. If it may be read, initially, as a strategy to set the narrated world apart from the 'real' world of the reader, the fact of its intrusion into the processes of narration itself must prompt some suspicion about the accountability of the narrator.

This impression is enhanced by regular flickerings of uncertainty and ambiguity in the language about the veracity or reliability of what is reported: the Duchesse de Valentinois *might be said* to be the real power in France (p. 26); *one might say* that the Prince de Clèves fell in love at first sight (p. 31); after the vicious quarrel between the Prince and the Princesse following his discovery of the Duc's visit to the estate at Coulommiers, Nemours tries to visit her, but finds the door barred: 'He learned that nobody saw her and that she had even forbidden them to tell her who had come to visit. *It might be* that these instructions had been given precisely because of the prince' (p. 158) – a turn of phrase which goes against the grain of the apparent precision that marks so many descriptions. A particularly revealing moment occurs when the Princesse's decision to have some paintings copied for her pavilion is narrated: on one of them, as mentioned earlier, the Duc de Nemours also features, 'and this, *perhaps*, was what made Mme de Clèves wish to have the painting' (p. 145; my italics). Occurring precisely at *this* point, the 'perhaps' is particularly striking. And that this is no stylistic accident is proved by its recurrence – in the emblematic pavilion scene itself, when the Princesse has the impulse 'to go back into the room and look in the garden to see if anybody was there. *Perhaps* she hoped as much as she feared finding M. de Nemours.'

More pointers to the unreliability of language, even – and now especially – on the narrating level itself, occur in the frequent admission that language cannot meet the challenge of a given reality: 'It is impossible to describe the pain she felt' (p. 56); 'her feelings and agitation of mind cannot be described' (p. 72); 'M. de Nemours's feelings at this moment cannot be described' (p. 148); 'the disgust she felt for herself and for M. de Nemours cannot be described' (p. 158); 'It is impossible to describe the feelings of M. de Nemours and Mme de Clèves on finding themselves alone' (p. 164),[14] and so on. Against the background of so many other situations where the narrator *does* describe, in fine detail, the emotions of the characters, moments like these cannot be read as narrative incompetence or laziness, but indeed as significant revelations of inadequacies within language itself.

7

There is yet another way in which the authority of language of *La Princesse de Clèves* is subtly interrogated in the text. One is struck by the prominence of letter-writing in the narrative as a key component of the endless process of intrigue at the court: but these letters appear almost never to be signed. This is most pertinently the case in the Vidame's lost letter, which functions as such an important trigger in the story as to become an almost emblematic episode. It is the fact that the letter is unsigned which makes it possible to ascribe it to the Duc de Nemours and for it to become such a potentially dangerous floating signifier in the text. This also makes it possible for others (in this instance the Princesse and Nemours) to copy it, that is, in Derridean terms, quite literally to 'iterate' it: *to dramatise its iterability.*

And can one not discern the same process of *de-authorising* at work behind most of the messages and rumours which determine so largely the rise and fall in the fortunes of major actors in the great play of life at the court? Anyone can plant a piece of information, and then back away from it, allowing it a lethal life of its own in the form of *écriture.* Even that urge of characters like Nemours to look without being seen, to hide the physical self behind bushes or in the dark, might be read as attempts to 'de-authorise' their actions. An important consequence is that language, once again, becomes suspect. And there is a piquant extension of this strategy beyond the text in the fact that Madame de Lafayette persistently refused to acknowledge authorship: even today we cannot be *absolutely* sure that she wrote the novel. No wonder that, even when we encounter intradiegetic 'authorised speech' where the speakers are present in the scene, we may perceive an interval between speaker and speech – because from the very beginning the nameless narrator herself merges with a possible, or presumed, author who has also, noticeably, withdrawn from the text. Two hundred years before Barthes *La Princesse de Clèves* hints at the death of the author 'as the past of his own book', which leaves the text as 'a tissue of quotations drawn from the innumerable centres of culture' (Barthes 1988: 169–70). It is, admittedly, a far cry from those texts of Postmodernism where *différance* is the very condition of language, but *La Princesse de Clèves* becomes all the more fascinating by, at least tentatively, pointing a possible course for future exploration of the languages of the novel.

3

'The Woman's Snare'

Daniel Defoe: *Moll Flanders*

1

Traditionally regarded as the father of the English novel,[1] more particularly by those who choose to ignore that the genre also had mothers, Defoe tends to be seen as an early exponent of realism. This would imply that his narrative language is transparent and representational, words standing in a more or less one-to-one relation to facts, events or characters. But a closer reading of his novels brings to light surprisingly original, and surprisingly 'modern', aspects of the author's exploitation of language. Especially in *Moll Flanders* (1722), as later in *Roxana* (1724), the leap of the imagination in adopting the voice of a female narrator appears to stimulate in Defoe a new self-consciousness in the exploitation of language as a means, not simply of representing the real, but of fabricating it.

2

There is a small revealing episode in *Moll Flanders* where the redoubtable heroine, her whoring days (as she herself would call them) behind her, has to leave Harwich in something of a hurry with the spoils of a thieving trip. Informing her landlady that she is departing for London on a vessel known as a wherry, she boards, instead, a boat headed for Ipswich. The whole episode is gravid with deceit: Moll has stayed at the inn disguised as a gentlewoman; her luggage consists of a parcel of linen acquired under false pretences in Cambridge, a gold watch filched from a lady who has feasted too merrily at St Edmund's Bury, a portmanteau stolen from a foreigner and his drunken footman; in the turmoil of comings and goings she leaves without paying her bill, and the well-intentioned fellow summoned from the street to transport her load does not suspect that he is aiding and abetting a wily criminal. In the midst of all this narrative business Moll finds the time to reflect on something which at first sight seems to be of little consequence: the designation of the boat she is to travel on:

> These wherries are large vessels, with good accommodation for carrying passengers from Harwich to London; *and though they are called wherries, which is a word used in the Thames for a small boat rowed with one or two men, yet are these vessels able to carry twenty passengers, and ten or fifteen tons of goods, and fitted to bear the sea.* (p. 290, my emphasis)[2]

The passage is interesting for its almost casual reflection of Moll's familiarity with an unexpected dimension of London's seamier regions (part of a formidable accumulation of information about a diversity of social and economic strata in the life and topography of the city); but even more interesting for its focus – at such a moment – on a detail of language. What initially may appear irrelevant, becomes significant if one considers that in this almost throwaway line on the meaning of *wherry* is encapsulated a view of language which permeates the whole novel, namely that words mean different things to different people (or in different contexts); or, more radically, that words are not fixed in their meanings but interchangeable and ultimately unreliable. They are there for mere convenience and may be changed at a whim; they exist not so much to circumscribe meaning as to manipulate or even to camouflage it. In other words, language is not primarily representational, as one would expect in a novel from the Age of Reason, but a *condition* (and even a strategy) for the construction of reality according to the needs or designs of the speaker or the inclination of the reader.

This instability of meaning is reflected throughout the novel. If there is one syntactic device which must strike even the casual reader of *Moll Flanders*, it is, in Jakobson's paradigm of communication, the metalingual, that is, the privileging of the speech act itself over the content of what is transmitted to the reader. A sentence like the following is the rule rather than the exception: 'I *assure* you, if I find a woman so accomplished as you *talk* of, I *say*, I *assure* you, I would not trouble myself about the money' (p. 21, my emphasis).

In a typical paragraph near the beginning, Moll reports (or is reported to be reporting) that she was 'terrified with the *news* that the magistrates (*as I think they called them*) *had ordered* that I should go to service [...] for I had a thorough aversion to going to service, *as they called it* [...] though I was so young: and I *told* my nurse, *as we called her*, that I *believed* I could get my living without going to service' (p. 10, my emphasis).

Initially, it may be simply a matter of misunderstanding or mis-reading: as many commentators have pointed out, the course of Moll's life is determined from the outset by her resolve to be a 'gentlewoman [...] as [she] understood the word' (p. 11): while, as everybody knows, much of her conflict with society stems from other definitions of the same word, 'for they meant one sort of thing by the word gentlewoman, and I meant quite another' (p. 13). But as her exposure to language increases, and as she comes to discover that her very survival may depend on her constructions of reality through language, this process becomes increasingly com-plex. In a typical passage near the end Moll describes a criminal of her acquaintance:

I knew one fellow that, while I was a prisoner in Newgate, was one of those *they called then* night-fliers. *I know not what other word they may have understood by it since*, but he was one who by connivance was admitted to go abroad every evening, when he played his pranks, and furnished those honest people *they call* thief-catchers with business to find out next day [...] *If he had told* all the particulars, and given *a full account* of his rambles and success, to any comrade, any brother thief, or to his employers, *as I may justly call them*, then all was well with him. (p. 358, my emphasis)

But if this is true of the use of language in *Moll Flanders* in general, its functioning concerns her status as a woman in a very specific way. In a very revealing passage, strategically placed just after her disastrous marriage to the gentleman draper and before she meets and marries the man who turns out to be her brother, Moll dis-cusses the (limited) options available to a woman who wishes to take revenge on a man who has left her in the lurch. Her justifica-tion (which leads directly to the kind of deceit she will exercise on her next suitor) is the observation, arrived at through bitter experi-ence, that 'as the market ran very unhappily on the men's side, I found the women had lost the privilege of saying No [...] The men had such choice everywhere' (p. 73). In the dog-eats-dog society of early eighteenth-century London in which she has to survive,[3] freedom is gendered, and it is predicated on language: on the possibility of choice, on the right to say No. Males have appropriated language; they make the rules in which women are invariably ensnared. And the only way for a female of Moll's intelligence and talents to survive is to repossess language and to turn 'woman's rhetoric' (p. 351) into a snare of her own.

This seems to be the deeper meaning informing her tirade against the bondage of marriage – a bondage prompted by the fear of a *word*: the term 'old maid':

> I would fain have the conduct of my sex a little regulated in this particular, which is the thing in which, of all the parts of life, I think at this time we suffer most in; 'tis nothing but lack of courage, for fear of not being married at all, and of that frightful state of life called an old maid, of which I have a story to tell by itself. This, I say, is the woman's snare. (p. 82)

The word, read against the background of all the 'discourses of matrimony' that constitute the text, can only be viewed as the threat it is if it is seen as constitutive of its own reality – not because it designates a pre-existing reality, but because the term *constructs* a social perception of which woman becomes the target and the victim.

3

The process of highlighting this function of language is introduced in the Preface, with its presentation of two (and subsequently even three) distinct speaking voices in the narrative. Numerous commentators have explored Moll's dual role as character and narrator (see especially Robert Alan Donovan's 'The Two Heroines of *Moll Flanders*': 1969); several have pursued this to the perception that, 'An editor is required to separate Moll from her life, to create a Moll who can speak about her life without being what her life implies' (Richetti 1975:97). And, within the discourse of the novel, many have examined what they perceived as Defoe's and/or Moll's 'casuistry' (Starr 1971), or the codes of disguise and deceit in the text (Blewett 1979). But it seems to me that the true focus of such an enquiry should be the strategy of narrating as such, as this is the nexus between story and discourse, as well as the point where, traditionally, the 'world' enters the text, or the text spills into the 'world'.

We know that almost no eighteenth-century English novel was published without a note disclaiming its fictitious nature and insisting on its being, as Defoe states in *Roxana*, 'not a story, but a history',[4] a distinction also honoured by Fielding, Richardson, Sterne and others, and already featuring in Aphra Behn's Introduction to *Oroonoko* in 1688: 'I do not pretend, in giving you the history of this ROYAL SLAVE, to entertain my Reader with the adventures of a feigned hero.'

In an age when the term 'novel' still designated primarily a small tale about trivial matters and when serious authors and readers alike were horrified at the idea of being associated with the levities and the extravagance of 'romance', writers of narrative were practically unanimous in their paranoia about 'fiction', about 'meddling with the Unclean Thing', as William Hazlitt (in Kelly (ed.) 1973:328) so charmingly termed it, going out of their way to present their texts as histories, letters, journals, diaries, memoirs, in fact, anything *but* 'novels' (see also Woolf 1919:338). This was the basis on which they constructed their fictions and metafictions; in fact, the history of the novel proper has known no other period, prior to Postmodernism, when metafiction and narcissistic fiction were so much in vogue.

For *Moll Flanders* it has peculiar implications.

It is necessary to look very carefully at the terms of the narrative contract proposed in the Preface. It is offered as an autobiography, a 'private history', an 'original [...] put into new words' (p. 1). The Editor, looking back from the early 1720s on a document dated 1683, cannot vouch for any authenticity, any Auctor, the existence of any signified, *behind* the written text; at most, he can offer it as an 'account' or a *version* of reality. 'The author is here *supposed* to be writing her own history', the Editor states, in a 'copy which first came to hand [...] written in language more like one still in Newgate than one grown penitent and humble, as she afterwards *pretends* to be' (p. 2, my emphasis). This preliminary, and already dubious, version is now offered, through the mediation of the Editor, as 'put into new words', specifically in 'modester words than she told it at first'; it is 'put into a dress fit to be seen',[5] and made to 'speak language fit to be read'.

What is important in this explanation-cum-warning is the early introduction of a code of dressing or dressing up that pervades the novel, most visibly in Moll's habit, especially during her thieving days, of masquerading in a wide assortment of costumes: a widow's weeds (p. 69), various gentlewoman's outfits (for example pp. 282, 325, 343), a 'very mean habit' (p. 261), a beggar's rags (p. 278), the dress of a poor but decent person (p. 343), even man's clothing (p. 235). Indeed, a code of masking and masquerading, of acting and dissembling and pretence, of lies and deceit and mis-representation, weaves the very fabric of the narrative. But what is especially important about this early reference is that the trope is here explicitly linked to the functioning of *language*.

Just as significant is the fact that through language the reader is drawn into the text: it is *'language fit to be read'*. Within another paragraph or two, 'the gust and palate of the reader' is given primacy above 'the real worth of the subject'; and the text is 'recommended to those who know how to read it' (p. 2).

Having activated this web of meaning in the text, the Editor specifies his intervention as twofold: on the one hand, the narrative 'is carefully garbled of all the levity and looseness that was in it' (p. 3); on the other, it is now explicitly 'applied, and with the utmost care, to virtuous and religious uses', a dual activity which has allegedly resulted in the excision of 'the vicious parts of her life' and the drastic shortening of 'several other parts', while inevitably – and implicitly – also necessitating the interpolation of moralising comment.

Rather than embark on a possibly futile exercise of trying to assess the distinct contribution of each of these two narrating voices, it would seem to me more useful to read the entire text as being spoken by two voices, or written by two pens; even if one appears to be more emphatic in some passages, and the second in others, *both are present throughout.*[6]

Neither can exist without the other, just as, within the narrated text, ultimately there is no hard and fast distinction to be made between the body and the clothes which disguise it, or between signified and signifier.

4

This leads straight to a problem of identity: *Moll Flanders cannot* be the 'autobiography' (or the biography, for that matter) of a person called Moll Flanders, because – even within the realities of the discourse – no 'Moll Flanders' exists. It goes further than the Editor's early warning about 'the reason why she thinks fit to conceal her true name' (p. 28), or the intradiegetic narrator's saucy announcement in her opening paragraph that,

> My true name is so well known in the records or registers at Newgate, and in the old Bailey, and there are some other things of such consequence still depending there, relating to my particular conduct, that it is not to be expected I should set my name or the account of my family to this work; perhaps, after my death, it may be better known. (p. 7)

After all, this narrator *must* be dead by the time her Editor takes up her memoirs some forty years after she allegedly completed them, by which time she was 'almost seventy years of age' (p. 376). For the purposes of a biography, or the annotation of an autobiography, any diligent researcher could have authenticated her existence if she had been a historical personage: however, as a fictitious narrator, she *invents* – and constantly reinvents – herself. This concerns not only the various personae she adopts in the course of her narrative for the sake of finding new consorts or new means of survival; and it also involves much more than the fascinating battle of the individual, most pertinently a *woman*, to assert herself in a situation of drastic social change.[7] What it ultimately concerns is Moll's uses of language to negotiate her place in the (male-dominated) world.

She first marks the conscious invention of a 'self' when, during her sojourn as a destitute woman at the Mint, she 'dressed [...] up in the habit of a widow, and called myself Mrs Flanders' (p. 69); soon the recourse to pseudonyms comes so naturally to her that even when she prepares to remarry her new husbands are not told her 'real' name (see pp. 163, 174). In due course the 'identity' associated with the adopted name becomes the fabrication of *others*, notably the inmates of Newgate.[8]

The use of floating signifiers instead of names is extended to other characters too: to the young man who will become her first husband and who is sometimes Robert and sometimes Robin (pp. 48–9); to 'Mother Midnight' who becomes the most lasting female companion of her life (pp. 177, etc.); to the series of husbands who all remain nameless in the text.[9] Later her own son is forced to refer to her as his 'aunt' (p. 368), for fear of revealing their real precarious bond, which derives from the confusion of the categories of 'brother' and 'husband' in her troubled relationship with his father.

This unreliability in the processes of naming is only to be expected in a narrative where most of Moll's actions are dictated by an awareness of being 'under constant constraint for fear of betraying myself in my discourse' (p. 368).

5

There is reason to fear discourse. Because as *Moll Flanders* unfolds, we discover that reality itself is dependent upon language – just as much as in Robinson Crusoe's various versions of himself, and in HF's 'invented history' (Boardman 1983:94) in *A Journal of the Plague Year*. The narrator's consciousness of this is made evident through numerous stylistic devices, among them the repeated use of the phrase 'in a word', which recurs more than a dozen times in the text.

Its first appearance is in the Preface, where it loops together the different voices of the narrative: 'In a word, as the whole relation is carefully garbled of all the levity and looseness that was in it, so it is all applied [...] to virtuous and religious uses' (p. 3). The 'word' in which the two discourses coincide is, of course, the singularly well-chosen *garbled*. Even if allowance is made for the older, now largely obsolete, meanings of the word as 'purified', 'refined', 'sifted', its ambiguity in the context of the narrative as a whole is obvious.

More spectacularly, the phrase returns in Moll's account of her seduction by the rhetoric of the elder brother at Colchester: 'Thus, *in a word*, I may say, he reasoned me out of my mind' (p. 61). This is no mere turn of phrase: it is *literally* true that she is won over by his eloquence, his use of words. The implications of this grammatical strategy are amplified in dazzling manner in the episode where Moll wins her third husband (the one who turns out to be her brother) through an elaborate language game in which they compose a poem of rhyming couplets by writing, first with a diamond ring on a window pane, then with pen on paper. Her object here is to be absolutely honest in describing her state of desperate poverty, while making him believe that it is only a stratagem to conceal an untold fortune:

Besides, though I had jested with him (as he supposed it) so often about my poverty, yet, when he found it to be true, he had foreclosed all manner of objection, seeing, whether he was in jest or in earnest, he had declared he took me without any regard to my portion, and, whether I was in jest or in earnest, I had declared myself to be very poor; so that, *in a word*, I had him fast both ways. (p. 87)

This is Moll at her most brilliant. This is language at its most treacherous. And everything is encapsulated in that wonderfully apt phrase, *in a word*.

In a later episode, Moll decides to place a solid new suitor, a banker, on hold while exploring the possibilities of an even better match; this requires turning down the banker's request for a signed declaration of intent – but it has to be done in such a way as to keep the man's affections firmly committed to herself. She does this, as always, not only by turning on the full extent of her sexual charm, but also by her superlative command of ambiguous language, so that, *'in a word*, I avoided a contract' (p. 154).

In the scene with the gentleman she beds in order to rob him of all his valuables, her scruples (if such they are) about succumbing to his sexual demands are won over, as so often happens in this story, by his eloquence – and so, inevitably, 'I little by little yielded to everything, so that, *in a word*, he did what he pleased with me; *I need say no more*' (p. 247). The interplay of what she previously called 'jest' and 'earnest' once again prompts a reading which is both literal and figurative.

Several other occurrences of the phrase in the narrative (see pp. 275, 303, 316, 347, 350, 375) all reinforce the reader's impression of a conscious manipulation of language in order to constitute a useful version of reality; and when Moll admits that, 'in a word, I grew more hardened and audacious than ever' (p. 288), the reference is not so much to her character as to her skill at handling language.

The bottom line of this argument is the point made by my initial reference to Moll's discussion of the word 'wherry', namely the fact that everything in the narrative world of *Moll Flanders* is predicated on *what it is called*. The first, and in the final analysis perhaps the most startling, demonstration of this, after Moll's early discovery of the different meanings attached to 'gentlewoman', comes in a crucial scene between her and her first lover, when it is becoming clear that having had his way with her he has decided to fob her off on his younger brother rather than marry her himself as he has promised. ' "Only then" ', he argues, ' "shall it be honest, and

perfectly just to my brother you shall be my dear sister, as now you
are my dear –" and there he stopped' (p. 42).

He cannot mouth the right word to express her position in the
present situation. But Moll, who previously hasn't flinched from
defining a role in which she might be 'a whore to one brother and a
wife to the other' (p. 33), is the one who speaks what is unspeakable to the gallant:

> 'Your dear whore', says I, 'you would have said if you had gone
> on [...] If I have been persuaded to believe that I am really, and
> in the essence of the thing, your wife, shall I now give the lie to
> all those arguments and call myself your whore, or mistress,
> which is the same thing?'. (p. 42)

From this moment on there can no longer be an 'essence of the
thing' to any experience: everything, and every relationship, will
henceforth be defined only by *what it is called*. One of the word-
pairs most acutely put to the test by the rest of the narrative, is *wife*
and 'that unmusical, harsh-sounding title of *whore*', as she calls it
on p. 127, one of the crucial relationships interrogated and placed
under stress by the changing mores of the society Defoe lived in.

As a result, experience means the learning of a new vocabulary,
as Moll affirms with disarming frankness when she talks about the
dépaysement she and Jemmy feel after their deportation to America:

> My husband was a perfect stranger to the country, and had not
> yet so much as a geographical knowledge of the situation of the
> several places; and I, that, till I wrote this, did not know what the
> word geographical signified. (p. 359)

More precariously, the confrontation with a language-shaped
world drives home, in one episode after another, the acknowledgement that whatever we term or come to accept as 'real' is constituted by the way in which we talk about it. Moll is made aware of
this at a tender age when the discovered *fact* of her beauty is seen
as dependent on her first lover's *account* of it:

> He began with that unhappy snare to all women, viz. taking
> notice upon all occasions how pretty I was, *as he called it*, how
> agreeable, how well-carriaged, and the like; and this he con-
> trived so subtly, as if he had known as well how to catch a

woman in his net as a partridge when he went a-setting; for he would contrive *to be talking* this to his sisters when, though I was not by, yet when he knew I was not so far off but that *I should be sure to hear him.* His sisters would *return* softly to him, 'Hush, brother, she will hear you; she is but in the next room.' Then he would put it off and *talk* softlier, as if he had not known it, and begin to *acknowledge* he was wrong; and then, as if he had forgot himself, he would *speak aloud* again, and I, that was so well pleased *to hear it*, was sure to *listen* for it upon all occasions. (pp. 20–1, my emphases)

This brother manages to get away with the affair because he never discusses it with others; the younger brother's love becomes scandalous because it is given shape in language. Eavesdropping, gossip, and the avid reporting of events determine the entire course of their ensuing relationship; and inevitably the conclusion is drawn that each individual's reality is shaped by what he or she says and hears about it. As soon as the mother informs the daughters of Moll's version of 'the whole story', their reactions are predictable: 'One said she could never have thought it; another said Robin was a fool; a third said she would not believe a word of it, and she would warrant that Robin would tell the story another way' (p. 55).

One piquant consequence of this course of events in the unfolding of Moll's first experience of love is that the denouement of the wedding night becomes entirely dependent on what language makes of it:

My husband was so fuddled when he came to bed, that he could not remember in the morning whether he had had any conversation with me or no, and I was obliged to tell him he had, though in reality he had not, that I might be sure he could make no inquiry about anything else. (p. 63)

Given the common usage of the term in Defoe's time, and the general tendency towards ambiguity in this novel, there is a nice convergence of linguistic and sexual intercourse in the word 'conversation'.

The entire course of the case history of a woman's revenge (which Moll uses to justify her calculated economic exploitation of men after the departure of her second husband) depends on the possibilities of language to *misrepresent*, and in the process to *invent*: encouraged by Moll, a young woman left in the lurch by a fortune hunter spreads all kinds of unsavoury rumours about him – that is, 'turning the tables upon him, and playing back upon him his own game' (p. 79) – which so restricts his possibilities for amorous manoeuvring that in the end he is forced to beg her pardon and marry her.

This leads directly to the episode already referred to above: Moll's wooing by the man who turns out to be her brother, a courtship whose entire success (or failure, depending on one's point of view) is determined by games in written language. After their journey to America the breakdown of the marriage is caused by the *story* of the past told by the woman who is discovered to be her mother. As long as that distant past remained beyond the grasp of language it could not harm anyone, but turned into story the consequences are devastating, reverberating through the whole rest of the novel.

6

Once the reader has been alerted to these processes a crucial strategy in the structuration of the novel comes to light, and that is the tendency, which resides in whatever is conceived of as reality, towards story. Most of the characters indulge this tendency in 'telling' versions of their past to others – sometimes too late, as in the case of Jemmy, who plays the part of a swashbuckling hero in the story he enacts in Moll's company during their courtship and after their marriage, holding back the criminal version of his past until he and Moll both find themselves in prison (pp. 328, etc.).

The tendency features most spectacularly in the portrayal (or invention) of Moll herself. Once again the point at which it breaks into the larger narrative is Moll's first sojourn in America, when her mother-in-law's *story* leads to the discovery of Moll's *history*; when at first she refuses to divulge it to her husband, giving only an evasive answer ('he told me I had given him a mortal wound with my tongue': p. 102) he reports her anguish to his mother as another *story* (p. 102), which obliges Moll to confront the old woman directly: 'Then I told her *my story*, and my name' (p. 103) – and in due course this leads to further processes of storifying between Moll and her husband, until history and story are indeed indistinguishable.

On several crucial occasions during her life Moll transforms events already narrated into a new rudimentary story in front of the reader's eyes. Faced with the trusting banker she has so callously deceived (to the point of 'marrying' another man and having a child with him while the banker is arranging a divorce from his promiscuous wife in order to marry Moll), our narrator recasts her whole life story thus far in the moralising light of contrition, which may or may not be real or lasting (p. 199).[10]

And later, in Newgate prison, there is another move from history towards story, that is, another step on the way that leads from experience to language:

> My course of life for forty years had been a horrid complication of wickedness, whoredom, adultery, incest, lying, theft; and, in a word, everything but murder and treason had been my practice from the age of eighteen, or thereabouts, to three- score [...] and yet I had no sense of my condition. (p. 306)

This 'sense of a condition' can only be arrived at through the processes of story; and this is where the 'living Moll' and the 'writing Moll' acquire the same kind of narrative weight as the experiencing self and the narrating self of the narrator in Proust's *A la recherche du temps perdu*; the novel even becomes an early signpost that points the way towards Beckett's *Malone Dies* in which, famously, the narrator strives to make his last words coincide with his words *about* his last words. Such an extreme one cannot expect from an early eighteenth-century novel, which is why the Editor of the Preface finds it necessary to refer to 'a third hand' (p. 5) which enters the manuscript as it approaches both its own end and Moll's. But surely it is no less remarkable that such an early text should already find itself propelled by the same urge one tends to identify with Modernism, and even more so with Postmodernism: history's urge towards story.

Moll's notion of freedom, as viewed from within the woman's snare of language, is to be liberated from language. After the death of her first husband she believes that the moment has arrived: 'I had money in my pocket and had nothing to say to them' (p. 65). Of course this proves illusory. But even in the depths of her later snares (those prepared by others as well as those of her own making) she looks forward to settling in America as an arrival of a paradise beyond language:

this where we should look back on all our past disasters with infinite satisfaction, when we should consider that our enemies should entirely forget us, *and that we should live as new people in a new world, nobody having anything to say to us, or we to them.* (p. 334, my emphasis)

This proves even more of illusion. For having herself made her entire life dependent upon language – its treachery, its falseness, its cover-ups, its misrepresentations; but also its sense of security, of shielding one from the 'real' world of causes and consequences – she cannot, ever, exist beyond the need for it. That is why her ultimate recourse is not America, and not returning to England, but the writing of her own story, which is the final resolution of language.

Upon reflection, this outcome in *Moll Flanders* is inevitable: for having at such an early stage recognised the determining influence of language upon events, Moll sets in motion a process of accumulation – that is, of 'adding up', of 'telling', in the eighteenth-century meaning of the verb – in a word, of *accounting*. Her entire life evolves *towards* the writing of it; and in the final analysis it is her only *raison d'être*.

7

At this point we should return to a passage from Barthes's *S/Z* already quoted in the Introduction to this study: 'One narrates in order to obtain by exchanging; and it is this exchange that is represented in the narrative itself: narrative is both product and production, merchandise and commerce, a stake and the bearer of that stake' (Barthes 1975:89).

Moll Flanders and its characters function in the world of transition from the 'theocentric authority of Puritanism to the historical authority of culture, a world where divine order by itself no longer suffices to constrain the individual, but where "culture" and "history" have not yet attained sufficient conceptual clarity to take its place as the acknowledged frame of human destiny' (Ray 1990:74). In this context, various possibilities of 'self-fabrication' (ibid: 75), even 'self-narrativation' (p. 90) emerge, and this becomes a main preoccupation of Defoe's central characters. The key to all this, which Ray does *not* develop, is that this self-fabrication and invention takes place – can only take place – in language, in the processes of narration. And the language of narration is itself informed by the notion of *transaction*, which Ray (p. 79) describes as follows:

> At the core of the program of self-determination which structures *Moll Flanders* [...] lies a subset of interpersonal discourse we can call, *negotiation*, and a form of interpersonal relationship we can call, *transaction*. Personal relationships are in [this novel] incidental to the main business of negotiating one's place and fortune in the world.

Once again the point to be made is that language is the key to this 'business': language is not used only, as Ray suggests, as 'one instrument of (Moll's) repentance' (p. 75), but as the instrument of fabricating a self as well as of negotiating its interaction with the world. This is, at heart, an economic transaction.

A whole critical tradition, in which Ian Watt figures prominently, has already established that, for Moll Flanders, narrative is inextricably entangled with finance; with the reality of money. She first becomes aware of it when, a mere child in the foster-care of a kind woman in Colchester, she is rewarded with a shilling by the Mayoress who is charmed by the little girl's (mis)use of the word 'gentlewoman' (p. 13); other ladies follow her example. But the crunch comes when Moll's first seducer (or, as the Editor of the Preface would have it, the first victim upon whom she unleashes her 'depredations'), offers her words and money at the same time: 'So he got off from the bed, lifted me up, professing a great deal of love for me, but told me it was all an honest affection, and that he meant no ill to me; and with that he put five guineas into my hand, and went away downstairs' (p. 25).

From this moment money and speech are equated in her mind. Not that her attitude towards either language or money is ever simplistic – much of the narrative triumph resides in the increasing complication of their interdependence – but the starting point remains the fact of the relationship. *This* is why the vicissitudes of a long life debouch into the *telling* of a story, an *account* – in the strictly economic sense of the word – of experience.

The word 'account' is introduced with something of a flourish on the second page of the novel when it features no less than five times in as many paragraphs: and in each instance the notion of exactitude and precision normally associated with the word is subverted by the ambiguities of its context. The first reference is to her mother (although it is also prophetic of a decisive turn towards the end of her own life story):

> My mother was convicted of a felony for a certain petty theft scarce worth naming, viz. having an opportunity of borrowing three pieces of fine holland of a certain draper in Cheapside. The circumstances are too long to repeat, and I have heard them related in so many ways, that I can scarce be certain which is the right account. (p. 8)

Her own recollection of her origins, she confesses, is vague as it depends on 'hearsay'; 'nor can I give the least account of how I was kept alive' (p. 8). This does not prevent her from offering one possible version of those years:

> The first account that I can recollect, or could ever learn of myself, was that I had wandered among a crew of those people they call gypsies, or Egyptians [...]. but I am not able to be particular on that account; only this I remember, that being taken up by some of the parish officers of Colchester, I gave an account that I came into the town with the gypsies. (p. 9)

Everything in this version is uncertain, even the designation of the people who brought her up ('those people they call gypsies, or Egyptians'), which not only sets the tone for the autobiography which follows, but strikes the reader through the repeated use of a word normally associated with exact reckoning. More to the point, in my present argument, is that even before any episode occurs to connect the world of finance with that of narrative, the language already establishes this link. *Account* will figure over thirty more times in the text. There are long tracts in the narrative where it fades from view; but whenever it reappears it is almost invariably in the same form of clustering that marks its first appearance, to ensure that it is firmly imprinted on the reader's mind.

This functioning is reinforced by an extensive vocabulary from the world of money and economics: an almost random scanning of the text would come up with *number, interest, returns, bonds, loss, gain, portion, amounts, value, debtor, credit,* and many more. In a particularly revealing episode, the whole development of a relationship between Moll and Jemmy is determined by the meticulously nurtured rumour that she is 'a fortune' (pp. 139, 141, 155, 156, 159 and elsewhere). The narrator even makes sure that the reader is reminded of the mercenary roots of that key word of narrative, *telling*, by using it as a synonym for *counting* ('telling us the number of women', p. 80; 'I had mistold my money', p. 143; 'when I told them, there were threescore and three guineas', p. 287). If this is read in conjunction with the many episodes in which the use of language (especially by potential benefactors and lovers) is part of a transaction in which money changes hands, it is unavoidable that *language* should come to be viewed as the primary currency of exchange in the text. Both language and money represent value systems.[11] The problem, however, is that unlike real money, this currency is not only fluctuating in its market value, but *essentially* unreliable. Accounting remains a precarious business, whether in purely financial terms (as in the three versions of an account for the same services rendered produced by Mother Midnight on pp. 179–80), in the different versions offered of a single episode (as in the conflicting testimonies of Moll and her accusers in one of the most vividly dramatic episodes of the novel, when she is wrongly accused of having stolen wares from a shop in Covent Garden, pp. 264–77), or in the calculations and accumulations that constitute Moll's narrative of her life.

8

One consequence of this equation is that it reinforces the economic nature – supply and demand; offer and response – of the narrative contract, the interdependence of 'self' and 'other', of speaker/writer and listener/reader, which again foregrounds language as a *transaction* (see Richetti 1975:139: 'The self can only be aware of itself as such when it sees itself operating upon others').

Unfortunately, perceptive as many of them have been, some commentators may in the past have oversimplified the issue by noting no more than the fact that Moll Flanders 'reduces everything to the level of economics' (Van Ghent 1961:35). It is true that every relationship with another person, male or female, is in due course converted into a code of pounds, shillings and pence, and that Moll's interest seems to reside solely in the calculation of what she can gain from any given situation, or of what she has spent on it.[12] But I suspect that the opposite approach, namely, interpreting

Moll's economic calculations as her encoding of emotional values, might lead us more deeply into the text; from the time that her first lover's declaration of love is accompanied by a gift of five pounds, Moll *knows no other language*: her only means of articulation is money. Literally to 'sum up' a relationship in terms of financial loss or gain, may well be Moll's way of articulating *love*. Among other things, this would support Lerenbaum's thesis (1977:117) that the course of Moll's life embodies, not 'freedom from the require-ments of the female role', but on the contrary, 'a tribute to the very femininity – unglamorous but not inglorious – that modern readers deny her'.

It is true, as many critics have shown, that economics is the driving force behind almost all Moll's actions.[13] But to insist only on the immediacy of Moll's desire for security and her fear of indigence (or, in another terminology, her wish for female inde-pendence based on the exploitation of male economic power, and her fear of being placed, as happened in her first relationship, at the mercy of male power), is to miss the translation of this con-sciousness into linguistic terms, and the way in which the whole discourse of the narrative is informed by it.

As a form of economic transaction, language enters the realm of power-play in the novel. In the acknowledgement of this process lies the discovery of the woman's situation as a dual experience of being *ensnared* by the power of male language, and of retaliating by preparing, oneself, the snares of female language. Woman is both the subject and the object of the processes of snaring and entrap-ment demonstrated by the language of *Moll Flanders*.

Underlying this narrative strategy is an awareness of language as *rhetoric*, as an instrument of persuasion, that is, of domination and subjugation. It begins, as we have seen, with the eloquence of Moll's first lover, who persuades her with the power of his speech (reinforced by the money that accompanies his entreaties) to yield to his sexual advances; and when he decides to free himself from her by passing her on to his younger brother, it is the combined linguistic force of his arguments (significantly constructed around his addressing her as 'child': pp. 36, 59 and elsewhere) and his brother's pleading which finally breaks down her resistance and sets her on the way which will prove both her downfall and her triumph.

Throughout the rest of the novel each change of direction, the outcome of each moment of choice in Moll's life, is determined by the persuasive or coercive power of language. 'Kind words trigger passionate and moral enthusiasm' (Miller 1950:18), deceitful language seduces. This explains the hold Mother Midnight gains on Moll through 'such a bewitching eloquence, and so great a power of persuasion' (p. 188), the wily old lady 'being a woman of a rare tongue, and withal having money in her pocket' (p. 233). It also endorses Jemmy's influence merely by using 'such language indeed as I had not been used to' (p. 156), or Moll's manipulations of her banker suitor. A clear demonstration of the power of rhetoric is Moll's impressive ability to talk herself out of tight situations: after the attempt to steal a gentlewoman's watch, or the robbery perpetrated on a young girl, or in response to the false accusation in the case of mistaken identity at Covent Garden, or even (with Mother Midnight's eloquent help) the death sentence in Newgate prison.

This language is propelled not only by the energy of its rhetoric but by a phenomenon we have already noted in another context: its treachery, its deceit, its *misuse*. This is pursued so far, in fact, that at many points in the novel language, in its fruitless pursuit of vanished signifieds, loses all meaning. *Opposites* come to mean the same thing, or nothing: 'being now, as it were, a woman of fortune, though I was a woman without fortune' (p. 115); 'I lived six years in this happy but unhappy condition (p. 131); 'she is a wife and no wife' (p. 147); 'this was a robbery and no robbery' (p. 279). No wonder that the news of the hanging of an accomplice who might testify against Moll is described as 'joyful [...] the best news to me that I had heard a great while' (p. 241). When another woman is taken to prison for a theft committed by Moll, 'I had the satisfaction, or the terror indeed, of looking out of the window [...] and seeing the poor creature dragged away' (p. 242).

Contemplating a sleeping gentleman she has just robbed, Moll reflects:

[T]here is nothing so absurd, so surfeiting, so ridiculous, as a man heated by wine in his head [...] and he acts absurdities even in his view; such as drinking more, when he is drunk already; picking up a common woman, without regard to what she is or who she is, whether sound or rotten, clean or unclean, whether ugly or handsome, whether old or young, and so blinded as not really to distinguish. (p. 248)

Here everything runs together, not merely because the man is drunk, but because *language* has suspended all powers of distinction.

The way in which language 'takes over' is illustrated by what is often cited by critics as a famous example of Defoe's 'carelessness': the expression of Moll's reaction to finding herself in the hell of Newgate prison:

> I degenerated into stone; I turned first stupid and senseless, then brutish and thoughtless, and at last raving mad as any of them were; and, in short, I became as naturally pleased and easy with the place, *as if indeed I had been born there.* (p. 305)

Now, as many commentators have pointed out, Moll *was* born in Newgate, which would show up an uncomfortable internal contradiction in her choice of words – unless the phrase is seen as a revelation of her confused mental state. But another consideration is that Moll 'was' born in Newgate *only if we take her word for it in the first place.* Everything in the narrative is her invention; and she is one of the most notoriously unreliable narrators in the history of the novel. Whatever one reads into the passage, the starting point of all argument should be, surely, that it foregrounds *language-as-language,* and the way in which all the narrative 'facts' of the novel are reduced to the processes of their narration.

9

At the root of these processes lies, once more, the transactional nature of the language in *Moll Flanders,* or, in other words, the dialogic impulse in it. This is expressed in various forms of dialogue embedded in the text: that, already noted, between a supposed narrator and a presumed editor; more significantly, that between an 'experiencing' Moll and a 'narrating' Moll (which is to say, younger and older versions of herself).

Such tensions surface in many ways, some predictable, others surprising. A readily identifiable strategy is that of a description impossible in its context and justifiable only in view of the impression it may make on the reader. A typical example occurs on p. 30 where Moll describes how her 'colour came and went', which she could not possibly have observed herself. One of the more subtle devices through which the dialogism is made visible is in the writing of 'devil': the word occurs many times in the text, always in diegetic passages; on the single occasion when it is incorporated in direct speech it is written 'd——l', which imposes on the reader a consciousness of the dialogue waged between two mentalities, two narrative attitudes.

This appeal to the reader (in a situation where not one of the *dramatis personae* in the scene in question is affected by the spelling of the word) is symptomatic of a focus established from the first references, in the Preface, to 'language fit to be read', to 'the gust and palate of the reader', to the text being recommended 'to those who know how to read it (pp. 2–3). For whatever other participants and/or impulses in dialogue may be evoked in the course of the novel, the definitive relationship on which any dialogic narrative text is constructed remains that between narrator and reader. This means that all the transactional relations in the story, all the negotiations Moll enters into with the men and women in her life, all the conversations, all the arguments and battles with the self, replicate this ultimate relationship. The economy of the novel itself predestines a final transaction between narrator (or narrators) and reader, which means that, through the act of writing her story, Moll demonstrates that everything that has happened to her (the 'facts of her life') propels that history towards the story she must make out of it. This is the last, and most difficult, and most obvious, transaction the text must negotiate. But it works in the opposite direction as well: *because* the life exists here as story, as a transaction between narrator and reader, it defines, before the fact, all the business of the narrative as adumbrations of such a relationship. Economy and narrative become signs for each other.

And it is in this economy that, from beginning to end, we are encouraged to recognise the position of Moll, not only as victim of her society but as heroine of her story, not only as predator but as manipulator, and not only as individual but as *woman*, as much snaring as ensnared.

4

The Dialogic Pact

Denis Diderot: *Jacques the Fatalist and His Master*

1

As the Age of Reason drew to a close in the turbulence of the French Revolution, the publication of *Jacques the Fatalist and His Master* in 1796, almost a decade after the great Encyclopedician Denis Diderot had finished writing it, represented a kind of stock-taking of a century's avid novel-writing in England and France. At the same time, and this is perhaps Diderot's most remarkable achievement, his novel is a radical subversion of a genre that in a relatively short period had taken Europe by storm. Looking back at it from the end of our own century *Jacques the Fatalist* demonstrates the consciousness, and most of the processes, we have come to associate with Postmodernism. Indeed, together with Sterne's *Tristram Shandy* it defines an age, and a concept of the novel, without which Postmodernist fiction – or at least those versions of it that are informed by the notions of self-consciousness, metanarrative and intertextuality – may not have taken the form it has.

In one of the most informative essays written on these two texts, Robert Alter indicates that Diderot explores primarily the possibilities of language as *speech*, whereas Sterne, judged to be 'more radically modern' (Alter 1978:72), focuses on language as *writing*; read in this way, Diderot would seem to anticipate Modernism, Sterne the Derridean *écriture* of Postmodernism. But it seems to me that a more incisive reading brings to light the opposite. Sterne is indeed preoccupied with the processes of writing, with the whole spectrum of techniques involved in writing as a *visual* medium, but his pervasive concern is with writing as the representation of *presence* and *authority*, that is, the presence and authority of the 'writer',[1] Tristram Shandy. Diderot, on the other hand, constructs his whole novel on the principle of dialogue, but this interactive process, even if it is based on verbal exchange, on speaking and listening and responding, presents language throughout as an activity cut loose from the moorings of the here-and-now, the identity of speakers, the reliability and authority of speech. Apart from the fact that every minute incident in the novel is unfailingly (if ironically) referred to a Great Scroll *written* somewhere 'above', there is at no moment of the text any biographical, psychological or historical weight or presence of a speaker invested in a single speech. The components of dialogue are interchangeable, whatever is said is unfailingly subverted; the very 'substance' of the plot lies in interruption, evasion, digression, while many of its details are spectacularly lifted from other texts, recognisable to the contemporary reader (not least among these is *Tristram Shandy* itself, with which Diderot's story begins and closes).

It is in this very respect that *Jacques the Fatalist* most emphatically belongs to the Age of Reason ('for Diderot,' says Alter (1978:74), reality 'is analytic and intellectual, even as it bears on the emotional nature of man as a moral animal'): it places narrative language, and in fact the genre of the novel, under scientific scrutiny as relentlessly and assiduously as Newton observed, and reported on, the laws of nature, Galileo the relations of bodies in the universe, or Descartes the machinations of the mind. Yet *at the same time* it brilliantly subverts the very object of its scrutiny by bringing to it, not only that consciousness of an observer which will later shape Heisenberg's Uncertainty Principle, but an insight which radically questions the foundations of Reason, the reliability of the Great Machine posited by Newton, and the logic of language which made the whole Enlightenment possible.[2]

2

'With all your questions', Jacques reprimands his Master when the latter once again interrupts his narrative, 'we'll have gone round the world before we've finished the story of my loves.' The Master replies: 'What does that matter so long as you are speaking and I am listening to you? Aren't those the two important things?' (p. 53).[3]

Everything, but everything, in this novel – plot, characters, time, space, all the strategies of narration – is determined by this basic situation, this 'poor theatre' of the word, in which human communication is defined by dialogue, that is, an utterance and its anticipation of a response. As Lacan (1977:40) specifies, 'All speech calls for a reply [...] There is no speech without a reply, even if it is met only with silence, provided that it has an auditor.' Later in the same essay it is elaborated: 'Man's desire finds its meaning in the desire of the other [...] because the first object of desire is to be recognized by the other' (p. 58).

In some of his earlier writing Diderot had already structured a narrative on the principle of dialogue: the whole story of *Le Neveu de Rameau* is produced by the tension between an 'I' and a 'He'; and in the witty *Les Bijoux indiscrètes* there is a constant dialogue between the polite conversation uttered by the mouths of the female characters and the rather more plain speech spoken by their vulvas (the 'indiscreet jewels' of the title). But in *Jacques the Fatalist* this approach is taken to a brilliant extreme.

There is an almost emblematic illustration of the dialogic relationship in the episode where Jacques, recovering from his knee wound, overhears the conversation and lovemaking of his host and hostess (pp. 35–7). It is a delightful, and characteristic, scene in which language and sex become metaphors for each other, hinging on the wife's reference to her ear: ear-ache is first used as an excuse for not yielding to her husband's advances; soon the sound *ee...ee...aaah* represents her voluble orgasm; and eventually 'ear' becomes a euphemism for her vagina. Through dialogic interaction (that is, an interaction which is itself predicated on 'the ear of the other': Derrida 1982), the text requires only three lines to turn linear meaning against itself, as the husband's emphatic 'No, no' is changed into a fervent 'Yes, yes' (p. 36). Barely twenty pages later, in response to Jacques's question, 'Do you find something sinister in me?' (p. 55), the Master says, 'No, no' (p. 56), which Jacques immediately translates as, 'Yes, yes.'

In the first example an initial 'No' is *transformed* into its opposite, 'Yes'; in the second it is *translated* as its own opposite. In both cases the discovery that meaning in language is a free-floating function of it, not a fixed entity, is the result of dialogue, the product of a transaction between two speakers. Without dialogue this intrinsic instability of language could not have been discerned. Behind these discoveries lies the driving force of the Age of Reason: 'Do not exclaim, do not get angry, do not take sides. *Let us reason*' (p. 150). We reason, therefore we are.

It is through the act of reasoning, and the dialectical process which determines it, that the novel comes into being in the first place:

How did they meet? By chance like everyone else. What were their names? What's that got to do with you? Where were they coming from? From the nearest place. Where were they going to? Does anyone ever really know where they are going to? What were they saying? The master wasn't saying anything and Jacques was saying that his Captain used to say that everything which happens to us on this earth, both good and bad, is written up above. (p. 21)

No fewer than four dialogues, or four levels of dialogue, are engaged in this famous opening paragraph: a question-and-answer session between 'representatives' of the Narrator and the Reader *in* the text; Jacques and his Master, in what is to become the narrative present of the novel; Jacques and his Captain in what will be clarified as the novel's narrative past; the interaction between what happens in the world and what is 'written up' above. Further dialogic relationships hover just at the edges of the passage: in an elucidation of the Captain's philosophy Jacques will quote the line 'that every shot fired from a gun had someone's name on it' (p. 21), which is taken from *Tristram Shandy*, activating another dialogue between Diderot's text and Sterne's. And as the novel develops, numerous other dialogues will become embedded within the two defining frames named above, the one constituted by Narrator and Reader; and that of Jacques and his Master. Often these relationships will break into one another, even to the extent of involving a confusion of narrative levels: at one point, for example, the Narrator tells the Reader that Jacques tells his Master that the doctor told the lady that he'd had a discussion with a sick man (p. 179). As Ray (1990:298) phrases it,

> Writing and reading become in a sense the master metaphor for the conflicted historical consciousness caught up in its own passivity and activity, inscription and description: all the characters alternate between the role of narratee and narrator, recounting and relating their own stories to Others, structuring and being structured by the verbal constructs of their rivals and accomplices.

What makes it particularly intriguing is that *each* of these dialogues may be interrupted by any of the others, whether from the outside inward, or from the inside outward. In other words, the different dialogues are also engaged in dialogues *among themselves*. Binarity, and the *interruption* of binarity, is the key to language in *Jacques the Fatalist*, and language the key to its narrative.

This concept of language becomes a fulcrum which extends into, and in fact determines, the patterns of action in the novel (and conversely, actantial relationships constantly inform and amplify the reader's perception of the nature and possibilities of dialogue). All the love relationships in the narrative are, at heart, dialogic. This concerns, first of all, the relationships within the main narrative line: the young Jacques's desire for Justine and the frustrations of this desire by their mutual friend Bugger until the latter is given the slip and they meet in his bed behind his back; Jacques's seduction by Suzanna and by Marguerite; his developing relationship with Denise; his Master's attempts to consummate his love for Agathe, and others. But it also concerns the stories-within-the-story, notably the long yarn spun by the Hostess in the inn: the relationship between Madame de Pommeraye and the Marquis d'Arcis encapsulates a dialogue that dissipates itself; thereafter her intrigue with the Duquênoi ladies who adopt the name of d'Aisnon is essentially dialogic in nature; this is followed by a new developing 'dialogue' between the Marquis and the younger woman (with Madame de Pommeraye as facilitator or 'narrator'). Most pertinently this kind of relationship is expressed in the story of Jacques's Captain and his friend whose deep attachment to each other is expressed most dramatically in their incessant duelling:

> There were days when they were the best of friends and others when they were mortal enemies [...] They would consult each other on the most intimate subjects [...] And then the next day they would pass each other by without looking, or they would glare fiercely at each other, draw their swords and fight [...] two gallant men, two sincere friends each facing death at the other's hands'. (pp. 68–9)

This story, it turns out, is modelled on, and enters into a dialogue with, an historical account, presumably known to Diderot's readers, concerning the Comte de Guerchy and his duelling companion; and when the Master confesses that he hasn't heard about it, Jacques proposes to tell both stories simultaneously. That is, by offering a single narrative it can be read as the story of the Captain *as well as* the story of de Guerchy (pp. 116–17). This doubling enhances the emblematic force of the story and, *ipso facto*, the presentation of a dialogic relationship *in action*.

There are situations when binarity appears to be eschewed by presenting a threesome within a relationship. But when this happens, it invariably functions in the form of two-plus-one, that is, a couple plus its surplus, which re-establishes a dialogue between the two 'groups': for example, Jacques and Bugger, in the story of one of his early loves, scheming to get Justine in bed, or the Master and his friend Desglands plotting the seduction of Agathe. But soon it will be Jacques and Justine, with Bugger left out in the cold; or the Master and Agathe, with Desglands in the antechamber. In a dialogue there is only place for two at a time; otherwise the force of language, and narrative, is dissipated. In all these instances the vicissitudes of the plot are produced by the dialogic nature of the *language* which constitutes it.

It comes as no surprise that, near the end, after Jacques and his Master have spent considerable time reflecting on the nature of their relationship, Jacques should point out how he, the servant, has acted as puppeteer to his superior. The Master is flabbergasted: 'What, it was a game?' And Jacques calmly confirms: 'A game' (p. 249). Because this is what language amounts to in the end: a ludic enterprise, no more. *This* is why meaning can never be stable, and relationships neither lasting nor real. We have our exits and our entrances, and a man in his life plays many parts.

3

The dialogic link between Jacques and his Master, as the key to all the relationships and events of the text, derives its *raison d'être* from the fact that it is shaped by the crucial question about fate/fatality/ fatalism explored by the novel: it does not simply 'happen' but is 'written up above'. Following the remarkable scene in the inn where Jacques categorically refuses to obey his Master, rebelling against the role that defines his position in the world, the two attempt to formalise their relationship in a contract which anticipates Hegel's enquiry, a century later, into the indissoluble bond between master and slave:[4]

JACQUES: Whereas it is agreed: Firstly, considering that it is written up above that I am essential to you, that I know it, and that I know that you cannot do without me, I will abuse this advantage each and every time the occasion presents itself.

MASTER: But Jacques, no such agreement was ever made.

JACQUES: Made or not, that's how it has been for all time, is now, and ever shall be [...] Whereas it is agreed: Secondly, considering that it is just as impossible for Jacques not to know his ascendancy over his master as it is for his master to be unaware of his own weakness and divest himself of his indulgence, it is therefore necessary that Jacques be insolent, and that for the sake of peace his master not notice. All of this was arranged without our knowledge, all of this was sealed by Fate at the moment when nature created Jacques and his master. It was ordained that you would have the title to the thing and I would have the thing itself [...]

MASTER: What relevance has our consent got if it's a law of necessity?

JACQUES: A lot.

(pp. 160–1)

This brings into focus what is, arguably, the most profound, and certainly the most problematic, of all the dialogic relationships in the novel: that between the Great Scroll of Destiny and the unfolding of events in reality. What Diderot examines in *Jacques the Fatalist* is as momentous as the enquiries of Kant: the relation between destiny and free will. At the same time it concerns the very nature of narrative (the relationship between a 'real world' and a 'fictitious' one, which was so important to novelists of the eighteenth century), and the nature of language: does meaning ('out there', 'up there') *precede* the word (which is *here*) – or does the word enjoy the freedom of deciding about what meanings it wishes to activate in any given situation?

Initially the relationship between the Scroll and the here-and-now of events appears to concern both chronology (first the Scroll, *then* the predicted or predestined events) and causality (first the Scroll, and *as a result of it* the events): 'If the thing had been written up above, everything which you are about to say to me now I would already have said to myself...' (p. 25). And the Master wonders, logically, 'whether your benefactor would have been cuckolded because it was written up above or whether it was written up above because you cuckolded your benefactor' (p. 25).

It is (of course) Jacques, the alleged Fatalist, who suggests that, 'The two were written side by side. Everything was written at the same time. It is like a great scroll which is unrolled little by little'[5] (p. 25) – an insight as modern as that of the twentieth century biochemist Jacques Monod (1979:137) who explains the nature of causality in the processes of evolutionary biology by asserting that, 'Destiny is written as and while, not before, it happens.'

There are indeed moments in the text when it would seem, briefly, as if Jacques fatalistically submits to the inscrutable dictates of Destiny: 'We travel in darkness underneath whatever it is that is written up above, all of us equally unreasonable in our hopes, our joys and our afflictions' (p. 87). But the text as a whole tends to subvert these whimsical hints – which, more often than not, function purely as ripples of *play*.

The first intimations about the dubious metaphysics involved concern a questioning of the Author of the Scroll:

MASTER: And who is it up there who wrote out this good and bad fortune up above?
JACQUES: And who created the great scroll on which it is all written?

(pp. 29–30)

Merely asking the question does not, of course, suggest the absence – or death – of an Author, an Auctor, a Maker, a Prime Cause; but posing the question *does* convey, at the very least, an uncertainty about the nature, or even the existence, of such an Author,[6] and the first casualty of such an uncertainty is the stability of meaning in language.

There are more than enough indications in the text of precisely such a process of questioning; in fact, if narrative is seen, as it traditionally is, as *quest*, the quest of *this* narrative is not directed towards finding a Grail, but an inner process of questioning of whether such a Grail exists at all.

If it does, it may be a purely subjective illusion, rather than objective truth. When Jacques proposes to return, in the telling of the story of his loves, to the house of the surgeon who tended him, his Master mockingly asks, 'Do you think that is what is written up above?' And Jacques replies, 'That depends on you. But down here it is written: *Chi va piano va sano*' (p. 84). Not long afterwards he confirms his scepticism: 'We never know what Heaven wants

or doesn't want, and perhaps Heaven doesn't even know itself'
(p. 98).[7]

As Jacques appears to move closer to the story of his loves,
ostensibly the 'point' of the narrative, he mockingly addresses the
great Author up there: 'Thou who mad'st the Great Scroll, whatever Thou art, Thou whose finger has traced the Writing
Up Above.' But when his Master angrily confronts him, he is
quick to explain: 'I pray on the off-chance' (p. 155). For, after all,
'Destiny for Jacques was everything which touched him or came
near him – his horse, his master, a monk, a dog, a woman, a mule, a
cow' (p. 44).

The Narrator himself intervenes at one moment to explain that
Jacques, the archetypal Fatalist, constantly subverts his own code
of conduct:

> Like you and me he was often inconsistent, and inclined to forget
> his principles, except, of course, in the moment when his philo-
> sophy dominated him and then he would say: 'That had to be so
> because it was written up above.' (p. 166)

Even more cynical is the remark that, 'When his Destiny was silent
in his head, it made itself known through his gourd' (p. 202). And
when the Master begins to displace the story of Jacques's loves
with the account of his own, he is interrupted by the Narrator, 'if
only to annoy Jacques by proving to him that it was not written up
above, as he believed, that he would always be interrupted and his
master would never be' (p. 223).

The final subversion of the notion of a preordaining Scroll of
Destiny occurs at the end when all the characters are described as
living happily ever after: 'for thus it was written up above' (p. 154).
But the ending in which this is so piously affirmed is only *one of
three* possible endings proposed by the text and left to the reader's
discretion. At this point the definitive concept of traditional narrative, *closure*, is turned inside out, referring the reader back to the
very roots of the process of subversion, which began with a subversion of the stability of meaning in *language*. Jacques the Fatalist
and his Master do not meet, initially, on a plain, or a blasted heath,
or in some undulating valley of *la belle France*; they do not come
from a town or travel to a castle or an inn: they meet *in language*,
they come from a noun, and move, in a verb, towards the possibility of meaning – a meaning which is deferred all the time, and

which differs all the time from whatever is here-and-now, in a remarkable demonstration of what will concern Derrida two centuries later.

4

The most visible strategy the text uses to foreground the instability of meaning as vested in language, what Hassan (1987:199) calls 'indeterminance', is that of interruption. It is noteworthy that a short story with a title which anticipates Magritte, 'Ceci n'est pas un conte' ('This is not a story'), presumably written concurrently with *Jacques the Fatalist*, also opens with an explanation of dialogue as the condition of narrative:

> *Lorsqu'on fait un conte, à quelqu'un qui l'écoute, et pour peu que le conte dure, il est rare que le conteur ne soit pas interrompu quelquefois par son auditeur. Voilà pourquoi j'ai introduit dans le récit qu'on va lire, et qui n'est pas un conte, ou qui est un mauvais conte, si vous vous en doutez, un personnage qui fasse à peu près le rôle de lecteur; et je commence.* [When one tells a story to someone who is listening, however short a time it may last, it is rare for the teller not to be interrupted by his listener. That is why, in the story you are going to read, and which isn't a story, or which is a bad story, in case you have any doubts, I have introduced a character who plays more or less the part of reader; and so I begin.] (p. 753, my translation)

In grammar, the basic urge of the sentence is towards syntactical closure, replicated in the urge of narrative towards denouement and conclusion. But in a novel like *Jacques the Fatalist*, just as in Calvino's *If on a Winter's Night a Traveller* two centuries later, this defining urge is constantly interrupted through a spectacular diversity of means. The grammatical integrity of separate sentences is undermined by the structure of questions and answers, or by the literal breakdown of one sentence when it is interrupted by another. A typical example:

'Jacques, you're drunk!'
'Or not far from it.'
'And what time to do you intend to go to bed?'

'Soon, Monsieur. It's just... it's just...'
'It's just that what?'
'There's a little left in this bottle which will go off.'

(p. 152)

Or, significantly:

MASTER: Could you not...
JACQUES: Carry on with the story of my loves?

(p. 82)

On the narrative level, the novel is structured on the expectation of
the story of Jacques's loves. It is an expectation shaped by a century
of fiction during which the 'horizon of expectations'[8] constructed
by novel readers was conditioned by this impulse towards closure,
this 'sense of an ending'.[9] And Diderot himself acknowledges this
anticipation in Jacques's anecdote about the little boy crying in the
laundry and accosted by a kind woman:

'Little man, why are you crying?'
'Because they want me to say "A".'
'And why don't you want to say "A"?'
'Because as soon as I say "A" they'll want me to say "B".'

(p. 197)

But almost simultaneously with the first announcement of this
theme in the novel the Narrator subverts it: having told his Master
that a shot in the knee first brought about his falling in love, the
Master begins to prod him for a full account.

MASTER: And has the moment come for hearing about these
loves?
JACQUES: Who knows?
MASTER: Well, on the off-chance, begin anyway...

(p. 22)

Whereupon the Narrator takes over:

Jacques began the story of his loves. It was after lunch. The
weather was very close, and his master fell asleep. Nightfall
surprised them in the middle of nowhere [...] So you can see,

Reader, that I'm well away and it's entirely within my power to make you wait a year, or two, or even three years for my story of Jacques's loves, by separating him from his master and exposing each of them to whatever perils I liked. (p. 22)

The story of Jacques's loves, as the *product* of the dialogic interaction between Jacques and his Master, is the carrot designed to keep the reader reading (that is, a reader shaped by a tradition of narrative quest and narrative closure). But, famously, this story is never told: it is always there, just beyond the edge of the narrative; and one has the illusion of constantly drawing nearer to it – but it is never realised. Every time the narrative makes a move in that direction, it is interrupted, not so much *in* the text as *by* the text. These interruptions are of different duration, sometimes for a few paragraphs, usually for much longer, once for more than fifty pages or one-fifth of the novel as a whole (pp. 99–153). Jacques may be interrupted by an event (the arrival of a surgeon and his female companion who promptly falls from her horse; a rowdy crowd conjured up to appear in pursuit of the travellers, only to be written out of the text as promptly as they were first introduced; a funeral procession; a sojourn at an inn; a drinking session; sleep), or by the conversation of third parties, or by comments from other speakers in the dialogic chain, or by the telling of other stories. Whatever the nature of the interruption, they all have the same function, postponing *ad infinitum* the telling of the story of Jacques's loves. As the end of their journey begins to loom (even though it is a journey from nowhere to nowhere) the Master substitutes for Jacques's story the account of his own loves – or at least the story of his thwarted love for Agathe. In more than one respect it *displaces* the story Jacques might have told, as the lives of Master and servant become so intertwined that the experiences of the one may well be substituted for those of the other. Or, phrased differently, the experiences of the one come to *signify* those of the other (just as the spaces of their loves come to coincide within that of Desglands's castle, where both Master and Jacques appear to arrive at some consummation).

It should be said that after innumerable frustrated attempts the Master does succeed in coaxing from Jacques the story of three loves. *But these are not the loves whose narration is promised during the novel.* Jacques has been steering the account of his life, from the moment he was shot in the knee, via his sojourn with a peasant and his wife, and another in the house of a surgeon, towards a possible denouement in the castle of Desglands, where he meets the seductive, or seduceable, Denise. But instead of pursuing this narrative line, Jacques proposes, by way of digression or diversion, an account of his loss of virginity. The problem is that not one of the three 'loves' he relates can be taken at face value. Certainly, the second and third versions (his sexual 'initiation' through the generosity of a woman sometimes called Suzanne and sometimes Suzon, which in itself betrays a lack of credibility; and yet another 'initiation' at the hands of Marguerite) are openly presented as travesties, since he was no longer a virgin at the time of either memorable occurrence. But the same may just as well be true of his story about his amorous dalliance with the lusty Justine behind the back, and in the bed, of Jacques's friend and her lover, young Bugger: it may or may not have been Jacques's first taste of sex; or, indeed, the whole account may be a fabrication conceived merely to entertain and delude the Master – and, by extension, the reader.

The story of Jacques's loves, says Fuentes (1990:80), is

> only the pretext for the author and the reader to show themselves naked, radically an *Author* and radically a *Reader*, bereft of the realistic, psychological, or melodramatic disguises that they should wear if the subject of *Jacques le Fataliste* were the 'Loves of Jacques'.

It is true that the story of Denise is resumed, after numerous interruptions, right at the end of the novel; and that, this time, it is taken to what seems to be its logical conclusion in a love scene. But this account is but one of three versions offered the reader by the narrator, after consulting his 'source', that is, 'the written record, which I have reason to hold suspect' (p. 251). The first version is rather flat, creating the impression of a deliberately contrived anticlimax: Jacques responds to Denise's declaration of love by leaving it 'to her love to choose the moment to reward his own' (p. 252). The third version is so far-fetched as to be quite obviously a fabrication in the style of the more extravagant romances of the age so regularly satirised or contemptuously dismissed in Diderot's novel: Jacques lands in jail, from where he is rescued by a band of brigands, and when they chance one night upon Desglands's castle (where the Master and his mistress Agathe are now living happily together), all the missing links are reunited. Appointed as concierge, Jacques marries his Denise, 'with whom he occupied himself in raising disciples of Zeno and Spinoza, loved by Desglands, cherished by his master and adored by his wife, for thus was it written up above' (p. 154).

The middle passage of the three proposed endings comes closest to bringing together the threads of what could possibly be the story of Jacques's love. But this passage is paraphrased, explicitly, from *Tristram Shandy*. Sterne's episode, figuring Trim and Beguine (Part 8, chapter 22), leads to a climax when the young woman's stroking of her lover's thigh causes his passion (and presumably not only his passion) to rise 'to the highest pitch' – and there the story breaks off, to be deftly concluded by Uncle Toby : 'And then, thou clappest it to thy lips, Trim [...] and madest a speech' (p. 467). In Diderot's version[10] the young woman moves her hand higher and higher until Jacques grabs it. At this point, regrettably, the English translation fails its original. 'He threw himself on Denise's hand ... and then kissed her ... hand' (p. 253). The French is incomparably more dense: '*Il se précipita sur la main de Denise ... et la baisa*' (p. 710), which could have one of at least three meanings – that he grabbed her hand and '*kissed it*', or that he grabbed her hand and '*kissed her*', or, quite bluntly, that he grabbed her hand and '*fucked her*'.

There is a moment of comparable intensity, caused by the same word, in the last scene of Shakespeare's *Henry V* when Henry insists on kissing Catherine, who refuses as it is not the custom for French ladies to kiss a future husband before marriage. She explains this to him in Shakespeare's rather garbled French ('*Les dames et demoiselles pour être baisées devant leurs noces, il n'est pas la coutume de France*'), and her lady Alice interprets to the King: 'Dat it is not be de *façon pour les* ladies of France – I cannot tell vat is *baiser en* Anglish.' There is a whole subtext throughout the play informed by coarse and bawdy sexual references, as an accompaniment to the refinements and courtly manners on the surface. And indeed much of one's reading of the play hinges on Lady Alice's line: 'I cannot tell vat is *baiser en* Anglish.' If the English king interprets it as 'kiss', gender relations may be saved; if he interprets it as 'fuck', Henry will be definitively discredited.

In *Jacques the Fatalist* it is not a question of credit or discredit, nor of a choice between crude action and a long tradition of *cortesia*; it is, rather, a (re)discovery of the world in the word. *Baiser* is the product of a dialogic relationship, not only between Denise and Jacques, but between Jacques and his Master – ultimately, between narrator and reader.

5

To the reader conditioned by the kind of narrative the eighteenth century came to identify as 'the novel', it may seem as if *Jacques the Fatalist* never really fulfils its original promise of telling the story of Jacques's loves; that is, it never deals with what has been proposed as its main business. As a result it appears to get bogged down in 'secondary business', in what in most conventional novels would be considered mere bridging passages, digressions or interpolations, an excess or surplus of material surrounding whatever the narrative 'is really about'. But just as Cervantes adopted the tradition of the picaresque merely to subvert it, Diderot exploits the reader's conventional horizon of expectations in order to turn it upside down – just as surely as Robert Musil will later in *Der Mann ohne Eigenschaften* (*The Man without Qualities*), of which the author stated that, '*Die Geschichte dieses Romans kommt darauf hinaus, dass die Geschichte die in ihm erzählt werden söllte, nicht erzählt wird* [The story of this novel comes down to this, that the story which should be told in it is not told]' (Musil 1952:1640). The very notion of 'main business' derives from a mind-set used to binaries and hierarchies; in short, from the logocentric tradition so radically questioned by Diderot.

The apparently aimless journey undertaken by Jacques and his Master with the sole 'purpose', it would seem, of telling the story of the servant's loves, would in a conventional novel be no more than a frame for the story; that is, in Derridean terms, a 'supplement' to it. But what Diderot achieves is more than an inversion of the hierarchy between 'main business' and 'secondary' or 'supplementary' business: he does away with the very mentality that resorts to hierarchic thinking. The narrative *is* the process of narrating; and if anything like a 'story' is presented as it is written, then its meaning is written in the interstices, as surely as it will happen in Calvino's *If on a Winter's Night a Traveller*.

A kind of Scheherazade strategy is employed to establish an *oblique* story. In the *Thousand and One Nights* the primary diegesis – the 'main business' – concerns the relationship between Scheher-

azade and Shahriar, since her stories are merely told as a stratagem
to stay alive and keep their relationship going (among other things,
by producing three children). Her continuing action in narrating
constitutes the text, and also ensures that she survives. In a comparable manner *Jacques the Fatalist* is not 'about' the servant's loves:
it is no more, and no less, than what it is, a multi-layered dialogic
process. The narrative text is itself the action which it purports to
'tell', and *il n'y a pas de hors-texte*. Once again Diderot predefines
what will become crucial concerns of the late twentieth century: 'In
the universe of Postmodernism, words invent our world, words
shape our world, words are becoming the sole justification of our
world' (Fokkema: 1984:45).

Fuentes (1990:83) reads the freedom of a novel like *Jacques the
Fatalist* in its choice to narrate some things and not others: 'We
choose to tell a story by sacrificing all the other stories we might
tell.' But it seems to me that Diderot is determined, precisely, to
extend this narrative freedom by demonstrating that this restriction
of choice is not always inevitable: instead of *excluding* such 'other'
stories, they are all here, part of the text, precisely because there is
nothing outside of the text.

Through the way in which story is subsumed by text, narrative by
narration, 'main business' by supplement, Diderot succeeds in
releasing another set of meanings which very much preoccupies
Postmodernist theorists, and that is the conflation of desire and
language, 'the intimate connection of narrative with love' (de Lauretis 1987:70).[11] In what may easily be read as a succinct characterisation of *Jacques the Fatalist*, de Lauretis (1987:71) explains that,
'Desire is founded in absence, in the tension-forward rather than
the attainment of the object of love, in the delays, the displacements,
the deferrals.' Phrased differently, by *not* writing 'about' Jacques's
loves, Diderot's text *as such* becomes a text of love, in which the
narrative motion itself becomes the expression of desire. By apparently avoiding the narration of his loves, the text becomes a Derridean collection of *traces* of love.

In this observation the circle is completed: this kind of desire
finds its most adequate expression in the dialogic relationship
between narrator and reader, Jacques and his Master, Captain
and friend, and so on, where language embodies the anticipation
of, or the desire for, the response of the Other. Because the Other is
the supplement to the self, just as, in this kind of text, the self is
supplementary to the Other.

6

As conventional narrative linearity falls away *Jacques the Fatalist* offers the reader another structuring device instead, that of what Eco (1985a:179) called 'variations to infinity'. Most of these variations are constructed on the frustration of narrative expectation, the substitution of anticlimax for climax. Jacques buys a horse which twice leads him to a gallows, in what seems to be a demonstration of fatality, opening an expectation of a bad end – but then the animal's previous owner turns out to be a hangman (p. 76); Jacques is attacked by robbers who believe him to be rich and who proceed to beat him up because he is poor (p. 86); in the Hostess's tale the Marquis expects a bride who is the symbol of purity, only to discover that he has married a prostitute (pp. 107–44); getting into bed with Auguste, the Master expects consummation but experiences betrayal instead (pp. 224–8, 240–1).

It is in this context that one may reread the story of Jacques and Denise: if all the others are constructed around frustration rather than fulfilment, anticlimax rather than climax, one would be hard put to justify a definitive 'happy-ending' reading of that episode – in which case the one story which appears to fulfil the initial promise of an account of Jacques's loves would also be an avoidance of the issue. Because in this novel avoidance *is* the issue.

This vindicates the trope of deception as a key to the narrative construction of the novel: deception within the overall pattern of frustrated expectations, but also in the many instances of false perceptions or false identities (the prostitutes masquerading as pious ladies in Madame de Pommeraye's story; Suzette who is also Suzon, or Fourgeot de Mathieu who may just as well be Mathieu de Fourgeot; a funeral procession which turns out to be an elaborate ruse by a band of brigands to shake off their pursuers; the Master who creeps into Agathe's bedroom at night leaving her under the impression that he is Desglands...). And, as in all the other episodes I have already referred to in various contexts, this narrative trick is based on the fact that the *language* of the text is demonstrated to be a complicated game of falsification and deceit – precisely because language is represented, not as a set of fixed, reliable meanings assigned and guaranteed by an Author, but as something *produced* through infinitely variable and unstable processes of dialogic interaction.

At most it is subjective, and by that very token unreliable, as we discover when the Master has suffered a knee injury which for the first time helps him to understand Jacques's earlier suffering. '(Jacques) was trying to make his master conceive that the word pain does not refer to any real idea and only begins to signify anything at all at the moment when it recalls in our memory a sensation which we have already experienced' (p. 34).

Ultimately, life – and consequently narrative – is presented in *Jacques the Fatalist* as no more than 'a series of misunderstandings' (p. 66),[12] which is a persuasive subversion of any vestige of fatality or Destiny or a Great Scroll above. Inasmuch as a scroll may be perceived to operate in Jacques's mind (if hardly in his life), it is perceived *wrongly* – and demonstrated to be thus, in one episode after another. Life as it is lived, or written, 'down here' simply does not match its pattern 'up there', just as meaning does not ever quite match language.

5

Charades

Jane Austen: *Emma*

1

Ever since Henry James invented Jane Austen as one of his predecessors, and even more so since she was done the dubious honour of being incorporated into Leavis's Great Tradition, her novels have enjoyed both popular success and avid critical scrutiny. More recently, a whole industry has sprung up around film adaptations of her work. Within her *oeuvre* pride of place is often accorded to *Emma*, of which two film versions have been completed in one year (1996). At the same time there is often a curious diffidence in critical approaches to the novel, as if it were admired but not loved. In quite a number of studies on Austen it is simply acknowledged as Austen's masterpiece before the critic moves on to a detailed discussion of other titles. It may indeed be true, as Craik (1979:125) notes, that *Emma* is Jane Austen's 'best and most misunderstood novel'.

When discussion does focus on it, the subject, with good reason, tends to be either Austen's architectural skills[1] or her consummate use of irony;[2] in addition, in recent years, Feminism has produced some particularly stimulating readings of *Emma*.[3]

Understandably, Austen's language is often singled out for comment, usually as a barometer of social relations or class distinctions. But it does not go far enough to observe, as Craik does, that Austen's style 'is the result of clear thinking and a firm purpose' (ibid.:165); or that she creates characters 'whose every movement of thought finds its verbal equivalent in a nuance of speech' (Butler 1976:250). At another extreme there is the sociolinguistic enquiry undertaken by Stokes (1991), which reveals much about vocabulary, but little about narrative language.

For our present purpose it is necessary to venture more deeply into the interaction between language and narrative in *Emma*. In my discussion I shall inevitably revisit much of the territory previously explored by others, but I hope the difference in angle will also bring to light a different kind of discovery.

2

In the seemingly placid and predictable little world of Highbury, the most exciting events on the social calendar are weddings and balls, picnics and rides, or the comings and goings of visitors to and from an almost unreal outside world: Frank Churchill, Jane Fairfax, Emma Woodhouse's sister and brother-in-law; and once, only once, shockingly, unnervingly, a band of wild gypsies.

The scene figuring the gypsies, in Chapter 39, is indeed a most remarkable event, not only in *Emma* but in the whole of Jane Austen's *oeuvre*. What makes it even more remarkable is that most commentators appear to feel so uncomfortable about it that they tend to ignore it. (Which is most significant in the light of the reading we are embarking on here.) And on a first reading it does appear rather clumsy and out of place, particularly since, subsequently, so little is made of it in the narrative. Yet closer scrutiny suggests that it may actually be the most crucial incident in the novel.

In comparison with the rest of the novel it is indeed 'a very extraordinary thing! Nothing of the sort had ever occurred before to any young ladies in the place, within her memory; no rencontre, no alarm of the kind' (p. 331).[4] Yet in itself, it is almost ludicrously insignificant: on the morning after a ball, Emma's protégée Harriet and Miss Bickerton take a walk along the little-frequented Richmond road where they are accosted, in a particularly isolated spot, by a beggar child from a band of gypsies. Miss Bickerton, scared out of her wits, runs off screaming, leaving Harriet behind. The latter, incapacitated by cramps after too much dancing the previous night, is immediately surrounded by half a dozen ragged children, a stout woman and a hulk of a boy. She tries to buy them off with a shilling, but the gang demands more. At that moment Providence brings Frank Churchill to the rescue, and that is that. 'This was the amount of the whole story', the narrator announces demurely (p. 331).

But if this truly was the whole amount of it, what is the scene doing in the novel?

Harriet's rescue by Frank may briefly appear to promote a budding relationship fondly imagined by Emma; but this soon turns out to be entirely unimportant, as Frank is already secretly engaged to Jane Fairfax, while Harriet is only superficially interested. In other words, the scene makes no contribution whatsoever to the development of the narrative. Its only importance may reside in the fact that it marks the break in Harriet's position of subservience in relation to Emma: compared to her reaction at the time when the misunderstanding with Mr Elton came to light, she is hardly perturbed at all to learn the truth about Frank's real amorous interest; and the moment the young Mr Martin returns to the scene, she quite independently, without consulting Emma, accepts his offer of marriage. But it need not have taken such a drastic event to nudge Harriet from meek compliance to decisiveness. This suggests that, if the episode does mark the turning point for Harriet, it can hardly be construed to prompt or motivate it. So once again there seems to be little 'point', whether in terms of narrative or of psychology or of structure, in the irruption of the gypsies into the otherwise so neatly structured world of Highbury.

On careful rereading, however, new possibilities begin to emerge – if not on the level of narrative then certainly within the dimension of language. Is it not striking that in all the clamour raised by the gypsies, the begging and importuning and (possibly) threatening, not a word is reported of what was *spoken* during the encounter? On the contrary, we are specifically alerted to the discovery that the band were 'all clamorous, and impertinent in look, *though not absolutely in word*' (p. 331, my emphasis). The scene is set in a space from which language is studiously excluded. The gypsies are part – the most clamorous part – of the novel's (literal) silences.

One is reminded of the well-known terms proposed by Pierre Macherey in *A Theory of Literary Production* (1978):

> The speech of the book comes from a certain silence, a matter which endows it with form, a ground on which it traces a figure. Thus, the book is not self-sufficient; it is necessarily accompanied by a *certain absence*, without which it would not exist. (p. 85)

Whatever may be said in *Emma*, as its elaborate web of words unfolds, certain things have to be kept out of it altogether. This means that one has to be particularly meticulous in one's reading of what *does* surface in language, since quite clearly what is said is articulated only by virtue of what is *not* said. Approached from the other end, the *not-said* can (and must) be deduced from the *said*.

What Colin MacCabe (1978:22), talking about Joyce, says of the role of dreams in psychoanalysis, is directly applicable to the narrative manipulation of the gypsy scene in *Emma*:

> It is the gaps in the narrative of the dream that make evident the workings of a censorship which suppresses those elements of the dream that would carry traces of the unconscious desires into consciousness. But the gaps themselves bear witness to an activity of repression.

And *Emma* is remarkably self-revealing in its demonstration of these gaps through the workings of language. We need only look at the way in which the silence of this gypsy episode is invaded, and dealt with, by language after the event.

In the first place, whereas the gypsies themselves decamp immediately after the brief confrontation, they persist in the text as *language*. This happens in the form of stories told to Isabella's children, who insist that no variations be introduced 'from the original recital' (p. 333); and in gossip. In the transposition of event into story the main consideration clearly is the entertainment value of the account. This implies that it must be stripped of what initially was the key to the episode as such: its *threat* to genteel society, its otherness. In such a situation language sheds all claims to being representative as it displaces, and replaces, the very thing that first prompted it. In the most literal sense language becomes a game (the rituals of storytelling or gossip) to smooth over an unmanageable reality.

It is also revealing that the event is discussed not so much by Emma's immediate middle-class circle as by 'those who talk most – the young and the low; and all the youth and servants in the place were soon in the happiness of frightful news. The last night's ball seemed lost in the gypsies' (p. 332). Considering that servants in Emma's world are largely written out of *Emma* (something to which we shall return in due course), this disturbance from outside, which also concerns the lower *classes*, acquires additional significance – and all the more so as servants enter, briefly, into an alliance with *youth*: the two fronts on which the received traditions and structures of this tight little society, like any other, may in the long run be most vulnerable.

But above all, the irruption of the gypsies becomes significant through the way in which the Highbury society turns it into a *non-event*: that is, by all the strategies and subterfuges of word-games, the concentration on trivialities. In this way an elaborate structure of relationships is kept in place solely through the machinations of language, and without any foundation in 'reality' (that is, the kind of reality represented by the gypsies).

The first intimation of the adventure is brought home to Emma when, safely ensconced inside the grounds of her father's splendid home, 'the great iron sweepgate opened' (p. 329) to let in Frank and the trembling Harriet: this is an emblematic invasion of her whole familiar world. And it comes immediately after the ball scene which celebrates gentility, good manners and security just as it confirms a new-found state of tranquillity in Emma's mind: it is one of the only moments in the novel when she is not plotting either her own life or those of others. This juxtaposition makes the impact of the disclosure about the gypsies all the more dramatic. Yet, as I have indicated, after the initial excitement everything is immediately contained in the language by which this small society sustains itself.

After the gypsy scene one returns to the world of Highbury with a heightened awareness, for one knows, now, the fears that have to be kept at bay. In this society the language game *must* be played, for there is no language available, apart from this 'parade of insincere professions' (p. 209) with which to face such another *kind* of reality. Hence the recourse to 'such extreme and perpetual cautiousness of word and manner, such a dread of giving a distinct idea about anybody' (p. 214), which makes of *Emma* an infinitely richer, more complex, and darker text than the light, pleasant, teasing, sardonic, well-mannered novel tradition has conditioned us to read.

3

Against this background of silenced, darker forces lurking on the fringes of the familiar world, one returns with deeper understanding to Emma's acceptance of Frank Churchill's assurances about returning to Highbury: 'If it were a falsehood, it was a pleasant one, and pleasantly handled' (p. 203). The repetition of 'pleasant'/'pleasantly' highlights one of the conditions of survival in this small sealed society, a world in which language must necessarily be a diversion, a game, part of an elaborate network of ludic activities all designed to keep unmanageable reality at bay. The game is best played when everybody acknowledges it as such; but the test lies in playing it well, 'pleasantly'. What unspeakable chasms may lie behind the game cannot be faced, at least not openly, in *this* society, or by *this* narrator.

Alerted especially by the gypsy episode, we know these silences are there, and we can now sense them behind Emma's existence of small intrigues, domestic preoccupations and social intercourse informed by superficialities and restricted by the boundaries of the genteel classes. Behind these seeming frivolities, as behind the apparently even tenor of Jane Austen's own life, rage the Napoleonic wars, slaughter, disease, famine, poverty. And through mere flickers of signification the text conveys an intimation of these silences.

To begin with, there are the references to the Campbells, the *military* family who brought up Jane Fairfax: incidental and down-played as they may appear, they keep alive, at the back of the mind, the existence of another world, remote from Emma's field of vision, yet not wholly excluded; and whatever happens in that world, causes ripple-effects even in Highbury. Captain Weston, too, brings with him a reminder of military life; and Frank Churchill himself has done military service. It is merely mentioned, but the very silence that surrounds the hidden world of what must have been a profound and devastating part of the experience of Englishmen in the early nineteenth century, charges that absence with meaning.

Also, Emma's circumscription within the boundaries of her class keeps the narrated world under firm control – but without obliterating an awareness of another kind of society altogether beyond the periphery of her existence. The hint of a threat which Frank Churchill poses to the tranquillity of her world and her mind is quite apparent in her evaluation of 'his indifference to a confusion of rank [which] bordered [...] on inelegance of mind' (p. 210); and the description of the Cole family sounds another subdued warning: 'The Coles were very respectable in their way, but they ought to be taught that it was not for them to arrange the terms on which the superior families would visit them' (p. 218). There is more than a subtle hint here of the narrative grammar at stake in the social relationships that determine Emma's world: there is a decisive gulf between those ('the superior families') who operate in the active voice, who 'arrange the terms' of intercourse, and those on the receiving end, who exist in the passive voice.

In fact, much of the narrative action is determined by this social syntax which defines the range of possible action available to various characters: Emma, born into the active voice, consciously exerts herself to stay in command. And it is only towards the end, as she enters into a give-and-take relationship with Mr Knightley, that a grammatical balance is struck in the presentation of her character. This is expressed particularly vividly in her loss of control over Harriet's life. Harriet's entire *raison d'être* as a character lies in the initial ambiguity of her social position: imagined by Emma to be of superior descent ('There can be no doubt about your being a gentleman's daughter, and you must support your claim to that station by everything within your own power': p 60), she yet finds herself in a position of inferiority where Emma herself allows her no access to the active voice. She is, instead, constrained to be acted upon by Emma – whether in pursuing Mr Elton, turning down young Martin, or in attending functions, consorting with people or responding to whatever challenges may come her way. To Emma, Harriet is no more than an *object*, 'exactly the something which her home required' (p. 56). This forms part of the whole narrative approach: 'Jane Austen never tells the reader what Harriet really feels, but only what Emma thinks she must feel' (Craik 1979:144).

Only at the end, she eludes Emma's domination and turns herself from the object to the subject of her own life by refusing further interference and choosing herself to accept Martin's offer. In an extension of the actantial model of narrative relationships proposed by Greimas (1973),[5] the narrative 'line' represented by each individual character in *Emma* may be defined in terms of this syntax, namely in terms of being active or passive, or of moving from one position to the other.

But what concerns us at the moment is the representation of characters from beyond the boundaries of Emma's own space: in narrative terms, they are generally dealt with rather severely by keeping them in the grammatical position of passivity. The poor exist, in the novel, only as an occasion, or a pretext, for the rich to bestow charity and thereby to keep them firmly in their place. In Chapter 10 Emma has 'a charitable visit to pay to a poor sick family who lived a little way out of Highbury' (p. 108), but in the course of the chapter even the misery of the poor is exploited merely to advance Emma's real (and trivial) concern in promoting Harriet's chances of marrying the vicar; again, in Chapter 23, Emma proceeds 'to give that portion of time to an old servant who was married, and settled in Donwell' (p. 199).

The only other function permitted to the poor is that of agents providing food and comfort as they prepare and dish up food, clear tables and tea things and so on, but here, too, they are almost invariably relegated to the passive voice: 'The hair was curled, and the maid sent away' (p. 153); 'parcels [...] were bringing down and displaying on the counter' (p. 211); 'Tea was carrying round' (p. 310), and so on. They are lumped together with the objects and possessions of a household: 'The nature and the simplicity of gentlemen and ladies, *with their servants and furniture*, I think is best observed by meals within doors' (p. 351, my emphasis);[6] 'the appearance of the servants looking out for them to give notice of the carriages was a joyful sight' (p. 367).

But they are there. Like the war, and all the upheavals of the age, they cannot be denied. At best they can be kept in their place through processes of syntactical relegation; but in their *absence* they remain uncomfortably present. And the gypsy scene represents the eruption of all these restrained forces in the novel.

4

The discovery of the potency of such absences in the text brings a new understanding to the obsessive playing of word-games, which forms one of the main diversions of Emma's world. Particularly revealing are the charades in Chapter 9. This chapter opens with a focus on the portrait Emma has painted of Harriet, and which is the emblem of the triangular comedy of errors that first brought the two young women and Mr Elton together; and it ends with the three participants in a new scene that pursues the underlying misreading. Framed in this way, the main business of the chapter is a succession of word-games. Most prominent is the charade in which 'woman' as a word composed of 'woe' and 'man' provides a clue to the gender relationships that are so often the focus of Austen's novels. Emma, 'quite mistress of the lines' (p. 97), turns out to be, significantly, the one who can decode all the hidden meanings – and yet she misreads the whole, believing it to be directed at Harriet rather than herself. In this small scene everything in the novel, from characterisation to narrative organisation to the strategies of language, is brought into sharp focus. Language is here revealed primarily in its function as *play*, as a game of charades and cover-ups, in which nothing is as it seems – and consequently it lends itself to constant misreadings of the kind which in the Postmodernist novel will resurface in highly sophisticated forms.

In this scene, what initially appears to be a charming and eloquent conceit will be perceived on p. 153 as 'a jumble without taste or truth'. Considering Austen's acute awareness of her position as a woman trying to demarcate her own space in a man's world, the remark may well be read as a comment on the female author's efforts to manage reality; at the very least it reflects on Emma's own enterprise in the novel, that is, to organise the grammar of other people's lives and the narrative of their relations. A key to her involvement in this network of relations that characterises Highbury, is provided in Chapter 41 when Mr Knightley muses on Cowper's revealing line, 'Myself creating what I saw' (p. 340).

In this same chapter word-games occupy a central place in the orchestration of the characters, that is, in the interaction between their private spaces and the social space in which they meet. In the first of these games – a scene observed, but not understood, by Harriet – Frank tries to communicate to Jane the fact of his 'blunder':

> Disingenuousness and double dealing seemed to meet him [the observer, Knightley] at every turn. These letters were but a vehicle for gallantry and trick. It was a child's play, chosen to conceal a deeper game on Frank Churchill's part. (p. 344)

Once again this may be read as a comment on the function of language throughout the text. And the same is true of the riddles and conundrums in Chapter 43. Possibly the most revealing comment prompted by this scene is Emma's remark, 'Let me hear anything rather than what you are all thinking of' (p. 363). The episode proves to be a turning-point in the unmasking of interpersonal relationships (Emma and Miss Bates, Emma and Knightley, Mrs Elton's position at the intersection of several other lines, and others); and that word-games – the maskings and charades and subterfuges of language – should be the agent to effect this, has implications for the narrative as a whole.

5

But if these games capture the attention because they are presented with so much narrative self-consciousness, they are no more than the crystallisation of the less obvious play of language in the novel, where it functions, from beginning to end, as the condition of social intercourse. As many commentators have pointed out, the novel is structured through the eddying of narrative around events where the private and the public intersect. Language is persistently presented in its preoccupation with the trivia that characterise this interface: 'half an hour's uninterrupted communication of all those little matters on which the daily happiness of private life depends' (p. 138) – and life itself is a game 'of being always interesting and always intelligible, the little affairs, arrangements, perplexities, and pleasures' of people in a close network of relationships (p. 138). This focus on trivia is presented as particularly characteristic of *female* society (see the reference to 'all the minute particulars, which only woman's language can make interesting' on p. 453).

Emma is very much an English novel of the early nineteenth century; consequently there is no doubt in the narrator about the ability of language to communicate 'truth' – except when the truth becomes so uncomfortable or menacing that language must be used to obscure it. In this respect it functions as a blanket – but a blanket never quite big enough to cover entirely the nakedness beneath. And one of the ways in which the text signals this is through its insistent focus on 'the contrast between what is and what is believed' (Lerner 1967:102). Kroeber (1975:39) comments on Austen's 'concern with exactness of language dependent upon a conservative estimate as to what words can do – and her belief that they ought never to be used to muddle our perception'.[7] What is invariably conveyed is the 'discrepancy between words on the one hand, truth on the other' (Butler 1976:256). This means that Austen distinguishes clearly between 'subjective and objective modes of perception' – and 'it is only in *Emma* that she consistently contrasts two styles, making language itself enact the disharmony between the false and the true' (ibid.:264).

This is borne out by Mr Knightley's habit of frank speaking, which is equated with speaking the truth. He is the only character in the novel who consistently says, particularly in his dealings with Emma, what he means: on p. 368 he expressly tells her, 'This is not pleasant to you, Emma – and it is far from pleasant to me; but I must, I will – I will tell you truths while I can.' Soon afterwards he warns against what has become the most characteristic feature of the narrated world: 'the miserable state of concealment that had been carrying on so long' (p. 389). In the same scene, Emma confirms that the basis of her admiration for him is 'that strict adherence to truth and principle, that disdain of trick and littleness which a man should display in every transaction of his life'.

Mr Knightley makes an impression on her, as on others, precisely because he does *not* conform to the norm in the language of social intercourse foregrounded by Austen; and it is sadly noteworthy that his frankness, his use of language to provide direct access to 'truth' ('You know what I am. You hear nothing but truth from me': p. 417), appears to be available only to men, not to women. It is no accident that his speech should be characterised as 'plain, unaffected, *gentlemanlike* English' (p. 432, my emphasis). In this respect, of course, it is a comment not only on Emma's world but on Jane Austen's as well.[8]

That Knightley's privileged access to truth is based on his position in society as a *male* is to a certain extent comparable to the way in which even Frank's letters are presented as at least an approximation of truth (Chapter 50), although such a perception may be undermined by the way in which language hedges its own bets in the letter to Mrs Weston which concludes the chapter:

> 'Circumstances were in my favour, the late event had softened away his pride, and he was, earlier than I could have anticipated, wholly reconciled and complying; and could say at last, poor man! with a deep sigh, that he wished I might find as much happiness in the marriage state as he had done.' (p. 428)

No wonder that Knightley should comment: 'Humph! A fine complimentary opening: but it is his way. One man's style must not be the rule of another's' (p. 429). And on p. 166 Emma herself will refer disparagingly to Frank's habit of sitting down to 'write a fine flourishing letter, full of professions and falsehoods' – exactly what she herself is so adept at doing.

The problem with the language through which the characters communicate in their given milieu, is that it is (literally) circumscribed by a sense of social propriety – by 'due decorum' (p. 394) and 'the general opinion' (p. 402) – based, as we must acknowledge by now, on a deep-seated fear of the unsaid and the unsayable.

The novel as a whole is constructed on 'the tension between the stable communal values ideally at the heart of patriarchal society and the moral relativity implied by the individualistic defense of that society' (Butler 1976:324). As a result, not only in polite social intercourse but even in private conversations between parents and children, close friends, 'lovers' or married couples, language is presented in the form of elaborate games of pretence, dissimulation, evasion and masking, if not of downright cheating and lying. Everything is enmeshed in 'schemes, and hopes, and connivance' (p. 340). The reader soon discovers that such actions and interactions are supported by a social contract of subterfuge and pretence, a 'system of hypocrisy and deceit, espionage and treachery' (p. 390). This is all the more ironical in view of the fact that all the characters fancy themselves to be 'on an equal footing of truth and honour' (p. 390).

As in *La Princesse de Clèves*, but in a less formalised way (because a different set of power relations is at work), there is in *Emma* always the existence of *another system of meanings* behind the façade. But because of the distortions of the surface these hidden meanings are invariably misread.

Much of the narrative is determined by this double play. Quite early in the novel (Chapter 10) Emma and Harriet come past Mr Elton's home (ostensibly on their way to a poor family who live some distance from Highbury); Emma would dearly love to go inside in order to further her scheme of pairing off Elton and Harriet, but the lack of an acceptable reason, that is, the lack of the appropriately deceitful language in which to mask her real intent, thwarts the attempt: 'I wish we could contrive it [...] but I cannot think of any tolerable pretence for going in; – no servant that I want to enquire about of his housekeeper – no message from my father' (p. 108).

Shortly afterwards, when 'something in the name, in the idea' of Frank Churchill prompts Emma to reconsider her resolve not to marry, she is persuaded 'that Mr and Mrs Weston did think of it' (p. 139): she needs no proof, intuition suffices; the point is that there is always a suspected, or a possible, language *behind* that of the surface. In the very next paragraph, forced to cope with Mr Elton's 'ill-timed' civilities, 'she had the comfort of appearing very polite, while feeling very cross'. This will become Emma's defining strategy in dealing with society – to the point of habitually 'taking the other side of the question from her real opinion' (p. 163). And on p. 362 'she laughed because she was disappointed': it is presented *as a matter of course*. Appearance is all; and this is confirmed by Emma's father when he says on p 230: 'I have no pleasure in seeing my friends, unless I can believe myself fit to be seen.'

The subtlety of the ironies and double-ironies of such a world (a world defined primarily by the innuendos and *doubles entendres* of language) is well conveyed at the beginning of Chapter 17, where 'a long, civil ceremonious note' from Mr Elton to Emma's father announces the vicar's journey to Bath. His real motive is, of course, the need to get away from Highbury as quickly as possible after the shocking discovery of the double misreading in the intrigue linking Emma, Harriet and the vicar: while Emma was promoting a relationship between Elton and Harriet, the vicar saw in it the fulfilment of his own desire to be linked to Emma. As might be expected by now, the letter's eloquence lies in its silences, that is, in its loquacious avoidance of all direct reference to these events, without even mentioning Emma by name. It pretends only to convey to Mr Woodhouse, with the vicar's best compliments,

> that he was proposing to leave the following morning in his way to Bath; where, in compliance with the pressing entreaties of some friends, he had engaged to spend a few weeks; and very much regretted the impossibility he was under, from various circumstances of weather and business, of taking personal leave of Mr Woodhouse, of whose friendly civilities he should ever retain a grateful sense; and had Mr Woodhouse any commands, should be happy to attend to them. (p. 158)

The 'checker-work' of this text (the phrase is used on p. 171 by Miss Bates to describe her mother's stock reaction to letters from Jane Fairfax) requires decoding. And the account of Emma's reaction is particularly revealing, once again, in its communication of the ambiguity of language as text *and* subtext, or words *and* silence:

> Emma was most agreeably surprised. – Mr Elton's absence just at this time was the very thing to be desired. She admired him for contriving it, though not able to give him much credit for the manner in which it was announced. Resentment could not have

been more plainly spoken than in a civility to her father, from which she was so pointedly excluded. She had not even a share in his opening compliments. – Her name was not mentioned; – and there was so striking a change in all this, and such an ill-judged solemnity of leavetaking in his grateful acknowledgments, as she thought, at first, could not escape her father's suspicion.

It did, however. – Her father was quite taken up with the surprise of so sudden a journey [...] and saw nothing extraordinary in his language. It was a very useful note, for it supplied them with fresh matter for thought and conversation during the rest of their lonely evening. (p. 158)

At least five readers are involved in this situation: Mr Elton as the reader of his own letter; Mr Woodhouse to whom it speaks purely on the surface; Emma, who reads only the silences; the narrator, who manipulates the commentary; and the reader of *Emma*, who can decode all the strategies of interpretation brought to the letter by the previous four participants in the charade. This ultimate reading is made possible by Austen's remarkable skill. As Craik (1979:152) points out, 'At the same time as Emma misreads what she sees, she helps the reader to understand it.'

So conditioned is Emma by the conceits (and deceits) of her world that even when there is nothing to conceal, she *imagines* something concealed below the surface: what may be a perfectly natural reticence in Jane Fairfax is misread by Emma as being 'disgustingly, [...] suspiciously reserved [...] Emma saw its artifice, and returned to her first surmizes. There probably *was* something more to conceal than her own preference' (p. 182).[9] Butler (1976:254) places particular emphasis on Emma's functioning in such scenes: 'From the beginning there is perversity and injustice in the manner in which Emma meets the challenge of Frank and Jane. Because Emma fears critical, rational friendship, she tries to avoid evidence that would be in Jane's favour.'

The game of pretence, of saying one thing and meaning another, is played throughout: upon hearing that the vicar is going to be married, Emma – 'as soon as she could speak' – remarks, 'He will have everybody's wishes for his happiness' (p. 187). Even a simple question like 'Is he a tall man?' she turns inside-out to reveal the ambiguities of language at work:

'Who shall answer that question?' cried Emma. 'My father would say, "Yes"; Mr Knightley, "No"; and Miss Bates and I, that he is just the happy medium.' (p. 188)

Frank Churchill briefly seems to be an exception to the universal game when, warned by Emma that he 'speaks too plain', he retorts, 'I would have her understand me. I am not in the least ashamed of my meaning' (p. 249), but the irony is, of course, that the whole scene in which these words are spoken is one of dissembling – he enters Emma's game about Dixon being Jane's secret lover, as he does not want her to discover his own engagement to Jane.

The inimitable Miss Bates may appear to be another exception, if at the opposite end of the scale, through excess rather than deficiency, that is, by being too garrulous rather than too discreet ('I am a talker, you know; I am rather a talker; and now and then I have let a thing escape me which I should not': p. 343). But in fact she proves the rule – not only by flagrantly, if unwittingly, transgressing all the rules by which Highbury's polite society must abide for its survival, but more importantly by demonstrating that just as much as all the other characters her life is defined by language and the way in which the language game is played.

As the novel develops towards its final movement, Emma for once resolves to act *against* appearances, as a sign of her love (see p. 370: 'She would not be ashamed of the appearance of the penitence, so justly and truly hers'): yet when the true feelings of the lovers are finally communicated, the *narrator* feels obliged to resort to a series of *as ifs*: 'It seemed as if there were an instantaneous impression in her favour, as if his eyes received the truth from hers' (p. 377).

More and more, in this final movement, language is tested. When Jane sends a brief note declining Emma's invitation to a walk, Emma is at a loss: 'Emma felt that her own note had deserved something better; but it was impossible to quarrel with words, whose tremulous inequality showed indisposition so plainly' (p. 381). The implication is clear: 'true' language *is* possible – Jane's note is an example of it – but in the society of this narrated world it has little or no place. At the very least there is no adequate *response* to it in a world that plays by the rules of charades.

This becomes even more obvious when Emma is confronted by the news that Harriet is in love with Knightley. 'When we talked about him', says Harriet, 'it was as clear as possible', to which,

'with forced calmness', Emma responds, 'Not quite [...] for all that
you then said appeared to me to relate to a different person'
(p. 396). It takes several more dissemblings and misreadings before
even self-knowledge turns out to be delusion:

> This was the knowledge of herself [...] which she reached [...]
> With insufferable vanity had she believed herself in the secret of
> everybody's feelings; with unpardonable arrogance proposed to
> arrange everybody's destiny. She was proved to have been uni-
> versally mistaken. (p. 402)

This is echoed in Emma's own words: 'I seem to have been
doomed to blindness' (p. 413) – but the delightful juxtaposition of
'seem' and 'blindness' should not escape the reader.

The final misreading occurs in Chapter 54 with Mr Knightley's
news of Harriet's decision to marry Martin; and the misreading
itself is packaged in another characteristic play of pretences and
appearances:

> 'I have something to tell you, Emma; some news.'
> 'Good or bad?' said she, quickly, looking up in his face.
> 'I do not think which it ought to be called.'
> 'Oh, good I am sure. I see it in your countenance. You are
> trying not to smile.'
> 'I am afraid', said he, composing his features, 'I am very much
> afraid, my dear Emma, that you will not smile when you hear it
> [...] Does nothing occur to you? Do you not recollect? Harriet
> Smith.'
> Her cheeks flushed at the name, and she felt afraid of some-
> thing, though she knew not what.
> 'Have you heard from her yourself this morning?' cried he.
> 'You have, I believe, and know the whole.'
> 'No, I have not; I know nothing; pray tell me.'
> 'You are prepared for the worst, I see; and very bad it is.
> Harriet Smith marries Robert Martin.' (p. 452)

The ultimate irony, here, is the equivocation about marriage
as 'good' or 'bad' news, in a novel that opens and concludes
with marriage as the main preoccupation of society and the language it has devised to contain its ceremonies, its rituals and
its epiphanies.

Inevitably, Emma's own deepening relationship with Mr Knightley should be read in this context, for marriage is, itself, an event loaded with several meanings. Many commentators have already explicitly placed Jane Austen's novels in the context of the shift that occurred in English social codes during the eighteenth century from the arranged marriage, or the marriage of convenience (that is, marriage as a purely social affair, negotiated to consolidate or promote family interests) towards a marriage based on personal choice. Bearing in mind Kundera's contention that each novel is structured on a selection of key words (see Kundera 1988:121ff and the section 'Words Misunderstood' in *The Unbearable Lightness of Being*), one may well read 'marriage' as just such a word in *Emma*. And in the state of social flux in which the novel inserts itself, it should come as no wonder that 'marriage' is to be read as a signifier pointing towards contradictory signifieds. The most illuminating reference in this regard must be the narrator's statement on p. 194, that 'a young person, who either marries or dies, is sure of being kindly spoken of' – an equation the significance (and subtext) of which the reader can hardly overlook.

But our immediate concern is still the tension between dissembling and 'real meaning'; and the alliance with Knightley inevitably leads to Emma's assurance on p. 417: 'I will hear whatever you like. *I will tell you exactly what I think*' (my emphasis). Yet only moments later comes one of the most deftly crafted narratorial interventions in the text: 'She spoke then, on being so entreated. What did she say? *Just what she ought, of course*. A lady always does' (again, my emphasis). On this last turn of phrase DuPlessis (1985:8) comments that, 'the lack of dialogue produces discretion and reserve from what had been a babbling girl hero'. But it seems to me that Austen's phrasing does much more in this scene than to depict character: it demonstrates a primacy of language over individuality, even that of Emma, whose narrative space is utterly circumscribed by linguistic convention. Certainly, at this moment it allows her very little of that 'saving irresponsibility' which Bayley (1968:8) translates as freedom.

The narrator's pregnant phrase is followed by a statement which may almost serve as an epigraph to the novel: 'Seldom, very seldom does complete truth belong to any human disclosure, seldom can it happen that something is not a little disguised, or a little mistaken' (pp. 418–19).

And from here on moments of direct communication will continue to alternate with instances of the old language of pretence and propriety. Emma's wish in the very last chapter to 'be respectable and happy' (p. 463) appears to confirm that the language of dissembling and appearances will continue.

It may be argued that, however paradoxically, towards the end, marriage offers Emma a prospect of *liberation* from 'the disguise, equivocation, mystery, so hateful to her practise' (p. 457) – but this appears to be contradicted by all the preceding evidence from other marriages. At the very least one has to bear in mind that from very early in the novel marriage is viewed, as far as *women* are concerned, as no more than domestic service ('Miss Taylor has been used to have two persons to please; she will now have but one': p. 42); John Knightley's happiness is assured by having 'such a worshipping wife' (p. 116); this same Isabella, Emma's sister, is restricted to visiting close friends, and spending evenings with her father and sister ('She had nothing to wish otherwise': p. 130). So it may seem, at first sight, ironical that marriage should also be presented as a woman's issue towards independence. Emma regrets that Jane seems to have 'no young man worthy of giving her independence' (p. 181). Yet if marriage as a concept, as a 'word', is to be read, like all the other social practices ensconced in, and legitimised by, language, this should come as no surprise. On the contrary, it would insert 'marriage' into the entire narrative vocabulary of a society based on pretence and dissimulation as its only means of survival.[10]

6

Against this background, there are also deeper and darker meanings attached to the interplay of active and passive positions in the novel, and especially in the crucial role played (in every sense of the word) by Emma herself.

As Brown (1976:37), among many other critics, has indicated, Austen reveals a predilection for female characters 'who are demonstrably unusual in their circle'. Among these, Emma has pride of place, being allowed, throughout the narrative, to 'act out her wilful errors' (Butler 1976:251). More than any other Austen heroine, she demonstrates 'the epistemological and ethical anarchy that unchecked individualism can produce' (Poovey 1984:200).

It is through the manipulation and the misreading of language that Emma also assumes her role in organising the lives of those surrounding her. She is 'an arranger, a manager of other people's affairs' (Mudrick 1968:187). In another essay by the same critic, Emma is pertinently accused of being 'moved to play God [...] she must feel herself to be central and centripetal' (Mudrick 1952:117), to which Claudia L. Johnson, in a particularly incisive study, retorts that what such critics really mean is that 'she plays man' (Johnson 1988:123). She continues: 'What makes Emma unusual, then, is not that she [...] is a woman freakishly endowed with self-love, but rather that she is a woman who possesses and enjoys power, without bothering to demur about it' (p. 125).

Translated into the terms of the present enquiry, Emma's sense of authority cannot be separated from her manipulations of language, both her own and that of others.[11] As Gilbert and Gubar formulated it, she manipulates others 'as if they were characters in her own stories' (Gilbert & Gubar 1979:158). And it is through the act of telling these imagined stories of others that she draws them into the fabric of her *own* narrative. A revealing example is the scene at the end of Chapter 10, where Emma, contemplating Harriet and Elton together, 'felt the glory of having schemed successfully' (p. 114). Once again one is referred to the quote from Cowper as a clue to this strategy: *Myself creating what I saw.* And the anagnorisis in Chapter 47 inevitably focuses on this crucial aspect of Emma's role: 'With insufferable vanity had she believed herself in the secret of everybody's feelings; with unpardonable arrogance proposed to arrange everybody's destiny. She was proved to be universally mistaken' (p. 402).

It is important to be reminded by Gilbert and Gubar that she has been forced into this role, as a woman, quite simply because 'Emma has nothing to do. Given her intelligence and imagination, her impatient attempts to transform a mundane reality are completely understandable' (ibid.:158). This is true also of Frank. When he confesses on p. 359 that, 'I am tired of doing nothing', Emma's response is as true of herself as of him: 'You are sick of prosperity and indulgence.' But their reactions to this situation, and the *scope* they are allowed for such reaction, are predicated on gender. Furthermore, Emma's strategies illuminate not only her own circumscription, but the scope and limitations of the *woman writer* of the age. And her 'punishment' is to find 'that she has all along been manipulated as a character in someone else's fiction [...] Not only does the female artist fail, then, her efforts are condemned as tyrannical and coercive' (Gilbert & Gubar 1979:159).

Every person Emma encounters, every situation in which she finds herself, she treats as a signifier to which she stands in a twofold relationship: first, as an assigner of meaning (only to discover that the signifieds she intends are often displaced by others); and second, as a *receiver* of meaning (only to find that her decoding is invariable defective). It is in this respect, more than in any other, that Emma's 'prodigious self-deception' is evident (Mudrick 1968:197). And this, too, is a consequence of the *language of dissimulation* which informs the novel as a whole.

Her intentions are stated quite openly as early as the first chapter: 'I promise you to make none [that is, no more matches] for myself, papa; but I must, indeed, for other people. It is the greatest amusement in the world!' (p. 43). Knightley teases her drily: 'Your time has been properly and delicately spent, if you have been endeavouring for the last four years to bring about this marriage. A worthy employment for a young lady's mind!' He also warns her, as far as Elton is concerned, to 'invite him to dinner [...] and help him to the best of the fish and chicken, but leave him to chuse his own wife' (p. 45). It is her disregard for the warning – and her misreading of the signs of the ensuing adventure – that leads to her first disillusionment, when she tries to arrange a liaison between Elton and Harriet, only to discover that Elton in turn misreads it as interest on her own behalf, leading to his proposal and embarrassment all round. (Not that even this disillusionment deters her.)

The moment she sets eyes on Harriet she resolves that, '*She* would notice her; she would improve her; she would detach her from her bad acquaintance, and introduce her into good society' (p. 54): all she really manages to achieve is to make Harriet's life miserable, to set her up as her own rival for Knightley's love, and in the end to see her restored to the man (the good honest farmer Martin) Harriet was set to marry at the very beginning of the novel.

7

Underlying all Emma's schemings, her use and misuse of language and of narrative, is the crude and inescapable fact that the social code by which all the characters exist and survive is different for men and women. This also intensifies the meanings of the gypsy scene: it could never have happened to a man, only to women, since the crude nature of the reality represented by the clamorous gang threatens most obviously the women who weave the language web of games through which genteel society keeps itself going.

Gendering works through all the layers of private and public life in the text. In a telling comment on Frank Churchill's decision to come on a visit against the wishes of his family, Emma remarks: 'One can hardly conceive a young man's not having it in his power to do as much as that. A young *woman*, if she falls into bad hands, may be teazed, and kept at a distance from those she wants to be with; but one cannot comprehend a young *man's* being under such restraint' (p. 143).

Men decide and act; women submit. This is most evident in the all-important space occupied by marriage in this society. It has been the subject of so much comment over the years that it does not need repetition here. What concerns us is the defining function of language in this regard, as in all others. When Emma is forced to come to terms with the fact that Frank Churchill is not available as a possible marriage partner, her reaction is revealing: 'I do not find myself making any use of the word *sacrifice*' (p. 268). The experience of sacrifice itself, which for women is the key to matrimony, is here turned into a *word*, as if it were part of one of Emma's charades. Indeed, she continues: 'In not one of all my clever replies, my delicate negatives, is there any allusion to making a sacrifice.' It is surely significant that even at a moment of emotional intensity like this, her primary concern should be her choice of words, her arrangement of language.

For Emma herself, life is all too readily reduced to the terms in which she summarises her contentment: 'Harriet rational [read 'understanding reason', that is, obeying Emma's instructions], Frank Churchill not too much in love [that is, not causing her any inconvenience], and Mr Knightley not wanting to quarrel with her, how very happy a summer must be before her' (p. 329). Even in spite of the narrator's light-hearted ironical tone, the egoism in the passage is quite staggering – until one begins to read it against the silences of the text. The alternatives, as the hackneyed phrase goes, are simply too ghastly to contemplate.

Reading in the same vein, one discovers the pathos below the surface of Chapter 53, where the prospects of the Westons' unborn child are examined: Emma wishes for a girl, with at least the submerged desire that she may one day resume her matchmaking. Even with her own future with Mr Knightley more or less secure (or precisely *because* of it?), the personal unfulfilment which initially drove her towards the language games and storytelling implicit in her compulsive matchmaking appears still to be unresolved. *Because she is a woman.*

For men, self-fulfilment in a patriarchal society may be measured in terms of Mr Weston's kind of 'success': making a fortune, buying a house, getting a wife (p. 47). For women, there is little prospect of 'obtaining' anything in the same sense, because in the processes of their fulfilment (that is, the stories into which they translate themselves) men remain firmly ensconced in the active voice; women, who can at most attempt to manipulate the stories of *others*, always run the risk of merely passive constructions.

In a situation where open revolt or defiance is ruled out, one of the only possible alternatives to compliance is silence, and on occasion Emma does resort to it. When she cannot agree with her father, 'she had resolution enough to refrain from making any answer at all. She could not be complying; she dreaded being quarrelsome; her heroism reached only to silence' (p. 135). But the problem with silence, as Cordelia also discovered, is that it can so easily be misread – as Emma is forced to acknowledge, to her chagrin, when Mr Elton takes it upon himself 'to interpret this interesting silence' (p. 150) and comes up with a complete, and deeply embarrassing, reading of her responsiveness to his ardours. If in these circumstances a woman wishes to succeed it can only be by outplaying her rivals in the constructs of language and the charades of social interaction.

At any rate, no amount of 'success' can *essentially* alter a woman's fortune: even for Emma with her fierce if often misguided and deftly ironicised sense of independence, marriage describes her horizon. There are no prospects beyond domesticity, a state which, if the female experience in *Emma* is anything to go by, lumps women together with 'the furniture' just as surely as it happens to servants. They belong categorically with those others who continue to live in the silence beyond the strictly demarcated language of propriety and genteel society. Those others who, in the form of a band of gypsy children, found one brief moment to break into the world of 'due decorum' and disrupt its elaborate word-games and charades to show up the inadequacies of the whole structure of language devised, not just to cope with the trivia of social intercourse, but to ignore, to deny, or actively to ward off those other existences, that other reality.

6

The Language of Scandal

Gustave Flaubert: *Madame Bovary*

1

Maître Ernest Pinard, the prosecutor in the trial of Gustave Flaubert on charges of 'offenses à la morale publique et à la religion', gave an eloquent performance in his denunciation of the novel's seductive style. His attack focused on four narrative clusters: Emma's relationship with Rodolphe and her first 'fall'; her recourse to religion afterwards; the affair with Léon; and her death. But throughout the learned man's diatribe it is clear that his concern is not, primarily, the incidents *as such*, but the style of their presentation. Maître Pinard himself rises to a considerable height of eloquence when he describes Emma's emotional reaction to her first extramarital relationship:

> *Ainsi dès cette première faute, dès cette première chute, elle fait la glorification de l'adultère, elle chante la cantique de l'adultère, sa poésie, ses voluptés. Voilà, messieurs, qui pour moi est bien plus dangereux, bien plus immoral que la chute elle-même!* [Thus from the moment of this first mistake, this first fall, she begins to glorify adultery, to sing the hymn of adultery, its poetry, its voluptuous pleasures. This, gentlemen, I find much more dangerous, much more immoral, than the fall itself!]. (Flaubert 1987:623, my translation)[1]

After quoting a passage on one of Emma's nocturnal encounters with Rodolphe (Part II, Chapter 10), the learned man concludes: '*Connaissez-vous au monde, messieurs, un langage plus expressif*? [Gentlemen, have you ever encountered language more expressive than this in the world?]' (p. 623). In short, the scandal provoked by *Madame Bovary* resides, for the state prosecutor, in the book's language; and this is borne out by the rest of his argument: the fact that Emma's temporary embracing of religion is described in the same language of love in which her adulterous relationships are presented (Part II, Chapter 14); the description of incidents from her relationship with Léon in Part III; and the way in which the sacred language of extreme unction is contaminated (or, in a key word from the novel, *compromised*) by profane language from the experience of sexual love (this concerns one of the most profoundly moving passages in the novel: p. 335).

If Maître Pinard, for quite the wrong reasons, was right about locating the source of scandal in *Madame Bovary* in the novel's language, he also wholly misread that language, an error not uncommon among prosecutors (the trials of Oscar Wilde, of *Ulysses*, and of *Lady Chatterley's Lover* provide three more reminders). A clue to the nature of his misreading is provided in the very passage in which he enquired from the court whether it had ever encountered 'un langage plus expressif'. To this rhetorical question he adds, '*Avez-vous jamais vu un tableau plus lascif*? [Have you ever seen a lewder painting?]' The point is, of course, that language is *not* painting, even though the language of realism – inasmuch as Flaubert was a realist – invariably appeals to the *reader's* visual sense. Certainly, in *Madame Bovary*, Flaubert is often at pains to explore distinctions between writing and painting, writing and music.

And in a way, paradoxically, even Flaubert's contemporaries were already aware, however confusedly, of a different functioning of language. This is suggested by the fact that the very first onslaught of censorship on *Madame Bovary* was the decision of the editors of the *Revue de Paris* (in which the novel was first published, in six instalments, from 1 October to 15 December 1856) to make certain cuts, the most important of which was the famous episode in the first chapter of Part III (pp. 255–7) when Emma and Léon leave the cathedral and board a fiacre in which, with curtains drawn, they follow, for the rest of the day, a crazy course through the streets of Rouen and the country roads beyond. This was evidently considered the most 'dangerous' scene in the whole novel. Yet, especially when compared to some others in which the naked Emma is described in the arms of her lover, there is in this scene not a single scabrous phrase or word about sex, adultery, or an illicit affair of any kind. There is only the description of the fiacre careering through the streets, its yellow curtains drawn; and of an ungloved hand which, once, emerges to toss away 'some scraps of paper, which were carried off on the wind and landed like white butterflies in a field of red clover in full bloom' (pp. 256–7). If this is a canvas, there is not even a human figure visible on it, except for the increasingly exasperated driver and the staring citizens. Yet, in a sense, the censors were right: for all its silences, and even more *because* of its silences, this is indeed the most erotic scene in the novel.[2] It provides a clue to one of the least visible, yet most significant, problems that preoccupy the narrator, and the narrative, in *Madame Bovary*: that of language.

2

Innumerable studies have been written about Flaubert's language; more specifically, there have been stimulating close readings of *Madame Bovary*, as of his other texts, demonstrating the ways in which Flaubert's very strong views on narrative style (as expounded notably in his voluminous correspondence, particularly with Louise Colet) are 'applied' to the novels in question. But that is not the focus in the present essay. What concerns me here, as in the other essays in the volume, is the theory or notion of language advanced by the novel itself, and the extent to which that concept becomes crucial to the nature and the shape of the narrative produced in it.

True to his famous – or notorious, as the case may be – conviction that the author in his work is like God in creation, omnipresent but invisible,[3] Flaubert is not interested in explicating his views on language (or anything else, for that matter), in his narrative. But the novel does so, as it were, of its own accord, because, like Luther, it cannot do otherwise: it lies in its very nature to reflect on language; it is, as I have been arguing, a generic imperative.

There are only two explicit comments on language in *Madame Bovary*, and this rarity makes them all the more inviting to close scrutiny. In the first, Rodolphe reacts to Emma's extravagant protestation of love in Part II, Chapter 12 (p. 203):

> He had listened to so many speeches of this kind that they no longer made an impression on him. Emma was like any other mistress [...] High-flown language concealing tepid affection must be discounted, thought he: as though the full heart may not sometimes overflow in the emptiest metaphors, since no one can ever give the exact measure of his needs, his thoughts or his

sorrows, *and human speech is like a cracked kettle on which we strum*
out tunes to make a bear dance, when we would move the stars to pity.
(p. 203, my emphasis)

The passage confirms an earlier image which describes Emma's
reading of a letter from her father:

> She stood a few minutes with the rough paper in her hands,
> following the kindly thoughts which went cackling through the
> tangle of spelling mistakes like a hen half-hidden in a thorn
> hedge. (p. 184)

One should be careful not to assign any absolute meaning to either
passage: Rodolphe is thinking of a particular kind of (female)
speech which 'sometimes' fails – although the step towards generalisation ('no one can ever', 'human speech', 'we'...) is readily
taken; Emma reflects on a specific letter from a half-illiterate
farmer. But read together, and in conjunction with a whole network of images throughout the novel, they do prepare the
reader for a notion of language very much at odds with the
received wisdom about realism at the time, and very much revealing the modernist approach with which Flaubert, together with
Mallarmé and Rimbaud, so radically shifted our appreciation of
literature and its implication in language. There is already more
than a mere hint of the modernist despair of language and its
incapability of communicating adequately the private perception
and experience. There is, above all, a tension, if not a split, between
intention and performance in language; meaning is reduced to the
random and haphazard cacklings of a hen in an untidy hedge, and
between the poles of this tension are captured all the major oppositions of the narrative: dream and reality, literature and actuality,
mind and body, female and male, individual and society, 'a desire
that impels' and 'a convention that restrains' (p. 101), the 'conventional morality of men' and 'the eternal morality' invoked by
Rodolphe,[4] lofty thought and the drab, unimaginative, wretched
and restricted world of the bourgeoisie (which largely coincides
with patriarchy). Most of these polarities have been copiously
discussed in the vast critical literature which has accumulated
around Flaubert and which makes it so difficult to read his texts
without their encrustations. But the important thing in the present
context is that all these essential tensions are, in the very first

instance, embedded in a specific view of language. Language itself conditions, and in fact predetermines, the experience of desire and unfulfilment, of the sublime and the banal, of hit and miss, of will and frustration. Much later, at the outset of that memorable journey in the closed fiacre, the cabby will ask, 'Where to, sir?' and Léon will answer, 'Where you like!' (p. 255), and from that moment the cab ride will become the metaphor of a ride within *language*, and its undetermined route will coincide with that randomness Rodolphe had already read into language.

Most pertinently – and this, too, lends a note of dire warning to the fiacre scene – the image of language as cackling hen or broken kettle emphasises its flatness, its staleness, its lack of infinite variety. It is linked to a series of other perceptions on monotony and drabness: 'Charles' conversation was as flat as a street pavement, on which everybody's ideas trudged past, in their workaday dress, provoking no emotion, no laughter, no dreams' (p. 54); 'Here [that is, in Yonville-l'Abbaye] you are on the borders of Normandy, Picardy and the Ile de France, a bastard region whose speech is without accentuation as its scenery is without character' (p. 83).

The second major explication of a view of language is closely linked to the first, but provides a more specific framework for discussion. It occurs in the first chapter of Part III, just prior to the decisive meeting between Léon and Emma in the cathedral and the cab ride in which the episode debouches. In response to Emma's vague religious yearnings ('I should very much like to be a Sister of Mercy') Léon romantically imagines the 'peace of the tomb':

> For this was how they would have liked it to be: they were both constructing an ideal of themselves and adapting their past lives to it. *Speech acts invariably as an enlarger of sentiments.* (pp. 245–6, my emphasis)

The startlingly modern notion of self-construction is significant enough in itself – and the novel amply demonstrates that the construction goes beyond an 'image' or an 'ideal', and beyond the relation of past to present – but the most important aspect of this insight is, once more, its relation to language. The ideal to which the self has to be measured, and in which it expresses itself, is *a construct of language*. In the most literal sense, to which we shall return, it begins in Charles Bovary's identification of himself in *defective* language ('Charbovari'), and in Emma's construction of herself as the heroine of her world from the heroines she finds in *literature.*

The mechanics of the process are revealed most tellingly in Part II, Chapter 9, at the height of Emma's infatuation with Rodolphe:

> She remembered the heroines of the books she had read, and that lyrical legion of adulteresses began to sing in her memory with sisterly voices that enchanted her. *She was becoming a part of her own imaginings.* (p. 175, my emphasis)

Language here defines the condition of her self-construction: as a bridge to the imagination, and to fiction; at the same time it bolsters her confidence in transcending the boundaries that circumscribe the individual woman in order to be united (once again in singularly modern terms) with a 'lyrical legion' of 'sisterly voices'. Her functioning within the deadening dullness of her society is that of a *voice*, a female *vox clamantis*.

This is also a danger signal. Because we know by now that language not only enlarges or exaggerates sentiment (and everything else it visits), but also banalises and reduces experience, turning a star into a dancing bear or a kindly thought into a cackling hen. The two processes are not only simultaneous but interdependent; each becomes a condition of the other. No wonder there can be no escape for Emma, or anyone else, from this double bind.[5] The authenticity of either dream or identity is ruled out a priori; what remains is the precarious balancing act of trying to remain upright in the hideous world of the bourgeoisie and the platitudes of its language.

3

It is surely no coincidence that in so many instances where a character or a scene is described, the categories of such description either include, or lead up to, language. When Charles first encounters Emma, she is presented as a young woman who can 'embroider', who can 'be clever' and *'who could talk'* (p. 31, my emphasis in this and the following quotations). Binet 'was a good shot, an expert at all card games, *and he wrote a fine hand'* (p. 88).[6] As one should expect, it features particularly prominently in the presentation of the men who excite Emma's sexual interest: reflecting on the dinner party where he first had the opportunity of making an impression on her, Léon wonders 'how on earth had he managed to expound – *and with such a flow of language* – a hundred things that he could never have said before' (p. 98); and when in the full bloom of their love he thinks, not only of her 'quiet taste in dress', her 'languid drowsy-dove postures', 'the elevation of her soul', or 'the lace on her petticoat', but of her '*grace of language*' (p. 276). In the elaborate if extremely rapid seduction of Emma, Rodolphe relies more on speech than on anything else (this is particularly evident in the decisive conversation at the Agricultural Show, Part II, Chapter 8); and when he thinks of it afterwards, 'he was thinking of *the things she had said, and of the shape of her lips*' (p. 164). (The linkage of language and the organs of speech will become particularly significant later in the narrative.) And when Emma's face and body begin to show the signs of the passion she is living, it is inevitable that the change should also be described in terms of language: 'There were softer inflexions *in her voice* and in her figure' (p. 207); 'her eyes grew bolder, *her talk freer*' (p. 204).

Emma Bovary's eyes invite another comment. They have fascinated critics for many years, especially since Enid Starkie's rather nasty remarks about Flaubert's alleged lapse in presenting them first as brown, later as blue. Barnes (1985:74ff) deals delightfully with this kind of pedantry by citing the account, by a more or less contemporary writer, Du Camp, of the woman on whom Emma Bovary had presumably been based. This woman's eyes, wrote the authoritative Du Camp, were 'of uncertain colour, green, grey, or blue, according to the light' (quoted in Barnes 1985:81). But do we really need such external evidence? All that concerns us is the functioning of these eyes *in the text*: sometimes they appear brown (p. 28), sometimes black (p. 62), or blue (p. 46 or p. 246); sometimes large and dark (pp. 95, 175), sometimes piercing (p. 144), sometimes flaming (p. 292); in death they fade into a 'viscous pallor' (p. 341).

These changing colours and intensities are sometimes a trick of light, sometimes a trick of the emotions, but in the final analysis *they are a trick of language*. Because we have only the word(s) of the narrator to go by, and not an image to which we have direct access, if 'error' there be, it can only be error of language. Read in this way, it is an early pointer towards the novel's constant preoccupation with language as shifting and unreliable. As early as in *Mém-*

oires d'un fou (*Memories of a Madman*), written when he was a mere
teenager, Flaubert warned that '*les mots ne sont que des balbutiements
et le langage est impuissant* [words are only stammerings and language is impotent]' (quoted in Bollème 1979:122); and for the rest of
his life, most dramatically in *Madame Bovary*, his concern, and often
his despair, remained the conviction that '*le langage est inapte à
rendre compte d'une expérience que l'effort de l'expression altère et com-
promet* [language is incapable of accounting for an experience
which is changed and compromised by the attempt to express it]'
(ibid.:127).

4

In *Madame Bovary* the interrogation of language is effected in various ways. One, extremely subtle, is the use of imagery. It is noteworthy that although different worlds, or different kinds and levels
of experience, are constantly juxtaposed in the text, there are very
few full-blown metaphors in the novel.[7] Similes, on the other hand,
abound. This means that whereas the *fusion* of (contrasting) elements so characteristic of metaphor is eschewed, an explicit *comparison* of disparate givens is favoured: Charles's mother and wife
are 'at him like a pair of knives' (p. 32); 'he felt dreary as an empty
house' (p. 44); 'life was as cold as an attic facing north' (p. 57);
'sorrow sank deep into her soul with a muffled wailing, like the
winter wind in a derelict chateau' (p. 136); 'gasping for love, as a
carp on a kitchen table' (p. 143); 'her dreams dropping in the mud
like wounded swallows' (p. 197); or that stunning image which
anticipates T. S Eliot: 'her whole existence was spread out like a
corpse at a post-mortem' (p. 306). Although such similes occasionally come close to the density of metaphor ('the grand passion into
which she had plunged seemed to be dwindling around her like a
river sinking into its bed; she saw the slime at the bottom': p. 183),
there is this profound difference: in metaphor the combining force
that brings together the separate images is so strong that the reader
is not primarily aware of the agent which effects it, namely language. In a simile, through the obtrusive verbal manipulation of
the separate images ('like', 'as' . . .) the reader is kept conscious of
the *act of comparison*, that is, the intervention of language. And
through this awareness of language we are also reminded of the
manipulatory presence of a narrator.

Since our attention is so explicitly directed towards the *fact* of language, it becomes legitimate to enquire into *how* that language is perceived in the text, and how it functions in different situations.

Now if a predilection for simile rather than metaphor were the only strategy used in *Madame Bovary* to foreground – and, in the process, interrogate – language, my case wouldn't be very persuasive. But it happens in more overt and dramatic ways, one of the most obvious being the italicising of certain words or phrases. Thibaudet (1935) was the first to comment on this usage as marking deviations from the clichés of Yonville, or quotations from the bourgeoisie; but as Llosa indicates, the use of italics goes far beyond this, in order to mark substitutions in the narrative position or, most particularly, the composition of a rhetorical level in the narrative: *'ce sont des expressions marquées au sceau d'une communauté, non à celui d'individus isolés* [these expressions are marked with the seal of a community, not that of isolated individuals]' (Llosa 1978:197–8, my translation). Italics draw attention to the phrases and expressions as slang, as forms of regional or colloquial language, the turns of phrase of a particular class or social or professional category, *'cette région de l'opinion publique* [this region of public opinion]' as Butor (1984:80) defines it; or, in the definition proposed by Frey (1987:71), *'la mentalité d'une époque* [the mentality of a period]'. As a result, *'rien n'échappe à la socialité, donc il n'y a plus de parole authentique. Tout est aliénation, tout est dévalorisé* [nothing escapes from sociality, and so there is no authentic language left. Everything is alienation, everything is devalorised]' (Gengembre 1990:72, my translation). All the italicised passages together form a weave within the text, a collective borrowing from a language foreign to that of the narrator, establishing an intertextual dynamic, as Duchet (1976:153–7) indicates.

In the first paragraphs of the novel Charles is designated as a *'nouveau* habillé en bourgeois'; promotion to a higher class is described as '[passer] *dans les grands'*; the custom of flinging one's cap to one's bench in a particular way is explained as 'c'était le *genre'*. From time to time the English translator tries to find equivalents, often with less than impressive results: the opening paragraph refers to 'a new boy dressed in "civvies"', and the two other terms highlighted in the French text are translated in unremarkable pedestrian terms. This may promote an easier flow of narrative, but the point of the somewhat eccentric presentation of the original text is that *language draws attention to itself as language.*

Fortunately this is not entirely lost in the English version. A typical example is the elder Madame Bovary's assessment of her daughter-in-law 'who had "ideas above her station in life", and ran away with "enough firewood and sugar and candles for a mansion"' (p. 55). This goes beyond mere reported speech, as it isolates phrases in order to dramatise the functioning of speech in social relations, which becomes quite evident when, later, Léon visits Yonville from Rouen, and Homais 'talked slang to impress [...] the bourgeois; saying "digs", "outfit", "swell", "slick", "Breda Street", and "I'll cut along" for "I'm going"' (p. 289).[8] And it becomes particularly effective when in the representation of Emma she becomes, as it were, a quotation from one of her own favourite novels: 'She was the "woman in love" of all the novels, the heroine of all drama, the shadowy "she" of all the poetry-books' (p. 276). In passages like these (and they define the fibre of the narrative), the questionable, second-hand nature of language subverts the characters' (and notably Emma's) attempts at achieving some kind of authenticity in their definitions of self.[9]

The problem derives from the acknowledgement that, however strongly language marks character through individual usage, it is primarily a form of social currency, devised and used and put at one's disposal by *others*. Charles first becomes aware of it at school when his alienation is defined by his exclusion from the language of the other boys; later he will experience it in a different way when Emma takes control: 'His wife was master. He had to say this, and not that, in company' (p. 24). It is a profound, if depressing, truth of *Madame Bovary* that 'we must take some notice of what the world thinks, and conform to its morality', as Emma tells Rodolphe in Part II, Chapter 8 (p. 157); and this process, as we have seen in the reference to Emma's very sense of self as a consequence of her identification with the norm of novel characters, is predicated on language.

And because this is so, language becomes a social force which can punish, or even destroy, the individual who tries to deviate from the norm by corrupting the accepted with private definition: *this* is the locus of the scandal sensed by Maître Pinard in his condemnation of the confusion of two languages – that of religion, and that of love. In Part II, Chapter 14, on the rebound from her failed affair with Rodolphe, the confusion is Emma's; in

the scene of her death (Part III, Chapter 8), the narrator is the
manipulator:

> The priest recited the *Misereatur* and the *Indulgentiam*; then he
> dipped his right thumb into the oil and began the unctions: first
> on the eyes, that had so coveted all earthly splendours; then on
> the nostrils, that had loved warm breezes and amorous per-
> fumes; then on the mouth, that had opened for falsehood, had
> groaned with pride and cried out in lust; then on the hands, that
> had revelled in delicious contacts; lastly on the soles of the feet
> that once had run so swiftly to the assuaging of her desires, and
> now would walk no more. (p. 335)

The very notion of 'scandal', in *Madame Bovary*, long before Maître
Pinard made his attempt to define it (a reaction which, in itself,
replicated the 'scandals' *within* the text), resides in the possibility of
a clash between such different languages, notably those of the
individual and of society. The danger is signalled with wonderful
subtlety when, soon after first meeting Léon, Emma goes on a walk
with him, 'and Madame Tuvache, the mayor's wife, declared in her
maid's hearing that Madame Bovary was *compromising herself*'
(p. 104). The italicising of the phrase (this time retained in the
English translation), classifies it with those many instances
throughout the narrative when the 'common speech' of a class, or
a group, in society is cited as a norm. And as in so many other
respects, Emma's deviation is here a contravention not just of social
propriety, but of social propriety *ensconced in language*. The danger
is heightened by the hint of gossip which will take up Madame
Tuvache's story and spread it throughout the community: for language is at its most dangerous when activated and socialised in
this manner. Every further decisive moment in Emma's story will
be accompanied by gossip, that is, by language's own revenge on
individual transgression. The very particular threat in Emma's
demeanour, highlighted by the phrase 'compromising herself'
acquires even greater, and more ironic, meaning when, a few
chapters later, at the height of her first affair, none other than
Rodolphe himself will try to scare her off from visiting him by
warning her, in identical terms, that 'she was compromising herself' (p. 177). And the danger is extended to Léon when Emma asks
him to pawn part of her dowry on her behalf, and he is said to be
'afraid of compromising himself' (p. 300).

5

In all these situations language functions as the marker of specific realities. As far as society is concerned, there is no great distance from what is regarded as 'acceptable' (or, for the individual, 'desired') to what becomes accepted as 'real'. Phrased somewhat differently, whatever is real in a given context, is determined by the language in which that context is defined, and which is in turn produced by that context. One of the most revealing ways in which this is imparted to the reader is the narrator's use of the designations 'Emma' and 'Madame Bovary' for the heroine.

That the very title of the novel suppresses all sense of Emma's individuality by integrating her into the 'social discourse' of the narrative, has been noted by many critics: it utterly 'socialises' her, draws her into the realm of the plural, turns her into the novel's 'Other', says Duchet (1976:144–6), making it impossible for her, even before her story has been told, to achieve any form of authenticity (Gengembre 1990:34, 43). But within the text, the tussle between private identity and the forces of socialisation is relentlessly fought on every page, marked by the distinction between 'Emma' and 'Madame Bovary'.

It is used to particular effect in the ball scene of Part I, Chapter 8, where she enters the dining-room as 'Emma' (the young country wife overwhelmed by all that is strange and wonderful), then becomes 'Madame Bovary' (the socially aware guest who 'noticed that several of the ladies had not put their gloves in their glasses': p. 61), then involuntarily reverts to 'Emma' who 'shivered all over at the cold taste of [the champagne] in her mouth' (p. 62), and later, invited to dance by the Viscount, adopts again the public persona of 'Madame Bovary', before having her outsidership confirmed when, as 'Emma' she adopts the – for her – telling and characteristic pose of standing at the window to stare out at the vast, unknown, magical night outside (p. 67).

How eloquent the appellation becomes when, after many pages of a purely private, and deprived, existence as 'Emma', she accompanies Charles at the end of Part I, leaving Tostes to travel to Yonville, and the narrator announces that 'Madame Bovary was pregnant' (p. 81).

Not long afterwards, in the tour de force of the chapter on the Agricultural Show, the whole complicated process through which Emma alternately yields to Rodolphe's seductive language and tries to keep a distance, are conveyed (in the midst of several other narrative strategies) by the revealing interplay of 'Emma' and 'Madame Bovary'. Already, within the larger contours of the scene, we have the juxtaposition of different realities (the official world of the pompous speakers, and the private world of the would-be lovers; in addition to the pretences of politics, and the crude facts of animals, manure and mud); now the reader discovers that such splits are replicated within the two principal characters of the scene as well: Rodolphe the callous schemer and Rodolphe the lover; Madame Bovary, the medical officer's wife, and Emma, the passionate and frustrated, but desperately scared, young woman.

And once again it is not a byproduct of the narrative, but part of its main business; and it is emphasised when Rodolphe first ventures to call her by her name, explaining that, ' "that name that fell from my lips – the name that fills my heart – is forbidden me. Madame Bovary: everybody calls you that! And it isn't your name, anyway, it's somebody else's. Someone else's" ', he repeated; and he hid his face in his hands' (p. 168).

The reader cannot but remember that, eight chapters earlier, in the first days of her marriage to Charles, Emma was already musing about that name: 'She would have liked this name of Bovary, that was hers, to be famous, on view at the bookshops, always cropping up in the papers, known all over France' (p. 74). It is a wish, one should be reminded in passing, that was ironically granted: not so much by Homais's prudently distorted account of her death in a provincial newspaper, as by Flaubert's novel, which granted her name passage into the very dictionaries of the French language.

Perhaps the final irony of the Agricultural Show lies in the discovery that the different worlds, the different realities, designated by the languages used with such dazzling mastery in the chapter, turn out to be distressingly similar. Rodolphe's language of seduction is no more, and no less, calculated, or hollow, or mendacious, than the rhetoric of the speakers on the platform; and the lofty flight of dreams is, in the final analysis, not so remote from the dung of the beasts or the trampling of the crowds. There is a *'négation réciproque* [a reciprocal denial]' of both worlds, reality and dream, in this scene, argues Cigada (1989:128) – and Emma is as much the victim of the one as of the other. This will be confirmed by her rudest awakening when she eventually rediscovers 'in adultery all the banality of marriage' (p. 301). In the same chapter Léon comes to acknowledge that, 'Not a lawyer but carries within him the débris of a poet.' And how can it be otherwise? Is not human speech – the speech in which we address the angels or herd the cattle – a cracked kettle on which we strum out tunes to make a bear dance, when we would move the stars to pity? *This* is the heart of the tragedy of Flaubert's human condition: not that dreams fail us, or flights of the imagination end in the mud, but that we have only one language in which to attempt to say it all. Our most private utterances are soiled (*souiller* is one of Maître Pinard's favourite words) when their expression is determined by a language already devaluated by others; our social intercourse, at the other end of the scale, is rendered suspect by the idiosyncrasies of the private stamp we place on public utterance.

6

All this flows from the specific concept of language that informs the novel as a whole, namely as primarily unreliable and defective, a broken kettle. More often than not language is unmasked as a web of lies. What begins, not without a touch of humour, with the discovery that Charles's first mother-in-law has lied about her daughter's inheritance, will soon gather momentum to destroy the main characters (with the exception of those who have always been masters of mendacity themselves, Rodolphe or Homais; or those like Léon who have gradually succumbed to the lie). Emma's early knack of finding 'an extraordinary name for some quite ordinary dish' (p. 73) may appear innocent, even charming; but because this deceit is vested in language, and language defines everything she regards as important, from social standing to romantic love, the end is predictable:

> From that moment her existence became nothing but a tissue of lies, in which she hid her love from view.
>   It became a need, a craving, an indulgence: to the point that if she said she had gone along the right side of a street yesterday, it was to be inferred that she had in fact taken the left. (p. 281)

And since a lie, like truth, is not a 'thing' in itself but the expression of a relation, this phenomenon in *Madame Bovary* is linked, as a narrative device, to the use of similes as a barometer of dissonance;

and to that entire dimension of the novel concerned with 'reality' and 'illusion', desire and frustration, appearance and concealment:

> What caused this inadequacy in her life? Why did everything she leaned on instantaneously decay? [. . .] There was nothing that was worth going far to get: all was lies! Every smile concealed a yawn of boredom, every joy a misery. (p. 295)

Words become empty signs. Even at a very early stage of her life 'Emma wondered exactly what was meant in life by the words "bliss", "passion", "ecstasy", which had looked so beautiful in books' (p. 47); more and more, below the 'flow of courteous phrases' (p. 116), she discovers *other words* – those terms which so revolted Maître Pinard, 'the soilure of marriage and the disillusionment of adultery' (p. 236).

There is little need to elaborate on the concealing effect of language in *Madame Bovary* (an effect, it should be said, which flies in the face of most of the accepted wisdom on 'realism', in which the opposite, namely the *representative* faculty of language, is usually the starting point). Almost every episode, in one way or another, is constructed around this functioning. A single brief illustration would illuminate some of the various ways in which this is done.

In Part II, Chapter 4, soon after Emma has first met Léon, in the dawning of the first possibilities of love, there is a small scene in which she has her baby girl brought down to her, 'and Madame Bovary undressed her to show off her fine limbs. She declared she adored children' (p. 119). It is not the lie as such that comes a surprise: even at this early stage the reader has come to expect it of Emma. It may not even, in this context, be much of a lie, since Emma is probably quite convinced, at least for the moment, that she does love her child in particular and even children in general. But at best, what she says is irrelevant: her talk about loving children is really a way of saying that she is in love with a man – but within the act of articulating it, language is also *concealing* what it means. *Instead* of saying what she has in mind, she expresses something entirely different. The categories of signification become confused. And the 'scandal' of the scene resides in the juxtaposition of the child's nakedness and the concealments, the clothing and trappings, of language.

What is implied in this scene, is stated explicitly in the presentation of one of Emma's encounters with Rodolphe. There has been an upheaval in the house after Charles's mother has, ironically, caught Emma's maid in the arms of a suitor; and when Rodolphe is summoned to the garden with the sign-language they have agreed on (fastening, significantly, a sheet of paper to the blind), Emma's emotions reflect that confusion in the categories of meaning she has become accustomed to:

> She threw herself into his arms.
> 'Take care!' he said.
> 'Ah, if you only knew ...' she answered, and then she told him everything, *hurriedly, disjointedly, overstating the facts, inventing several, with such a wealth of parentheses that he couldn't make head or tail of it.* (p. 205, my emphasis)

The problem lies in the hit-or-miss nature of language: sometimes it 'works' (as it would seem in Emma's view of the canon of romantic love, or in Homais's view of the scientific truth of his books), but there is no guarantee. Even the unscrupulous Rodolphe experiences something of it when he rummages through Emma's letters – 'A word would bring back a face, a gesture, a tone of voice; but sometimes he could recall nothing' (p. 213) – and the full significance of the scene is driven home when he then sits down to write the fatal final letter to Emma, ending their affair at the very moment she is preparing to elope with him. Almost every phrase in the letter is revealed to be the product of Machiavellian calculation, in a remarkable display of the power relations at work between man and woman, and between language and whatever passes for 'reality'.

Such demonstrations of the language of concealment find their narrative extension in some of the key scenes of the novel: lovers' trysts which are invariably set in secluded spots whose 'meaning' cannot be probed from outside (in arbour or forest or garden, or otherwise in secluded rooms 'behind drawn blinds and locked doors': p. 267); the Agricultural Show with its syncopation of public speeches and declarations of love, all of them equally false; the scene in the cathedral where the guided tour conceals everything that is really happening between Emma and Léon; and, inevitably, the splendid scene of the fiacre driving through the streets of Rouen. And just as the good citizens of that city misread the signs of the sight before them, the morally minded Maître Pinard read into these concealments whatever *he* pleased. This is the danger of the empty sign.

What makes the strategies of concealment particularly striking (and often poignant, and sometimes amusing) is that the major indictment of *Madame Bovary* at Flaubert's trial was the opposite, namely the author's shameless exhibitionism: '*Chez lui*', said Maître Pinard, '*point de gaze, point de voiles, c'est la nature dans toute sa nudité, dans toute sa crudité* [With him, no gauze, no veils, it's nature in all its nakedness, in all its crudeness]' (Flaubert 1951:627). This accusation is, in fact, belied by evidence the advocate himself advances elsewhere, to demonstrate the extent to which Flaubert's narrator relies, for the dangerous seductions of his style, on suggestions and hints rather than overt description – 'Emma put out her arms to steady herself as she crouched down, and the material clung to her here and there following the curve of her bosom' (p. 141) – which may indeed be read as a metaphor for language itself. In another incident, 'Rodolphe [. . .] had his eyes on the dainty white stocking that showed like a morsel of her naked flesh between the black cloth and the black boot' (p. 172). Like Madame de Lafayette and others before him, Flaubert already appreciated what Barthes (1976:9–10) would express over a century later in the famous observation on the gaping garment. But he goes even further: what is visible, in the scene just quoted, is no more than 'the dainty white stocking' – but to Rodolphe's eyes (and Maître Pinard's, inevitably) it *looks like*, and is read as if it were, a morsel of naked flesh. It is a conjurer's trick in which a *lack* in language is read as an *excess*.[10]

Even when, upon occasion, language does serve some function of communication or explication in *Madame Bovary*, it is demonstrated, invariably, as going only *so* far – and then no farther; sooner or later it runs into the blank wall of the unintelligible or of silence. Nowhere is this manifested more intensely than in Part II, Chapter 9, where Emma for the first time 'abandons herself' (Mr Russell's English translation regrettably says 'surrendered': p. 173) to Rodolphe. For a brief moment they exist in total, splendid isolation from the world, and everything is turned inward:

> Silence was everywhere. Sweetness seemed to breathe from the trees. She felt her heart beginning to beat again, and the blood flowing inside her flesh like a river of milk. Then, far away beyond the forest, on the other side of the valley, she heard a strange, long-drawn cry that hung on the air, and listened to it in silence as it mingled like music with the last vibrations of her jangled nerves. (p. 174)

This sound, from a dimension where realism cannot reach, anticipates that equally unexplained, and inexplicable, breaking of some cosmic string in Act II, and again at the very end, of Chekhov's *Cherry Orchard*.[11] It comes from beyond language, and *signals* the limit of language, in a text where the very faculty of language is constantly placed at risk. It belongs to the same realm as that roar from the other side of silence we shall encounter in *Middlemarch*.

Less dramatically, the limits of language, certainly of the tellable, are signalled throughout *Madame Bovary* whenever an experience is acknowledged but not told. This may occur with reference to the narrator himself (there is sufficient evidence, from the very first chapter, to suspect that the narrator is male), as in Part III, Chapter 7, when he refers to 'one of those indescribable ivory carvings which are composed of crescents and spheres fitted one inside the other' (p. 316). In a different vein the fiacre scene also reflects on the narrator's presence, not merely in almost literally drawing a veil of discretion over the event but in implying that the limits of his language have been reached.

More often the strategy is used in connection with the characters in scenes they cannot adequately handle. This is a very eloquent device in those many scenes where the reader finds Emma at a window, looking out.[12] But there are, of course, many other instances as well, and it is hardly necessary to offer a full catalogue. An especially poignant moment occurs in Part II, Chapter 3 when Emma's child is born and Charles announces it to be a girl. Emma's only reaction is to turn away and faint (p. 101).

The bourgeois Charles, whose speech, we know, is as flat as the *trottoir* or the countryside, has no problem in translating the experience into language. To Emma, the woman, this kind of language is inadequate; whatever she feels – including, the reader can only presume, the full extent of her revulsion of replicating herself, of bringing another girl-child, doomed to frustration and futility, into a world circumscribed by male speech – exists *beyond* language.

There are other episodes in which her silence may be less extreme, but even there it marks the limits of speech. When in Part II, Chapter 6, Emma is forced to acknowledge, for the first time, and against her will, that the old village priest is incapable of helping her, 'Her wandering gaze slowly alighted on the old man in the cassock, and they looked at one another face to face, without speaking' (p. 127).

After Emma's death, her father arrives to console Charles, but as might be expected language soon breaks down again: 'Do you remember me coming to Tostes once when you had lost your first wife. I comforted you then. *I found something to say, then. But now...*' (p. 350, my emphasis).

This is the ultimate function of death in the novel: it signals the end of language; and, as Carlos Fuentes once remarked, the theme of death *in* a novel is also a metaphor for the ending of the novel itself, which imposes the sense of a double silence on the text. This is particularly relevant to *Madame Bovary*, where the narration, both of Emma's death and of Charles's, focuses very specifically on the mouth, the organ of speech.

After the extreme unction, which included, as we have noted, the blessing of the mouth 'that had opened for falsehood, had groaned with pride and cried out in lust' (p. 335), Emma goes through the final spasms and indignities of death. At the crucial moment the hideous old blind man[13] who has haunted the coach in which she so regularly travelled between Yonville and Rouen for her love-meetings with Léon, returns with his silly little song about 'a maiden's thoughts (of) love', ending with the innuendo of her petticoat blown away by the wind (p. 337). Within its flimsy contours the ditty encapsulates, once again, the futility of language with which the novel as a whole has been preoccupied. And it is Emma's desperate amusement at the song that brings on the final spasm which causes her death. Afterwards she is left in silence, and much of the activity surrounding her has to do with language: Charles's written instructions for her burial; Homais's attempts at an obituary; the bickering of the priest and the chemist on the authority of 'texts' (p. 340). Then the narrator returns to the corpse: 'Emma lay with her head on her right shoulder. Her mouth hung open, the corner of it showing like a black hole at the bottom of her face' (p. 341).

It is no coincidence that soon afterwards, when Charles, too, dies, the description of his corpse should include a reference to the fact that 'his mouth was open' (p. 360). The twice-repeated mention of an open mouth brings together, from the whole extent of the text, the many threads of imagery concerning holes, gaps, chasms – all those openings from which language has disappeared.

To compound the impact of this final image we have the description of the corpse after it has been washed and dressed and laid out by the maid, the innkeeper Madame Lefrançois, and Charles's mother:

> They bent over to put on her wreath; they had to lift her head a little, and as they did so a stream of dark liquid poured from her mouth, as though she were vomiting. (p. 342)

Scandalous! – not, as Maître Pinard would argue, because of the impropriety of the scene, the violation of Emma's integrity in death, the 'extreme realism' of the passage, but because of the way in which, in the black hole of silence, language is replaced by no more than a dark fluid. There can hardly be a more horrible representation of the final meaninglessness of language.

7

And yet language is all we have to articulate the world, including the black holes of the unsayable. Because language, however flawed, however finite, however threatened by that ultimate silence that surrounds and pervades it, is also the only act of restitution – restitution through memory – available to the Flaubertian narrator.

The novel as a whole may be regarded as an act of language 'with the lengthening of perspective that things attain in memory' (p. 115). And that an act of memory is involved, constituted by falsification and invention as much as by representation, may be extrapolated from the many examples of Homais's reporting on current events in Yonville in his regional newspaper. More importantly, it is evident from the perspective behind the text as a whole: when the novel opens, it is narrated by one of the boys in the class into which Charles Bovary irrupts; there is a body of observation and of observers, a *we*, incorporated in this speaking voice.[14] Very soon, still in Chapter 1, the immediacy of this perspective is interrupted when the narrator steps further back to provide a background to Charles's family (p. 18); and once Charles leaves the school and moves on to Rouen (p. 21), whatever is narrated from that point on can be construed only – as innumerable commentators have argued – as recollection and/or fabrication.

There seems to be a tendency towards the latter. On p. 21 there is, after all, the curious remark that, 'It would be impossible for any of us to remember the least thing about him now.' And yet the

whole rest of the novel is involved in the extremely detailed rein-
vention of precisely what has just been designated 'impossible'.
This means that *Madame Bovary* as a whole becomes, itself, one of
those written texts so often invoked in the narrative, whose authority resides entirely in the fact that they are written. More precisely,
it becomes a novel like those novels Emma so compulsively reads,
a text whose claims to authority are subverted in every fibre of its
own narration.

And this, without any doubt, must be regarded as scandalous,
even if the word here acquires yet another meaning of which our
Maître Pinard could have had no inkling.

7

Quoted in Slang

George Eliot: *Middlemarch*

1

For all its preoccupation with trivia and with the business of what is traditionally regarded as 'realism', the opening passage of *Middlemarch* is a remarkable revelation of the structures and concerns of the whole massive novel that is to follow. And from the outset there is a subtle but significant awareness of the functioning of language in the kind of narrative Eliot handles with such consummate skill:

> Miss Brooke had that kind of beauty which seems to be thrown into relief by poor dress. Her hand and wrist were so finely formed that she could wear sleeves not less bare of style than those in which the Blessed Virgin appeared to Italian painters; and her profile as well as her stature and bearing seemed to gain the more dignity from her plain garments, which by the side of provincial fashion gave her the impressiveness of a fine quotation from the Bible – or from one of our elder poets, – in a paragraph of today's newspaper. She was usually spoken of as being remarkably clever, but with the addition that her sister Celia had more common-sense. Nevertheless, Celia wore scarcely more trimmings; and it was only to close observers that her dress differed from her sister's. (p. 29)[1]

The passage as a whole (of which this is only the beginning) is built on a grammar of observation, perception and (re)presentation: Miss Brooke's beauty *seems to be* of a certain kind; the Virgin *appeared* to painters in a certain light; her profile and bearing *seemed* to gain dignity from her dress, which lent her an *impressiveness*; she was *spoken of* as being clever; only *close observers* noticed the difference between her dress and her sister's.

147

At one remove another layer of words, less obvious or directly informative than the first, supports the slowly emerging concept of the object of description (Miss Brooke, or her sister) as being constituted, not in terms of an inner substance, but as a construct of observation and reporting: *beauty* is such a word, since convention has already established it as the product of interaction between an object and a beholder; *relief* is another, as it depends entirely on an act and an angle of observation; so is *painter*, a term which, through a sleight of hand, introduces the agent of observation and reporting into the passage, as a stand-in for the narrator, whose presence is perceived in every turn of phrase. Other words in this category are, of course, *poor, kind, style, remarkably, addition, differed, fine, provincial fashion*, each of which, to some degree or other, implies the presence of an adjudicator or observer. Even terms like *finely formed, stature, bearing, dignity* are far from innocent.

Initially, the perceptions are mostly of a visual order, culminating in the introduction of the *painters* who are primarily involved in such activity; but gradually the weight shifts towards the aural and the verbal, and the evocation of the Bible, the line of poetry, and the newspaper, firmly establishes language and the act of writing as the process which mediates in the act of communication between an observer and her/his public. As the novel unfolds, the visual and the aural will often merge (a particularly felicitous example is the description of Rosamond Vincy, who 'seemed to have the true melodic charm': p. 121), to attain its greatest metaphoric density in the code of the theatre which informs so much of the structuration of *Middlemarch*. Ultimately, even those perceptions informed by the visual (in the opening passage just as much as in the rest of the novel), also depend on language: in the novel they can only be communicated to the reader if the visual itself has been translated into the verbal. This is made explicit in the narrator's injunction on p. 470: 'Let those who know, tell us exactly what stuff it was that Dorothea wore in those days of mild autumn – that thin white woollen stuff soft to the touch and soft to the eye.'

An important consequence of this persistent strategy of witnessing, that is, of perception-and-reporting, is that everything is relational, as Newton (1981), among many others, has pointed out. This has become a commonplace in readings of Eliot, but one which remains important in our present context. What is said of Rosamond on p. 196 really applies to everybody around her: 'Rosamond, in fact, was entirely occupied not exactly with Tertius Lydgate as he was in himself, but with his relation to her.' As many critics have argued, if 'character' itself is merely the nexus of innumerable intersecting lines of observation, it loses all notion of fixed identity ('Character is not cut in marble – it is not something solid and unalterable. It is something living and changing': pp. 790–1). It exists, in fact, wholly in the eye, and in the language, of the beholder. In one of the most illuminating – and most startlingly 'modern' – comments of the novel, the narrator describes an individual as 'merely a cluster of signs for his neighbours' false suppositions' (p. 171). And, as she reminds the reader elsewhere, 'signs are small measurable things, but interpretations are illimitable' (p. 47). Everything is dependent on perception, but as perception itself depends on language, 'we all of us, grave or light, get our thoughts entangled in metaphors, and act fatally on the strength of them' (p. 111).

In her illuminating essay '*Middlemarch*: An experiment in time', Sally Shuttleworth argues that, 'The unity of *Middlemarch* is based, primarily, not on relations of direct effect, but on the shared community of language [...] Through language characters articulate both their individual and communal identity [...] Individual psychology is defined, in accordance with Lewes' theories, both by the accumulated beliefs and prejudices stored within language, and the contemporary functions of gossip' (Shuttleworth 1984:147–8).

But this offers no more than a starting point for the enquiry I propose, as it seems to me that the very concept of 'language' itself is under scrutiny in Eliot's novel. Colin MacCabe has argued for what he sees as the 'transparency' of George Eliot's language, based on '[t]he claim of the narrative prose to grant direct access to a final reality' (MacCabe 1991:159).[2] In a novel like *Middlemarch*, he avers, 'The metalanguage [...] refuses to acknowledge its own status as writing' (p. 158). This has already been adequately refuted by David Lodge (1991:160): 'There is never a perfect fit between language and the world.' But I believe one can go much further, in demonstrating the virtuoso exploitation, in *Middlemarch*, of a dense and opaque metalanguage supremely aware of itself, and unremittingly problematising its own relation to the other languages in the novel, and to reality. As D. M. Miller (1991:189) puts it:

The main force of the pluralism in *Middlemarch* [...] is surely to make us aware of the perspective itself. What traditional form shows us is no longer exhibited in a spirit of naïve realism, as simply what is there to be seen. Instead it must now be taken as a function of a perceiving system with its own desires, disguises, deletions, and disinterests, *which might have been organized otherwise.*

All the defining terms in this passage ('pluralism', 'perspective', 'perceiving system'), I propose, should be read as functions of language.

Once again the opening passage provides a useful starting point. It is no coincidence that Dorothea's appearance in her provincial context is described as conveying 'the impressiveness of a fine quotation from the Bible – or from one of our elder poets – in a paragraph of today's newspaper': apart from equating the world of Middlemarch with writing, with the texture of newspaper reportage, with narrative, and even apart from introducing at a very early stage the discrepancy between the sublime (or, on the platonic level so often invoked, the Ideal) and the mundane, it is particularly significant that Dorothea should be compared to a 'quotation'. Almost compulsively language in *Middlemarch* will come to function *as* quotation: it comes from elsewhere, points elsewhere, refers to a source located elsewhere.

This source may often seem to be identifiable: the Bible, Shakespeare, Chaucer, or whatever. But more often than not the source remains anonymous, whether in the epigraphs that constitute the chapter headings, or in quotations within the narrative, or quite simply in the functioning of speech by characters and narrator alike. For language in *Middlemarch*, as Shuttleworth and others have already argued, is primarily a common possession of society. Read in its full significance, this means that whatever is said has already been said by others: it is, as Derrida would have it, *iterable*. If, as innumerable commentators have so eloquently demonstrated over the years, Eliot's fiction is primarily a representation of the interaction between the social and the individual, the *site* of that encounter is language.

These are some of the aspects – all of them already activated in the opening passage of *Middlemarch* – of the argument I propose to develop and illustrate in what follows.

2

Characterisation through processes of interactive perception, or what Shuttleworth, borrowing Lydgate's term, calls 'organic interdependence', occurs within each of the major narrative lines of the novel: Dorothea Brooke's disillusioning marriage to the pedant Casaubon and her subsequent devotion to 'good works' before she dares to accept Will Ladislaw's love in what Gilbert and Gubar (1984:530) describe as 'the most subversive act available to her within the context defined by the author'; Tertius Lydgate's search for self-fulfilment in his medical practice and research, which is temporarily shipwrecked in public humiliation as a result of his increasingly desperate attempts to satisfy the exorbitant needs of his puppy-wife Rosamond; the hypocritical banker Bulstrode's confrontation with his less-than-commendable past, resurrected when the unscrupulous Raffles turns up in Middlemarch and threatens to spread the news; Fred Vincy's attempts to overcome his penchant for irresponsible self-gratification and to reform himself in order to be worthy of the love of Mary Garth. There are many links among these narratives. Most obviously, there are family relationships: Dorothea and Celia are siblings, as are Fred and Rosamond; Bulstrode married Ladislaw's grandmother, and his present wife is Caleb Garth's sister. More intricately, it happens on the level of plot: Dorothea's high-minded honesty links her with Mary Garth; her passionate pursuit of an ideal runs parallel to Ladislaw's; Rosamond's naïveté invites comparison with that of Dorothea's sister; Bulstrode backs Lydgate financially and also gets drawn into the social advancement of the Garth family; Mrs Garth and Rosamond show a strong, if unexpected, resemblance in their observation of strict grammatical rules; Ladislaw's mother was stage-struck, and a French actress was the great love in Lydgate's life.

But what concerns us here is the fact that each narrative line may also be read as 'witnessing' – that is, observing and commenting on – the others: their relationship is one of narrative syntax, a grammar informed essentially by Auguste Comte's Positivism – an enterprise every bit as ambitious, and in retrospect, surely, as ridiculous, as Casaubon's *Key to All the Mythologies*. It is as true of Comte as of Casaubon and of Lydgate, that 'the more he became interested in special questions [...] the more keenly he felt the need for *that fundamental knowledge of structure*' (p. 177, my emphasis.) It is a grammar structured by the binarities of cause and effect, active and passive, command and obedience, as succinctly summarised in the unattributed epigraph to Chapter 64 (p. 697), ultimately by the Comtean distinction between altruism as the highest good and egoism as the basest evil.

The triumph of *Middlemarch*, I should propose at this early stage, is that it both follows *and* subverts Comte, as it follows and subverts Wordsworth, and Lewes, and several other scientists, philosophers and poets of the age; and in the final analysis it also both confirms and radically disrupts all notions of the nineteenth-century realist novel, of which it has been held by many critics to be the supreme specimen (see Lodge 1991:169). Narrative closure, rooted in linguistic closure, is the very last thing *Middlemarch* demonstrates.

But in order to arrive at such an appraisal it is necessary to return to that multi-faceted act of witnessing at work throughout the text, in which language is so fundamentally implicated.

In this regard, the opening passage of Chapter 27 has proved deservedly popular with commentators. The narrator presents a 'pregnant little fact' demonstrated to her by a philosopher friend:

> Your pier-glass or extensive surface of polished steel made to be rubbed by a housemaid, will be minutely and multitudinously scratched in all directions; but place now against it a lighted candle as a centre of illumination, and lo! the scratches will seem to arrange themselves in a fine series of concentric circles around that little sun. It is demonstrable that the scratches are going everywhere impartially, and it is only your candle which produces the flattering illusion of a concentric arrangement, its light falling with an exclusive optical selection. These things are a parable. The scratches are events, and the candle is the egoism of any person now absent. (p. 297)

The narrative structure of the novel as a whole, as the imposition of a pattern of numerous small, closed, egocentric acts of observation on a surface of innumerable events 'going everywhere impartially', is clearly mirrored here, as is the overall conception of events perceived as components of an overarching parable.[3] The crux, for the present argument, comes at the moment when the language in which the whole passage is communicated – for it is, after all, a verbal, not a visual, image – becomes conscious of itself: *These things are a parable*. Observation as such becomes potent only when it is translated into language.

The negative implications of the image are illuminated in the last chapter devoted to Casaubon's wretched, self-centred life in which his own perception is blamed for all his miseries:

Will not a tiny speck very close to our vision blot out the glory of the world, and leave only a margin by which we see the blot? I know no speck so troublesome as self. (p. 456)

Once again the leap from the visual to the verbal, specifically the allegorical, is obvious.

But that there is also a potential for positive experience in this kind of observation is clear from a passage in Chapter 76, where Dorothea sits among Casaubon's books in the library,[4] which, through Casaubon's close identification with the place, has come to signify language gone wrong. She is thinking about Lydgate as she waits for him to arrive:

> These thoughts were like a drama to her, and made her eyes bright, and gave an attitude of suspense to her whole frame, though she was only looking out from the brown library on to the turf and the bright green buds which stood in relief against the dark evergreens. (p. 818)

There is a triple process of observation involved in the scene: Dorothea, physically and psychologically immured among her dead husband's dead books, is looking out into the space of the Spring scene; but at the same time there is a narrator at work, observing the observer, noting her 'bright' eyes and her 'attitude of suspense', and turning this perception into language as she stares out into the space of the reader. The third process at work in the scene is that of Dorothea contemplating her own thoughts as though they were being acted out on a stage, 'like a drama', one of the key patterns of imagery active throughout the novel. Thought (presumably in the form of language) is turned into visual experience which is then reshaped into language. And it is through this process, in which language is twice involved, that the novel assumes the structure it has (on the one hand, its convoluted frames of witnessing; on the other, its urge towards philosophising).

The dual nature of the process is illuminated with particular force in another scene where interior and exterior are linked in the observation. This time it concerns Bulstrode at the moment when he faces ruin through the irruption of his past into his present:

> [H]e felt the scenes of his earlier life coming between him and everything else, as obstinately as when we look through the

window from a lighted room, the lighted objects we turn our
backs on are still before us, instead of the grass and the trees. The
successive events inward and outward were there in one view:
though each might be dwelt on in turn, the rest still keep their
hold in the consciousness. (p. 663)

Among other things, the passage derives its impact from the way
in which the levels of the visual and the verbal – 'scenes' and
'consciousness' – find parallels on the level of syntax, in the shifts
from 'he' to 'we', and between past to present tense.

3

The importance of witnessing as a structuring principle in *Middlemarch* lies in the demonstration of its power in determining human
relations. This is spelled out in the Guizot epigraph to Chapter 38:
'*C'est beaucoup que le jugement des hommes sur les actions humaines; tôt
ou tard il devient efficace* [Men's judgement on human actions is a
serious thing; sooner or later it takes effect]' (p. 413). On the
narrative level it is demonstrated most spectacularly in the downfall of Bulstrode and Lydgate as a direct result of 'public opinion';
and Will, too, is haunted by the idea of being 'grossly insulted in
your eyes and in the eyes of others' (p. 680). Bulstrode fully realises
that he has nothing to fear by way of legal punishment or of
beggary; what drives him into the deepest darkness of self is the
acknowledgement that 'he was in danger only of seeing *disclosed to
the judgement of his neighbours and the mournful perception of his wife*
certain facts of his past life which would render him an object of
scorn and an opprobrium of the religion with which he had dili-
gently associated himself' (p. 663, my emphasis). This is inevitable
in a society constructed on the conviction 'that everybody must
watch everybody else, and that it would be well for everybody else
to reflect that the Almighty was watching him' (p. 338) – a society,
in short, which functions as 'a huge whispering-gallery' (p. 448).
    As many critics have pointed out, the device through which
public opinion (that is, incessant interpersonal observation translated into language) is converted into a destructive narrative force
is gossip. Characters like Mrs Cadwallader exist in the novel
almost solely in function of their promotion of gossip as a demonstration of the distortive and destructive consequences of witnes-

sing. Many chapters are structured in their entirety on the generation and transmission of rumour; and in one of the landmarks of Eliot criticism, Gilbert and Gubar (1984:478ff), illuminated quite startlingly the destructive forces of violence, cannibalism and murder at work below the seemingly gentle surface of, the novel. A single example is the much-quoted ending of the famous dinner scene of Chapter 15 where George Eliot first brought together the previously separate narratives of Dorothea and Lydgate: 'Middlemarch [...] counted on swallowing Lydgate and assimilating him very comfortably' (p. 183).

Eliot would not be the writer she is without zooming in from the general to the particular, especially where a broad, inchoate phenomenon like gossip is concerned; and quite often the reader is allowed very precisely to witness the unfolding of the process. The narrator is indeed interested in the global view of the phenomenon: 'News is often dispersed as thoughtlessly and effectively as that pollen which bees carry off (having no idea how powdery they are) when they are buzzing in search of their particular nectar' (p. 645). But she is also concerned with the detail. The secret of the money Bulstrode paid Lydgate to buy his silence is propagated 'by innocent Mrs Bulstrode herself, who mentioned the loan to Mrs Plymdale, who mentioned it to her daughter-in-law of the house of Toller, who mentioned it generally' (pp. 773–4).

Elsewhere, a nameless 'old servant' is reported to be an active link in transmitting the news that Casaubon's will has excluded Dorothea from all inheritance should she marry Will Ladislaw (p. 645). At first sight there may seem to be nothing unusual about this. But only a few pages earlier, as in numerous other scenes of the novel, servants were noticeable only by their traces in the text: '[Lydgate] waited till *the tray was gone, the candles were lit*, and the evening quiet might be counted on' (p. 639). Whoever removed the tray or lit the candles was written out of the narrative, just as they were relegated to the margins of Austen's *Emma*. And surely this must be significant in a novel whose stated preoccupation is with 'insignificant people', with 'the number who lived faithfully a hidden life, and rest in unvisited tombs' (p. 896). Only through language, that is, through the novel's process of telling a story, can some of these insignificant individuals can be rescued from obscurity: *but the servants are not allowed this redemption*. That is, except when, as in the scene referred to, they are drawn into the web of gossip, where even if they remain nameless they can contribute to the making or breaking of the more (or less?) fortunate. These are Eliot's 'low people by whose interference, however little we may like it, the course of the world is very much determined' (p. 448). Whatever the moral implications of this functioning, it does suggest that only when they are acknowledged by language can the obscure be marked with humanity.[5]

So powerful a force – both in society and in narrative – is gossip that characters remain aware of being observed even when they are most alone. Bulstrode 'felt that he was performing a striking piece of scrupulosity in the judgement of his auditor, and a penitential act in the eyes of God' (p. 671); alone in the library (once again) before the final breakthrough in her relationship with Ladislaw, Dorothea's entire concern is with the absent other: 'What she was least conscious of just then was her own body: she was thinking of what was likely to be in Will's mind, and of the hard feelings that others had had about him [. . .] there was a voice within her saying this to some imagined audience in the library' (p. 865).

In one of the most moving passages of the novel, revealing, as in so many other instances, Eliot's acute sense of a theatrical *mise-en-scène*, Mrs Bulstrode prepares herself in total seclusion for the decisive confrontation with her husband. Taking off all her ornaments and putting on a severely plain black dress, she becomes most herself when she imagines that self exposed to others: her actions, we are told by the narrator, amount to little acts which 'were her way of expressing to all spectators visible and invisible that she had begun a new life in which she embraced humiliation' (p. 807).[6]

This makes perfect sense. Because in the final analysis all the characters are exposed, every moment of their lives, including the most intimate, to the scrutiny of a narrator who instantly translates observation into language.

4

George Eliot does not allow the reader for a minute to underestimate the extent of the narrator's determining role in the shaping and presentation of characters and events. Even when focalisation occurs via a specific character, the narrator is visible – or, rather, audible – as the final interpreter and decision-maker. Chapter 53 offers a typical instance: after an initial observation on Bulstrode's interest in the acquisition of Rigg's newly inherited property, the focus characteristically broadens to general comment ('But how little we know what would make paradise for our neighbours! We judge from our own desires, and our neighbours themselves are not always open enough to throw out a hint of theirs': pp. 563–4), only to return, a moment later, to Joshua Rigg's reasons for selling the property. And then the narrator interrupts her own account:

> Enough. We are concerned with looking at Joshua Rigg's sale of his land from Mr Bulstrode's point of view, and he interpreted it as a cheering dispensation. (p. 564)

Even if the 'point of view' that concerns the reader is announced to be Bulstrode's, the phrasing of the intervention directs our attention to the strings that manipulate the puppet. What we are offered is *the narrator's view of Bulstrode's view.*

This is illustrated in another form in Chapter 62: Will and Dorothea have just parted and she is left to herself; but even if there is no person with her, the narrator remains to observe what others cannot: 'Any one watching her might have seen that there was a fortifying thought within her' (p. 683).

Even when the narrator does not obtrude in a scene, the very framing and phrasing of that scene, the choice of perspective and priorities, mark her manipulative presence. The predilection, for instance, for interiors with a view through a window (or without the view, when Casaubon is involved), suggests an impression of theatrical staging (see Chapters 42, 58, 76, 77, 83, among others): and this has less to do with the much vaunted 'objectivity' of the realist tradition than with mapping the mind of the observer-narrator. The attentive reader is led not so much to observe, passively, what is presented in the scene, as to enquire *why* the scene has been staged in this particular way and what has prompted the narrator's choice of rhetoric. Using again the example of the passage involving Bulstrode in which we are made conscious of both the exterior and the interior of the lighted room, the interior becomes a metaphor for the narrator's mind, and once more the act of seeing merges with the act of language.

The strategy is made even more obvious by the constant concern, not just with the narrated world, but with the processes of narrating which constitute it: 'And here I am naturally led to reflect on the means of elevating a low subject' (p. 375); 'Will had – to use Sir Thomas Browne's phrase – a "passionate prodigality" of statement' (p. 396); 'Thus Mr Casaubon was in one of his busiest epochs, and as I began to say a little while ago, Dorothea joined him early in the library' (p. 315); 'The group I am moving towards is at Caleb Garth's breakfast-table' (p. 434); 'Much of Fred's rumination might be summed up in the words, "It certainly would have been a fine thing for her to marry Farebrother"' (pp. 728–9)...

But the narrator's manipulation of the reader's perception of scenes or characters goes well beyond a biased choice of words (in a single paragraph describing Raffles the reader's perception of the man is coloured by 'a jocose snuffle', 'cunning', 'calculates', 'the meanest feelings', 'the blurting rallying tone with which he spoke': p 573): it amounts to quite passionate pleading for or against the presented narrative evidence. A meticulous description of Caleb Garth is interrupted by the interjection, 'Pardon these details for once – you would have learned to love them if you had known Caleb Garth' (p. 265); and arguing against the grain of the way in which Bulstrode has been presented the narrator offers in mitigation the plea that

> He was simply a man whose desires had been stronger than his theoretic beliefs, and who has gradually explained the gratification of his desires into satisfactory agreement with those beliefs. If this be hypocrisy, it is a process which shows itself occasionally in us all. (p. 667)

The appeal to what is presented as 'common humanity' in order to explain the particular is especially characteristic.

In examples like these, narratorial comment reaches a significant threshold. To interrupt description in order to offer comment or draw a moral; to use the presentation of a particular scene or character as a basis, or even a pretext, for generalisation; to coax the reader into accepting a particular version – all of this had become standard narrative practice in the realist novel. But when the narrator's perception is argued in terms which contradict not only the intradiegetic views of characters who operate on the same level as the character concerned, but the evidence of the narrative itself as presented to the reader, there is a shift in function from one of overall and decisive control to one of merely another viewpoint among others. As Newton (1981:167) concludes, '*Middlemarch* does not present us with reality as such, but with reality as seen through the medium of the narrator's mind; *it is one interpretation of the world and the narrator is aware of this*' (my emphasis). It means that the narrator, who in the tradition of realism has come to be regarded as omniscient, may here be *seen*, by the reader, to be biased, even to be wrong – a kind of relativisation more often associated with the Modernist or Postmodernist novel.

The presentation of the relationship between Rosamond and Lydgate is a good example. For all the acknowledgement of her flightiness and his lofty aspirations, the *narrative* is neither entirely unsympathetic towards her nor entirely sympathetic towards him: Rosamond may be silly and spoilt, but she is also cruelly trapped in a male world that allows her little if any breathing space, and this lends a desperation to the way in which she uses the only means at her disposal to save herself from an impossible situation; Lydgate regularly behaves like a cad towards her and towards others. Without ever, before it is too late, discussing with her his deteriorating financial position, he persists in treating her like one of 'these creatures that are bred merely as pets' (which is Dorothea's reaction to a Maltese puppy, p. 52). Not only does he indulge her as, at best, 'a thoughtful kitten' (p. 877), which inevitably encourages her in her attempts at self-gratification, the only means of articulation permitted her, but he replaces adult conversation with 'the "little language" of affection' (p. 708). More often than not, in dealing with his wife, he moves beyond language altogether: 'He did not say anything, for what was there to say?' (p. 718). His only response in such situations is to pet or caress her, denying her humanity and even her intelligence.[7] 'It was inevitable that [...] he should think of her as if she were an animal of another and feebler species' (p. 719) – to which the narrator adds maliciously, 'Nevertheless she had mastered him.'[8]

This means that when the narrator concludes, with reference to Rosamond and Ladislaw, that 'shallow natures dream of an easy sway over the emotions of others [...] confident of making the thing that is not as though it were' (p. 834), she is, quite simply, wrong – not only because it is a questionable account of the Rosamond the reader encounters in the text as a whole, but also because the description as it stands would be just as applicable to Dorothea.

And this is not Rosamund's narrative fate alone. Dorothea's sister Celia plays a much smaller role in the narrative, but she,

too, is treated dismissively if not contemptuously by the narrator:
she is another 'thoughtful kitten' (p. 877) (Dorothea indeed calls
her 'Kitty'), depicted condescendingly as a limited creature whose
world is defined by the little details of domesticity and mother-
hood. Like Rosamond's, her features are invariably described as
'small', her hands as 'little', and so on. And yet, flying in the face of
the narrator's overt attempts at belittling her, Celia reveals herself a
much better judge of character than Dorothea herself: she immediately sees Casaubon for what he is; she is a shrewd if loving
observer of her own sister ('She likes giving up', p. 41; 'Dodo
would perhaps not make a husband happy who had not her way
of looking at things', p. 43); she is eminently sensible in her appraisal of marriage ('I don't think it can be nice to marry a man with a
great soul', p. 79). More significantly, in Celia's habit of constantly
extrapolating generalisations from specific situations (nowhere
more evident than in Chapter 84, where whole passages in Celia's
speech are constructed around the words 'always', 'never, 'ever'
and 'nobody'), we recognise the basic principle of the narrator's
own *modus operandi*. And if the narrator is herself linked to a
character she tries to present as risible in so many ways, her own
status and reliability are placed at risk.

There does seem to be a general tendency to be less tolerant of
females than of males: even the most exemplary of women characters, Dorothea, is gently mocked as 'quixotic' and myopic. For
the male of the species, on the other hand, even the most repre-
hensible (with few exceptions, Raffles being one), special pleading
in mitigation of one kind of another is usually advanced. This is
most obvious in the presentation of Casaubon, presented as a
ridiculous bore, a pretentious fool, an unbearable egoist from his
first entry into the text; yet in Chapter 10 the narrator intervenes to
counter the impression she herself has so meticulously constructed
through the narrative. After cautioning the reader against judging
Ladislaw too hastily, she turns to Casaubon:

> I protest against any absolute conclusion, any prejudice derived
> from Mrs Cadwallader's contempt for a neighbouring clergy-
> man's alleged greatness of soul, of Sir James Chettam's poor
> opinion of his rival's legs, – from Mr Brooke's failure to elicit a
> companion's ideas, or from Celia's criticism of a middle-aged
> scholar's personal appearance. I am not sure that the greatest
> man of his age [...] could escape these unfavourable reflections

of himself in various small mirrors; and even Milton, looking for his portrait in a spoon, must submit to have the facial angle of a bumpkin. (pp. 110–11)

As an example of rhetoric (notably in promoting Casaubon's cause, most especially through the shrewd reference to Milton; in exposing the flaws in the arguments of his detractors; and in revealing the essential unreliability of the various commentators) the passage as a whole is a *tour de force*. But in the dazzle of the performance the reader is encouraged to repress the most telling evidence in the matter: Casaubon's own words, in speech and writing (particularly his letter of proposal to Dorothea, later followed by his letter severing relations with Ladislaw, and his will), and his own actions.

This is radically different from the wonderful understanding of and sympathy with a poor, lamed creature evoked in the final scene between Casaubon and Dorothea at the end of Chapter 42 (pp. 464–5): there the reader, even if still gently prodded by the narrator, is allowed to evaluate for her/himself the actions and motivations of the characters; while in the plea of Chapter 10 the narrator's view becomes *one interpretation among many others*. This is followed by later narratorial protestations on Casaubon's behalf, for example on p. 314: 'For my part I am very sorry for him. It is an uneasy lot at best, to be what we call highly taught and yet not to enjoy: to be present at this great spectacle of life and never to be liberated from a small hungry shivering self'. The crucial phrase here is *for my part*. It is a statement, and an act, which ultimately amounts to a relinquishment of total narrative control, precisely because the narrator's voice is exposed to the same kind of doubt that may affect the reader's evaluation of any other opinion in the text.

The implications of this narratorial stance are subtly embedded in this reference to Dorothea on p. 408:

She was blind, you see, to many things obvious to others – likely to tread in the wrong places, as Celia had warned her; yet her blindness to whatever did not lie in her own pure purpose carried her safely by the side of precipices where vision would have been perilous with fear.

This is more than a (re)statement of the novel's narrative truth, first suggested in the Platonic pattern of Ideal and paradigm announced

in the Prelude and confirmed in the Finale. More significant for the
present argument is the shrewd juxtaposition of *She was blind* and
you see. What in normal speech would be a throwaway phrase here
craftily shifts the balance, and responsibility, towards the *reader*: *she*
may have been blind, but *you* should see. If the narrator herself, as
has been amply demonstrated by now, is not to be trusted, the
reader is not merely the final, but the only, arbiter.

5

It is a tenet of narratology that a narrator's stance can never be
neutral, never innocent; that 'a writer's handling of reality is
affected by his basic philosophic outlook on nature and society
and his method of investigating that nature and society' (Ngugi
1986:78). In *Middlemarch* much of this ideological position is
revealed in the choice of epigraphs to the chapters (to which we
shall return in due course); among these, a particularly revealing
passage is the exchange at the beginning of Chapter 64, referred to
earlier and featuring two Gentlemen who also make their appearance elsewhere:

> 1ST GENT. Where lies the power, there let the blame lies too.
> 2ND GENT. Nay, power is relative; you cannot fright
> The coming pest with border fortresses,
> Or catch your carp with subtle argument.
> All force is twain in one: cause is not cause
> Unless effect be there; and action's self
> Must needs contain a passive. So command
> Exists but with obedience.

This vision of the power relations which determine both personal
affairs and the functioning of society as a whole lies behind most of
the narratorial strategies of *Middlemarch*, and it is particularly felicitous that the argument itself should emerge from a dialogue
between two persons. Like several others, but unlike the majority,
the quotation is not attributed to a source; and there is a wide-
ranging suspicion among critics that such epigraphs have been
fabricated by George Eliot herself. To the implications this has for
the novel's theory of language, I shall return later; what is relevant
at the moment is that, if the passage is indeed by the author, the

link between the narrator's ideological stance and the philosophy of Comte becomes very direct indeed. Whatever other sources from Eliot's omnivorous reading informed her writing, we know that Comte always occupied a central place, to the extent that much of her fiction may be read as adumbrations of his Idea, formulated in the convolutions of the *Cours de Philosophie Positive*.[9]

This would, among other things, validate the preoccupation with the way in which individual behaviour is constantly linked to norms emerging from social action. Lydgate is most obviously concerned with this, in his search for 'primal matter': '[T]here must be a systole and diastole in all inquiry'; 'a man's mind must be continually expanding and shrinking between the whole human horizon and the horizon of an object-glass' (p. 690).

The vision is first articulated in the Prelude with its comparison of the original Saint Theresa whose 'passionate, ideal nature demanded an epic life' to the innumerable 'later-born Theresas' (of whom Dorothea will become the primary focus of the novel) whose ardour 'alternated between a vague ideal and the common yearning of womanhood' (p. 25). After all the vicissitudes narrated in the novel, the Finale returns to the vision of the Ideal, Saint Theresa, this time coupled with another heroic female prototype, Antigone, and their joint example to 'we insignificant people' and the 'unhistoric acts' of 'the number who lived faithfully a hidden life, and rest in unvisited tombs' (p. 896).[10]

These statements of intent illuminate the great patterns of the novel's structure: the pendulum movement (the systole and dia-stole) of the social and the individual; the tension between lofty ideal and humdrum, or failed, or sordid, actuality, between inner and outer worlds, between an act and its observation and inter-pretation; the interplay between the centrifugal motion of altruism and the centripetal force of egoism, between the strong and the weak, the flamboyant and the timid, male and female, young and old. It determines much of the syncopation of mimesis and diegesis, of theme and variation, of example and imitation (whether successful or failed). In other words, the narrator's manipulation of scenes and characters is the outcome, not of mere whim or power-play, but of an awe-inspiring sense of struc-ture and of hierarchy, inspired by a grasp of contemporary science and its methodologies, and determined by a (Comtean) conviction of what is 'good' and what 'bad', what is socially fecund and what barren.

In much of this enterprise the narrator's views, as expressed in her direct commentaries as well as in her techniques of highlighting and foregrounding, may be said to coincide with the author's, as we know it from her letters and other writings. But there is, also, a fascinating *interval* between George Eliot, the enthusiastic disciple of Comte, and the narrator of *Middlemarch*.[11]

This emerges with particularly striking effect in the parallel drawn in the text between Casaubon and Lydgate: if it lends a (dubious) measure of respectability to Casaubon's enterprise, it certainly subverts Lydgate's own stature as a paradigm of Comte. If gossip is evil, as the author would hold, the narrator's depiction of the delightful Mrs Cadwallader's implication in it makes it altogether more palatable. If Dorothea's altruism is commendable, the narrator presents her also as a fool and a prig. If Mrs Garth is a model wife and mother, the narrator's presentation of her strict adherence to the niceties of grammar adds a touch of humour to her narrative presence, persuading the reader to take her, like everybody else, with a pinch of salt. And once the narrator's manoeuvrings and manipulations invite the reader to question detail after detail of the narrative, the whole philosophical edifice is open to subversion. Which is why, in spite of the smug-sounding Finale, there can be no possibility of real narrative closure: at every point of the narration the novel begins to interrogate itself and its processes – and, by extension, the grand schemes and philosophies that inspired it in the first place.

The clue to this process of deconstruction – for it is nothing less – lies in the interval between author and narrator. And the nature of this interval is defined by the novel's concept of language, and its realisation in the text.

6

At first sight, George Eliot is wholly an author of the nineteenth century in her apparent faith in language and its relation to reality ('The right word is always a power, and communicates its definiteness to our action': p. 336). And when characters in *Middlemarch* find themselves unable to pronounce the redeeming words, the narrator can speak on their behalf, as in the final confrontation between Ladislaw's 'mute rage' and Rosamond's 'mute misery' (pp. 834–7), or in the consummation of the Bulstrodes' newly found unity on p. 808: 'They could not yet speak to each other [...] His confession was silent, and her promise of faithfulness was silent [...] She could not say, "How much is only slander and false suspicion?" and he did not say, "I am innocent."'

But the narrator of *Middlemarch* is much more ambiguous about the status of language and the range of its possibilities than it may appear from such scenes; and there is an intimation of this when she refrains from her customary role as interpreter in an important moment shared by Dorothea and Ladislaw on p. 427. In response to Dorothea's attempt to explain her view of the individual's involvement in the larger battle between good and evil, Ladislaw terms it 'a beautiful mysticism'; but she passionately stops him short: '*Please do not call it by any name* [...] You will say it is Persian, or something else geographical. It is my life.' This goes beyond a specific reaction to Casaubon's style of reducing all experience to pat formulas and deft definitions: at the very least it intimates, in the narrator just as much as in Dorothea, an acknowledgement of a territory between 'life' and 'name' where language cannot venture. If there were any doubt about this, it should be dispelled by one of the most remarkable passages in Eliot's writing, in which the Prelude and the Finale of *Middlemarch* (concerning the relationship between the great and the mundane, the extraordinary and the ordinary, the Saint Theresas of the world and the nameless multitude which clutter the periphery of history) are subsumed in an early formulation of the unbearable lightness of being, and the terrifying, ultimate impotence of language:

> That element of tragedy which lies in the very fact of frequency, has not yet wrought itself into the coarse emotion of mankind; and perhaps our frames could hardly bear much of it. If we had a keen vision and feeling of all ordinary human life, it would be like hearing the grass grow and the squirrel's heart beat, and we should die of that roar which lies on the other side of silence. (p. 226)

It may be argued that *Middlemarch* as a whole represents an attempt at bridging the silence of the 'unvisited tomb' (compare the last lines of the Finale), that is, at translating the 'great roar' into language. But it is doomed to remaining, ultimately, a *failed* attempt; and the reason for this is that language, by its very nature, can only ever say what has already been said. And this is where I

should argue that author and narrator are most alarmingly at odds
with each other.

As early as p. 61 we are informed that Mr Brooke's 'usual
tendency to say what he had said before' is, in fact, a 'fundamental
principle of human speech'. It is repeated with a different emphasis
in the narrator's comment on Rosamond's ingenuous response to
Lydgate's attempt at long last to be completely frank with her:

> 'What can *I* do, Tertius?' said Rosamond, turning her eyes on
> him again. That little speech of four words, like so many others
> in all languages, is capable by varied vocal inflexions of expres-
> sing all states of mind from helpless dimness to exhaustive
> argumentative perception, from the completest self-devoting fel-
> lowship to the most neutral aloofness. (p. 640)

The emphasis here is on the subjective contribution of each speaker
to the already-said of language, in the conviction that the most one
can hope for is to add a little reminder of the speaking self, through
a different inflection, a different syntactical or narrative configuration. Anticipating Saussure, it presents the relationship of *parole* to
langue, and in this regard it would confirm Ladislaw's urge 'to put
something of my own in' (p. 245), to the point of fabricating songs
by suiting 'some words of his own' to some 'ready-made melody'
(p. 512). But in the final analysis individual nuance merely serves
to confirm language as a 'general rule', as the already-spoken
('speech is representative: and who can represent himself just as
he is . . .?': p. 763) – and it is borne out, with a touch of wry humour,
when the Finale records the writing of a children's book by Mary
Garth, attributed by all of Middlemarch to her husband
Fred, and that of a farming manual by Fred, attributed by
everybody to Mary: 'In this way it was made clear that Middlemarch had never been deceived, and that there was no need to
praise anybody for writing a book, since it was always done by
somebody else' (pp. 890–1). The authority of authorship itself is
undermined, if not entirely ruled out, by the fact that speech
belongs to all, and that language is, by definition, the language of
everybody – that is, the language of others. Narrative itself is a
'telling (of) what had been' (Chapter 11, p. 123), not an invention of
anything new.

Speech is, at best, slang, as is spelled out in a much-discussed
conversation between Mrs Vincy and her daughter Rosamond

about the propriety of using 'shopkeeper's slang' in the choice of a word like 'superior':

'Are you beginning to dislike slang, then?' said Rosamond, with mild gravity.
'Only the wrong sort. All choice of words is slang. It marks a class.'
'There is correct English: that is not slang.'
'I beg your pardon: correct English is the slang of prigs who write history and essays. And the strongest slang of all is the slang of poets.' (p. 126)

Below the playful surface lies much more than a keen sense of the niceties of social intercourse or the forces at work in social construction: what ultimately lurks there is the deeper concern of our raids upon the inarticulate, of that roar which lies at the other side of silence, and of language whose very validity is challenged by all the doomed attempts (by Dorothea, by Will Ladislaw, by Lydgate, by Casaubon, by Auguste Comte, by George Eliot) to grasp a sense of originality and of beginnings, whether of primal matter, of mythology, of good and evil, or of words.

If all language is slang, then each utterance is a mere quotation from it. This is why I suggested early in this essay that *Middlemarch* is not only a web of social relations but a weave of quotations. Even Caleb Garth, who comes closer to independent or original thought than most of the other characters, and who only speaks when he clearly knows his own mind, is inhibited by the second-hand nature of language: 'In his difficulty of finding speech for his thought, he caught, as it were, snatches of diction which he associated with various points of view or states of mind; and whenever he had a feeling of awe, he was haunted by a sense of Biblical phraseology, though he could hardly have given a strict quotation' (p. 447).

In the iterability of language, and in the eternal repetitions of story, we are reminded, lies the fascination of literature itself – because 'what's the use of writing at all if nobody can understand it?' (p. 611):

We are not afraid of telling over and over again how a man comes to fall in love with a woman and be wedded to her, or else be fatally parted from her. Is it due to excess of poetry or of stupidity that we are never weary of describing what King James called a woman's 'makdom and her fairnesse'...? (p. 173)

The use of a literal quotation to make the point is characteristic of Eliot. And the text of *Middlemarch* is sprinkled throughout with all manner of literary, philosophical, scientific and other borrowings, whether by way of direct quotation or through less obvious allusion – to Goethe and to Cromwell, to the Bible and to Shakespeare, to Byron and to Shelley, to Drayton or to collective wisdom in the form of a proverb, or to some anonymous wag, as the case may be. It is part of the narrative procedure itself, relating the private and the individual to some more general norm, and the personal utterance to some larger verbal framework – expressed, ultimately, in the most profound lesson Casaubon has to learn, 'when the commonplace 'We must all die' transforms itself suddenly into the acute consciousness 'I must die – and soon' (p. 461).

7

Apart from direct citation within the narrative, quotation features most prominently in the epigraphs to each of the eighty-six chapters. These may be read, and have been read in a century of criticism, as appeals to 'higher authority', the authority of the wisdom of humanity as distilled in its literature, 'almost as if Eliot were obsessively stating her credentials' (Gilbert & Gubar 1984:531). They certainly affirm the narrator's strategy of appealing to the sanction of common approval in the form of what has been canonised by being written down (which may be either the truth, or, as the narrator points out with subversive wit, 'this power of generalizing which gives men so much the superiority in mistake over the dumb animals', p. 638). In this way they ironically endorse Casaubon's enterprise by perpetuating 'a hierarchical genealogy whereby an original Text fathers forth subsidiary and subordinate texts' (Gilbert & Gubar 1984:502). This would be a particularly effective demonstration of patriarchy's appropriation of literature, which is the bottom line of Gilbert and Gubar's argument.

But the argument about authority may also be approached from the opposite end. Instead of reading the narrative as being 'authorised', through reference to a canonised source, it may be seen to convey the impossibility of coming up with anything new. In this reading the epigraphs become a highly visible demonstration of the fact that nothing can be said, and no story told, that has not been said or told before. And the processes of iteration – as well as of *textualising* the narrative world – are taken a step further when an epigraph at the head of a chapter is itself quoted in the text that follows (see p. 880), or when an epigraph is taken from a book earlier referred to in the text (on p. 172 *Rasselas* is mentioned among Lydgate's reading matter, later the epigraph to Chapter 61 is quoted from it).

In this context, possibly the most significant epigraphs are those not attributed to any source and generally taken, as I have mentioned before, to be devised by George Eliot herself. What they effect is to turn the author herself into an anonymous text and her original creation into secondary quotation – surely a highly dramatised illustration, *avant la lettre*, of the postmodern 'death of the author', of language as the embodiment of alterity. In such a configuration, as Toril Moi, paraphrasing Lacan, would have it, 'The sentence "I am" could therefore best be translated as "I am that which I am not"' (Moi 1985:99).

The most spectacular demonstration of this view of language in *Middlemarch* is to be found in Casaubon who, initially at least, indulges Dorothea, 'usually with an appropriate quotation' (p. 55), who 'dreams footnotes, and they run away with his brains' (p. 96), and whose very books 'looked more like immovable imitations of books' (p. 306). *Ceci n'est pas un livre.*

At his very entry into the narrative he is described as being '*noted in the .county* as a man of profound learning, *understood* for many years to be engaged in a great work concerning religious history; [...] and having views of his own which *were to be more clearly ascertained on the publication of his book*' (p. 33, my emphases). In the same passage the reader is informed that 'his very name carried an impressiveness hardly to be measured without a precise chronology of scholarship'. The 'impressiveness' of this name derives, of course, from an Italian Renaissance scholar (with, for the postmodernist reader, an ironical surplus of meaning informed by Eco's *Foucault's Pendulum*): even the poor man's name is a quotation from another source.

But in an important respect most of the other key characters may also be said to figure in the text as quotations. From Prelude and Finale, and from a number of other references in between, we are forewarned to read Dorothea, in a manner of speaking, as a quotation from Saint Theresa; but it is a composite quote, as she also refers us to Don Quixote, through the Cervantes epigraph to Chapter 2 (which, in addition, links Dorothea with Casaubon), and explicit comments on her 'quixotic' nature (p. 458; also p. 820). And Don Quixote, of course, refers to a tradition of chivalric romance going back far beyond Cervantes – so far back, in fact, that whatever original 'source' or signifier there may have been has now become trammelled up in the consequence.

To complicate the Dorothea quotation even further, she is read elsewhere as 'Imogene or Cato's daughter' (p. 470) – just as Will Ladislaw, in spite of declaring, 'I hate copying' (p. 245) and trying his damnedest to be his own man, is one moment read as Pegasus (p. 107) and another as Byron (p. 415). And if both Casaubon and Lydgate can be read, as suggested earlier, as quotations from Auguste Comte, they can also be approached as quotations from each other, trapped in a circle in which signifiers are constantly transformed into signifieds, and vice versa.

Even apart from functioning as she does in these relationships, Dorothea is quite literally reduced to a quotation by Casaubon who reacts to whatever she says 'as if she had given a quotation from the Delectus familiar to him from his tender years' (p. 396).

8

An important demonstration of this process would lie in reading the characters as actors in a play, mouthing the words an absent author has devised for each. (The only choice a character like Mary Garth is allowed, is in deciding 'not to act the mean or treacherous part': p. 349.) Such a portrayal of the processes of alienation and alterity which inform Eliot's notion of language in *Middlemarch* would be pleasingly consistent with the imagery of the theatre that underlies the narrative web, and the construction of the novel as a series of theatrical scenes. It would also lend additional weight to the decisive moment from Lydgate's earlier life on which Gilbert and Gubar (1984:499ff) base so much of their brilliant discussion of the violent subtext in the novel – what Byatt (1991:76) calls 'a saving savagery in her vision of man's normal and natural inhumanity to man'. Because Lydgate meets his *femme fatale*, the actress Laure,[12] at a performance of 'a melodrama *which he had already seen several times*' (p. 180). On this occasion, of course, the action onstage deviates from the plot of the play: it may be read as the equivalent (the 'quotation'?) in Laure's life of Ladislaw's urge to insert 'something of his own' into the songs he copies from other sources. It is her shocking and ultimately paltry *parole* pitched against the *langue* of her role, both as actress and as wife, as woman. But her very deviation from the plot, as she kills the actor she was supposed to kill as a character, confirms the iterability she has tried to escape – *if* that is what she has tried to do: in the end Lydgate, and even more so the reader, has only her word to go by, among the many others offered during and surrounding the case. In terms of her relationship with Lydgate she is killed by language – its ambiguities, its unreliability, its iterability – as certainly as her husband has been killed by a dagger. And as certainly as Bulstrode and Lydgate himself are subsequently (symbolically) killed by the language of gossip.

The only characters who openly resist these forms of quotation may be said, not surprisingly, to be the members of the Garth family. When Fred reproaches Mary that, 'I suppose a woman is never in love with any one she has always known [...] It is always a new fellow who strikes a girl', she responds with exuberant irony,

> 'Let me see...I must go back on my experience. There is Juliet – she seems an example of what you say. But then Ophelia had probably known Hamlet a long while; and Brenda Troil – she had known Mordaunt Merton ever since they were children [...] Waverley was new to Flora MacIvor; but then she did not fall in love with him. And there Olivia and Sophia Primrose, and Corinne [...] altogether, my experience is rather mixed.' (p. 167)

Precisely because her 'own' experience is presented as purely literary, her originality and independence are asserted – but even so the assertion can be made *only* by using the conventionalities of language-as-quotation, which highlights the entrapment of the full cast of *Middlemarch* in their play.

In a different way, the habitual silence of her father Caleb endorses the crucial dilemma in which all the characters are caught: to refrain from speech exposes him to misunderstanding, sometimes to ridicule, even to hostility; but to express himself in speech forces him to use a devalued and debased currency which places his integrity at stake – a dilemma most poignantly exposed through his position of confidence in Bulstrode's affairs. In one way or another this affects all the characters: in order to 'be themselves', they have to break out of language which is everybody's; yet it is only through language that they can possibly fulfil themselves, as it is the sole medium in which they can express and realise their full humanity.

In the final analysis, language itself constitutes that 'element of tragedy' which marks the narrative world of *Middlemarch*. It holds the key to the past, whether in the shape of myth (Casaubon's doomed enterprise) or of history (Bulstrode's past is safe until it erupts into language). It defines and in fact determines the interactions of the present. And it circumscribes – through the sharing or frustration of visions and schemes, through gossip, through common pursuit – the possibilities for the future. In the Prelude it refers the reader back to times and territories before the beginnings of the narrative; in the Finale it reaches forward past the lives and the deaths of the *dramatis personae*. Through its view, and its uses, of language, *Middlemarch* is never contained in a here-and-now, but always involved in processes which refer, not to origins and conclusions, but to an ever-elusive beyond.

8

The Tiger's Revenge

Thomas Mann: *Death in Venice*

1

If there is a problem Thomas Mann's exquisitely crafted short novel *Der Tod in Venedig* (*Death in Venice*) poses to the reader in search of clues about the relationship between language and narrative, it is that – at least at first sight – the text seems to say too much rather than too little. The novel, which draws in many respects on Mann's own visit to the Lido in April–June 1911 (Lehnert 1968:122), can be, and has been, read as an essay on the birth of art, on the creative process, on the way the rough 'marble mass of language' has to be worked on to liberate 'the slender forms of [...] art' (p. 50).[1] But behind this obvious level of meaning, and behind the spectacular struggle between Apollo and Dionysus highlighted by the novel, lies another tension which seems to me to lead us closer to the text's subtler and more profound concerns with language – and that is the dialectic between Aschenbach, the author *in* the narrative, and the narrator who manipulates and articulates it.[2]

It is this dialectic, much more than the split between reason and emotion, logic and passion, Apollo and Dionysus, the dual legacy of a Silesian father and a Bohemian mother, within Aschenbach's artistic personality, which demonstrates the novel's problematising view of language, and its embodiment in the narrative.

The first time this is intimated in *Death in Venice* is in the opening scene where Aschenbach notices in the portico of the Byzantine mortuary chapel in the North Cemetery of Munich (a building which presages Venice as his destination and his destiny), the curious figure of the stranger, the traveller, the pilgrim. Later in the novel adumbrations of this figure will reappear in the 'ghastly young-old man' who joins him on the boat to Venice (p. 25), and in the 'half bully, half comedian' musician who performs in the hotel gardens one evening (p. 67); at the end, when Aschenbach has his hair dyed and his face made up, his lips changed to 'the colour of ripe strawberries' (p. 78) in a vain attempt to recover his own lost youth, he will himself become this enigmatic, hideous figure.[3] In the process, the course of his life, which has always veered between the poles suggested by his name ('Aschenbach' can be literally translated as 'Ashbrook', which, as many commentators have noted, signify both death and life), will take a decisive turn towards death. But on this first occasion the stranger, this marker of death-in-life, provokes in Aschenbach the urge to travel, to move away from the familiar environment and the strictly ordered existence he has led as a respected and honoured writer, to a wilderness which seems to come straight out of a painting by the Douanier Rousseau:

> He saw. He beheld a landscape, a tropical marshland, beneath a reeking sky, steaming, monstrous, rank – a kind of primeval wilderness-world of island, morasses, and alluvial channels. Hairy palm-trunks rose near and far out of lush brakes of fern, out of bottoms of crass vegetation, fat, swollen, thick with incredible bloom. There were trees, mis-shapen as a dream, that dropped their naked roots straight through the air into the ground or into water that was stagnant and shadowy and glassy-green, where mammoth milk-white blossoms floated, and strange high-shouldered birds with curious bills stood gazing sidewise without sound or stir. Among the knotted joints of a bamboo thicket the eyes of a crouching tiger gleamed – and he felt his heart throb with terror, yet with a longing inexplicable... (pp. 9–10)

What Aschenbach *sees* the narrator *describes*: and in his choice of words he echoes those writers of the colonial experience, ranging from Rider Haggard to Conrad, who evoked the dark places of the earth as virgin, female, lush, fertile territories to be invaded, penetrated and colonised by the male enterprise. In terms of conventional symbolism it is a female landscape, and its emblem is the tiger. It is also a landscape which at first sight appears to be without language (even the birds are 'without sound or stir'), but this may not be altogether true: *to Aschenbach* it is without language, because it lies beyond the reach of *his* language: but it is not beyond reach of the narrator who can name what Aschenbach focalises as pure image.

Only a few pages later Aschenbach has made up his mind to depart – even if the journey need not be far: 'not all the way to the tigers' (p. 12) notes the narrator with characteristic dry irony.[4] But there is no *need* to go far, as Venice itself turns out to be exactly this landscape of dream, of 'alluvial channels', 'lulling and lascivious' (p. 63), its 'sultriness' (p. 40), its air 'heavy and foul' (p. 62), with 'water [...] gurgling against wood and stone' (ibid.), its 'evil exhalations' (p. 41), under the spell of the goddess Eos, 'ravisher of youth' (p. 55). And moving through it, with all the effortless rippling androgynous grace of a tiger, will be the young boy Tadzio whose explicitly feline and feminine appeal is unmistakeable.

This needs closer scrutiny. As Heller (1958:111), among many others, indicates, the 'homosexual and incestuous' nature of Aschenbach's love of Tadzio is more than obvious, and it also replicates various similar relationships in Mann's other novels. Tadzio is, and must be read as, a beautiful *boy*. In many respects his function in Aschenbach's life confirms the 'genealogical imperative' which Drechsel Tobin (1978) investigates in Mann and other authors (with the important difference that Tadzio is *not* Aschenbach's son, and that the outcome of the relationship is, not the perpetuation of patrilinearity, but death). But Tadzio's *function* in the text is to represent the feminine: not only because we know that Mann based this decisive encounter in Aschenbach's life on the pathetic last love in Goethe's life, for a young girl he'd met at Marienbad (see Lehnert 1968:122–4), or because of the explicit influence of the female figure in Erwin Rohde's *Psyche* on *Death in Venice* (ibid.:109), but because Mann's text *produces* Tadzio in the terminology conventionally associated with femininity. There are abundant references to his 'chaste perfection of form' (p. 31), his 'slender legs' (p. 37), his 'sweet and wild' name (p. 39), his body 'virginally pure' (p. 39), his 'delicate [...] sickly' air (p. 40), his habit of 'tossing his curls' (p. 49), his armpits 'still as smooth as a statue's' (p. 50), his 'lips just slightly pursed' (p. 58), his characteristic 'exquisite movement, one hand resting on his hip' (p. 83) – all of this surrounded, constantly, by the 'foul-smelling lagoon' (p. 40) and 'the progress of the disease' (p. 64).

Significantly, the plague which besets Venice, first to enhance Aschenbach's fascination with the boy and then to bring about his death, originates in the very Asian landscapes of the writer's first dream image:

> Its source was the hot, moist swamps of the delta of the Ganges, where it bred in the mephitic air of that primeval island-jungle, among whose bamboo thickets the tiger crouches ... (p. 71)

This is, once again, a conspicuously feminised world: specifically, it may be associated with femininity as menacing and dangerous and subversive, even destructive: the kind of femininity associated with witchcraft and sorcery and poisoning – that is, a femininity which becomes threatening *because it has been excluded from, or denied by, the masculine world*. This is something the narrator realises only too well, but which Aschenbach cannot acknowledge since he has repressed it in himself. It undoubtedly has its biological origins in the writer's mother, 'the daughter of a Bohemian musical conductor' (p. 12), since the other women in his life – his dead wife, his daughter – have simply been written out of the text. If it was the *union* between his mother's 'ardent, obscure impulse' (p. 12) and his father's strict discipline – 'a life of self-conquest, a life against odds, dour, steadfast, abstinent' (p. 64) – that produced Aschenbach the artist, his increasing tendency to acknowledge only reason, rectilinearity, propriety and 'honour' (p. 16) has led to the ascendancy of Apollo over Dionysus, severing 'the delicate connection between discipline and licence, which is at the root of being an artist' (Fokkema & Ibsch 1988:299). More pertinently, Aschenbach's development as a writer has led to the suppression of the female by the male. And if there were still any doubt about the alliance between Dionysus and the fertile female forces of the earth, it must be dispelled by the extravagant bacchanalian dream in which Aschenbach reacts to the final acceptance of the plague as reality (pp. 74–6).[5]

The revenge of the tiger, and ultimately the revenge of Tadzio's threatened beauty and innocence, is the revenge of the female force. But primarily, as I shall try to argue, it is the revenge of the narrator on the narrated life: that is, *the revenge of human language* (when relegated to silence) on the pretensions of art. This is all the more evident if we consider that in Mann's aesthetics 'the artist's creative material is the mass of sensuousness, impulse and longing which threatens the form and morality he craves. The substance of creation is chaos, and this chaos can destroy the creator' (Apter 1978:57).

2

Gustave Aschenbach is presented in the novel, and honoured in the story, as author of several notable works in the grand German tradition of Goethe and Schiller to which Mann himself belonged: a 'lucid and vigorous prose epic on the life of Frederick the Great', a 'richly patterned tapestry' in an ambitious novel called *Maia*, 'a powerful narrative' about the triumph of moral resolution following a descent into the abyss of knowledge in *The Abject*, and an 'impassioned discourse on the theme of Mind and Art' (pp. 12–13).[6] He has always been 'remote from the banal' (p. 13); and even when in later years his style assumed a 'new austerity [...] an almost exaggerated sense of beauty, a lofty purity, symmetry and simplicity' (p. 17), there was clearly nothing of the common touch in the man. It would seem that especially from the time when his fiftieth birthday was marked by the authorities with an elevation in rank which entitled him to a 'von' before his name, he 'banished from his style every common word' (p. 18). As von Gronicka (1964:47) indicates, this is true of Mann himself as well, since his stylistic combination of 'mythos plus psychology [...] calls for a language that is cleansed of the colloquial and the commonplace, is marked by epic pathos, or evokes the monumental and the statuesque'.

To his comment on Aschenbach's abandonment of 'every common word' the narrator adds, wryly, that 'It was at this time that the school authorities adopted selections from his work into their text-books' (p. 17). This amounts to a form of betrayal of *language* in the name of *art*, just as surely as Aschenbach's suppression of his mother's influence in favour of his father's dourness represents a betrayal of femininity. In this way, subliminally, woman and language (or, the wild places of the earth, and silence) become associated in the text.

The voyage to Venice, the splendid city of art (which, of course, is also the city of decadence and pestilential vapours), confirms the distance between the writer as aesthete and the lives and language of ordinary humanity. From the moment the gondolier, the latest avatar of Charon, rows Aschenbach across the lagoon to his hotel on the Lido, the narrator subtly emphasises this process of distancing and estrangement. The gondolier 'was talking to himself' (p. 26), and keeps muttering throughout the trip (pp. 27–8), but the writer understands no word of it. Apart from a few brief and unsatisfactory exchanges, the gondolier does not even answer his passenger's questions and remains 'obstinate, tongue-tied, uncanny' (p. 27), which reinforces Aschenbach's linguistic isolation. Their only meaningful exchange may be said to be

Aschenbach's question: 'How much do you ask for the trip?' and the gondolier's enigmatic repy, 'The signore will pay' (p. 27). Soon afterwards, when they arrive at the Lido, the gondolier is sent off by the hotel staff and Aschenbach appears to have had 'a ride for nothing' (p. 29). But it proves to be more complicated than that: in the end the signore will indeed pay, and with his life.

The first sign of the entry of Tadzio's family into the text is on the level of language: the writer discovers that he is surrounded by foreigners. As in the case of the tiger landscape, this places the scene beyond the reach of Aschenbach's language. There are a few Germans in the hotel (even their children have French nannies), but most of the guests are Americans, English, and Russian. 'In Aschenbach's neighbourhood Polish was being spoken' (p. 30) – and it is via this observation that the young boy, beautiful as a Greek sculpture, is introduced. Aschenbach cannot even be sure of his name: what initially sounds to him like 'Adgio; or 'Adjiu' (p. 37), he subsequently, 'with the help of a few Polish memories' (p. 38), but without any certainty, surmises to be 'Tadzio' (p. 38). And in the writer's dream near the end of the novel the boy's name will once more be dissolved into sound, 'a kind of howl with a long-drawn *u*-sound at the end' (p. 75).

This is inevitable, since for Aschenbach, the man *par excellence* 'of the gift of words and their power to charm' (p. 40), the man with such tremendous 'native eloquence' (p. 45), Tadzio's beauty (as, in another context, the fetid lagoon and the swamps of the East) marks the *limit of language*. In 'a world possessed, peopled by Pan (p. 56), that is, in a world of pure instinct, of curiosity, desire, love, and craving (p. 57) – the boy is 'lovelier [...] than words could say [...] and so often as the thought visited Aschenbach, and brought its own pang, that language could but extol, not reproduce, the beauties of the sense' (p. 58).

But behind Aschenbach, whose language cannot grasp the boy's beauty, stands the narrator, who *can* (at least up to a point). And this illuminates the boy's position in the text *vis-à-vis* language: throughout the novel there will be at least two competing strategies to articulate him as a narrative experience: first, there are Aschenbach's attempts to appropriate him by means of high-flown rhetoric borrowed from Homer and other classical authors; second, there is the narrator's approach, based on that 'ordinary' human language from which Aschenbach has so fatefully distanced himself that it became, for him, relegated to the domain of silence.

In the passage above, as in the first scene with the herald-stranger, the reader registers that when Aschenbach is most silent the narrator is most consciously present through his language.

Aschenbach's increasing isolation, in and through language, dominates all the later movements of the text. Surrounded in the hotel by an incessant 'chattering in many tongues – French, Polish, and even some of the Balkan languages' (p. 38), his only recourse is his memories of classical mythology or the dialogues of Plato (to which we shall return in due course). When the children, including Tadzio, are frolicking on the beach, 'Aschenbach understood not a word' (p. 49); he is conscious of 'nothing but foreign words' (p. 59). In this manner Tadzio himself, for Aschenbach, if not for the narrator, is removed from language, into a realm of pure aesthetics: 'Thus the lad's foreign birth raised his speech to music' (p. 49).

As the city reels more and more under the onslaught of the plague, tourists depart; 'the German tongue had suffered a rout, being scarcely or never heard in the land' (p. 59), leaving Aschenbach almost totally isolated.

Among his first reactions to the inspiration of Tadzio's uncanny beauty was, inevitably, the urge to create: 'He felt a sudden desire to write, Eros, indeed, we are told, loves idleness' (p. 52); using the lad as a model and a muse, he sets up his table on the very beach where Tadzio is playing and ventures into a noble display of linguistic passion. It is to him a new experience: 'never had he known so well that Eros is in the word' (p. 53). But his 'page and a half of choicest prose, so chaste, so lofty, so poignant with feeling, which would shortly be the wonder and admiration of the multitude' (p. 53)[7] is accompanied by the narrator's unfazed comment:

> Verily it is well for the world that it sees only the beauty of the completed work and not its origins nor the conditions whence it sprang; since knowledge of the artist's inspiration might often but confuse and alarm and so prevent the full effect of its excellence. (p. 53)

The effort, significantly, leaves Aschenbach 'exhausted [...] as it were after a debauch' (p. 53), as if the excesses of creativity and of physical passion are indeed closely connected, and both equally remote from the saner experiences and pleasures of the word. The result is revealing: for the first time Aschenbach feels the need to forsake the lofty betrayals of aesthetics and 'to address (Tadzio) and have the pleasure of his reply and answering look' (p. 53). But of course this is beyond him: in his state of isolation from ordinary language, and without the narrator's ready access to it, it is only in total darkness and remote from all other human beings, that he dares to whisper

> the hackneyed phrase of love and longing – impossible in these circumstances, absurd, abject, ridiculous enough, yet sacred too, and not unworthy of honour even here: 'I love you'. (p. 59)[8]

Language, when shorn of all possibility of communicating, is not language any more, and can only be recovered through the narrator's intervention. As Josipovici (1971:288) puts it, 'For Mann himself *the end is not silence but the articulation of silence.'*

For Aschenbach the last movement begins with the intimation, then the confirmation, of the conspiracy of silence about the plague. The first public ordinance he reads about the danger of certain infections, the recommendation to avoid certain foods and not to use the canal water, 'showed every sign of minimizing an existing situation' (p. 60). He traces a few reports in German newspapers (their publication explained by the fact that the first tourist to fall ill was an Austrian who returned home to die there), but 'the foreign-language sheets had nothing', and he concludes that, 'It ought to be kept quiet [...] It should not be talked about' (p. 60). As the plague spreads, there is still 'no definite information [...] to be had' (p. 64), and 'the persistent official policy of silence and denial' (p. 72) proves impenetrable. If this is an extension of his earlier isolation, when the foreign languages surrounding him excluded him, it is also of a different and more insidious kind. *And this time Aschenbach colludes with it.* Upon his return to the hotel after first becoming aware of the conspiracy of silence he resolves not to breathe a word about it, in order not to alarm Tadzio's family:

> These things that were going on in the unclean alleys of Venice, under cover of an official hushing-up policy – they gave Aschenbach a dark satisfaction. *The city's evil secret mingled with the one in the depths of his heart* – and he would have staked all he possessed to keep it, since in his infatuation he cared for nothing but to keep Tadzio here, and owned to himself, not without horror, that he could not exist were the lad to pass from his sight. (p. 61, my emphasis)

This is the key to Aschenbach's real betrayal, and to the dialectic between him and his narrator: not his corrupting love of the innocent boy, not even his sacrifice of life to the pursuit of the aesthetic, but his *betrayal of language* as he colludes with silence, its original enemy and antithesis.

Curiously, if also ineluctably, the more he allies himself, for personal reasons, with the officially imposed silence, the more urgently he is driven to subvert it by discovering the truth about the plague. The last step in his Oedipal road of enquiry leads him to ask the hideously fascinating old musician, the leader of the band come to entertain the hotel guests, about the plague. The musician, whose songs have all been 'in impossible dialect' (p. 69) – even though 'they took on meaning' through the accompanying performance (p. 67) – answers with a point- blank lie: 'A plague? What sort of plague? Is the sirroco a plague? Or perhaps our police are a plague? You are making fun of us, signore!' (p. 68). But *through* the lie Aschenbach receives confirmation of the truth he has so perversely been seeking, and which is allied with death; and the following day it is explicitly concluded by an Englishman in the tourist office. Here, again, the Lowe-Porter translation leaves the reader in the lurch: 'He continued in a lower voice, rather confused' (p. 71) – which has nothing at all in common with Mann's text: *'Und dann sagte er in seinen redlichen und bequemen Sprache die Wahrheit* [And then, in his reasonable and honest language, he told the truth]'. It is precisely this 'reasonable and honest language' which Aschenbach has abandoned as his fame increased; and given the links the text has by now established between different layers of meaning, it is only natural that the Englishman's tale, in the sadly betrayed language of ordinary human beings, should begin with an evocation of the swampy female regions of Asia where the plague has been conceived and the tiger lurks.

After the imaginary 'abyss of knowledge' which Aschenbach renounced in his writing of *The Abject* (cf. p. 17), this is the true abyss he has to plummet, and cannot. The final crisis comes just before his death when he remembers a key passage from Plato's *Phaedrus*:

> For you know that we poets cannot walk the way of beauty without Eros as our companion and guide. We may be heroic after our fashion, disciplined warriors of our craft, yet are we all like women, for we exult in passion, and love is still our desire –

our craving and our shame [...] So then, since knowledge might destroy us, we will have none of it. For knowledge, Phaedrus, does not make him who possesses it dignified and austere. Knowledge is all-knowing, understanding, forgiving; it takes up no position, sets no store by form. It has compassion with the abyss – it *is* the abyss. So we reject it, firmly, and hence-forward our concern shall be with beauty only. (pp. 80–1)

But this pursuit of beauty depends, as the text has shown, on a betrayal of language, the condition of knowledge: nowhere is it illuminated so distressingly as in the decisive episode where the beautiful youth silently, without saying a word, leads Aschenbach through the female labyrinth of the streets of Venice – from which he will emerge only to take his last farewell. In pursuing beauty at the expense of language (which, initially, was its condition) Aschenbach betrays everything that has made him what he is. It is all the more striking as he acknowledges it, in the passage quoted above, in a quotation from *written language*. The paradoxes are multiplying.

3

This trope of *writing*, which introduces a metalingual element, a process of writing-about-writing, into the text, constantly alerts the reader to the activities of the narrator. Aschenbach of course, being himself a writer, a man of words, ensures that we never lose sight of the way in which writing is permanently interposed between the observer and the world: his world is always, already, a *written* world. The crux comes when, as I have suggested, he begins to be isolated from, and even actively to withdraw from, language (at least from language in its everyday aspect of human communication), forcing the narrator to intervene more openly on his behalf and in his stead. But this process is manifested from the opening paragraphs of the novel, even if it is not always so highly dramatised as in the later movements of the text; however, it is much more complicated than the move from consonance towards dissonance suggested by Cohn (1978) and others. It tends, rather, towards a dialectical relationship throughout – and it is thanks to this that aspects like the tension between male and female forces, and the tiger's revenge, are made visible.

The first acknowledgement of writing in the text comes in the opening paragraph in the form of an explanation by the narrator of the productive mechanism that drives Aschenbach, 'that *motus animi continuus* in which, according to Cicero, eloquence resides' (p. 7). Only a few lines later more writing figures in the text, in the form of inscriptions on tombs in the graveyard, 'a symmetrically arranged selection of scriptural texts in gilded letters, all of them with a bearing upon the future life' (p. 8). In this way, even before the action proper has begun, written language circumscribes its space as a present, not only *between* classical past and life after death, but *informed* by both. 'Mann's cultivated mind', says von Gronicka (1964:48), is 'oriented Janus-like toward the past as well as toward the present.' Moments later the stranger will extend this present into the future when he makes his appearance among the 'apocalyptic beasts' of the Byzantine mortuary chapel.

The reference to the past was quite explicitly the narrator's; the evocation of the future is based on Aschenbach's observation. And these represent at least the opening gambit in the dialectic which is to follow: a dialectic not only between different views (of art, of life, of beauty) but between different notions and practices of language. It is complicated by the fact that the two 'intelligences' at work do not hold stable positions, but may actually change places or switch arguments.

Springing from the first reference to the classical world, a pre-occupation with mythology, especially that of ancient Greece, will mark much of the ensuing narrative. This is but one sign of what will become such a defining characteristic of Modernism, its involvement with the already-written, with the world-as-book, a world increasingly weary with the weight of accumulated literature, which will culminate much later in the century, after two world wars, in the *nouveau roman* of Sarraute, Robbe-Grillet, Butor and others.

In the death's-head appearance of the boatsman in Venice and the coffin-like appearance of his gondola we are prepared for recognising the gondolier as Charon. In the case of Tadzio the link with antiquity is much more explicit. He is, as von Gronicka (1964:54) phrases it, 'the creature of the two worlds of reality and myth, a creation of Mann's bifocal view'. Tadzio is observed through the lenses of antiquity in Aschenbach's exaggerated, pompous language; but also, much more directly, through the 'common language of humanity' in the narrator's articulation. What this double vision achieves is to posit Tadzio as an ambiguous textual presence. Tadzio is Tadzio, the beautiful girlish boy of flesh and blood and lingering looks and golden locks and charm enough to turn a worldly-wise elderly aesthete into a doting lover: but he is also Hyacinthus, and Narcissus, and, in the final scene, Hermes (von Gronicka 1964:55). Upon his first appearance he is described as resembling 'the noblest moment of Greek sculpture' (p. 30: once again the image is Aschenbach's, the words are those of the narrator), specifically that of the Spinnario (p. 31). Soon after first setting eyes on the boy Aschenbach mentally addresses him as 'little Phaeax', that is, 'Bright Arrival' (p. 34: this time the words, too, are Aschenbach's) and is prompted to quote from the Eighth Book of the *Odyssey* (even if it is in German translation) a line spoken by the king of the Phaeacians to describe the delights of his island of pleasure: '*Oft veränderten Schmuck und warme Bäder und Ruhe* [Often changing jewellery and warm baths and rest]'.

As Lehnert (1968:118) points out, this is only one of several overt or covert quotations from Homer in the novel; but for a number of reasons this one is particularly significant. It is taken from a description of Alkinoös on the leisurely and luxuriating life of the Phaeacians; but what most commentators seem to have missed is the way in which this line echoes two others in the same book of the *Odyssey*. One concerns the sexual relationship between Ares and Aphrodite, after which the Graces bathe the love goddess and apply sweet-smelling oils to her body and lovingly clothe her; the other refers to Odysseus who, after a warm bath, is oiled and clothed in garments bestowed on him by the lovely Arete, wife of Alkinoös. In both these instances female sexuality, or at least sensuality, is involved; and this heightens the informed reader's perception of Tadzio as the most important female presence in the novel.

In the same paragraph the image changes again: now it is described in the narrator's words, possibly as a slight correction of Aschenbach's initial reading of the boy; and the likeness is said, most significantly, to be that of a sculpture of Eros, 'with the yellowish bloom of Parian marble' (p. 35).

When Aschenbach's literary style takes over again, in poetry pushed to that extremity where language begins to dissolve into music ('this poesy hymning itself silently within him': p. 39), the boy's figure is said to conjure up 'mythologies, it was like a primeval legend, handed down from the beginning of time, of the birth of form, of the origin of the gods'.

The passages inspired by Tadzio become increasingly elaborate as the narrative develops, and this is where an uneasy discrepancy develops between the German and English texts: in Mann's German the language aspires more and more towards a lofty rhetoric derived not only from Homer but from the great tradition of German Romanticism:

> *Nun lenkte Tag für Tag der Gott mit den hitzigen Wangen nakkend sein gluthauchendes Viergespann durch die Räume des Himmels, und sein gelbes Gelock flatterte im Zugleich ausstürmenden Ostwind...*
> (Mann 1954:38)

Lowe-Porter's English is unabashed purple prose:

> Now daily the naked god with cheeks aflame drove his four fire-breathing steeds through heaven's spaces; and with him streamed the strong east wind that fluttered his yellow locks... (pp. 46–7)

In due course this becomes even worse:

> But that day, which began so fierily and festally, was not like other days; it was transmuted and gilded with mythical significance. For whence could come the breath, so mild and meaningful, like a whisper from higher spheres, that played about temple and ear? Troops of small feathery white clouds ranged over the sky, like grazing herds of the gods. A stronger wind arose, and Poseidon's horses ran up, arching their manes, among them too the steers of him with the purpled locks, who lowered their horns and bellowed as they came on; while like prancing goats the waves on the farther strand leaped among the craggy rocks. It was a world possessed, peopled by Pan, that closed round the spellbound man, and his doting heart conceived the most delicate fancies. (p. 56)[9]

This is quite obviously the narrator speaking, adopting, for the time being, what must be Aschenbach's usual manner of writing. In English this comes across as an almost devastating act of debunking through ridiculously overblown prose; in the process Aschenbach loses all stature he may have had in the reader's mind – while in German, in spite of the unmasking effect of a shrewd and subtle irony, the notion of his 'honour' remains intact. 'Such deliberately exemplary language', says Heller (1958:99), 'is the parodistic idiom of *Death in Venice* itself [...] a literary intelligence superbly succeeding in this extreme experiment with parody.' Aschenbach is revealed to be *out of touch* with the world of ordinary people: not ludicrously so, as in English, but rather with a touch of grand pathos. As a result, the impression of a dialectical relationship between narrator and protagonist is undermined in English. And if this is undermined, and the brilliantly controlled functioning of language in the narrative lost, the full measure of the tensions produced by this dialectic cannot be convincingly communicated.

Mann infuses his use of language itself with quite remarkably nuanced 'male' and 'female' overtones: this means that the text's portrayal of male and female forces in juxtaposition, and the narrator's attempts to restore Aschenbach's suppressed female dimension, cannot properly work through to the level of language, remaining instead a matter merely of *imagery* and of *thematics*.

5

This is particularly regrettable, as language is as decisive in Aschenbach's life as in the narrator's interpretation of that life. Aschenbach is a man who travels with a *book* on his lap (p. 22), and who persists in *reading* even while he is on the beach in the presence of the object of his love and admiration, the boy who holds the key to either his redemption or his damnation (p. 39). His reach towards a mythological past, like his reach towards an apocalyptic future, is defined by *writing* (his entire life prior to the voyage to Venice is summarised in terms of his writings: see pp. 12–15). Even his apprehension of nature requires the intervention of the written word: the coming of dawn is described (ostensibly by the narrator, but in a wryly ironical re-presentation of Aschenbach's own thought processes) as the arrival of

> a breath, *a winged word* from far and inaccessible abodes, that Eos was rising [...] She neared, the goddess, ravisher of youth, who stole away Cleitos and Cephalus and, defying the envious Olympians, tasted beautiful Orion's love. (p. 55, my emphasis)[10]

And when the writer recalls a mythological context for Tadzio, it is more often than not in the form of direct or indirect quotation:

> Has it not been *written* that the sun beguiles our attention from things of the intellect to fix it on things of the sense? The sun, *they say*, dazzles. (p. 51, my emphases)

This leads to a memory of the dialogue between Socrates and Phaedrus in Plato (that is, a dialogue reported by Plato, recollected by Aschenbach, narrated by the narrator): a dialogue in which Socrates 'held forth', he 'told' the youth about desire and 'spoke of' the corruption of beauty (p. 51). And in the final pages of the novel the narrator will return us to this dialogue, now in a direct quotation from the *Phaedrus* (but still spoken in three voices: that of Socrates, of Aschenbach, and the narrator):

> 'For mark you, Phaedrus, beauty alone is both divine and visible [...] For you know that we poets cannot walk the way of beauty without Eros as our companion and guide [...] but detachment, Phaedrus, and preoccupation with form lead to intoxication and desire, they may lead the noblest among us to frightful emotional excesses, which his own stern cult of the beautiful would make him the first to condemn'. (pp. 80–1)

It is this triad of voices which prompts the final denouement: voices not speaking but *written*, distanced from their authors, mediated by layers of language poetic and ordinary. In the final analysis it is this discovery of the impossibility of original articulation which kills Aschenbach and concludes the novel. That beauty which Aschenbach so desperately sought to confront directly, to possess, to commune with, remains forever elusive; and for the artist who has only the word – a word which defiles beauty as certainly as Tadzio is besmirched with sand by his companion in the last scene – this is too much to bear. Yet the ultimate irony remains: the word *has* the final word: the narrator describes what Aschenbach cannot. And if the novel is 'about' the failure of language, it is also its affirmation. We are left, in the end, holding a novel – just as Aschenbach set out on his travels with a book on his lap.

Aschenbach goes in search of a beautiful tiger in a dangerous swampy jungle. What he finds is Tadzio amid the pestilential vapours of Venice. But he also sets out, through the involvement of the narrator, in search of a language beyond the obsolete grandeur of his own writing: *this* he cannot grasp – but the narrator can, and does. And in the end this is the revenge of a tiger Aschenbach could never have anticipated: the tiger of language.

9

A Room without a View

Franz Kafka: *The Trial*

1

'Somebody must have made a false accusation against Josef K., for he was arrested one morning without having done anything wrong': in these stark and precise terms begins one of the most enigmatic and remarkable novels of the twentieth century, Franz Kafka's *Der Prozess*, known to English readers, since the first wooden and often erroneous translation by Willa and Edwin Muir in 1935, as *The Trial*.[1]

The apparent contradiction between 'stark and precise terms' and 'a most enigmatic novel' defines the territory to be explored in this chapter, in the conviction that 'the text is situated on a particular linguistic level at which only its own language is adequate' (Rolleston 1976:6).

Even a cursory rereading of the opening sentence reveals an alarming lack of precision and reliability in what has seemed, at first sight, to be so factual and solid a statement. The 'somebody' lurking behind the entire plot, real or presumed, will remain just as vague and murky to the very end: there may not even be a real Author behind it all. *Must have* is a phrase from a world where logic has a place, where causes and consequences can be calculated, seen or at least surmised, but as *The Trial* unfolds, the reader, like Josef K, is drawn ever more inextricably into a morass of the *un*foreseen and the *un*foreseeable, the illogical and the absurd, a world in which sequence is replaced by the *non sequitur*. *Must have* signals, in fact, the very mind-set the reader has to be divested of before the story, inasmuch as there is a story, can begin. *False accusation* is another marker of importance, signalling as it does the hazardous and unreliable nature of the narrated world we are about to enter: to the very end we will not be sure that the accusation has been false, or whether there has even been an accusation. The very premises and guiding principles of a criminal

189

investigation and a trial will be ignored and subverted as the plot develops. The main character himself, the key figure of the entire text, is only half-identified as a man whose surname is never disclosed and whose individuality becomes suspect as a result. A near-empty signifier. This Josef K. is reported to have been 'arrested', yet as it turns out there is nothing in his state of arrest which bears any resemblance at all to what one normally understands by the term. Except for the first hour or so after he is informed of his arrest, he is free to come and go almost as he wishes (he will be summoned, by an anonymous voice on the telephone, to attend a hearing-which-is-not-a-hearing in a courtroom-which-is-not-a-courtroom on the following Sunday; but never again), he may continue in his work at the bank without any obvious interference; he will never be furnished with details of the case against him, if any; in the end he will be executed *without* the trial the title has led us to anticipate. It happens 'one morning', in a nameless city; and it takes place 'without [his] having done anything wrong' – perhaps the most contentious assertion of all in this sentence. K himself will in due course begin to assume his guilt, not as a *reason* for his arrest, but as the *result* of it. As Kundera (1995:208) puts it, 'K is guilty not because he has committed a crime but because he has been accused.' He will certainly, at the beginning of Chapter 7, decide to compose an extensive *apologia pro vita sua* (p. 89) just in case an almost forgotten, trivial incident from his past – or, alternatively, his life as a whole – constitutes his transgression. Because, exactly as has happened with the use of words like 'false' or 'arrested', 'wrong' will gradually be revealed to have shed all conventional meaning it may have had. It is like discovering, via quantum physics, that all is relative, all is uncertain; that the too, too solid flesh must soon be resolved into a dew; that the solid table on which I lean consists, 'in reality', of a vast collection of subatomic particles moving about at a dizzying speed in unpredictable directions. So much, indeed, for the stark and precise terms of the opening sentence.

2

The ensuing conversation between Josef K and his two rude captors (whom, inexplicably, he will only later recognise as colleagues from the bank in which he holds a position of importance) confirms the first impression: directness and factuality on the surface of the reportage – and a shifting, fluid world of uncertainty and indefiniteness below.

As the guards requisition K's nightgown, 'they' (without further specification) explain:

> 'It's better to hand these things to us than to the depot [...] because there's a lot of thieving in the depot, and, apart from that, things are sold after a specified time regardless of whether the relevant proceedings have been concluded or not. And how cases of this kind do drag on, especially as we've seen in recent times. Of course you would get the money eventually from the depot, but these proceeds are small enough in the first place because it's not the size of the offer which determines the sale but the size of the bribe, and secondly we know such proceeds dwindle as they are passed from hand to hand over the years.' (p. 3)

It is all extremely lucid: there appears to be no ambiguity in the language. *And yet (like most officialese) it makes no sense at all.* K offers them his identity papers, in which they do not show the least interest: 'What have they got to do with us?' asks the guard (p. 5). And immediately they plunge into further obfuscation by way of 'explanation':

> 'We are junior officials who hardly know one end of an identity document from another [...] That's all we are, but we are capable of seeing that the higher authorities we serve would not order such an arrest without gathering exact information about the reasons for the arrest and about the person to be arrested. Our authorities, as far as I know them, and I know only the lowest grades, do not go in search of guilt in the population but are, as it says in the law, drawn to guilt and must send us warders out. That is law...' (p. 5)

No wonder that K finds himself 'even more confused by the twaddle of these lowest of instruments' (p. 5); they, in turn, react to his eloquent protestations of innocence and his angry questioning merely by warning him not to 'make such a palaver about your innocence' (p. 9). In fact, as they point out, language in their situation has become totally superfluous:

'You should be more restrained in what you say too, nearly everything you said just now could have been inferred from your conduct even if you had said only a few words, and in any case it was nothing of great advantage to you.' (pp. 9–10)

With this, the tone has been set for all the conversations to follow.

When K tries to explain the puzzling events to his landlady, Frau Grubach, in the belief that 'it's only to an old woman that I can mention it' (p. 15), he gets lost in his own empty verbosity:

'What you have said, Frau Grubach, is not stupid at all, at least I too share your opinion to some extent, but I judge the whole thing more strictly than you and I consider it to be not even scholarly but nothing at all.' (pp. 15–16)

The same happens when he desperately tries to explain the situation to Fräulein Bürstner (' "That's too vague", said Fräulein Bürstner. "What's too vague?" K. asked': p. 21). And when he attends a session of the court for his first examination his whole passionate outburst – played to the gallery of a huge crowd, half of whom are applauding, the rest apparently disapproving – is just another burst of hot air (pp. 32–6).

In the third chapter K has an encounter with a young washerwoman, as seductive as she is victimised, who disrupted the proceedings of the first examination by making love with a student on the floor of the courtroom; not only is there an urgent discussion about the machinations of the court, but below the surface there is a subtext of sexual play which almost literally comes to a climax when the student, who has returned to assert his 'rights', forcibly carries her away; but in spite of the exemplary precision of Kafka's grammar, once again nothing is really communicated. There is no exchange of ideas to prompt further narrative development: in fact, as soon as the woman is carried off, K 'had to assume [she] had not only deceived him but had also lied to him' (p. 47). And in K's extended visit, immediately afterwards, to the labyrinth of court offices, the game is extended. What seems like a wealth of information from 'behind the scenes', ostensibly to guide K through the further stages of his case, amounts to a staggering amount of wholly useless detail from which no coherent pattern of meaning emerges. The various conversations in this labyrinth – with the usher, with the helpful girl, with none less than the information officer – all turn out to be further meanderings through a maze of mere verbiage. When the experience makes K so dizzy that he has to be dragged out for fresh air, the oppressive atmosphere and stale air of the offices become quite obvious metaphors for the *linguistic* claustrophobia the scene has induced in him.

Each new chapter operates on the *illusion* of discovering more about the amazing processes of the court: the interview with K's uncle creates an opening for engaging Herr Huld, an advocate, on his behalf; an old acquaintance, a merchant, directs him to the painter Titorello who (like practically everybody else in the novel) finds himself in a hereditary position in the huge machinery of the court; the advocate's assistant, the strangely bewitching Leni who seduces all her employer's clients, offers advice and illumination; the priest in the cathedral, who turns out to be the prison chaplain, provides him with what seems like a new and deeper understanding of the process in which he is ensnared.[2]

Yet not a single encounter or conversation truly *advances* the process or provides understanding: what at first sight, sometimes (as in the interview with the merchant, or with the painter) looks like useful information, invariably turns out to be no more than deferral. Each new glimpse illuminates a few new passages, detours or tunnels within the all-encompassing labyrinth of text and language, without any hint of an overall pattern to this proliferation of forking paths. There is no minotaur in the centre; there is no centre. In an emblematic scene, as the dizzy K is dragged from the offices by the girl and the information officer, 'he noticed that they were talking to him, but he did not understand what they were saying, he could hear only the noise which filled everything' (p. 57).

Each time the reader gleans an impression of progress – most particularly in the scene with the painter, the only possible helper who seems capable of *personally* intervening in the process through his access to the judges who sit for their portraits – it turns out to have been an illusion. Titorelli offers the choice between 'apparent acquittal' or 'prolongation' (pp. 125ff) – but ultimately even this is illusory: ' "What both methods have in common is that they prevent conviction of the defendant. But they also prevent actual acquittal" ' (p. 127). The key to the fascinating interview with the painter Titorelli lies in the painter's warning that,

'The court can never be persuaded to change its opinion. If I paint all the judges in a row on a canvas, and you argue your defence before this canvas, you'll have more success than you would have before the actual court.' (p. 117)

In short, language *means* nothing, *signifies* nothing. As Titorelli reveals elsewhere, the only 'weight' that could possibly be attached to an argument submitted to the court, would derive from legends of the past; but legends are not permissible evidence (p. 121). Or again: 'That's not just a superficial surety, it's really binding [...] But of course it's not absolutely certain every judge will believe me' (p. 123). In this context it is not surprising to find, in the penultimate chapter, 'In The Cathedral' that K is designated to show a visiting Italian businessman the sights of the town, but that he knows very little of the language, and nothing at all of the dialect spoken by the visitor. No wonder the man doesn't even turn up for their appointment in the cathedral – another legitimate narrative expectation thwarted by the emptiness of language.

It comes almost as a relief, in that terrible last chapter, when K's two executioners, as they silently lead him to his end, should be wholly inarticulate. Their muteness epitomises the silence, the blankness, that has informed all the excessive effusions of speech throughout the novel.

For every step forward in the narrative grammar of *The Trial* there is a step back as well; 'the distinction between advantages and disadvantages is extremely fine' (p. 127). Or, as Fräulein Montag puts it, 'That's true [...] or rather, that's not how it is at all' (p. 63). Language turns against itself, cancels itself all along the narrative. And this same impression of blankness is repeated on other levels of signification in the text – most obviously, perhaps, in Titorelli's paintings of judges (which are all variations of the same posture: pp. 114) or of moorland landscapes (which are all absolutely identical: pp. 128–9). Distinctions, notions of *difference*, amount to no more than prestidigitation, exercises in semantics, empty linguistic play.

One of the most extensive illustrations of this feature occurs in the account of K's interviews with the advocate in Chapter 7, 'speeches as useless as they were boring' (p. 89). In the form of reported speech the narrator gives an account of one such demonstration in a paragraph which runs to more than seven pages (pp. 90–7) – a quite dazzling performance in which *absolutely no sense* is communicated. Not surprisingly, a key anecdote in the speech presents a variation on the Sisyphus myth, concerning an elderly gentleman of the court who hurls down a flight of stairs all the advocates who pester him to admitted – and every time a man is flung downstairs he comes running back, 'and, after a great show of what was really passive resistance, he let himself be thrown down again' (p. 94). If there is a lesson to be drawn from the speech, the narrator intimates on behalf of the advocate, it lies in recognising that,

> Even if it were possible to rectify certain details – *but that was just a senseless delusion* – the best one could hope for would be to achieve something for the benefit of future cases, but that would be at the expense of doing oneself immeasurable harm. (p. 95, my emphasis)

The whole speech, which relentlessly wears down the reader's faculties of understanding as much as it devastates Josef K, is itself *demonstrated* to be 'just a senseless delusion'. And after seven and a half pages of such densely argued nonsense the narrator, in his inimitably correct manner, informs the reader that,

> The advocate had an inexhaustible supply of speeches like this. They were repeated at every visit. Always progress was being made, but the nature of this progress could never be communicated. (p. 97)

It is only natural that 'K. could not understand a word of this speech' (p. 81).The point is, after all, that *there is nothing – no 'substance' – to understand*. Once again the reader is invited to read such statements as metalanguage: in commenting on the advocate's speech, the text exposes its *own* usage of language. And *this* is the blankness and obfuscation on which the whole novel is constructed. In many other novels discussed so far – whether *La Princesse de Clèves* or *Moll Flanders* or *Emma* or *Madame Bovary* – we have discovered the novelistic exploitation of language as a game of deception, of masking, of lying. In *The Trial* the 'problem' of language is presented not as its tendency to prevaricate or mislead, but as *its inability to communicate sense*, to establish meaning, to convey a content. At best it is inconclusive. In the final analysis it remains as blank as a bare room, as issueless as a closed door. And some of the narrative consequences of this discovery should now be examined more closely.

3

What strikes one first about *The Trial* – accepting that it is a text which, as Camus said, 'offers everything and confirms nothing' (in Gray 1962:155) – is that it is unfinished. There is a beginning and an ending,[3] but the eight chapters between them are clearly not a full or a final story; and there is considerable doubt about their sequence. (Max Brod: 'Whether it was the author's intention to retain this order or to relinquish it must remain forever doubtful': quoted in the Introduction to Kafka 1976:8.) Rather than joining the academic debate about the likely sequence of the narrative events, I prefer to take the position that the point is not that the novel is physically incomplete, but that it is textually *incompletable*:[4] even if Kafka had added ten or twenty additional chapters, the story could never have been 'rounded off': it is the very nature of this text that the missing links *can* never be filled in; there can never be a solution to its riddle; there can never be a completeness of information. As surely as Diderot's *Jacques* is constructed around notions of interpolation, postponement and evasion, *The Trial* is constructed around the image of gaps and silences; even the chapters we have are simply supplements to silence. And not only is the novel essentially incompletable, but the sequence of its events – traditionally, arguably, the defining characteristic of narrative – is not important.[5]

The events Josef K is drawn into, from the first irruption of the two bumbling court messengers into his room on the morning of his thirtieth birthday until the night of his execution by two clown-like theatrical characters on the eve of his thirty-first birthday, present no logical narrative chain at all.

The key to the story is the *randomness* of its events: unlike most other narratives, they eschew linearity. If Josef K continues to believe that whatever happens is controlled by some mysterious and above all *absent* authority, it is the given of his situation that no pattern, no causality, no meaning at all can be deduced from his experiences. There is no logical, narrative 'need' for Josef K to have a discussion or make a sudden desperate attempt at an amorous liaison with his neighbour, Fräulein Bürstner, immediately after his initial arrest. The visit from his uncle, the meeting with the advocate, the sexual encounter with Leni, could have happened much earlier in the story, or later. His meeting with the merchant, his visit to the painter Titorelli, even his visits to the courtroom may be moved around in the text without effecting any change in his condition, or his story. Love relationships 'lead' to nothing; all attempts at soliciting help and summoning helpers end up in cul-de-sacs; even the processes of the court follow no predictable 'line' and lead to no predictable end. Josef K's death is not the 'outcome' of a story but at most the intensification of a condition.

In *The Castle*, K's entire existence is described as 'a mistake'; in *The Trial*, Josef K's life is an unanswered – an unanswerable – question. He demonstrates the breakdown of semiotics: nothing 'refers' any longer to anything beyond itself; it is a signifying process with empty signifiers, and the novel's ' "meaning" is its lack of "meaning" ' (Pascal 1982: 153). In the penultimate chapter in Brod's version of the text, as we have already noted, Josef K goes to the cathedral to meet an Italian businessman to whom he is supposed to show the city; he takes with him an album of 'municipal sights' (p. 155); but in the course of his conversation with the priest he 'threw it away so violently that it flew open and slid some way across the floor on crumpled pages' (p. 164): this is the final renunciation of conventional reality with its expectations and its chain of logic.

What motion there is in the story, is neither forward nor backward, but inward. We are reminded of Henry Miller (1957:12): 'There is only one adventure and that is inward, towards the self.' And it appears significant that in the first encounter with the guards sent to arrest him Josef K is warned to 'think [...] more about yourself' (p. 9), a warning repeated in several other forms in the course of the novel. Yet this is the one thing Josef K. does *not* do. His only defence against the infernal machinery of the invisible court lies in a resolution to produce a chronology of his life, but he never actually brings himself round to doing it – probably because there is no coherent self to begin with, and very little sense of any development in time.

If language constantly turns back on itself as it does in this novel, unfailingly denying and even erasing itself as it progresses, time itself is placed under threat, since language is the primary signifying system through which our existence in time can be negotiated. In *The Castle*, too, time is often disrupted: when K sets out from the Inn in the early morning, he discovers within an hour or two that night is falling (Kafka 1962:23); or when the narrator mentions that K wakes up on the 'fourth day since his arrival in the village' (ibid.:47) when the narrative facts themselves indicate that it is

only the second day. But in that novel, unlike in *The Trial*, chronology still matters – even if it is mainly there to note the disruptions
in its flow. In *The Trial* chronology has very little significance at all.
In fact, the action may be said to unfold spatially, rather than
temporally.

An oppressive awareness of being confined in space characterises *The Trial* from beginning to end, and in this, it seems to
me, the novel produces its most persistent metaphor for its understanding of the prison-house of language. With the exception of a
few brief bridging scenes only the final episode of the novel, Josef
K's execution, is set outdoors – and that is, significantly, a night
scene illuminated only by moonlight.[6] On the few other occasions
when something occurs outside, it seldom involves more than the
brief traversal of a space which is either left vague and nondescript
or darkened by night or gloomy weather. The only longish description of such a venture outside is that of Josef K walking through the
suburban streets on his way to his first examination in court (p. 26),
and even then the sky is overcast, looming over the scene like a
ceiling. Moreover, in this episode, as in other brief passages where
the reader follows K between one indoor scene and the next, there
is an awareness of people observing K's movements from the
interior of adjacent buildings. This happens most ominously in
the execution scene, in which the desolate quarry, beyond the
fringes of the nameless town, is suddenly discovered to be overlooked by a building:

> His eyes fell on the top storey of the house at the edge of the
> quarry. The casement window flew open like a light flashing on;
> a human figure, faint and insubstantial at that distance and
> height, forced itself far out and stretched its arms out even
> further. Who was it? A friend? A good man? One who sym-
> pathized? One who wanted to help? Was it one person? Was it
> everybody? Was there still help? Were there objections which
> had been forgotten? Certainly there were. Logic is of course
> unshakeable, but it cannot hold out against a man who wants
> to live. Where was the judge he had never seen? Where was the
> high court he had never reached? He raised his hands and
> spread his fingers wide. (p. 178)

In this final flurry of unanswered – unanswerable – questions
which represent the ultimate failure of language, K's extreme lone-

liness is overseen by an anonymous spectator. It is almost *for the sake of this spectator* that the whole execution is enacted, just as the narrative as a whole is enacted for, and overseen by, the final observer, the reader.

4

It follows that even to be outside is not to be free: in the absence of confining walls *the gaze of others* – in the final analysis, the gaze of the reader – circumscribes whatever little movement K is still allowed. This forms part of an elaborate code of observation which increases Josef K's sense of being constantly under some form of menacing surveillance. Translated into the terms of language, this may be associated with the public dimension of language – that is, language as the speech of *others* – which ceaselessly confines and invades the space of individual perception and expression.

For the rest, all the scenes of the novel are situated indoors: in Josef K's room, his landlady's kitchen, his female neighbour's room, the offices at the bank where he works, his advocate's home, the apartment building where the court offices are located, the painter's garret, the cathedral illuminated only by the small lamp of the priest. These spaces are invariably gloomy, oppressive, cramped; on at least two occasions Josef K suffers so badly from claustrophobia that he almost loses consciousness. The first is in the court offices where 'there was no direct source of daylight' (p. 49) and where K's dizziness is shrugged off since 'nearly everybody suffers an attack like this on their first visit' (p. 53). The second is in Titorelli's attic with its 'feeling of being completely cut off from fresh air' (p. 122), aggravated by the awareness of the Furies in the shape of the host of demonic girl-children thronging outside on the landing.

It might seem that the persistent noting of the presence of a window in almost each of these interior scenes should alleviate the sense of oppression; but the effect is, in fact, the opposite. These windows do not so much provide access to an open space beyond as confirm the closeness of the interior. Titorelli's window is no more than 'a pane of fixed glass, it can't be opened' (p. 122), a discovery which increases K's claustrophobia:

Now K realized he had been hoping all the time that either the painter or he himself would suddenly go to the window and fling it open. He was prepared to inhale even the fog through his open mouth. The feeling of being completely cut off from fresh air in this place made him dizzy. (p. 122)

In the court offices the helpful girl opens a small skylight, 'but so much soot fell in that the girl had to close the skylight again without delay' (p. 54).

At some stage, in almost every scene, a character – usually Josef K himself – attempts to stare out of a window, yet there is no hint that he ever sees anything significant.[7] There is, at most, perhaps, 'the empty street' (p. 18), or 'a stretch of blank house-wall between two shop-windows' (p. 72), or a heavy fog which obscures everything but 'the snow-covered roof of the next house' (p. 113); in the bedroom occupied by the wretched merchant Block in the advocate's house the window opens into 'an air-shaft and there's hardly any light' (p. 151). K almost obsessively spends time in front of the window in his office, without ever discovering anything of note. His view is restricted to the courtyard, itself a confined space; when he looks out, it is almost invariably gloomy. On one occasion, 'a very wet and stormy morning' (p. 155); on another, 'snow was still falling, the sky was still dark' (p. 104) – and when he does, once, risk opening it, 'a mixture of fog and smoke poured [...] into the room and filled it with a faint smell of burning' (p. 105).

In the opening scene, when he looks out, he becomes aware of the neighbours staring fixedly at him: first an old lady, 'observing him with a curiosity quite unusual for her' (p. 1), keeping watch 'with true senile inquisitiveness' (p. 2), then joined by 'an even older man' (p. 5), later by yet another who 'was saying something which was incomprehensible at that distance' (p. 10). Once the link between windows and language has been established, the reading of this trope is significantly expanded: windows open up the space of private experience to invasion by the language of Others, which remains forever incomprehensible. Through the presence of windows an outside is *acknowledged*, but it provides as little illumination or understanding as any amount of exposure to the esoteric workings of the closed system in operation in the court.

This is anticipated from the beginning. When K emerges from his bedroom in the first scene, one of the guards is sitting in front of the window (p. 2); when he approaches with his identity docu-

ments, both guards are obscuring the view (p. 4). Another significant blocking process is suggested on p. 8, when K discovers 'a
white blouse [...] hanging on the latch of the open window' in
Fräulein Bürstner's bedroom: the hint of sensuality in the scene is
fulfilled that night when K makes his sudden and violent sexual
advance in the same room (p. 23).

On many occasions what view there is turns out to be at least
partially obscured – by curtains (p. 75), by Fräulein Bürstner's
blouse draped across it, as we have already noted (p. 8),[8] or by
placing someone with his/her *back* to the window (Fräulein Montag on p. 63, K himself on p. 113).

But if Josef K cannot get out, others can get *in*, invading his space
in incessant thrusts and jolts, 'coming closer and closer to me
personally' (pp. 145–6).[9] This lurks behind the overwhelming
sense of *menace* in the novel: the awareness of being trapped inside
one confining room after the other, replicates Josef K's unsettling
experience of being caught inside a system – a judicial system, a
system of life, a *language* – to the interior of which he is doomed,
and from which no escape is possible. In the beginning he feels 'a
desire to ascertain whether this judicial system was just as loath-
some on the inside as it appeared from the outside' (p. 53); soon he
discovers that he is already trapped inside. 'At this very window',
the advocate informs him, 'you could have seen gentlemen [...]
gazing miserably down the alley while the advocate was studying
at his desk in order to offer them learned advice' (p. 93) – advice
which will only, ever, lead more deeply inward, never outward.
The result is inevitable: 'the client forgot in the end about the
outside world and merely hoped to drag himself along this illusory
path to the end of his case' (p. 151).

The search leads inexorably to the deepest darkness of the book,
the interior of the cathedral where the priest, who is no priest, tells
him the parable of the door-keeper whose 'ideas [...] about the
interior are held to be childish' (p. 170). In this ultimate paradox of
the novel, inside and outside merge, as in Derrida's concept of the
'hymen':[10] K discovers, in this setting of innermost darkness from
which all notions of an outside have fallen away, that he is still
outside the truth. Caught inside this legal trap, as inside language,
he is still kept outside of meaning, because language, like an onion,
is hollow, and keeps no secret hidden in its centre.

All Josef K's attempts to get *out* only result into his intrusion into
the spaces of others – in his visits to the courtroom, the court

offices, the advocate's house, the painter's room, the cathedral – while at the same time he can never be sure that his own space will remain inviolate. There is no end to the threats from outside. In fact, this unmitigating menace becomes more 'real' than Josef K's own life; and even though almost all the scenes in the novel are set 'inside', the weight of the novel resides in the 'outside' – as surely as the absent Godot determines the lives of Vladimir and Estragon. This is why Kundera suggests that Josef K's true problem lies in the question: 'What possibilities remain for a man in a world where the external determinants have become so over-powering that internal impulses no longer carry weight?' (Kundera 1988:26).

This explains the particular significance of the parable of the peasant which is told in the darkest heart of the novel, Josef K's meeting with the priest in the cathedral: the peasant arrives at a building whose sole entrance is barred by a door-keeper; he is never allowed to enter ('It is possible', the doorkeeper tells him, 'but not now': p. 166) – and yet the door is there only for him, and no-one else! This illuminates Josef K's frantic attempts, throughout the novel, to *reason* his way into the conundrum of his arrest: the interminable attempts to use language in order to *explain* his situation (repeated in K's obsession in *The Castle*) represent precisely the wrong approach. Because the problem begins where the language traditionally associated with knowledge, wisdom and rationality, ends. Some problems of life, someone once said, do not permit of any solution: they can only be lived. Among many other things, *The Trial* defines the failure of nineteenth-century Positivism and reason to provide an answer to the problem of living.

Even the parable in the cathedral provides, in the final analysis, no illumination: it is another dead end. For the text of the parable is surrounded by a proliferation of suggested 'readings': opinions, interpretations, possibilities, all of them dependent on the language of reason, hence doomed from the outset. Once again we end up in a blank room; and even the momentary illusion of a window provides no view of a coherent meaning beyond.

Once Josef K has been drawn into the empty space of the language which constitutes the reality of the court, its ramifications and processes and obfuscations, he must remain in the hymeneal margin of two dimensions: inside, there is the sound and fury of senseless action; outside, the threat of an incomprehensible power, of life, of history.

And instead of turning towards the possibilities of the self, as Fräulein Bürstner urges him to do, Josef K keeps on groping for help from outside – mainly from women: Fräulein Bürstner herself, her 'replacement' Fräulein Montag, the promiscuous washerwoman, the wife of the court usher, and the advocate's housekeeper Leni who finds 'nearly all accused men handsome [...] is attracted to them all, loves them all, and seems to be loved by them too' (p. 143). One problem is that all these women are, in one way or another, in league with the processes of the court. Even of the barely nubile girls swarming through Titorelli's building the painter asserts that, 'These girls too belong to the court' (p. 118). Fräulein Bürstner, who appears the most benevolent of them all, is the very one who points him to his place of execution in the end.

Curiously enough, the narrator presents nearly all the women in the text as persons of suspect morals: Josef K's first mistress Elsa appears to be a prostitute (p. 14); Fräulein Bürstner is reported by the landlady to have been observed twice in the street, 'each time with a different gentleman' (p. 17); the court usher's wife makes her first public appearance in a sexual embrace in the courtroom; Leni goes for every man who visits the advocate. This can hardly be ascribed to any misogyny in Kafka (although we know from his diaries and letters how problematic his relationships with Felice or Milena were):[11] after all, he has created quite a gallery of more wholesome female characters in his other stories, which means that this portrayal in *The Trial* must be deliberate. And it seems to me that the key lies in the provocative sexuality, the 'utter depravity' (p. 111)[12] of the girl-children surrounding the artist, and in the reference to Leni herself as a 'witch' (p. 81).

We know that witches, originally the worshippers of the Earth-Mother, that is, representatives of the fullness of the female principle in the world, were relegated to a position of alleged menace, depravity and immorality by and in a patriarchy which could not cope with femininity (Farrar 1987). In *The Trial* the functioning and all the processes of the presented world are phallocentric: the court is the primary expression of male Law and Order, Authority, Power, and of course Language. The women in the text have been drawn into its system and perverted into its image; their only possibility of revolt lies in subverting *other* males and taking delight in their destruction; at best they can act as tormenting Furies, as the girl-children do. Instead of remaining faithful to his relationship with Elsa (even if she is a prostitute), Josef K engages in a sexual contest with Fräulein Bürstner, the court usher's wife, and Leni: he *cannot* call himself 'innocent' after this, which means that he has no defence against the indictment – even if its terms are never divulged to him. And in this way, once more, the relationship between outside and inside becomes perverted, and the women as markers of space (witches traditionally find themselves on the periphery of society, both inside and outside) suggest to the reader that what we are confronted with in *The Trial* is the textual equivalent of a Möbius strip.

What makes the female characters particularly significant as markers within the space traversed by Josef K is the way in which their sexuality presents an escape, however temporary, *from language*, an alternative epistemology. In the scene with Fräulein Bürstner all the organs of speech are engaged by the violent lovemaking with which K responds to the threat of an eavesdropper:

> K [...] kissed her on the *mouth* and then all over her face like a thirsty animal who scours with his *tongue* the surface of a spring he has found at last. Finally he kissed her on the *neck*, on her *throat*, and lingered there with his *lips*. (p. 23, my emphasis)[13]

In the case of the promiscuous Leni – the 'witch', the 'freak of nature' with the webbed fingers (cf. p. 87) – sex, initially presented as no more than a *supplement* to speech, soon takes over from language as an incomparably more persuasive form of communication (cf. pp. 86–7).[14] Titorelli's young rabble of Lolitas[15] threatens *meaning* not only by constantly interrupting K's interview with the painter but by contributing a darkly disturbing subtext to the conversation. In a real sense this subtext subverts the 'information' the painter is supplying and turns language against itself in the ways we have already noted. In all these instances female sexuality, at the very least, provides both a non-verbal commentary on language and an alternative to it. But because K feels constrained to devote all his energy to the pursuit of his case, which involves all the vagaries of language, he neglects the women (we learn that 'his relationship with Fräulein Bürstner seemed to fluctuate in parallel with the case', p. 99; he turns down Leni's advances; he no longer visits Elsa),[16] turns away from sex, and remains committed to the main reason for his entrapment: the blankness of language.

The text itself becomes a space into which the reader enters only at his/her peril. In this respect there is one remarkable short chapter in *The Trial* which, in the force of its imagining, reveals more about the novel's concept of language than any other. It is one that might have been thought up by the physicist Erwin Schrödinger, who imagined an experiment set in a box containing a live cat and a lump of radioactive material, which may or may not decay. If it does, the experiment is set up in such a way that a poison phial will be broken and the cat killed:

> In the everyday world, there is a fifty-fifty chance that the cat will be killed, and without looking into the box we can say, quite happily, that the cat inside is either alive or dead. But now we encounter the strangeness of the quantum world. According to the theory, *neither* of the two possibilities open to the radioactive material, and therefore to the cat, has any reality unless it is observed. The atomic decay has neither happened nor not happened, the cat is neither killed nor not killed, until we look inside the box to see what has happened [...] Nothing is real unless it is observed. (Gribbin 1984:2–3)

In *The Trial* the equivalent of this theory is the scene in which Josef K enters a small storeroom in the bank to find a whipper flogging his two original tormentors; when he flees from it (in order to avoid attracting other bank officials to the scene), the screaming stops and there is silence behind him; but when he opens the door again the following day, it is as if no time has elapsed:

> Everything was unchanged, just as he had found it on opening the door the previous evening. The printed forms and inkpots just over the threshold, the whipper with his cane, the warders still fully dressed, the candle on the shelf, and the warders began to wail and cried out: 'Sir!'. (p. 71)

Without his presence, there is no room, nothing at all: his presence *makes it happen*, just as the text, existing as a room or a space constituted by language, is dependent on its narrator – and, as we have deduced from the positioning of the observer in the execution scene – on the reader who opens the magic door into its innermost recess. If there is a presence it is the presence of absence: in the blank space of language nothing happens, at least not 'by itself' or 'for itself'; but through the gaze of the reader anything, and everything, may happen – and does happen.

This is the only reality we are left with in the world of *The Trial*: not the room you are in, the wall you skirt, the blouse you see, the blow you feel, the scream you hear, not the body your body makes love to, but the place where you are not, the dream you do not wake from, time past or time future, never time present, the absent love, the present fear, the present guilt, and not the candle, not the moon, but the darkness which makes it visible – all of which is inscribed on the blank walls of the closed room of language.

10

The Perfect Crime

Alain Robbe-Grillet: *Le Voyeur*

1

The aestheticism that had been the hallmark of much Modernist fiction reached an extreme in Alain Robbe-Grillet's concept of *'une histoire qui n'avait d'autre réalité que celle du récit* [a story which has no other reality than the narrative]' (Robbe-Grillet 1963:132). But there is, at the same time, an opposite impulse in the *nouveau roman*, which places it on the cusp between Modernism and Postmodernism, that is, the urge to democratise the novel, to offer at least an illusion of accessibility which will lure the reader across the threshold of the narrative: hence especially Robbe-Grillet's regular recourse to versions or inversions of popular forms like the detective novel. *'En somme'*, says Janvier (1964:49), *'le Nouveau Roman, c'est le policier pris au sérieux* [In short, the Nouveau Roman is the detective story taken seriously]'.

On the one hand, as Garnham (1982:61) argues, Robbe-Grillet presents the reader with 'an enquiry into the art of writing a novel, and more specifically an enquiry into how the novel can liberate itself from its traditional function of "telling a story" and with what it might replace that function'. On the other, the vestiges of story do seem to indicate that 'pure textuality' is unattainable. At almost every point of its development the plot in *Le Voyeur* breaks down if one tries to read it within the framework of traditional narrative, yet the novel demonstrates just as persuasively that it is precisely the *lure of a story* which keeps the reader reading.

For many years after its first publication in 1955, *Le Voyeur* remained a strangely misunderstood and misread novel; and even today, after being flogged to near-death by generations of critics, it still preserves much of its initial sense of mystery.

Among the questions that have remained unanswered are these: Why is the novel titled *Le Voyeur* – and who is the voyeur in the story? What 'really' happened during the lost hour at the heart of

the novel? Or, put in different words, is there a crime in the novel?
What was it, and who committed it? Is Mathias a psychopath? a
cold-blooded, calculating murderer? a victim of circumstances?
How reliable is the narrator, and from whose point of view is the
narrative presented?

At least some of these problems, I hope to demonstrate,
have never been resolved satisfactorily for the simple reason
that they are based on wrong assumptions and phrased incorrectly.
It may well be that such questions arise as part of the game
proposed by the text. But if so, one should attempt to establish
why this is so.

2

The very nature of the problems presented by *Le Voyeur* is illuminated the moment one attempts to paraphrase the story. It appears
to follow a salesman, Mathias, on his travels on a rented bicycle
across the island on which he was born but which he hasn't seen
for many years. He arrives just after ten on a Tuesday morning,
spends the day trying to sell the watches he has brought with him,
misses the afternoon ferry and has to wait until the Friday to return
to the mainland. At about lunchtime on the Tuesday, it would
seem, a precocious young girl, Juliette Leduc, who has had invol-
vements with several men on the island, is tortured and murdered.
Whether Mathias has had a part in the event appears to be the
'business' of the story. In a synopsis proposed by Jean Alter
(1966:241), Part I represents the planning of a perfect enterprise,
which then breaks down in reality; Part II the fabrication of alibis;
Part III Mathias's attempts to undercut suspicion by removing all
available traces.

But any attempt to reconstruct what Morrissette (1963:84) terms
'la ligne rationelle qui relie les éléments de l'action [the rational line
which links the elements of the action]', is doomed to failure.
Trying to explain the uncertainties by blaming them on Mathias's
unreliable memory[1] only leads to new dead-ends. Even if one
agrees with Garnham that 'the centrepiece of this [novel] is a
crime, and the novel's structure is dictated by the anticipation of
that crime and the reactions to it once it has been committed'
(Garnham 1982:42), it would still sound, simply, like another
Crime and Punishment, missing precisely those elements which

combine to make Robbe-Grillet *different* from Dostoevsky. Garnham seems to me to come closer to the crux of the matter when he says that

> Robbe-Grillet is raising questions about the nature and the function of the novel itself and hopes to lead the reader to view *Le Voyeur* not as a puzzle ingeniously presented, containing one acceptable solution, *but as an enquiry into the capabilities, limits and methods of prose fiction.* (Garnham 1982:43, my emphasis)

This is why any attempted paraphrase soon breaks down. To begin with, it has to dispense with detail, and detail provides one of the most revealing entries into the text, not necessarily for the amplitude it provides, but for what it *covers up*, for what it *suppresses*, not for what it says, but for what it does *not* say. In a scene which should serve as a clear warning to the reader, Mathias enters a shop only to find the whole space between him and the counter barred by 'the most unrelated articles [...] piled side by side in great confusion' (p. 56).[2] Even more pointedly, two sailors in the bar near the lighthouse explain to him how to reach their houses, but in the process 'they probably gave him a number of useless or redundant details, but with such exactitude and such insistence that Mathias was completely confused' (p. 105).

Moreover, in reducing the narrative to its ostensible 'facts', the elaborate structure of *trompe-l'oeil* on which the novel rests, is sacrificed. And *trompe-l'oeil* is indeed a key phrase in Robbe-Grillet's *oeuvre*, even explicitly so. On p. 27 of *Le Voyeur*, in Mathias's first imaginary visit to the Leduc household (if, indeed, one may read the text in terms of the distinction between 'real' and 'imaginary'), the two circles or knots in the wood of the front door, recalling the iron rings on the slipway of the harbour, 'looked like two rings painted in *trompe-l'oeil* with the shadows they cast on the wood panel and the two nails on which they hung'; and near the end, the concrete blocks below the surface of the water look 'as if they had been painted in *trompe-l'oeil*' (p. 218). Once again the warning to the reader is quite explicit.

And furthermore, any paraphrase must omit the novel's smooth and sometimes almost imperceptible shifts between tenses (so imperceptible, in fact, that the English translator sometimes misses them altogether). The possible oscillations between narrative past, present and future, between a 'reality' Mathias shares with characters surrounding him and what may be mental projections, are lost if these shifts are not accounted for.

Most pertinently, any kind of reading that produces a paraphrase must be conditioned by a tradition of Realist fiction; and there is evidence enough that Robbe-Grillet wrote *Le Voyeur* the way he did because he *did not want* it to be read in this manner. If he retained some of the outward trappings of the traditional plot, they serve precisely to demonstrate the dead-ends they lead to in the *nouveau roman*. This, as I hope to illustrate in due course, also has a direct bearing on one's reading of the title, *Le Voyeur*.

Many of the deficiencies of a reading based on obsolete notions of plot may be traced quite simply to the impression it creates of an action directly accessible to the reader, not mediated by narrative processes, and in the final instance by the language on which such processes are predicated. For example, it would be wrong to say that, as the boat approaches the landing, Mathias 'stands apart from the other passengers'; there is somebody, or an instance, *who makes this observation and registers it in language*. (The very syntax of the sentence in question, with the deferral of its subject, establishes the distance between Mathias and the others: 'Slightly to one side, behind the area in which the steam had just appeared, one passenger stood apart from the expectant group': p. 3). This observer cannot be Mathias himself, and this immediately invalidates the many readings which have seen the text as the product of a narrator who is at most an extension of Mathias. Quite often the narrator and the observer may appear to occupy the same space; but from the outset it is clear that there are two separate functions involved.

Furthermore, the narrative information conveyed by the narrator (whether 'on behalf of' Mathias or not, as the case may be from one scene to the next)[3] is shaped, not in neutral language – because, as should be clear after the preceding chapters, such a thing simply does not exist – but in a language heavily loaded with certain possibilities and deprived of others. It is these sets of possibilities which will determine my proposed reading of the text.

If in this discussion I persist in taking the elements of 'story' as a starting point, it is done deliberately, in order to engage with the text on its own terms.

3

In the first place, it soon becomes clear that language is not a one-way street in *Le Voyeur*, but very much a two-way process, a give-and-take, in which speaker/narrator and listener/narratee are both heavily implicated. Meaning is the product of this interaction, and as this interaction more often than not turns out to be faulty, or prejudiced, or intermittent, meaning inevitably becomes distorted, tenuous and riddled with gaps. Thus, as we shall see, the 'portentous gap at the heart of the novel' noted by Sturrock (1969:182),[4] is only the most spectacular instance of a whole series of gaps produced by the language of the novel.

It is a feature of the reported language in *Le Voyeur* that at some of the most crucial moments of the narrative sentences should drop away into silence, leaving only phrases or words behind, practically inviting misunderstanding. The first time this is highlighted in the text is during Mathias's morning visit to the café *A L'Espérance*, just after his prurient imagination has been kindled by a cinema poster featuring a man in the process of assaulting a woman beside an unmade bed, and by the sight of the timorous young waitress. From a table where some sailors are seated, comes the sound of 'air whistled between clenched teeth – preceding the imminent return of speech', a signal which deftly picks up the blasts of the ship's siren[5] which announced the start of the novel:

> Passionately, though in an undertone, syllables picked out [one] by one: '...would deserve...' began the youngest, who was continuing some long-drawn-out argument begun elsewhere. 'She deserves...' A silence...A little whistle...Squinting from the effort of choosing his words, he was looking into a dark corner where the pin-ball machine stood. 'I don't know what she deserves'. (p. 46)

This is followed by other disjointed phrases: 'A good smack...', and, just after the waitress has placed her hands behind her back in one of the novel's pivotal images of torture, 'The whip!'.

When Mathias meets old Madame Marek at the crossroads, his speech assumes an existence of its own, quite independently of himself:

A sentence jolted out of his mouth – obscure and overlong, too sudden to be altogether friendly, grammatically incorrect – in which he could make out, nevertheless, the essential formulas: 'Marek', 'good morning', 'not recognized'. (p. 78)

This will happen on many other occasions too (including, significantly, the scene in which Mathias overhears an old fisherman recounting the local legend about a young girl sacrificed annually to the storm god: p. 189). A particularly eloquent scene is the one in the café near the lighthouse, where Mathias overhears two sailors speaking:

Mathias could not hear him clearly. Several syllables, however, *took shape in his mind*, resembling the word 'cliff' and – less positively – the verb 'to bind'. (p. 90, my emphasis)

and as if it is not enough that these words should be shaped 'in his mind', he is then reported to start ruminating on the very language in which he imagined this speech:

He tried to imagine what it could be about. But suddenly he was afraid to guess [...] as if their words, without their knowing it, might have concerned him. It would not be difficult to go a good deal further along this irrational course: the words 'without their knowing it', for instance, were superfluous, for if his presence had caused them to fall silent – although they were not embarrassed to speak in front of the proprietress – it was obviously because they...because 'he'...'In front of the proprietress', or rather 'with' her. (p. 91)

Before the reader's eyes the perceived details of the event are transformed into language, a language as broken and disjointed as the first utterances Mathias may or may not have overheard.

Moments later, still in the same scene, Mathias's thoughts presumably start wandering again, back to his visit to the Leduc home. In the form of free indirect speech the narrator's perception and that of Mathias momentarily overlap, and language actually breaks down into a stammered repetition of one word, gathering into it much of the novel's network of signifiers concerned with observing, gazing, looking:

[...] the rectangular frame on top of the sideboard, the shiny metal support, the photograph, the sloping path, the hollow on the cliff sheltered from the wind, secret, calm, isolated as if by thick walls...as if by thick walls...the oval table in the middle of the room, the oilcloth with the many-colored little flowers, the pressure of his fingers on the suitcase clasp, the cover opening back[6] as if on a spring, the black memorandum book, the prospectuses, the shiny metal frame, the photograph showing...the photograph showing the photograph, the photograph, the photograph, the photograph, the photograph...(p. 98)[7]

Even when language appears to be tracing a smooth grammatical course, this very smoothness suggests another kind of gap – this time on the level of the signifieds. Forced to acknowledge that the boy Julien knows 'all' about whatever has taken place on the cliff during the fateful central gap in the story, Mathias glibly tries to explain himself out of his predicament. But halfway through he is described as starting to interrogate his own language:

He might just as well have said that the gray sweater was not lying 'on the rocks', but 'on a projection of the rocks' – or that only one of the mahonias was budding at the Marek farm. He might have said: 'The road is not altogether level, nor entirely straight, between the crossroads and the fork leading to the mill' – 'The bulletin-board is not precisely in front of the café-tobacco shop door, but slightly to the right, and does not block the entrance' – 'The little square is not really triangular: the apex is flattened by the plot of grass around the public building so as to form a trapezoid' – 'The enameled iron skimmer sticking out of the mud in the harbor is not the same color blue as the one in the hardware store' – 'The pier is not rectilinear, but turns in the center at an angle of one hundred seventy-five degrees'. (p. 187)

This is not being finicky. Each of these descriptions refers to earlier, and often extremely elaborate, and repeated, attempts at describing observed features of the island, and by correcting them (without any guarantee whatsoever that the rephrased descriptions are more 'accurate' than the earlier ones) the narrator is questioning the entire relationship between signifier and signified. It may be linked to the famous 'repetitions' of descriptions, in this novel as in *La Jalousie* and others, commented on by practically all Robbe-Grillet's critics, especially those fascinated by the notion of the so-called 'l'école du regard'. But it would seem to me, instead, that the point of these apparently compulsive repetitions lies not in their sameness but in the *differences* they illuminate. Far from demonstrating 'pure vision' (Weiner 1962:220) they illuminate an *unreliability* of vision in its utter dependence on language. An eloquent example is the description of the landing on p. 6:

> The stone rim – an oblique, sharp edge formed by two intersecting perpendicular planes: the vertical embankment perpendicular to the quay and the ramp leading to the top of the pier – was continued along its upper side at the top of the pier by a horizontal line extending straight toward the quay.

At the end of Part II the description recurs:

> [...] the inner rim of the parapet, the angle formed by the jetty and the base of the parapet, the side of the pier that had no railing – rigid horizontal lines, interrupted by several openings, extending straight toward the quay. (p. 140)[8]

In Chomskian terminology, the 'deep structure', is unchanged in the two passages. But the surface structure has shifted, to reveal an inadequacy of language. After all, if language cannot deal with the representation of a scene that remains immutable, how can it be expected to capture the innumerable small shifts of nuance which occurs in perception, in emotional flickerings, or above all, in the processes of signification themselves?

The most dramatic instance of the dissolution of links between language and reality occurs during the meeting with Julien:

> And Mathias still went on talking, though without the slightest conviction, carried away by the flood of his own words across the deserted moor, across the series of dunes where no trace of vegetation remained, across the rubble and the sand, darkened here and there by a sudden shadow of a specter forcing him to retreat. He went on talking. And the ground, from sentence to sentence, gave way a little more beneath his feet. (p. 184)

What really gapes, vertiginously, below his feet, is *the* Void. And most of the strategies of language – some dazzling, others almost unobtrusive – converge in this signification. It is evident as much in the meticulous description of the dead frog at the crossroads (p. 75)[9] which soon afterwards turns out to be a toad (p. 85), as in the inscription of the name 'Jean Robin' (hitherto a fictitious character in Mathias's mind) above the door of the fisherman's cottage. It *may* refer to a cousin of the proprietor of *A L'Espérance* (see p. 48), but that man is already dead, and it would seem unlikely that the fisherman Pierre would have kept another man's name on his house; the most reasonable deduction, inasmuch as reason itself can be trusted, is that the text presents the name, quite deliberately, as a signifier that *proclaims* its emptiness.

4

This effect is enhanced by the whole strategy of contradictions and 'corrections' which characterises the use of language in the novel. The very first spoken utterance in the text, innocuous as it may seem at first sight, illustrates this, when the arrival of the boat is announced with the statement, ' "She's on time today", only to be qualified in the very next sentence: "Almost", someone corrected – perhaps it was the same voice' (p. 5).

In the case of the man who rents Mathias a bicycle this kind of speech is said to be habitual:

[he] had an odd way of answering, always beginning in agreement, even repeating his own words in a tone of conviction, only to introduce some doubt a second later, and then deny everything by a contrary, more or less categorical, proposition. (p. 37)

But far from being the ideolect of a particular individual, it turns out to be a feature of speech in general in *Le Voyeur*. The description of the fisherman who may or may not be Jean Robin, may even be read as another example of the *mise-en-abyme* device for which, throughout his *oeuvre*, Robbe-Grillet shows such a predilection:

[t]he fisherman had again begun on some general considerations of life on the island – oddly contradictory though they were. Each time that he seemed to want to illustrate what he was saying by some more personal detail, the latter contradicted the

very point of view he was defending. *In spite of this, the general tone of his remarks retained – in appearance, at least – a coherent structure, so that a distracted attention would not realize the anomalies involved.* (p. 128, my emphasis)

A particularly precarious moment results from this kind of speech when, still in the fisherman's cottage, Mathias responds to the argument about Jacqueline's visits to his host's wife by saying, 'She won't come now' (p. 120). Realising the implications of his own words, he hurriedly adds, 'I mean, she must have gone to lunch by now', followed by the even more confusing remark, ' " ... with the crabs...". which seemed to have no relation to anything at all'. The incident is both rounded off and compounded when, running into the fisherman's young companion again the following day on the cliff, she ascribes the words, not to Mathias but to 'Pierre': 'Tell me again what he said at dinner. "She won't come back any more..." ' – which Mathias 'corrects': '... now. She won't come back any more now' (p. 157).[10]

Another dramatic moment based on the severance of links between signifier and signified, resulting in an aporia, occurs when during Mathias's visit to the Marek farm the boy Julien gives a full account of the earlier, fictitious, visit (p. 170). This may be, and has consistently been, read as a lie, told to reveal some kind of complicity between the boy and the salesman in the murder; and such a reading appears to be corroborated by their meeting on the clifftop, later, when the boy admits that his earlier version was impossible (p. 186). But the pervasive pattern of faulty language, a language full of gaps and inconsistencies (not because of any wish on the part of the narrator to *deceive* the reader, but *because it is the nature of language to be unreliable*), suggests a different reading altogether. Either the two passages reveal a *language trap*, set by Julien, in which Mathias is caught as surely as the reader, or, more radically, they amplify the self-cancelling processes of language on which the whole narrative has been constructed.[11] At the very least it is significant that the moment after Mathias is said to have heard these words (spoken moreover, not by Julien, but merely by 'a voice'), he looks up to discover that 'he was alone on the moor' (p. 187) – as if Julien has never been there at all.

In a way all these breakdowns of language – whether they occur structurally, grammatically, or in the dissemination of some kind of meaning – pave the way for one of the most startling passages in the whole novel. It occurs just after the old fisherman has repeated the local legend (which, curiously and significantly enough, 'Mathias had never heard mentioned in his childhood': p. 189),[12] when the salesman has what seems like a blackout:

> He turned to face the fat woman, or the woman, or the girl, or the young barmaid, then set down the suitcase in order to pick up the suitcase while the sailor and the fisherman sneaked between, crept between, came between, Mathias and the sales-man... (p. 190)

In a 'straight' narrative this might well be read as a form of free indirect speech in which the failing mental faculties of the character are dramatised. But it seems to me that the passage has really nothing at all to do with Mathias and his perceptions: this is the language of the narrator, demonstrating that *everything* in the text so far has been, not an optical illusion or a psychological perception, but a trick of language.

Throughout Part I the central character was consistently called 'Mathias'; from the beginning of Part II, that is, from the moment a gap in the narrative has been established, he is alternately called 'Mathias' and 'the salesman': these are the terms the *narrator* has chosen to establish differences in distance within the focalising process. In other words, when the sailor and the fisherman are reported to sneak, or creep, or come between Mathias and the salesman, it is an interposition between two linguistic terms in which a narrative convention has been ratified. By now turning upon the terms themselves, the text is not 'representing' a process of mental breakdown in the character, but *a dissolution of language*. Thereby it – once again – questions its own premises, and alerts the reader to the need of inventing new processes of reading such a text.

5

To mark the dissolution of language the text often resorts to *showing* that it has nothing to say, or, paradoxically, *saying* that it has nothing to say. This happens on p. 91 in the café conversation where, as I have shown earlier, the words spoken (or believed to be spoken) are subjected to close scrutiny, not as referents, but simply as undirected acts of speech. 'To all intents and purposes', notes the narrator, 'no one had anything to say.' (A single paragraph later, the observation is repeated: 'Evidently no one had anything to say.')

More often than not, this is conveyed, not through comments but through a demonstration of language in action. This is evident from the garage .owner's perfunctory comment, 'Good-looking girl, isn't she?' (p. 36), apropos of an individual who turns out to be neither 'good-looking' nor, by any stretch of the imagination a 'girl'; later it is followed, and displaced, by the comment, 'Good-looking sign, isn't it?' (p. 144). The sailors in the café appear to have the same argument over and over again, 'with the same economy of words and the same deliberation, displaying neither progression nor conclusion' (p. 50). Mathias himself has 'the constant sense of talking in a void' (p. 52). Even the crucial newspaper cutting about the murdered girl offers no real information, being cast in 'the conventional language of the press for this category of news, and [referring], at best, to generalities' (p. 61).

Even when something specific is supposed to be signified, as in the café woman's description of where Jacqueline is tending her sheep, the phrase 'after the crossroads' is revealed to be 'an ambiguous expression, since it was impossible to know if she meant "after" in relation to her own village or the town where Madame Leduc lived' (p. 95). It conveys a blank, just like the fishermen who announce that they are going home for 'soup': 'It was just a figure of speech, probably; it had been several generations since the fishermen took soup at the afternoon meal' (p. 99).[13]

In the fisherman's cottage, Mathias listens to his host's description of the new lighthouse lenses, realising very soon that the entire description is impossible: 'It seemed to him that his host was using the words without understanding their meaning, satisfied to set one here or there almost at chance, into the surface of his discourse, which was itself quite vague and meaningless (p. 117).

This also determines the tenor, and the details, of the long conversation between Mathias and Pierre/Jean's female companion on the cliff:

'He said he had heard you.'
'Heard what?'
'What you told me.'

'And what did I tell you?'
'I don't know.' (p. 155)

The novel, one is reminded, dates from the decade of *Waiting for Godot* and *La Cantatrice Chauve*.

And all this leads up to the revealing moment in the scene, or non-scene, between Mathias and Julien, when, 'In order to fill in the blanks, he often repeated the same sentence several times. He even caught himself reciting the multiplication table' (p. 185).

In order to fill in the blanks: this may well be the clue to it all. And in this way we have come full circle in our argument.

6

It is in order to fill in blanks that the characters themselves are constructed, primarily, Mathias and his obsession with watches, his means of desperately attempting to establish the order and coherence of 'out there', the mainland, on the textual blank of the island, where nothing is 'on time'. Even when the boat is announced to be on time, it is, at best, 'almost'; when it leaves, it is five minutes late – when the bicycle is promised for a certain time, Mathias arrives late – all of which amounts to preparations for that signal 'lost hour' in the centre, which itself cannot be pinpointed: it may be fifty minutes, or forty, or more, or less; perhaps it doesn't exist at all. From the outset all his calculations are hampered by the fact that the very first time he opens his case there is already a blank inside, one watch missing (allegedly sold on the mainland, before his departure); which makes accurate mental arithmetic practically impossible.[14]

And as a fabrication of language himself, Mathias promptly sets about 'manufacturing' other characters as well. On the basis of some biographical details (which may be correct or false) furnished by the sailor on the mainland, aided and abetted by the newspaper cutting, an imagined scene of violence in the St Jacques district glimpsed on his way to the ferry that morning, the repetition of the phrase 'a real devil' applied to Jacqueline (for example on pp. 23, 68–9, 93, 161), and perhaps a suppressed memory from his childhood, all of these connected in some mysterious way to his passion for collecting twine and cord and string, he fabricates 'Violette', the archetypal young victim of male depredation and sadism. *This* may

well be the reconstitution of the 'story he had often heard [...]
before' (for example, pp. 3, 10, 122, 139), and which is only alluded
to, never *imaged*, in the text.

From the intersection of a number of words or phrases, which
constantly recur in named images (the length of cord, the gull, the
blue cigarette packet, the sweets, the figure 8 lying on its side like
the symbol of infinity and which recurs in the rolled-up string, in
eyes, in iron rings embedded in the landing, in wood-knots in a
door, *ad infinitum*) that fascinating gap in the heart of the novel is
constructed.

This is *not* a gap comparable to the cave scene in *A Passage to
India*, or to Stavrogin's confession excised from *The Possessed*, or to
the Great War in Musil's *Man without Qualities*. It is not primarily a
narrative gap, but a *language* gap. And it is prepared from the very
first scene in the novel.

7

Language itself marks and masks and designates, but also constitutes, gaps, absences, silences. It may be said that, as a consequence, the narrative itself becomes a fabricator of gaps; but it
may be equally true to say that the gaps in the narrative alert us
to those in language.

The first sign of an absence in the narrative comes as early as the
reference to the sound of the siren in the second sentence.[15] Only
the second blast is reported; the first belongs to the world outside
the text. It demarcates, as the *nouveau roman* is so fond of doing, the
world of the text from everything that does not belong to it – that
is, everything that has not been *verbalised*, transposed into language. It introduces an 'ear-splitting violence' which is, however,
at the same time, 'a violence without purpose that remained without effect' (p. 3). Yet it will soon start producing its effects, each one
of them as purposeless as the first, each one of them signifying an
absence. Above all, the absence of (traditional narrative) *meaning*.

An accumulation of such 'signs of absence' takes place as the text
unfolds. Quite elaborately, and very early, a childhood scene is
evoked in which Mathias spent an entire afternoon drawing a
gull – 'yet it seems as if something is missing' (p. 14). In the crucial
early morning scene in the St Jacques quarter, featuring what
appears to be the first act of physical violence, the girl on whom

the violence is supposedly perpetrated is invisible. (There may not even have been violence involved, because what is first described as 'moans, inarticulate sounds' turn out to be 'pleasant, not at all sad': p. 20.) Much is made of the neat arrangement of glasses behind the café counter on p. 103, but here, too, one is missing, and the 'empty place' appears to be more conspicuous than the presence of all the other glasses. Mathias goes to the cottage of the man called either Jean or Pierre, and while his back is turned 'something must have happened' between the man and the young woman (p. 115), because suddenly there is a tension between them which did not exist before, and no 'explanation' is ever given – nor, of course, need any be given, as nothing *has* happened; only the language has signalled the possibility of a gap. A few pages later, Mathias embarks on an account of his day so far, but by the time it ends he is no longer in the cottage and the reader realises that the 'events' in the cottage have imperceptibly been decanted into language. That is to say, once again, if there *were* any 'events' to begin with, as the entire incident appears to be fabricated, from the moment Mathias is said to close his eyes on p. 109. At this stage (p. 126) the visit to the cottage already belongs to the narrative past and is narrated in the pluperfect, together with a series of other events the reader now learns for the first time.

On p. 149, without any break in the text, there is a jump from the Tuesday evening to the following morning: the kind of jump that would be perfectly acceptable in any conventional narrative but which here, where the progress of time appears to have been so fastidiously noted, strikes one as curious. And from now on such gaps will occur more and more frequently, sometimes marked typographically, sometimes not.[16] If the spell of dizziness on p. 190 appears to be psychologically motivated, Julien's sudden 'disappearance' from the cliff (p. 186) has no explanation in conventional narrative terms, whereas the jump on p. 217 tends to direct the reader's attention back to language rather than to the flow of the narrative. Mathias is engrossed in studying one of his watches, described in a long paragraph of meticulous observation, then, unexpectedly, it is interrupted: 'The end of the extended finger approaches the circle formed by the face of the watch attached to...'. This is followed by a break in the text, before it resumes: '... circle formed by the face of the watch attached to his wrist and said: "Four-fifteen, exactly."'

As the end of his stay approaches, Mathias begins deliberately to obliterate signs of his presence through the disposal of whatever 'evidence' there may be against him (notably the cigarettes and the sweets). Most telling is the account of his burning of the newspaper clipping, which involves an obliteration of the very words that have helped to constitute *him* as a character:

> He reads this printed text from beginning to end, chooses a word in it, and after tapping the ash from his cigarette, brings the red tip near the selected spot. The paper immediately turns brown. Mathias gradually presses harder. The brown spot spreads; the cigarette finally burns through the paper, leaving a round hole ringed in black. (p. 202)

8

This passage is written in the present tense, like much of the final movement in the narrative, from the time following his dizzy spell in the café, when Mathias returns to the rented room which so disconcertingly resembles the bedroom of his childhood, 'this room where he had spent his whole life' (p. 197). There are fewer than ten shifts from the past tense to the present in *Le Voyeur*; and as this is one of the most noticeable markers in grammar of a change in levels of perception, the strategy demands special attention from a reader bent on discovering the links the novel establishes between language and narrative.

The first slip into the present tense occurs almost imperceptibly (so much so, in effect, that the English translation ignores it altogether): as the boat hovers alongside the quay, waiting to dock, 'On closer inspection, the stone rim drew almost imperceptibly closer' (p. 6); just over a page later, this sentence is repeated verbatim (a parallel regrettably missed in English, which replaces 'closer' with 'nearer': p. 7). The five paragraphs in between these two identical sentences are written in the present, as if placed in relief against the surrounding description in the past tense. The passage clearly does not belong 'naturally' to the description of Mathias's arrival on the boat; in a conventional reading it would be read as the evocation of a previous impression, which could date only from Mathias's last perception of the scene, thirty-odd years ago. This may intimate that nothing has changed in the interim, but the fuller implications will only become clear in the persistence of the archetypal image of the tortured Violette, on which all subsequent comparable images, whether real or imagined, have become superimposed. Certainly, one is reminded of Robbe-Grillet's discussion of cinematic imaging in the Introduction to *L'Année dernière à Marienbad*:

> *Une imagination, si elle est assez vive, est toujours au présent. Les souvenirs que l'on 'revoit', les régions lointaines, les rencontres à venir, ou même les episodes passés que chacun arrange dans sa tête en modifiant le cours tout à loisir, il y a là comme un film intérieur qui se déroule continuellement en nous-mêmes* [If an imagining is strong enough it is always in the present. The memories one 'sees again', the distant regions, the encounters still to come, or even the past episodes which everybody arranges in his/her mind, modifying their course entirely at one's leisure, all of this is like an interior film which continually unfolds in ourselves]. (Robbe-Grillet 1961:16)

It would also confirm Freud's assertion that the processes of the unconscious are '*timeless*; that is, they are not ordered temporally, are not altered by the passage of time; they have no relation to time whatsoever' (Freud 1974:187, translation slightly altered).

If this passage represents memory, or imagination, the use of the present tense would be the only technique available to *distinguish* it from the 'reality' of the scene witnessed by Mathias – a distinction which simultaneously emphasises the disconcerting way in which it overlaps 'with reality'. Both these observations are of the greatest importance for one's reading of the Violette scene(s).

A feature of the passage in question is its description of a curious mixture of ordered lines and confused outlines, of patterns regularly divided into two halves (two vertical surfaces in shadow, two in brilliant sunshine; the scene and its reflection; a parapet divided in two, one dark triangle and one bright; or the contrast between straight lines and curves, read by Bachelard (1957:136) as male and female), providing, *en abyme*, the interplay between the 'real' and the 'imaginary', and/or the present and the past on which so much of the narrative appears to be constructed. It becomes, in short, a geometrical schema of the novel as a whole.

This recurs quite soon, in the first description of the child Mathias drawing the seagull: in the middle of a paragraph flowing along easily in the past tense ('Mathias looked for the floating cigarette pack – it was impossible to tell exactly where it would surface again': p. 13), there is a sudden shift in the focus of the description, marked by the use of the present: 'He is sitting at the table wedged into the window recess, facing the window.' This continues for two paragraphs, concluding with a review of the drawing the child has made: 'Yet it seems as if something is missing' (p. 14) – repeated, more affirmatively, in the opening line of the following paragraph: 'There was something missing from the drawing.'

We have already noted the importance of objects or events 'missing' from the narrative, highlighting it in this way, through a switch in tenses, focuses the attention not only on the trope of gaps and absences, but on the processes of language through which it is brought to our attention. The process of drawing the gull has little interest as such: the 'point' of the whole scene is its conclusion about 'something missing', repeated in both present and past tenses.

These two brief excursions into the present tense (which, ironically, evoke the narrative *past*) should be sufficient warning to the reader to evaluate the first overtly 'imaginary' incident on pp. 25–6 in which Mathias visualises (and the narrator verbalises) the possible scene of his first sale to the Leduc family. Before the scene is concluded, the narrative reverts to the past tense. Having established its difference from the surrounding narrative, there is no need to maintain the present tense, it has fulfilled its function as a marker, and the rest of the incident can now be inserted into the ordinary flow of the narrative, illustrating the *lack* of definitive distinctions between 'real' and 'imaginary'. That is, if Mathias were to be considered as a person within a narrative, such distinctions would matter to *him*; but to the *narrator* (and, by extension, the reader) to whom everything in the text, real or imaginary in story terms, exists on the level of *language*, they are of little concern.

The next shift from past to present occurs in what appears to be the imagining of a scene of bondage and torture inspired by the newspaper report, and superimposed on Mathias's earlier visit to the (empty) bedroom above *A L'Espérance* where he saw a picture of a small praying girl, superimposed on the imagined violent scene in the St Jacques district on the mainland: from a number of scenes resuscitated from the past (whether in Mathias's mind, or purely in language), a kind of continuous present is created.

This collage effect is so strong that by the time the novel reaches the 'scandalous' experience in the Leduc household, where the photograph of Jacqueline on the sideboard merges with the ever-present, obsessive image of Violette,[17] there is no *need* to highlight it in the present tense. In fact, a shift to the present would have set apart the purported imagining so much as to lose the very scandal of its total insertion into the narrative reality of the moment. And it is only at the end of Part I that the present recurs, once again in a most striking fashion – and once again, irresponsibly, suppressed in the English translation – when Mathias is said to approach the crossroads near the lighthouse. Even before he arrives at that place of fatal choice he imagines (in the regular past tense) the road branching off to the Marek farm on the left, and the path turning to the right, 'where young Violette *is tending* sheep at the ridge of the cliff' (p. 71, my emphasis).[18] The concluding passage is written entirely in the present, leaving it to the reader to decide whether to read it 'literally', as a description of what is actually taking place in the story, or as the kind of construct introduced by the previous uses of the present tense.

Certainly, the latter kind of reading appears to be confirmed almost immediately after the reader's discovery of the famous gap, when on pp. 80–1 Mathias fabricates his first alibi about visiting the Marek farm (that is, once again, if one insists on reading it as 'story'), as well as in the account of the presumed visit to the fisherman's cottage, where Mathias's gift of a watch to the anxious young girl is again narrated in the present.[19]

Another highly significant switch of tenses, this time announced quite explicitly, comes in the café scene where the old fisherman narrates the legend of the annual sacrifice of a young girl: '*it was strange that he used only the present tense*' (p. 189, my emphasis). This must be a pretty clear pointer, both forward and back, towards one's reading of such passages.

We have reached the final movement in the novel: after his black-out, Mathias finds himself back in his room – this archetypal room which subsumes within it all the similar rooms of his life, just as Violette becomes the emblem of all the images of violated girls (pp. 191–4). The description switches to the present tense in a passage which, like the original one, is dominated by the perception of intersecting lines and planes, before it cross-fades, as it were, into another evocation of the 'primal scene'. As Mathias returns to his present, the narrative resumes in the past tense – but only for a few pages, when what seems like a recapitulation of the first seagull scene nudges the account back into the present

(p. 194). And now, as if suspended between times, the narrative remains in the present for most of the rest of the text. Briefly, on pp. 210–11, the tenses appear to go haywire, provoked by a recurrence of versions of the primal scene; but after this brief disturbance, 'everything becomes even calmer' (p. 211) and the present tense is maintained until, significantly, the previously signalled break in the description of the watch, the novel's primary emblem of time. Then, for the final two pages or so (pp. 217–19), the narrative reverts to the past in order to match as closely as possible the scene of departure with that of arrival, confirming the text as a whole as a feat of language. And it ends, as it began, with a sustained act of meticulous observation.

9

This passion of observation is expressed in the fixation with eyes, and of course with voyeurism, in the text. We know that Robbe-Grillet initially intended titling his novel *Le Voyageur*. In French, this still allowed him a play on both words (even if *voyeur* is never used in the text), whose different meanings depend on a single syllable: Vareille (1981:59) openly terms Mathias '*un voyageur voyeur*'. In English, regrettably, the choice of *salesman* sacrifices this important component of the ludic enterprise on the level of language.

Many critics have gone to great lengths to argue that *voyeur*, in addition to its psychosexual meaning, may also designate, simply, 'someone who looks', a spectator.[20] This is not implausible, given the obsession with gazing and observation throughout the text. In one way or another the function of looking, either unidirectionally or reciprocally, is exercised by every single character[21] (from the moment Mathias notices the small girl on the landing staring at him), as well as by seagulls or even inanimate objects.[22] But there is no doubt that Mathias is the main focalising agent of the narrative.

However, does this mean that he is also the psychosexual *voyeur* of the text?[23] For critics like Morrissette (1963), Stoltzfus (1964), Weil-Malherbe (1965), Sturrock (1969), Rault (1975) and many others there is no doubt about this; for them, consequently, there can also be no doubt about the (nature of) the crime committed between Parts I and II of the novel.[24] But, as Janvier (1964) and others have argued, even if there were a murder in the central gap in the narrative, it need not have been committed by Mathias; according to the deliberately vague information the narrative appears to provide, he might have *witnessed* a murder committed by someone else – the fisherman Pierre/Jean Robin, for instance, who clearly bore a smouldering grudge towards Jacqueline, or even young Julien, who has also had an humiliating involvement with the girl, as a result of which he either tried to commit suicide (p. 124), or was thrown into the sea by his jeering friends (p. 167). In each of these two hypotheses Mathias would indeed function as a stereotypical voyeur.

Another view, expressed by Morrissette (1963:103–4), is that the real voyeur of the story is Julien, whom he sees as a witness to the murder (and a possible replication of Mathias in his youth, '*jeune, innocent, mais déjà attiré vers la criminalité* [young, innocent, but already drawn towards criminality]'. But this seems to me tenuous, not only because in the overall plan of the story Julien[25] plays too minor a role to be singled out in the title, but especially because, as I have suggested earlier, there must be considerable doubt about the 'reality' of the whole scene on the clifftop between Mathias and the youngster.

An alternative solution may seem to lie in reverting to Mathias as the principal voyeur of the narrative, *whether he commits the murder or not.* Even if he is the murderer, and/or has committed similar murders in the past, what matters to the narrative is not the commission or omission of the crime, but the *witnessing* of it. In such a reading, Mathias may in fact commit the crime *with the sole purpose of watching it happen.* And everything leading up to the gap in the story, as well as everything that follows it, would then become part of the overall voyeuristic process of contemplating the crime, in actuality or in the mind, prospectively or retrospectively.

The main problem with all these approaches is that they persist in taking psychosexuality as their point of departure, *as if the narrative reality of the story were above suspicion* – precisely that part of novelistic writing which the practitioners of the *nouveau roman* most emphatically try subvert in their work, even if, as I have suggested, the move towards 'pure textuality' also, paradoxically, appears to emphasise the (reader's) need of story.

There exists, *behind* Mathias, another voyeuristic instance in the text: the narrator. His presence (in this context there seems to me no doubt about the male gendering of the narrator's gaze)[26] has already been signalled above, with reference to the passage in which Mathias and his perception are included within the broader focus of an observer *behind* him. And many critics have commented on the fact that the *regard* which informs so much of the *nouveau roman*, most particularly *Le Voyeur*, is by no means innocent. Robbe-Grillet (1963:65) may insist as much as he wishes that, '*Les choses sont là et [...] elles ne sont rien d'autre que des choses, chacune limité à soi* [The things are there and [...] they are nothing but things, each one restricted to itself]'. But the *selection* of 'things' which litter the pages of *Le Voyeur* represents a very deliberate act of choice. Mathias may appear randomly to fix his gaze on whatever comes into his field of vision, but he is not himself, as Sturrock (1969:182) would argue, the author of that field of vision. Its scope and its limits, and whatever is focused on within it, are most carefully chosen and circumscribed by the narrator. If, cumulatively, these objects constitute 'une machine infernale' and a suggestion of fatality (Alter 1966:23), this is the result of the voyeuristic impulse of the narrator, and no-one else.

This is confirmed by Morrissette (1963:87), even if he chooses to speak of the 'author' rather than the 'narrator':

> *C'est l'auteur lui-même, absent, impersonnel (mais doué d'une 'vision' spéciale de l'univers qu'il crée), qui ordonne le monde et les choses, les livrant ensuite à son personnage central* [It is the author himself, absent; impersonal (but endowed with a special 'vision' of the universe he creates) who controls the world and the objects, afterwards presenting them to his central character].[27]

It is demonstrated to singular effect in one of the last scenes of the novel, where Mathias looks out through the café window, observing a fisherman in red clothes walking along the pier outside (p. 207). The gaze is interrupted when the proprietor offers Mathias a cup of coffee; after their brief conversation, Mathias notices that while his attention has been elsewhere the fisherman 'seems to have stayed in the same place [...] yet his regular pace must have brought him noticeably closer during these last remarks'. The observation is repeated a second time. The only conclusion the reader can draw from this scene, is that all of 'external reality' in *Le Voyeur* depends on Mathias.[28] But, once again, a narrator has been observing, and commenting on, Mathias in the act of observation. Which means that Mathias's own 'reality' – not just what he observes, but his own observation of it – is produced by the narrator as a textual construct.

It is this same textualised narrator who chooses, not the objects of his narrated world, but the *words* to signify them, and who then arranges them in particular configurations which on the story level turn out to be fatal: the gaze of a young girl with large eyes (looking, possibly, at something – or someone? a narrator? – *behind* Mathias); sweets to lure her; a length of cord forming the pattern of a figure 8 with which she may be tied up, hands behind her back, legs apart; a gull hovering above, looking, looking; cigarettes which may be used to torture her... It amounts to what Kundera (1995:215), in a different context, calls 'a conspiracy of details'. The obsessive presentation to Mathias of all these 'objects', in ever-tightening loops of proximity, establishes the framework of reference within which the reader reads the absence in the heart of the novel: the words are the traces of that absence; the crime is the sign of its difference, and of its constant deferral. In this reading, Mathias is as much the subject as the object of voyeurism. *The true perpetrator of the crime is the language in which both 'Violette' and Mathias are ensnared.*

But this language can only be activated with the full complicity of the reader. Starting with a consideration of the title, Kelly (1993:6) proposes that at the very moment of being named, the novel 'also engages in a form of commercial exploitation by promising the satisfaction of the readers' desires; yet the title that draws the reader in comes in the course of the novel to reflect back upon the reader and interrogate his motives for reading the novel'. In this way the processes of voyeurism are both underscored and extended. Perhaps, as Kelly suggests, 'voyeurism is itself a formal characteristic of conventional realist literary tradition' (p. 24). In *this* text, the way that the story of Mathias's exploits is told, or not told, may well be an attempt to alert the reader to the mechanics of reading itself. In the absence of a central 'scandal' in the text on which to focus, the reader would thus have no choice but to focus on the body of the text rather than on any female body exposed in spectacle.

This is corroborated by Mathias's ritualistic burning of the newspaper cutting towards the end; in the reporting of his mental imaginings, Violette was burned (as witch); here, in the only 'real' act of burning in the text, not the girl but *the language that fabricated her in the text* is annulled.

If we accept that the narrator is nowhere visible in the text – that, in fact, the text is the manifestation of his absence – this disembodied creature cannot be a voyeur. The only, ultimate, voyeur produced by the text, in collusion with the reader, is language itself.[29] This is its scandal, and its crime. In the demonstration of its potent seductions of both characters and reader, language represents also the triumph of the text.

11

Making and Unmaking

Gabriel García Márquez: *One Hundred Years of Solitude*

1

'I merely wanted to tell the story of a family who for a hundred years did everything they could in order not to have a son with a pig's tail', Gabriel García Márquez explained, no doubt tongue in cheek, about the writing of *One Hundred Years of Solitude*, 'and [...] ending up having one' (quoted in Wood 1990:24). That there must be more to it is obvious from a mere glance at the veritable library of scholarly studies which have been accumulating ever since the first publication of *Cien Años de Soledad* in 1967.[1]

There have been illuminating studies on the relationship between the local and the universal in the novel, and on the relationship between Márquez and Cervantes; on the nature of magic realism; on the themes of incest, and genealogy, and taboo, and patriarchy; on characterisation, and tragedy, and comedy, and musicality; on mythology and history, and the mythology of history, and the history of mythology; on the temporal structure of the novel, and on its spatial structure, and on its spatio-temporal structure; there have been Marxist readings, and Feminist readings, and narratological readings, and deconstructive readings; psychoanalytical readings and mythopoeic readings and biographical readings. Yet in spite of all this, in one study after the other, there are admissions about the seeming inexhaustibility of the book, its 'elusive and enigmatic' nature (see Williamson 1987:45). It is, clearly, as Bell (1993:41) says, 'a work, like Kafka's novels, specifically designed both to invite and to resist interpretation'.

Within the context of the text's relationship with language one of the most stimulating essays is Aníbal González's study on 'Translation and Genealogy' (González 1987), which has the additional advantage of reading *One Hundred Years of Solitude* against the backdrop of the *Don Quixote*. González argues that not only the South American novel, but the novel as a genre, has its origins in the notion of translation, specifically 'in the transport – through violence or exchange – of meaning from other texts and other languages into the literary text' (González 1987:77; cf. also p. 65, and p. 79 n. 24).

From a close scrutiny of the many references to foreign languages in the text (a feature to which we shall soon return), González discusses the imperative of translation which arises from such confrontations. This concept is read against the background of three theoretical approaches: the first, suggested by Walter Benjamin, posits the existence of an overriding 'sacred text', an 'expressionless and creative Word, that which is meant in all languages' (González 1987:69); the second, derived from Derrida, focuses on 'a transgressive struggle between [...] two equally "proper" languages, one of which tries to deny the other's specificity' (p. 70); the third, based on Borges, proposes 'that the notion of translation is intimately linked to the nature of literature, and that translation can serve as an instrument of critical inquiry into the workings of literature' (p. 71).

On these premises González proposes an exciting extension of the notion of 'translation' by reading into the narrative of *One Hundred Years* a Derridean 'dissemination' of meanings from different signifying systems, discovering a parallel between the Buendías' task of translating the gypsy manuscript into 'the language of kinship (with all that it implies in terms of the incest taboo and of the importance of proper names)' (ibid.:72). This reading is motivated by the consideration that 'translation and incest both share a transgressive nature, both are "improper" acts that imply breaching the barriers between members of the same family or between two languages' (p. 75). He concludes this line of argument by asserting that

> translation, like incest, leads back to self-reflexiveness, to a cyclonic turning upon one's self which erases all illusions of solidity, all fantasies of a 'pure language', all mirages of 'propriety', and underscores instead language's dependence on the very notion of 'otherness', of difference, in order to signify 'something', as well as the novel's similar dependence on 'other' discourses (those of science, law and religion, for example) to constitute itself. (p. 76)

It is a seductive reading, even if one may question the parallel González assumes between sexual relations between individuals linked by kinship and intercourse between languages (like Sanskrit and Spanish) which belong to the same Indo-European family.[2] And it may come close to breaking down when the relationship also concerns, as it does in *One Hundred Years*, languages like Spanish and Guajiro (the indigenous tongue Arcadio and Amarante learn before they can speak their own) or Papiamento (which Aureliano junior speaks, haltingly, to the old West-Indian 'Negro'). Also, not all the languages that feature in the text impose a need for translation: in many episodes the function of those languages – ranging from Latin to English, or from the gypsy language to the one fabricated by Fernanda) – lies precisely in the fact that, at least in their specific context, they *cannot* be translated.

This does not mean that González's reading can be discounted; it remains one of the most stimulating contributions to the growth industry of writings about Márquez in general and *One Hundred Years of Solitude* in particular. But it does mean that reading language as translation does not go far enough towards illuminating the view of language presented by the text, and its relationship with the narrative that unfolds in it.

2

Certainly, the proliferation of references to foreign languages in the text (foreign, that is, to the Spanish spoken in Macondo) provides an important early pointer towards the role of language in this novel. As González (1987:66–8) already shows, an early distinction is made between the language of Macondo and that of the gypsies when the 'tender obscenities' whispered by José Arcadio in the gypsy girl's ear 'came out of her mouth translated into another language' (p. 35); Arcadio and Amaranta are taught Guajiro by the family's royal servant Visitación; when Rebeca arrives it turns out that she, too, can speak Guajiro; in addition to Spanish and the gypsy language, as well as several others, Melquíades speaks 'a complex hodgepodge' (p. 65); after being tied to the chestnut tree in the yard old José Arcadio Buendía speaks a strange tongue which turns out to be Latin (p. 75); José Arcadio's Spanish is 'larded with sailor slang' and his 'unusual masculinity [is] completely covered with tattoos of words in several languages intertwined in blue and red' (p. 80); Pietro Crespi translates the sonnets of Petrarch (p. 94); the manuscripts of Melquíades which provide the ultimate clue to the 'hundred years of solitude' of the Buendía family, are written in Sanskrit; and in his attempts to translate them, the youngest Aureliano has to learn, not only Sanskrit, but 'English and French and a little Latin and Greek' (p. 309), while he also picks up Papiamento (p. 311). In addition to the examples cited by González, languages other than Spanish obsessively intrude in the world of Macondo: Amaranta dreams of a Utopia 'of handsome men and women who spoke a childlike language' (p. 94); Arcadio speaks to the Indians in their own language (p. 97); what marks Mr Herbert as an outsider is that he speaks 'broken Spanish' (p. 186); Fernanda, as we have noted, invents her own language in order to avoid uttering words she regards as improper (p. 175); Mr Brown is marked by his 'strange tongue' (p. 208); Meme learns English from her friends in the enclave of the Banana Company (p. 225); the old Catalonian bookseller speaks his native tongue (p. 297); the labels on the bottles in the pharmacy are in Latin (p. 301); the encyclopedia from which Aureliano Segundo teaches his children is in English (p. 302), and so on.

But there is also what one may call a 'language of things' in many of the mysterious happenings in the Buendía household (like the empty flask which grows too heavy to be moved, or the pan of water which boils without any fire under it, observed by José Arcadio Buendía and Aureliano, 'unable to explain them but interpreting them as predictions of the material': p. 36). In the episode where Meme is taken away from Macondo to the convent, the young woman, having renounced speaking altogether, travels through what appears like a landscape without language, but in fact it is a landscape which has itself turned into a reified language, and on behalf of Meme (who registers nothing herself) the narrator reads it as if it were a book, allowing the reader to rediscover in it the whole history of Macondo (p. 240).

Once the reader has been alerted to the existence of such other signifying systems, the process is expanded. There is a language of the future read by Pilar Ternera from her cards. There is a language of the past which can only be read by deciphering codes like the galleon stranded in the moors or the submerged suit of armour. There is a language spoken by the ghost of José Arcadio Buendía which only his great-great- grandson Aureliano can understand (p. 216). There is a language of sex, markedly different from the

language of social intercourse, in the encounters between Pilar
Ternera and, first, José Arcadio, then Aureliano, as there is between
Aureliano Segundo and Petra Cotes (quite distinct from the articulation of his relationship with his emotionally repressed wife Fernanda); and ultimately a language of 'lyrical voracity' (p. 327)
between the youngest Aureliano and his aunt Amaranta Ursula,[3]
which begins, significantly, in an amorous encounter precisely
while her husband is writing a letter (p. 302), as if each activity is
a mirroring of the other. And, in confirmation of the language of
sex, there is a clear hint of a gendered language when it is said of
Remedios the Beauty that 'men's words would not penetrate her'
(p. 194).[4]

What all these moments cumulatively come to communicate, I
would argue, is both the *isolation* of Macondo from the outside
world and its distressing *vulnerability* to threats from that outside.[5]
Or, in different terms, the sense of *difference* imposed by language
on the reader's perception of Macondo and the rest of the world
(which in itself, of course, is shown to be multidimensional, or
stratified: the world of science and the world of intuition; Europe
and the 'Third World'; different experiences and definitions of
sociopolitics, commerce, history, culture, and so on).

This awareness of difference permeates, and determines, almost
every aspect of the novel, which presents difference in terms of
time and space (here-and-now as opposed to other places, other
times); in terms of inside and outside; in terms of beginning and
ending; in terms of whatever in a given situation is perceived to be
real and what as not-real, unreal, supra-real, imaginary, or magical;
in terms of the identity, of Self and Other. It quite literally establishes and subverts, creates and undoes, makes and unmakes the
narrative world. *Hacer para dehacer* (Márquez 1987:347) – 'to make
[or to do] in order to unmake [or undo]' – is a key phrase for *One
Hundred Years*. It designates specific actions of specific characters:
Colonel Aureliano Buendía who makes little gold fishes which he
sells for gold to make new fishes to sell for gold to make new
fishes, until he stops the selling and confines himself to manufacturing only two fishes a day 'and when he finished twenty-five he
would melt them down and start all over again' (p. 216); or Amaranta who weaves her shroud by day only to unweave it, like
Penelope in the *Odyssey*, at night (p. 212). But it also informs the
overall design of the novel, its patterns of creation and/or evolution (the founding of Macondo, the establishment of the Banana

Company, the love relationships, all the enterprises of the imagination) followed by decay, destruction and obliteration. The Banana Company grows into a monster until it is literally washed away by rain; consecutive attempts of José Arcadio Buendía, Colonel Aureliano and others to smash and destroy everything they have established during their lives are followed by the apocalyptic wind that blows Macondo from the face of the earth.

In the final analysis these creations or imaginings are obliterated by *language*. After José Arcadio Segundo's horrifying experience of the worst act of annihilation in the novel prior to its apocalypse (the massacre that ends the workers' strike and his discovery of the train of 'almost two hundred freight cars' transporting the corpses of the dead to be dumped in the sea: p. 250) he returns to Macondo where a woman dresses his wound and offers him some coffee; but when he tries to discuss the event, the woman cuts him short: 'There haven't been any dead here [...] Since the time of your uncle, the colonel, nothing has happened in Macondo' (p. 251).

This goes further than the earlier court decision in the dispute between workers and management of the Banana Company, 'that the workers did not exist' (p. 246), or the subsequent official announcement that, 'Nothing has happened in Macondo, nothing has ever happened, and nothing will ever happen' (p. 252), because these pronouncements merely establish the discrepancy between 'reality' or 'history' on the one hand, and its official versions on the other. When the woman addresses José Arcadio Segundo it is the ordinary language of ordinary people which accepts and disseminates as truth the 'fact' that nothing has happened whereas the reader has just been told that something *has* happened. The point is no longer whether something is 'officially' announced or 'popularly' believed, or even that the events witnessed by José Arcadio Segundo may be corroborated by at least some historical versions of the great United Fruit Company strike in Colombia in 1928 (see Martin 1987:107–8 or Wood 1990:vii): the point is that at one moment in the narrative a series of events (the strike and its outcome) is established by and in language, and that at another moment the same series is obliterated, once again in and by language.

Naturally, in such a situation, the reader's first reaction is to read the matter as a 'cover-up', whether imposed by the authorities or induced by shock among the population, and to trust what the narrator has just revealed about the massacre – especially when it concerns a character with whose viewpoint the narrator has persuaded us to sympathise. But what if the narrator's version of what Martin (1987:107) terms 'the central shaping episode of the entire novel', is just as suspect as that of the officials, or of the kindly woman?

Let us look at another episode, near the end of the novel, when the youngest Aureliano leaves the corpse of his beloved Ursula Amaranta, puts his new-born pig-tailed child in a basket and goes in search of help:

> He knocked at the door of the pharmacy, where he had not visited lately, and he found a carpenter shop. The old woman who opened the door with a lamp in her hand took pity on his delirium and insisted that no, there had never been a pharmacy there, nor had she ever known a woman with a thin neck and sleepy eyes named Mercedes. (p. 333)

Once again the reader still conditioned by a particular convention of reading might wonder who to believe: the woman of the pharmacy, or the narrator? Unlike the Good Samaritan encountered by José Arcadio Buendía this woman has no 'reason' to cover up. And the narrator does specify that she sympathises with his 'delirium'. Given the state Aureliano is in, he may well be suffering from a form of delusion. Yet the reader has encountered the pharmacy before, and knows about the girl Mercedes who has presumably left Macondo with her fiancé Gabriel Márquez when he went off to Paris 'with two changes of clothing, a pair of shoes, and the complete works of Rabelais' (p. 325). We may even know from a variety of sources, including a number of interviews with Márquez himself, that this Gabriel bears a strong resemblance to the 'real' Latin American author who left Colombia for Paris – the only apparent difference being that the Gabriel in the book carries a Rabelais with him while the Gabriel outside of it took *A Journal of the Plague Year* by Defoe.

'The suggestion', says Wood (1990:55), 'is not that history and fiction are the same, but that the borders take a lot of traffic, and have been known to shift' (p. 55). Certainly much can be made (and has been made) of the two texts which largely coincide in *One Hundred Years* while nevertheless retaining their differences: the manuscripts of Melquíades and 'the book of Gabriel' (Wood 1990:52).[6] But the two episodes I have referred to, and above all the stupendous apocalypse at the end (when it turns out that what the Buendía family has been experiencing over seven generations coincides exactly with what the old gypsy wrote down a century before, each the perfect supplement to the other, each perfectly cancelling the other), amount to more than a choice between two versions. What is really illuminated by them, and by countless other moments in the narrative, is that only by virtue of language do such versions, and such choices, become thinkable. On each occasion when the community of Macondo experiences a form of obliteration – whether in the form of the sleeping sickness, or the imposed amnesia following the massacre of workers, or the near-interminable rain which all but washes away the town, and ultimately the hurricane which obliterates the whole place (and Melquíades's manuscripts with it), *language* enters into the void to recover from silence everything that would otherwise have been lost – that is, everything which has been established by language to begin with. This goes far beyond what Martin (1987:104) and innumerable others have explored as instances of circularity. It demonstrates the awe-inspiring capabilities of language, through which a reality can be established by weaving together a textual world of signifieds, and then can be undone again by severing the link between signifiers and signifieds. It is an act of prestidigitation which outperforms anything the gypsies first brought to Macondo. It is both a celebration and a radical questioning of language. Language giveth and language taketh away. It establishes links in time and space, and cancels them. It does and undoes. *Hacer para dehacer.*

3

But language can only function significantly in this manner if it can be *seen* to be doing so – in other words, if it highlights itself, self-consciously, in the act of making and breaking. One of the ways in which language foregrounds itself, we have seen, is in consciously setting up Macondo (and its language) in distinction to the outside world (and its many languages). But there are other strategies as well, and each of them modifies, and adds different dimensions to, this general perception.

Perhaps the most visible of these strategies to highlight language is the trope of *writing*. It begins early in the first chapter, when not content with witnessing the marvels of Melquíades, José Arcadio Buendía insists on getting a set of *written* instructions from the gypsy, 'in his own handwriting [...] so that he would be able to make use of the astrolabe, the compass, and the sextant' (p. 11). At first sight writing appears to confer a sense of authority on the gypsy's language – which would be the exact opposite of Derrida's *écriture* – but this soon turns out to be, like most of the later instances of writing in the narrative, an illusion, because all the gypsy's instructions lead nowhere, or, if they may be said to lead anywhere, it is only into a Borgesian labyrinth of dead-ends and forking paths.

In Macondo, a world 'so recent that many things lacked names' (p. 9), an adamic process of naming is set in motion by the gypsy's instructions – and throughout the novel the activity, first of writing, and later of deciphering, the manuscripts of Melquíades, will form an undercurrent to all the multifarious other activities and incidents in the narrative.

When the sleeping sickness descends on the town, inherited from the Indians who have been silenced by the processes of colonisation, it becomes necessary to attach written name-tags to all objects:

> With an inked brush he marked everything with its name: *table, chair, clock, door, wall, bed, pan* [...] Little by little, studying the infinite possibilities of a loss of memory, he realized that the day would come when things would be recognized by their inscriptions but that no one would remember their use. Then he became more explicit: The sign that he hung on the neck of the cow was an exemplary proof of the way in which the inhabitants of Macondo were prepared to fight against loss of memory: *This is the cow. She must be milked every morning so that she will produce milk, and the milk must be boiled in order to be mixed with coffee to make coffee and milk.* Thus they went on living in a reality that was slipping away, momentarily captured by words, but which would escape irremediably when they forgot the values of the written letters. (p. 46)

If the danger appears to be averted when Melquíades arrives with a magic potion to dispel both the insomnia and its corollary, amnesia, we are reminded towards the end that the escape has been illusory too. This happens when the last Aureliano,

significantly named Aureliano Babilonia, is revealed to be 'a man
[...] holed up in written reality' (p. 314). The Spanish phrases it
even more strongly: '*encastillado en la realidad escrita*' (Márquez
1987:425). As Minta (1987:177) puts it,

> On the final page he discovers, in the words of Emir Rodríguez
> Monegal, that he is simply 'a ghost who has been dreamed by
> another man', just a fictional character, 'trapped in a labyrinth of
> words', and that his fate, completely conterminous with the
> Macondo that is dying, is to be annihilated so totally that not
> even a memory will remain.

Like Tweedledum and Tweedledee in Carroll's *Through the Looking-
Glass*, Aureliano turns out to be the product of another man's
dream, the prophetic writing of Melquíades – but at the very
moment of his reading about his end as he approaches the moment
of his end,[7] Aureliano is recovered, together with the whole written
history that has just been cancelled by his reading, by *another* text,
written by (a persona of) that Gabriel Márquez who earlier escaped
from Melquíades's text by leaving Macondo for Paris. Either way,
he remains a figment of writing – but in the process both his
writers, Melquíades and Gabriel, have also been transformed into
écriture: Melquíades who is written by Gabriel, and Gabriel,
who has first been written by Melquíades.[8]

No wonder that when the first government-appointed magis-
trate, Apolinar Moscote, arrives in Macondo with a flurry of written orders, José Arcadio Buendía calmly informs him that 'in this
town we do not give orders with pieces of papers' (p. 53). The
snowballing irony is that as language begins to draw more and
more attention to itself in the form of writing, it also increasingly
undermines its own validity. This is both the quandary and the
triumph of a text which 'establishes the frontiers of reality within a
book and the frontiers of a book within reality' (Fuentes 1990:192).

When Colonel Aureliano falls in love with Remedios and is
driven to writing poetry it would seem to offer an escape from
the developing conundrum:

> The house became full of love. Aureliano expressed it in poetry
> that had no beginning or end. He would write it on the harsh
> pieces of parchment that Melquíades gave him, on the bathroom
> walls, on the skin of his arms. (p. 61)

And poetry remains his most urgent activity throughout the years of his thirty-two armed uprisings, which would seem to lend credence to a view of written language as, at the very least, a search for meaning. But if the first of his love poems held no meaning for others because they were without beginning or end, his later outpourings remain strictly private and no-one is ever allowed a glimpse of them. And a central activity of his preparations for suicide, as he attempts to destroy 'all trace of his passage through the world' (p. 146) is the methodical burning of all his poetry. Far from being a demonstration of language as communication, Aureliano's writing wholly escapes from the public domain to become as much a secret and solitary indulgence as José Arcadio Buendía's habit (copied by several of his descendants) of talking to himself. This incident will, later, reflect new light on a small scene towards the end of the novel, when one of Aureliano Babilonia's intimate friends, Alvaro, leaves Macondo on 'an eternal ticket on a train that never stopped travelling' (p. 325); and as he watches the passing landscape from the window of his coach, and sends his friends postcards about these 'instantaneous images', he is described 'as if he were tearing up and throwing into oblivion some long, evanescent poem' (p. 325). Recalling the destruction of Colonel Aureliano's poetry, this would suggest that the whole world of geography and history through which Alvaro is travelling, is transformed into writing – which voids it of meaning and makes it destructible.

Acquiring the skill of writing appears to be an important concern in the Buendía household: Aureliano teaches it to Rebeca, Amaranta teaches Aureliano José, Fernanda teaches her children, Ursula teaches Amaranta Ursula; and sooner or later they all turn into more or less assiduous letter-writers. Yet for all their inveterate writing not one of them ever achieves anything in the process. In her old age, when Rebeca compulsively writes to the Bishop, she never receives any reply; Aureliano's letters to Ursula during his absence on his many wars communicate either a distorted image of what he is engaged in, or a totally false impression (receiving a note he has written from Santiago, Cuba, Ursula concludes: 'We've lost him forever': p. 124); and what General Moncada writes to him to remind him 'of their common aim to humanize the war' (p. 132) has so little effect that it might just as well not have been written. The same applies to the several letters written by Colonel Aureliano to the president after the war (pp. 150, 198). It is fitting that the terms for peace between Conservatives and Liberals (like, much later, the ultimatum to the striking workers, p. 248) should also be put in writing, only to be ridiculed and negated by both sides (p. 141). And as for the destructive consequences of writing, it is revealing that the prelude to Arcadio's rise towards eminence as an unscrupulous tyrant is his copying of his military uniform from a design in Melquíades's books (p. 91).

There are innumerable love-letters in the narrative, but they meet with no better fate. Rebeca, having finally won her family's consent to marry Crespi, writes 'a jubilant letter' to her fiancé (p. 64) – but the moment José Arcadio makes his appearance she forgets all about her earlier feelings and intentions. José Arcadio himself presents another form of writing, the tattoos all over his body, including his monstrous penis – to the extent that González (1987:73) speaks of his 'body-become-text', but this writing remains 'cryptic' (p. 80) and cannot be deciphered by anyone in Macondo. Crespi declares his love to Amaranta in 'wild notes' (p. 96), which she returns unopened. Aureliano Babilonia and Ursula Amaranta correspond during her absence in Brussels, but when she comes back they both discover that their 'real' selves, whatever these may be, have nothing at all in common with the imagined Other each has been writing to. Mauricio Babilonia is practically the only one truthfully to attempt declaring his love in writing when he sends Meme a card, but it is restricted to the merest statement of intent ('We'll get together Saturday after the movies': p. 235), and it is, moreover, characterised as a laborious inscription 'by someone who could barely write' (p. 235). To compound the situation, it is this tryst which leads to their discovery by Fernanda and results in the fatal retribution that puts an end to their love. Even when writing appears to 'mean' something, it has only devastating consequences.

Fernanda and her children dutifully correspond during all the years they spend away from home – but most of their writing amounts to barefaced lying, each communicating to the other a totally false image of their lives and emotions; in due course Fernanda even places her letters in the wrong envelopes (p. 292). This puts into perspective her habit, assumed since a very early stage in her strained relations with Amaranta, never to talk to her sister-in-law again, but to communicate only in writing (p. 175). Ultimately these letters 'mean' no more and no less than Fernanda's compulsive writing to a collection of 'invisible doctors' about her imaginary complaints,[9] a correspondence which, in any case, ends 'in failure' (p. 281).[10]

The whole business of letter-writing, and the function of language demonstrated and disseminated by it, is perhaps best summarised in the wonderful episode of Amaranta's death when she invites all the people of Macondo to bring her letters which she can deliver to the dead on the other side of the grave (p. 229).

These dead-end correspondences (together with others, like the old Catalan's letters to Aureliano and his friends, the last of which remains unopened because they do not want to read what they know it must contain (p. 331), or those exchanged between Amaranta Ursula and Gaston after he has left (p. 327) lend a particular effect of futility even to small throwaway scenes like the one in which Gabriel Márquez pays a prostitute in a brothel, not 'in money but in letters to a smuggler boyfriend who was in prison on the other side of the Orinoco' (p. 320). In a way *all* these many letters which, as Barthes might say, 'star' the text, are attempts to reach out from the *here* of Macondo to the *there* of the Outside and of Otherness; from the real to the unreal or the magical; from the known to the unknown; from present to past, or future, or timelessness (it is surely meaningful that Fernanda's writing 'made her lose her sense of time': p. 293).

4

All this accumulating mass of writing, within the overarching writing of the narrative itself, culminates in the deciphering of Melquíades's manuscripts. If it is a vast act of translation, as González (1990) has shown, it is above all a testing of the validity, and of the limits, of language as writing.

The first of the family to dedicate himself to this task, after the manuscripts have originally been entrusted to José Arcadio Buendía, is Aureliano Segundo. But he receives no help from Melquíades, who nevertheless visits him regularly for long discussions. 'No one must know of their meaning', the (ghost of) the old gypsy explains, 'until a hundred years have gone by [*Nadie debe conocer su sentido mientras no hayam cumplido cien años*]' (Márquez 1987:208) – which, unfortunately, as several critics have already pointed out, has been erroneously translated by Rabassa

as 'No one must know their meaning until he has reached one
hundred years of age', demonstrating once again, I suppose, the
unreliability of written language. It almost amounts to saying
that their meaning cannot be divulged within historical time (a
century, broadly speaking, comprises the whole history of
Macondo).

Even when, many years later, Aureliano Babilonia succeeds in
deciphering the original Sanskrit (with the help of books presumably 'last read [...by] Isaac the Blindman': p. 297) they remain
incomprehensible as they turn out to be 'predictions in coded
lines of poetry' (p. 316) – a dire warning, at the very least, to any
reader who has taken note of the fate of Colonel Aureliano Buendía's poetry. Only at the 'prodigious instant' of Amaranta Ursula's
death, following the birth of their pig-tailed son who is consumed
by ants,

> Melquíades' final keys were revealed to him and he saw the
> epigraph of the parchments perfectly placed in the order of
> man's time and space: *The first of the line is tied to a tree and the
> last is being eaten by the ants.* (p. 334)

This is 'the history of the family, written by Melquíades, down
to the most trivial details, one hundred years ahead of time' –
but written, not 'in the order of man's conventional time [...]
but [...] concentrated in such a way that they coexisted in one
instant' (p. 335). This is a Postmodernist reprise of Diderot's
'Great Scroll' which also moves from a chronological/causal
relationship with Jacques's life towards commensuration and
co-existence.

As Aureliano reads, he starts catching up with himself reading;
and outside the apocalyptic wind, which also exists in the writing,
springs up to obliterate him, and the whole Macondo, in the instant
of his reading about that obliteration. Genesis and Revelations
coincide in this moment. And everything is subsumed in writing:
language has led the reader from the opening page to this last one
where the writing consumes itself – only to be decanted from the
text of the gypsy into that of Gabriel García Márquez. We are
caught, here, in a bind as inescapable as the one between that
famous beginning which was no beginning, *riverrun, past Eve and
Adam's, from swerve of shore to bend of bay*... and that ending which
was no ending, *A way a lone a last a loved a long the*

5

The great act in which the narrated world (and the condition of its own narration, the manuscripts of Melquíades) is annihilated at the end of the novel, can be effected only if it has been constructed to begin with. In both processes, as I have begun to argue, language is implicated.

One of the most visible strategies of narrative construction in *One Hundred Years*, on which a host of critics have already commented, is what Wood (1993:18) terms 'almost a signature of the book', that is, its construction of 'loops' (ibid.:67), through which it becomes possible to look both forward and back in the same moment in order to achieve an impression, or at least an illusion, of Melquíades's motto: 'Everything is known' (pp. 302, 309). This strategy has been discussed as a feature of the time structure of the novel, as a marker of the interaction between the real and the imaginary, as a mnemonic device, as an indicator of decisive turns in the plot, as a clue to the philosophy of the epistemology of the novel ... Our present concern is to look at it as a device of language which marks the textualising process as decisively as the acts of conjuring performed by Melquíades and his band in the streets of Macondo. And, of course, in a very real sense, the language of the novel as a whole *is* a trick performed by the old gypsy himself, in the solitude of the study assigned to him: a trick of prestidigitation which requires a complementary action, the attempts of Aureliano Babilonia, before it can be completed – by obliterating itself. It is a block of ice melting under its own weight, in the heat of deciphering.

In a bleak moment during his many wars, Captain Aureliano Buendía expresses the confusion of his thoughts in the face of death in rhymed verse – poetry which will eventually be destroyed in a marvellous prefiguration of the self-destruction of Melquíades's world: 'Then his thoughts became so clear that he was able to examine them forward and backward' (p. 116).

This is precisely what happens in the syntax of the famous opening line of the book:

Many years later, as he faced the firing squad, Colonel Aureliano Buendía was to remember that distant afternoon when his father took him to discover ice. (p. 9)

– a variation of which will also introduce the second major movement in the narrative: 'Years later on his deathbed Aureliano
Segundo would remember the rainy afternoon in June when he
went into the bedroom to meet his first son' (p. 152).[11]

Just as Einstein invented, from the old Newtonian categories of
time and space, the new concept of spacetime, Márquez here establishes his own distinctive *language-time* which will come to define
the novel as a whole. The effect is immediately to dislodge the time
of the narrative from ordinary time, by subverting the possibility of
a fixed point of reference: is the episode narrated in a present from
which a glimpse of the future is offered, or is this 'present' *already*
viewed from a narrative future, with the advantages and disadvantages of hindsight? In the opening passage the issue is further
complicated by the consideration that the expectation of Aureliano's death by firing squad will be frustrated in the discovery, later,
that he was in fact freed at the last moment (to be repeated in his
'second' death when his attempted suicide also fails), and that the
first episode of the narrative does *not* concern the discovery of ice,
which only follows several pages later. But these are strategies of
narrative, whereas the description of looking forward-and-back in
the same sentence is a device of *language*. The compounded result
is an impression of drifting in time, of past and future simultaneously invading the present; or, phrased differently, of a present
constantly, and precariously, exposed to invasions by past and
future.

And this becomes a weave in the text as a whole. The first
reference to the Captain facing the firing squad will be repeated
many times before it 'actually happens' (p. 111); and it is entirely
in keeping with this weave that, when he is visited by his mother
just before he is to be taken out of his cell for his execution, he
should tell her, 'Don't beg or bow down to anyone. *Pretend that they
shot me a long time ago*' (p. 108, my emphasis). It is also fitting that
when he really dies in the story, he should again relive 'that
prodigious afternoon of the gypsies when his father took him to
see ice' (p. 218), but the important point about this event is that
when he finally dies, just after he has watched the sad circus going
by, the reader discovers that this moment, too, has already been
narrated:

He locked himself up inside himself and the family finally
thought of him as if he were dead. No other human reaction

was seen in him until one October eleventh,[12] he went to the street door to watch a circus parade. (p. 215)

Only three pages later in the text the narrator will describe how Aureliano goes to the door, watches the circus, returns to the chestnut tree in the courtyard where his father used to be tied up, urinates, and dies. On the level of the story it happens *now*; on the level of the text it has already happened.

Had this happened only a few times, it would have been easy to read over it; but it becomes a constitutive factor of the text. Little Remedios's death, soon after she has reached puberty and married Aureliano, is narrated on p. 77, *followed by* an account of events which preceded it, only to catch up with the narrative present two pages later. On p. 84 Aureliano, more or less out of the blue, remarks that, 'These are not times to go around thinking about weddings'; this is followed by a broad-ranging account of events from that period, before the narrative returns to the original statement: 'It was during those days that Ursula asked him his opinion about the marriage between Pietro Crespi and Amaranta, and he answered that these were not times to be thinking about such a thing' (p. 88). In these cases, as in so many others, language is shown to fold in upon itself, regularly signalling moments in time well ahead of their occurrence in the story, in order to catch up with them later. As many critics have shown, such circles and eddies are characteristic of the text; but it is important that they should also be read as flexions of *linguistic* muscles.

Sometimes this happens in a much more elaborate way. Chapter 6 opens with a remarkable synopsis of Colonel Aureliano Buendía's life as a soldier, beginning with the cryptic statement that, 'Colonel Aureliano Buendía organized thirty-two armed uprisings and he lost them all' (p. 91). Only towards the end of Chapter 9 is this particular loop completed, recapitulating the years of his thirty-two rebellions before he returns to attempt suicide (pp. 149–51) – which clears the scene for the novel's second major movement to begin. In this case, the synopsis serves as a Derridean supplement to the ensuing elaborations which will both consume it and restate its significance.

In numerous other instances this process of complicated prolepsis appears to be orchestrated to achieve an effect of *déjà vu* – by the time Meme's son is brought home (p. 243), we have already learnt about his arrival (p. 239); when Pilar dies in the story (p. 329), she has already been declared dead by the text (p. 322): this is more than what Genette would term iteration in the text, since it is more often than not accompanied by significant variation and deviance. By the time we learn about the conditions in which Aureliano Segundo found Fernanda in her parents' home (p. 172) we already know that they were married (p. 168), but the two accounts of his quest differ quite markedly. The first time it appeared straightforward; in the retelling, as the narrator warms up to his narrative, it becomes immensely complicated.

Ultimately, all these loops serve as a *mise-en-abyme* of the overall narrative situation: the history of the Buendías as the recapitulation of a story already written a hundred years before by Melquíades. This momentous discovery – the coincidence of 'life' and 'text', of 'story' and 'history' – turns out to be cataclysmic, resulting as we have seen in the total annihilation of both the world of the Buendías and the world according to Melquíades, and simultaneously in the eruption of the Márquez text from the ashes of the world which has just been declared destroyed (a 'declaration' as momentous, and as fallacious, as the court's finding that there were no workers in the plantations, or in the official assertion that no-one died in the massacre). As Drechsel Tobin (1978:177) phrases it in the context of a somewhat different argument:

> With this conversion of the past to a visionary future where all is guessed, we are confronted with the probability that our unobtrusive narrator has taken things so calmly because he is one incarnation of the gypsy Melquíades, to whom 'everything is known'.

The text is dead; long live the text.

6

But language connects people and events not only in the time of the narrated world but within its spatial dimensions as well.

When Colonel Aureliano Buendía finds himself in prison, awaiting the firing squad, there is a passage in which he is spatially related to his father in exactly the same way as they are related in time in the novel's opening sentence: 'He thought of José Arcadio Buendía, who at that moment was thinking about him under the

dreary dawn of the chestnut tree' (p. 109). The link is more complicated than it might seem at first sight. 'Obviously' the person –
the 'him' – referred to in the second part of the sentence, is José
Arcadio Buendía whom we know to spend his days under the
chestnut tree. But a number of years after this incident, having
survived both the firing squad and suicide, Aureliano will return
from watching the circus procession to sit down under the same
tree and succumb to death. And given the ceaseless uncertainties
and ambiguities of the narrative language, it cannot be absolutely
sure, in the shadow of death which hangs over the scene, whether
it is Aureliano thinking of his father tied up under the tree, or his
father thinking of his son who will one day die in the same spot. In
both readings there is a spatial connection, established by the
language, which carries some of the multiple meanings with
which the text abounds.

At the moment when Aureliano pulls the trigger to kill himself,
Ursula discovers that the pot of milk she has put on the stove
hasn't boiled yet and is, instead, full of worms; and her first reaction is to pronounce, 'They've killed Aureliano' (p. 149). The connection is inspired by her early discovery, when Aureliano was
only three years old, that he had the power of causing objects to
move by looking at them (p. 20). The intertwining of time and
space is complicated by the fact that in the same instant when
she believes Aureliano to be killed, she looks out into the courtyard
and sees her husband, 'soaking wet and sad in the rain and much
older than when he had died' (p. 149). In other words, when she
(wrongly) believes her son to be dead, she finds herself looking at
the spot where he *will* die, years later. Through the intricate ramifications of language time is fully spatialised.

The most spectacular spatial linkage of characters through the
manipulations of language occurs at the time of José Arcadio's mysterious death (shot either by himself or by his wife Rebeca). In one of
the most famous scenes in the novel (pp. 113–14), the dead man's
blood finds its way to his mother, trickling across half the village. She
retraces its course in a motion which precisely inverts the mean-
dering sentence in which the trail of blood has been described,
until she arrives at the body of José Arcadio. It is a remarkable to-
and-fro movement in which the progression of the first sentence is, as
it were, devoured by its counter-movement in the second – in a
brilliant anticipation of the two movements, forward and back,
which will explode in the moment of revelation at the end.

7

There is another linguistic force at work in this scene; behind what McMurray (1977:92) calls a technique of 'hyperbole and preposterous distortions' one discerns the workings of metaphor, not only as 'a kind of linguistic unconscious' (Bell 1993:51), but as a form of literalisation through which language in its communal or public form (de Saussure's *langue*) is appropriated for idiosyncratic personal use (*parole*). The notion of kinship, of blood-relationship, specifically the proverb about blood being thicker than water, is here concretised (just as, earlier in the story, the notion of memory is concretised in the form of an ancient galleon discovered in the swamps; or incest in the shape of a child with a pig's tail). The metaphor is turned into a *narrative performance*, theatrical and spectacular, which activates different levels of meaning in the text – most obviously those of the 'magical' and the 'real'. And once again this effect is not derived, in the first instance, from a kind of cultural or symbolical code interpellated by the narrative, but by a manipulation of language.

The text abounds with examples of this functioning, some comparatively brief, like the description of the rain of yellow flowers which marks José Aureliano Buendía's death (p. 120) or the yellow butterflies which accompany the comings and goings of Mauricio Babilonia (pp. 232ff), others much more ample, like the magnificent scene of the ascension of Remedios the Beauty. As a metaphorical elaboration of her untouchability, her 'lightness of being', *su impermeabilidad a la palabra de los hombres*, the narrator describes how one afternoon, while helping to fold Fernanda's Brabant sheets in the garden, a delicate wind springs up and Remedios begins to levitate. With delightful 'realistic' detail the scene unfolds:

> Ursula, almost blind at the time, was the only person who was sufficiently calm to identify the nature of that determined wind and she left the sheets to the mercy of the light as she watched Remedios the Beauty waving goodbye in the midst of the flapping sheets that rose up with her, abandoning with her the environment of beetles and dahlias and passing through the air with her as four o' clock in the afternoon came to an end, and they were lost forever with her in the upper atmosphere where not even the highest-flying birds of memory could reach her. (p. 195)[13]

Perhaps the give-away phrase in the passage is 'birds of memory' in which both the signifying and the signified dimensions of metaphor, tenor and vehicle, are explicitly linked to suggest that the rest of the scene may also be read as metaphor. All the more so as we are directly informed, in the narrator's characteristic dead-pan style, that

> The outsiders, of course, thought that Remedios the Beauty had finally succumbed to her irrevocable fate of a queen bee and that her family was trying to save her honour with that tale of levitation. (p. 195)

Once this practice has been established, it is no longer necessary to alert the reader to its machinations with phrases like 'birds of memory'; and by the time Amaranta Ursula arrives on the scene, we are prepared for the amplest possible reading of that delightful passage: 'Amaranta Ursula arrived with the first angels of December, driven on a sailor's breeze, leading her husband by a silk rope tied around his neck' (p. 305).

Once again, language foregrounds itself, in the form of a concretised metaphor ('she keeps her husband on a tight rein'), and by alerting the reader to the various layers of meaning embedded in a seemingly straightforward linguistic and narrative statement, we are prepared to acknowledge the decisive and defining function of language in the text as a whole.

8

This is not merely a powerful function; it is also a function of power – the power, as we have seen, to do and to undo, to create and to destroy. It is demonstrated quite specifically in the episode of old Ursula's death: after having been turned into a plaything by the children Aureliano and Amaranta Ursula (in a dramatic reversal of the relationship between generations), the wretched old great-great-grandmother practically reverts to a fetal state and remains lying motionless, but still alive, in her bedroom. From there, the children carry her out by the neck and ankles, pretending to lament her death, while ignoring all her feeble protests (p. 278). And eventually she succumbs – literally killed by language – the language of the children who have proclaimed her dead.

But they are merely adumbrations of old Melquíades, who, a hundred years earlier, already wrote characters into life and out of it; and he, in turn, of course, 'represents' the narrator looming behind him, that other Gabriel Márquez who resumes the narrative when Melquíades and his whole creation are written out of it.

It lies at the heart of storytelling, and this novel is not just a story told but a story about the telling of stories. From the first pages of the first chapter 'the children were startled by [Melquíades's] fantastic stories [...] lighting up with his deep organ voice the darkest reaches of the imagination' (p. 13). And when the inhabitants of Macondo are threatened by amnesia, one of their remedies is the telling of stories – even if it is only the senseless, repetitive game of the story about the capon which forms a verbal labyrinth without issue (pp. 44–5). Once they have been restored to the semblance of a normal, or 'real' existence,[14] the most significant irruption into their lives from abroad (apart, that is, from the visits of the gypsies), is that of Francisco the Man who transforms the history and the news of the outside world into song – a language of performance which adds a substratum of knowledge to their lives (p. 49). For many years after his last visit, his narrative songs – in which history has been transmuted into story – are still repeated by Aureliano Segundo (p. 285); and when he, too, disappears from the scene, the songs persist in the performance of 'an accordion group' (p. 333). Language has finally dissolved into music, into songs without words. Which is another form of obliteration, and of new creation; and at the same time, in the persistence of a memory reduced to the mere outline of a tune from which all traces of language have faded away, we discover, perhaps, *that language has always* been, 'essentially', empty and meaningless[15] – except when its power is harnessed in the form of narrative, of storytelling.

At the end, as we have now noted several times, all the stories and their telling are subsumed in the narrative action of the Gabriel who takes over from Melquíades (and who dreamed up Melquíades in the first place): making, unmaking, and then making again. It is the ultimate expression of solitude.

Because this is how language is conceived of in *One Hundred Years of Solitude*, in its functions, and its power, of summoning to life, and then assigning to death, in order to begin again. Text unto text. *Hacer para dehacer*.

12

Withdrawal and Return

Margaret Atwood: *Surfacing*

1

Margaret Atwood's *Surfacing*, described by Rigney (1987:38) as 'quite possibly, the best of all her work', has already been read in a great variety of ways: as a search for the self, as a female intro- version of the traditional male genre of the Quest, as a redefinition of the Oedipal relation, as an exploration of Canadian identity, a postcolonial showpiece, an enquiry into eco-relationships, an invo- cation of Amerindian mythology and shamanism. But in one way or another, sooner or later, all these approaches have to confront the novel's quite explicit problematisation of *language* – specifically as a *woman's* experience of (male) language. It is

> a search for a feminine discourse: [the narrator's] escape from, and challenge to, the patriarchal social order she has previously accepted as the 'norm', resulting in a 'double-voiced discourse' as [Atwood] depicts her protagonist gradually becoming 'silenced' in her inability to find expression through the domi- nant structure of patriarchy. (Spaull 1989:110)

Indeed, in a novel like *Surfacing*, 'language is both the vehicle of exploration and the site of combat' (Hutcheon 1988:143); and its presentation of 'a descent through space, time and water, and then a hazardous return to the surface' (Piercy 1988:63) is only possible in terms of the language in which it is invented or rein- vented.

As a background to the kind of enquiry involved, one should bear in mind Lacan's notion of the relation between the Imaginary Order, dating from the child's earliest experience of oneness with the mother, when everything is here and now, and the Symbolic

253

Order, linked to the Law of the Father and the discovery of language as something which invades the subjectively and imaginatively constituted world of the child (see, *inter alia*, Lacan 1991a (Book I) :174). This Father, as Jones (1981:248) so devastatingly puts it, is the supreme male figure who announces himself as, 'the unified, self-controlled center of the universe. The rest of the world, which I define as the Other, has meaning only in relation to me, as man/father, possessor of the phallus.'

A crucial moment in this whole process is marked by Lacan's famous 'mirror phase', in which the child discovers its 'self' in a mirror – that is, its existence 'out there' as opposed to 'in here'. In *Surfacing*, after the narrator has finally eluded her companions to remain behind, alone, on the island, she stops in front of the mirror for one last time, 'not to see myself but to see' (p. 169).[1] Then she reverses the mirror, which 'no longer traps me'. This is the decisive step before she systematically destroys all signs of her former entrapment in the world, and in her family, and returns to an Imaginary Order. This coincides with a (temporary) renunciation of language, because the mirror trap, in Lacan's view of the world, coincides with the entrapment of the self within language, 'I am' as opposed to 'you are' or 's/he is'. This is an acknowledgement of the distressing fact that the self will henceforth be defined from elsewhere, by an Other (see Lacan 1991b (Book II): 244, 246, 324). The very existence, and usage, of language already signals a deficiency, a lack in the speaker.

The Other is the site where speech is shaped, the locus of the signifier (Lacan 1977:185), and for the self there is no way out of this bind of language in which the ego is always, at best, an alter-ego (Lacan 1991b (Book II):321). Barthes (1972:xv), too, confirms, in a slightly different context, that 'Writing is, [...] on every level, the language of others.'

From this Lacan derives his notion of language as dialogue and interpellation:

> What I seek in speech is the response of the other. What constitutes me as subject is my question. In order to be recognized by the other, I utter what was only in view of what will be. In order to find him, I call him by a name that he must assume or refuse in order to reply to me. I identify myself in language, but only by losing myself in it as an object. (Lacan 1977:86)

2

The focus on language is immediately evident from the construction of the novel in three sections, distinguished primarily by tense; although the narrative flow is continuous, interrupted only by reminiscences of the past, Part I is written in the present tense; Part II largely in the preterite, reverting to the present only in the last three paragraphs on p. 153; Part III once again in the present. An important feature of the evocation of the past is the frequent suppression of a pluperfect (as on pp. 82, 135, among others): this effaces time boundaries to facilitate a return to an Imaginary Order, in which differentiation in person, time and space is absent.

The motivation for this structure is not obvious. In Part I the use of the present tense may be interpreted as the narrator's almost compulsive clinging to the present in order not to confront the truth about the past – notably her abortion and her relationship with the man involved. In Part II the use of the preterite imposes precisely the need to face the past, as it can no longer be avoided (although the truth is not yet told), but the preterite used in this section refers to the same time frame as the present of the first, which places it, through the suppression of a pluperfect, on the same level as the original past; a process of distancing becomes obvious, emphasising 'the dislocation of the narrator from her own personal history, past and present' (Campbell 1988:172). The return to the present tense in Part III may be interpreted as an acknowledgement of the need to assume the full burden of the here-and-now, into which the truth of the past has now been gathered and subsumed.

This is complicated by the discovery, on p. 45, that the *city* – increasingly associated with the Other, with alienation, with destructive masculinity – is linked to the present: 'There's no act I can perform except waiting; tomorrow Evans will ship us to the village, and after that we'll travel to the city *and the present tense*' (my emphasis). This present must be identical to the unspoken present in Part III, from which the excursion to the island is recalled retrospectively. One is tempted to insert the third-last paragraph of the novel into the same framework of narrative time: 'To trust is to let go. *I tense forward*, towards the demands and questions, though my feet do not move yet' (p. 186, my emphasis).

The reader should clearly beware of linearity and unambiguity in establishing links between language and experience, language and Imaginary and Symbolic Orders. Part of the problem explored in the novel is precisely the interpenetration of dimensions and languages, of past and present, male and female: simple oppositions are broken down, binary patterns subverted.

3

At the very beginning of the novel the subversion of language is already under way. The first demonstration of this process occurs as early as the first page, in the description of 'the last or first outpost depending on which way we were going', of which the main street is said to boast 'a movie theatre, the itz, the oyal, red R burnt out' (p. 1). This gangrene eating into language is a sign of things to come; and it is soon followed by another telling remark: 'Now we're on my home ground, foreign territory. My throat constricts, as it learned to do when I discovered people could say words that would go into my ears meaning nothing' (p. 5).

In this garbled or unintelligible language – the language of 'civilisation', the city, elections, social commerce, ultimately of phallocratic society – 'the district's entire history' is seen to be embedded in the slogans and graffiti covering the walls: 'VOTEZ GODET, VOTEZ OBRIEN [...] THÉ SALADA, BLUE MOON COTTAGES 1/2 MILE, QUEBEC LIBRE, FUCK YOU, BUVEZ COCA COLA GLACÉ, JESUS SAVES, mélange of demands and languages' (p. 9).

And the 'thing that isn't supposed to be here' is also announced in the written – and already increasingly meaningless – language of the city: 'MOTEL, BAR BIÈRE BEER...' (p. 10). This is symptomatic of the 'American' world to which it belongs: recyclable, collapsible, disposable, consumable.

In this new/old world the narrator is (re)entering, we are warned, a different language system operates, which imposes on her the need to lie (about her past relationship, about the baby): 'I sent my parents a postcard after the wedding, they must have mentioned it to Paul; that, but not the divorce. It isn't part of the vocabulary here' (p. 17). This vocabulary excludes all the primal facts of life: birth, love, even death (witness the lie about the baby, referred to above; the 'magic word' which is said to have become meaningless on p. 131; death reduced to a matter of 'arrangements' on p. 151). The problem is that by being forced to lie (not only to her parents, in the past; but here and now to the reader, when she writes about a marriage which never happened), the narrator is cut off from a significant segment of her own experience, of her own consciousness.[2] If city language is being corroded, it is also corrosive in turn. Which is why, among other results, 'there are no dirty words any more, they've been neutered, now they're only parts of speech' (p. 39): the signifieds are being peeled away from the signifiers. No wonder that, in this context, knowledge such as that which her father accumulated and transmitted to her (on survival, on co-existing with a natural order) is branded 'worthless', and superseded by that of the city, of 'the pulp magazines' (p. 42).

During the narrative, as it moves to its climax of silence, an increasing distance is signalled between the narrator and others, those she calls 'the Americans' (itself a misnomer!): 'I wondered what I would say to them, what could be said, if I asked them why it would mean nothing' (p. 111). And it also rules out communication with her friend David, when he tries to force his sexual attentions upon her and she refuses, a reaction he utterly fails to comprehend:

> There must be a phrase, a vocabulary that would work [...] he didn't know what language to use, he'd forgotten his own, he had to copy. Second-hand American was spreading over him in patches [...] He was infested, garbled, and I couldn't help him: it would take such time to heal, unearth him, scrape down to where he was true. (p. 146)

4

The key to her problem is that this corroded and corrosive language is not hers, that she is alienated from it; it is 'their' language, a 'caseful of alien words and failed pictures' (p. 158). This is stated explicitly when Joe asks her whether she loves him:

> It was the language again. I couldn't use it because it wasn't mine. He must have known what he meant but it was an imprecise word: the Eskimoes had fifty-two names for snow because it was important to them, there ought to be as many for love. (p. 100)

She consciously avoids using it, because that would mean entrapment: 'If you look like them and talk like them and think like them then you are them' (p. 123).

In this lies the danger of the complex of lies through which she has survived in 'their' world; through exposure to the language of 'pure logic' (p. 137) she used there, she lost her own identity, which makes the process of retrieval so particularly painful. This emerges on pp. 137–9, where she literally 'surfaces' from the water of the lake after the confrontation with her dead father (the Oedipal figure responsible, through his bonding with her, for her introduction into the natural world, but *also* for the disintegration of the Imaginary Order). Now, for the first time, she acknowledges the truth about her non-marriage and her abortion. Her refusal, at that time, to 'say no', that is, to counter their language with hers, 'made me one of them too, a killer' (p. 139).[3]

In the end, after her experience of mystical illumination – which in Iragaray's terminology would be equated with 'an experience of the loss of subjecthood, of the disappearance of the subject/object opposition' (see Moi 1985:136) – and her withdrawal into silence, her resumption of 'ordinary' language is infused with a different meaning: rejecting the notion of victim, which she previously assumed as part of her lie,[4] she also rejects 'the word games, the winning and losing games' (p. 185), which are the games of male language.

The specifics of male language[5] are revealed most eloquently in the almost caricatural functioning of the figure David: his 'yokel dialect' (p. 22), his patronising and domination of women. This happens even when he tries to be 'generous', as on p. 92: ' "Good girl", he said, "your heart's in the right place. And the rest of her too", he said to Joe, "I like it round and firm and fully packed." '

Sometimes it is overtly denigrating: 'What would we talk about? She's too dumb, she can't figure out what I'm saying to her' (p. 132). On yet other occasions it descends to unmitigated viciousness and destructiveness, culminating in the episode where he forces his wife to pose naked for the film he and Joe are making:

'Shut up, she's my wife', David said. His hand clamped down above her elbow. She jerked away, then I saw his arms go around her as if to kiss her and she was in the air, upside down over his shoulder, hair hanging in damp ropes. 'Okay twatface', he said, 'is it off or into the lake?' (p. 129)

In this episode, language spills from the verbal into the symbolic, as the posture in which he is holding Ann, upside down, recollects the 'language' of destruction used by the hunters in their senseless killing of a heron and their perversely ritualistic hanging of it from a branch (p. 109).

David's stale obscenities also reflect the corruption of the natural world by an alien and alienating language. A case in point is his limp attempt at a joke about 'a split beaver' as an emblem for the Canadian flag (p. 113).

There is a wide variety of connotations of 'maleness' invoked by the language associated with David's world, all of them related to the basic concept of power: the hunters kill a bird merely 'to prove they could do it, they had the power to kill' (p. 110), the kind of power the narrator herself has rejected very early ('I had no idea of what I would do with the power once I got it; if I'd turned out like the others with power I would have been evil': p. 31).[6] This world of power is structured dynastically (we are reminded that her father 'would have wanted a dynasty, like Paul's': p. 28), and the link with linguistic syntax is evident. It is, also, physical and material; even love is reduced to 'an exercising programme, athletic demonstration, ornamental swimming in a chlorine swimming pool noplace in California' (p. 145). Its ultimate sign is violence and war. It is notable how often specifically Hitler, Nazi Germany and the Second World War are evoked.

It is important, whenever 'their' language is signified in the text, to be alert to these meanings vibrating in it. It is equally important to remember that the narrator herself, notably through the atrophy of emotion after the abortion of her child, has become drawn into the vortex of this other world: although regarding herself primarily as a victim of it, she is forced to acknowledge ultimately her complicity in destruction and death and the use of 'their' language.

What makes 'their language' peculiarly 'male' is the way in which it functions to formulate a territorial imperative. This forms, in fact, an essential code in the text, first introduced, ironically, with reference to birdsong, in itself a revelation of the extent to which this language has invaded and corrupted the natural world: 'They sing for the same reason trucks honk, to proclaim their territories: a rudimentary language. Linguistics, I should have studied that instead of art' (p. 35).

The code reappears, with an extremely pejorative connotation, in a description of litter left by picnickers: 'It was like dogs pissing on a fence, as if the endlessness, anonymous water and unclaimed land, compelled them to leave their signature, stake their territory, and garbage was the only thing they had to do it with' (p. 104).

The next time we encounter the code is when the disastrous attempt at partner swapping results in Anna's apologetic offer to do the dishes: 'She rattled the cutlery in the pan, singing to avoid discussion, we were beyond the time for confidences; *her voice occupied the room, territorial*' (p. 149, my emphasis). The normal function of language is here taken over by pure sound (the rattling of dishes, the singing), that is by a system of signifiers deprived of signification, reducing communication to pure territoriality, a 'male' function now performed by the docile female, Anna, who has been totally co-opted into the male world.

Territoriality implies demarcation and division. And this may well be the most devastating characteristic of 'their' language. The key passage in this respect is the beginning of Chapter 9, which opens the second part: 'The trouble is all in the knob at the top of our bodies. I'm not against the body or the head either; only the neck, which creates the illusion that they are separate. The language is wrong, it shouldn't have different words for them' (p. 70)

This is only the starting point. The processes of division, imposed on the world by language, run through the whole novel: 'Language divides us into fragments' (p. 140) – which the narrator counters with her fervent desire for *wholeness*.[7]

Ultimately, 'their' language, male language, is the language of the city, of 'civilisation', of the 'Americans'. It represents the world in which, banished from the Imaginary Order, the narrator as a child first had 'to learn to be polite; "civilized", she called it' (p. 65),[8] a process regarded as completed on p. 102 ('I was civilized at last, the finished product'), when the mature narrator looks at early photographs of herself 'in the stiff dresses, crinolenes and tulle, layered like store birthday cakes'. The city world, that is, the world of 'the itz, the oyal, the red R burnt out', the world where sex smells of rubber and 'love is taking precautions' (p. 74), where everything is announced by – and reduced to – neon and other signs, where consumerism and the concomitant waste rely, as language does, on supply and demand, question and answer, is the very space from which the narrator is trying to escape in the course of the novel, not only in the few days of her 'return to nature', the search for the missing father, but in the *narration* of that quest, which represents its transposition into language.

5

This narration is both the result and the sign of what Spaull (1989:115) calls 'the two discourses' of the novel (that is, human speech and the unspoken language of natural things), and what the text itself terms 'two separate conversations' (p. 144). Hence the narrative itself may be read as a *third* layer or dimension of discourse in the novel, alongside the two on which it draws. In order properly to 'place' this discourse, which is the text the reader is primarily confronted with, it is necessary to trace more specifically the narrator's reaction to the first, that is 'their', language.

There are several dimensions to this reaction.

A significant aspect of it is the narrator's attempts to retrieve the lost father who, in terms of language, has come to represent that which can no longer be said, the lost or 'other' part of herself, notably through the abortion, in which she had the feeling of being 'cut in two', the divisive function of ('their') language began to operate on her: 'I came apart. The other half, the one locked away, was the only one that could live; I was the wrong half, detached, terminal. I was nothing but a head, or no, something minor like a severed thumb' (p. 102).

The lost half of herself is deprived of language like those deaf and dumb children she once refers to, whom nurses treat by 'locking them up in closets, depriving them of words, they found that after a certain age the mind is incapable of absorbing any language' (p. 70). It was to this silent self that her father directed her; he was the one who first made her aware of 'the cliff where the gods lived' (p. 143); he 'had left me the guides, the man-animals and the maze of numbers' (p. 143) – which, significantly, she first interprets as signs of madness.

On the linguistic level her father represents to her the language of traditional wisdom, what Barthes would term a 'culture code'. This father figure was the one who always responded to questions with maxims:

> There's more than one way to skin a cat, my father used to say; it bothered me, I didn't see why they would want to skin a cat even one way. I stared at the wall and thought of maxims: two can play that game, marry in haste, repent at leisure, least said soonest mended, traditional wisdom which was never any help. (p. 86)

The passage elicits two observations: on the one hand, the reader cannot but notice the *inadequacy* of her father's responses, which could only refer her to a language already established, even petrified, and which did not seem to apply to her specific circumstances. But on the other hand, her floundering is also the result of *misreading* his language, because she lacks the key, the code. If the stock phrases and clichés of her father baffle and disappoint her, it is at least to some extent because *she does not understand what they mean*, and not simply because they have inevitably become part of that 'other' language which so effectively excludes her.

The father's language, after all, includes in this text a collective unconscious wisdom in the form of stories, of 'serious books' (p. 32),[9] of directions on how to survive in, and with, nature, even though, as a Christ figure and a God figure (suggested by several references to 'Our Father'), he also represents the rationalised, institutionalised aspect of religion which she cannot come to terms with and which she opposes through her sense of magic, creative witchcraft or mysticism (a primitive *re-ligio*).

The important thing is that her father has also left her his drawings, his pictograms, a sign system beyond language, a map: 'He had been there and long before him the original ones, the first explorers, *leaving behind them their sign, word, but not its meaning*' (p. 120, my emphasis). And these signs, 'unlike language [...] do not trap her but release her and provide a means of deliverance' (Griffith 1979:89). And it is when she goes·in search of the spot he marked with an x, now submerged under the water of the lake, that she comes face to face, not only with the lost pictures from the Imaginary Order, but (presumably) with the body of the lost father himself, in whom is also subsumed the body of her lost child. 'She dives through language', comments Griffith (p. 89) 'to find an image transcending language.'

The scene in which she physically confronts the lost father is particularly rich in possibilities as it takes place in the *water* which, for a critic like Cixous, 'is the feminine element *par excellence*: the closure of the mythical world contains and reflects the comforting security of the mother's womb' (Moi 1985:117).

This suggests that she cannot find the father and learn to understand his language unless she is also reconciled with the mother and the mother's language: 'there had to be a gift from each of them' (p. 143). If the physical search on the island is for the lost father, as Rigney (1987:54) points out, 'the metaphoric search is for the mother'. But doubling the quest in this way at certain moments creates a somewhat mechanical, 'programmatical' tendency in the novel which is not always satisfactorily resolved. Its importance, however, notably in the context of the present enquiry into the dimension of language, is evident.

If the narrator assumes more and more, as 'mistress of the house' in which she lodges her guests, her mother's 'place' (p. 46),[10] she is also increasingly uncomfortable in this role:

> A lady was what you dressed up as on Hallowe'en when you couldn't think of anything else and didn't want to be a ghost; or it was what you said at school when they asked you what you were going to be when you grew up, you said 'A lady' or 'A mother', either one was safe; and it wasn't a lie, I did want to be those things. (p. 85)

As in the case of the father, in other words, the mother has also become drawn into 'their language'. Yet the implication is that this was not, as it were, their 'fault'; it is more a problem of perception, of the angle from which that language is experienced. *Inside* the language in which both father and mother have become ensnared, lurks their 'real meaning', the completion of the Imaginary Order. Which suggests that the wholeness which the significantly anonymous narrator is so desperately seeking, cannot be found within 'another' language but only *inside* the one she has inherited from her parents.

It is precisely this which the narrator initially, and for so long, rejects. Her primary urge, in response to the invasion and threat of 'their' language (in its verbal form, as well as its extensions into non-lingual semiotics: the dead heron, the debris, or other objects) is to find, and retreat into, 'another' language, an alternative language which is not human.

This is essentially a language of *signs* rather than words, and the early reference to Anna's reading of hands at parties (p. 2) – followed much later by the narrator's reading of her own hand, 'palm a network of trails, lifeline, past present and future' (p. 153) – alerts the reader to this. It is confirmed by the reference to 'the flight of birds [...] as a portent: augury' (p. 87). If Joe takes out his chewing gum, puts it in the ashtray and folds his arms, the narrator 'reads' the gestures: 'That means I'm not supposed to observe him' (p. 2). On the way to the island she reads the signs which guide them there, as surely as in her youth her parents had done so in the dark; on their later explorations she is specifically aware of early, original explorers, 'leaving behind them their sign, word, but not its meaning' (p. 120). What she is looking for from both her father and her mother is 'not money but an object, a token' (p. 30); when she is exploring the forest soon after their arrival on the island, she is bewildered because 'there's no sign; or there are too many signs' (p. 43); and all the noises she hears, later, in the wilderness are 'translated' (p. 118). Her father's drawings are immediately interpreted semiotically (p. 54). Even lovemaking is experienced as sign-language, 'crisp as a typewriter' (p. 62). To preserve her sanity she insists on maintaining 'at least the signs of order' (p. 72). One of the decisive lies of her life, the faked marriage, was encapsulated in the sign of a wedding ring.

The text, indeed, teems with signs of signs. And from beginning to end the narrator is tuned in to them.

What she tends (or 'tenses') towards, more and more, is the sign language of the *wilderness*, a preverbal or paraverbal state – that is, once again, an Imaginary Order: the 'rudimentary language' of birds (p. 35), 'the small waves talking against the shore' (p. 172), 'the other language' of the gods and myths (p. 182), the 'loon voice' in a natural world where 'everything echoes' (p. 34), and where through processes of Baudelairean *correspondances* language no longer divides but gathers, unites, unifies.

This alternative to the spoken language, to 'their' language, is, paradoxically, a space and a silence *beyond* language, an urge towards 'some indefinite thing with no name' (p. 67) which may be both terrifying (as in the case just cited), or infinitely reassuring ('I didn't know the names of the ones I was making the offering to; but they were there, they had power': p. 140); often it involves both these extremes of experience, as in Ann's cry of orgasm overheard by the narrator, 'not a word but pure pain, clear as water, an animal's at the moment the trap closes' (p. 76). In the final analysis, it is the space inhabited by the narrator herself, who has no name in the text, and who 'had to immerse myself in the other language' (p. 152) before she can converse with primordial gods and silence.

As the narrative enters its crucial phase, after the discovery of the father's body, when the narrator remains behind on the island, alone, reverting to primitivity and communion with nature, the battle between the languages becomes decisive: 'Sight flowing ahead of me over the ground, eyes filtering the shapes, the names of things fading but their forms and uses remaining, the animals learned to eat without nouns' (p. 144).

This is juxtaposed immediately with the memory of death, of coffins, of 'the stone with the name and the date [. . .] on them to weight them down' (p. 144).

She moves through a phase in which the whole of 'their' language and its incrustations and extensions must be destroyed. 'Everything from history must be eliminated, the circles and the arrogant square pages [. . .] all my artifacts' (pp. 170–1); she burns the books and photographs and drawings and papers, burns *language*, in an attempt, it seems, to follow the example of her mother who also moved beyond language: 'My father explained everything but my mother never did, which only convinced me *that she had the answers but wouldn't tell*' (p. 68, my emphasis).

What the narrator does in her apparently destructive mood is to create the space of silence for the 'waves talking against the shore' to make themselves heard (p. 172). This phase is most memorably evoked in Chapter 24:

> In one of the languages there are no nouns, only verbs held for a longer moment.
>
> The animals have no need for speech, why talk when you are a word
>
> I lean against a tree, I am a tree leaning
>
> I break out again into the bright sun and crumple, head against the ground
>
> I am not an animal or a tree, I am the thing in which the trees and animals move and grow, I am a place. (p. 175)

Her pursuers are reduced to pure sound, their boots crashing and their electronic signals described as 'language ululating' (p. 179). Her own reactions are mere sound: 'I laugh, and a noise comes out like something being killed: a mouse, a bird?' (p. 184).

But in the farthest extremity the turning point has already been reached subliminally; and a progress has begun, back to the integrated father/mother world where 'sanity' resides in the need 'to have someone to speak to and words that can be understood' (p. 184).

The significance of this discovery cannot be overstated. For she has now learned the lesson of her mother's retreat into silence, namely that it *solves* nothing. What it implies, above all, is that, in opposition to 'their' language, there exists no alternative: neither 'my' language, nor 'another' language. The only true alternative is silence, and that is aligned with death; it is everything language is not. In other words (quite literally, *in other words*): 'their language' *means* 'language'. For language to be language is already to be 'their' language, in its Lacanian existence as 'the Other'.

6

For a time the narrator (whose anonymity becomes even more eloquent in the light of this awareness) has crossed the limits of this language and the need for it. This goes far beyond the 'linguistic retrenchment' Cluett (1983:87) comments on in his syntactic profile of the text; it is not just a 'retreat from ornate "civilized" values' (p. 87), but a radical removal of the self from human language altogether; in this part of the narrative, she has become a savage, 'part of the land' (p. 172) – or, in 'their' language, a suspect 'naked woman wrapped in a blanket' (p. 177), a mad female, a witch. But the reader can only follow her into this silence once it has become translated into the language of the narrative text. Language can only be subverted by language. The 'magic', the 'madness' and the 'silence' into which the narrator temporarily retreats only assume meaning once they have been so *named*. But once named, they deserve, retroactively, the reader's particular attention.

The world of magic and witchcraft is activated in the text as early as Chapter 6, when she recalls the stories of her youth, 'bewitched dogs and malevolent trees perhaps, and the magic powers of rival political candidates, whose effigies in straw they burned during elections' (p. 48); the transition, in this passage, from the natural world to the city, from Imaginary to Symbolic Orders, is noteworthy. *This* is the key to the narrator's problem with language: that an initially 'natural' world has not been destroyed (that is, transferred to a dimension from which it might still be retrieved by memory), but imperialised; it now exists 'under erasure', contained by 'their' language. And to revalidate its earlier meanings it has to be wrested from this alien language. In the weeds, raked together, later 'to be burned, like witches, to keep them from reappearing' (p. 72), the problem is restated. In Chapter 18 the narrator sees herself, through the eyes of her companions, as a witch ('in a minute they would join hands and dance around me, and after that the rope and the pyre, cure for heresy': p. 148). But, as we have already noted in previous chapters of this study, witches are the image of femininity in a phallocratic society: original creativity, fertility, imagination relegated to the periphery of phallocracy, transformed into the Other, divested of language.[11] By *assuming* this position, reinvesting it with its original force, when at the beginning of the final movement in the novel the narrator finally makes love with Joe under a full moon to conceive a child (pp. 154–5), she reinscribes fertility into her previous failure and destructiveness, restores 'witch' to 'womanhood', returns to primary language.

But to persist in this state would be to deny the humanity she shares with others, a sharing to which language is the key: 'For us it's necessary, the intercession of words' (p. 186). In her return to the 'city' she reassumes the burden of language, accepting as it were Cixous's challenge to women 'to write themselves out of the world men have constructed for them by putting into words the unthinkable/unthought' (Tong 1989:224). For Atwood's narrator this means that even though she returns to the very language she once suspected and dreaded so much, she has transcended the facility of simple oppositions. She can now squarely assume the task defined by Ashcroft *et al.* (1989:39) in their discussion of postcoloniality, namely 'to convey in a language that is not one's own the spirit that is one's own'.

In the last lines of the text she hears both Joe's voice and that of the trees. *Within* human language she has reopened a spring of original meaning. Hence the paradox underlying the text as a whole: rejecting 'their' language, regressing into pre- and a-verbal silence, the narrator is still using language – because she has *nothing but* language – to communicate with a reader. Even language implies, particularly to women, 'a separation from a presumed state of nature' (Kristeva 1986:189); the narrator's assumption of its burden signals, not defeat, but a curious Sisyphean victory. Kroetsch (1989:50) formulates it with particular insight: 'Only when she has made herself unnameable in any traditional terms can she begin what might be a rebirth, a renaming into a valid vision or version of the world.'

Having transcended the binarities of a condition imposed upon her, this ultimate act of free choice demonstrates that, to her, there is no longer 'this' language and the 'other' language, no longer 'my' language and 'theirs': there is only language. Its flaws and lies and deceptions have been exposed; its logocentrism has been shifted and subverted. But it cannot be obliterated, as 'being human' is implicated in the faculties of speech and writing. Through this transcendence of binarities Atwood suggests a solution to the problem intrinsic to many early feminist views of essentialist distinctions between 'her' language and 'his' language. ('Once "women" are constituted as always and unchangingly subordinate and "men" as unqualifiedly powerful, the language structures of these groups are perceived as rigid and unchanging': Moi 1985:154.)

From the instant the narrator assumes responsibility for her abortion instead of regarding herself merely as a victim, and from the moment she ends her introversion into silence and returns to language, all easy distinctions are suspended. There is no longer nature/city: if the destructive impulses of the city have previously invaded nature, the creative possibilities of nature are now bestowed on the city. There is no longer the stark division man/ woman and the early image of the barometer indicating fair weather or rain in terms of femininity and masculinity (see p. 18) is replaced by something as useless, but at the same time as indispensable, as 'a third eye or a possibility' (p. 186).

By the same token the easy distinctions between past, present and future are also effaced: the *present* tense in which the end is narrated is an account of the narrative *past*, from which there are prospects opening up towards a *future*.

It is an acknowledgement of Kristeva's position on language and psychoanalysis, as summarised by Moi (1985:170):

If the Kristevan subject is always already inserted in the Symbolic Order, how can such an implacably authoritarian, phallocentric structure be broken up? It obviously cannot happen through a straightforward *rejection* of the Symbolic Order, since such a total failure to enter into human relations would, in Lacanian terms, make us psychotic. We have to accept our position as already inserted into an order that precedes us and from which there is no escape. There is no *other space* from which we can speak: if we are able to speak at all, it will have to be within the framework of symbolic language.

13

Taking the Gap

Milan Kundera: *The Unbearable Lightness of Being*

1

Like all the other novels we have examined in this study, *The Unbearable Lightness of Being* has been subjected to many kinds of reading. Especially after Philip Kaufman's film based on the novel, millions of people in many countries have read it as a poignant love story of the relationship between a brilliant young Czech doctor Tomas and a young waitress Tereza, who meet by pure chance (a series of six light coincidences which acquire the weight of fate), whose love survives his compulsive womanising, the Russian invasion of Czechoslovakia, the disruption of their domestic life through exile and return, his humiliation when he has to resign as a surgeon eventually to become a window-cleaner, and hers when she has to find work in a bar where all the men make passes at her and one seduces her – until they escape from it all by leaving Prague and settling, with their dog Karenin, in a remote country village, where at the moment when they finally seem to attain a state of peace and happiness they are killed in an accident, crushed by a truck. Interwoven with their story is that of one of Tomas's mistresses, the painter Sabina, who loves and leaves the Swiss academic Franz to settle in America, while he joins a great protest march to Cambodia and soon afterwards is murdered in a fortuitous mugging.

On another level, the novel can be read as one of the most eloquent testimonies of the Russian invasion of Czechoslovakia and the fate of the small nations of Central Europe in the grip of a totalitarian power; in this reading, it becomes a demonstration of *littérature engagée*, a sociopolitical document of great moral power.

It may also be read as a philosophical study, an enquiry into the lightness and the weight of existence, into the increasing ambigu-

269

ities of the notion that *Einmal ist keinmal* ('Once is never'), and that of its opposite, fate, represented by the key phrase in Beethoven's last quartet (Opus 135), *Es muss sein* ('It must be'). In this reading, the story line of the novel becomes an illustration of the philosophical thesis, the elaboration of an Idea – the idea of Being, of Nietzsche's Eternal Return, of the Oedipus myth, or whatever.

Or again, taking one's cue from the Beethoven reference, the novel may be read as the verbalisation of a musical composition, a fugue or a symphony with recurrent and interwoven motifs and melodies.

But in one way or another all these readings must take account of the fact that *The Unbearable Lightness of Being* highlights an engagement with the nature and the processes of language.

2

In *The Art of the Novel* Kundera himself provides several clues to our reading of *The Unbearable Lightness of Being*, specifically four 'appeals' to which he, as a novelist, responds: the appeal of *play* which constitutes the 'lightness' of the novel (Kundera 1988:15), and which in *Testaments Betrayed* (1995) is more specifically linked with laughter; the appeal of the *dream* ('the novel is a place where the imagination can explode as a dream': p. 16); the appeal of *thought*, 'not to transform the novel into philosophy, but to marshal around the story all the means – rational and irrational, narrative and contemplative – that could illuminate man's being' (p. 16); and the appeal of *time*, that is, 'to overstep the temporal limits of an individual life [...] and to insert in its space several historical periods' (p. 16).

What concerns us here is that all four dimensions outlined by Kundera emphatically concern language. Play, dream, thought and time are not simply 'expressed' in narrative language, or – conversely – 'shaped' by it, they *determine* language; they *are* language. If Kundera distinguishes three choices confronting a novelist – 'he *tells* a story [...] he *describes* a story [...] he *thinks* a story' (ibid.:139), his own choice is evidently the third. But it is a very specific kind of thinking he has in mind. As in his other novels – particularly *The Joke, The Book of Laughter and Forgetting, Life is Elsewhere, Immortality* and, most recently, *Slowness – The Unbearable Lightness of Being* is for Kundera a strategy of ludic thinking of what cannot be thought in any other way.

This process is self-conscious (a self-awareness that is not only filtered through language but wholly conditional upon it); and it is a curious combination of the metaphoric and the metonymic. In fact, what makes it uniquely Postmodernist, in a way inspired by Musil, is Kundera's use of metaphor *as* metonymy. While, as metaphor, a scene, a character, a description, a chapter 'stands for' something else, conjures up something else, displaces something else, it also exploits its contiguity with other metaphors to stimulate *narrative* (that is, metonymic) development along a horizontal axis. To illustrate in simple terms what might appear abstruse in this formulation: the love scene between Tomas and Sabina in which she is wearing a black bowler hat (pp. 87ff),[1] is a metaphoric expression of a variety of other meanings – her grandfather, her attitude towards the 'Grand March', authority, lightness, weight, and so on – but the meanings set in motion by this scene return to influence, to determine, a later scene between Sabina and Tereza photographing one another in the nude, and the disturbing implications unsettled by this metaphor, in turn, have a metonymic effect – a 'chain reaction' – on Tereza's later sexual encounter with the engineer (p. 155).

Each metaphor points towards possible signifieds in the story matrix, but at the same time it propels the narrative action and, more important, pursues new strands of the unfolding thought process. In the framework of the text, the bowler hat signifies (among many other things), the ultimate in propriety, conformity, 'dressing up': it is the world of the Great March, it is Weight, it is Tradition, it is History, it is Kitsch (that 'folding screen set up to curtain off death': p. 253); taken a step further, it is Pretence, Disguise, Concealment, a hypocritical Surface. The naked body of Sabina implies sexuality, identity, individuality, also exposure and vulnerability. Establishing a metonymic relationship between them by placing the hat on the woman, and confronting them with Tomas as a spectator or a 'reader', brings together two disparate worlds, two different paradigms of meanings and of values; it creates both *desire* (it leads, literally, to passionate lovemaking), and disturbance or disruption. Each becomes a surplus and supplement to the other; inasmuch as they create a supplement, they may fit into the notion Kundera designates with 'heaviness'; inasmuch as they leave a surplus, they may fit into a concept of 'lightness'.

At the same time they inform and extend the code of nakedness and clothing which runs, with many others, through the text and thereby metonymically influences scenes like those in which the prim young clothed Tereza confronts her gross naked mother (p. 45), or in which she is undressed by her would-be lover (p. 155), or in which she dreams of naked women in a pool threatened by a clothed man (who resembles Tomas) in a basket (p. 18). And this *heavy* basket, which contains a murderer, evokes that other *light* basket, the one in which a child is protected from drowning (p. 6); the stream that carries the child will, in its turn, later disturb and inform the 'stream of history' which converts the lightness of individual lives into the heaviness of eternal recurrence (p. 170).

The point, at this stage, is not the way in which all of these meanings are intricately meshed together, but the fact that this meshing *can only happen in language*. It is the *term* 'bowler hat' that triggers off its particular chain reaction, not the *object*. In a very explicit manner the text exemplifies a statement by Barthes (1982:295): ' "What takes place" in a narrative is from the referential (reality) point of view literally nothing; "what happens" is language alone, the adventure of language, the unceasing celebration of its coming.' This adventure involves, not only the cumulative meanings of words, but the processes of differentiation which distinguish them, and their internal disruptions.

3

The discourse of the novel opens with the initially simplistic distinction between the notions of 'heaviness' or 'weight' (expressed in Nietzsche's 'eternal recurrence') and 'lightness' expressed in the adage *Einmal ist keinmal*: '(A) life which disappears once and for all, which does not return, is like a shadow, without weight' (p. 3)... 'And what can life be worth if the first rehearsal for life is life itself?' (p. 8). Everything hinges on the possibility of 'return', 'repetition', which is a process of valorisation, the acquisition of meaning, and of weight.

This is linked to a philosophy ascribed to Parmenides from the 6th century BC, who 'saw the world divided into pairs of opposites: light/darkness, fineness/coarseness, warmth/cold, being/non-being' (p. 5). Much of the virtuosity of Kundera's novel depends on the exploitation of any number of such binarities, all of them subsumed within heaviness/lightness. Among the most active binarities in the narrative are: body/soul, chance/fate, sex/love, flirtation/sex, moment/eternity (or moment/duration), private/ public, shit/kitsch, death/kitsch, truth/lie, nakedness/clothing, strength/weakness, individual/history, constraint/freedom, speech/silence; and also, very significantly, male/female. These distinctions, which may fruitfully be read as Derridean *differences*, are not merely 'expressed' in language, but are in fact *established* by language, even imposed by language. They structure an internal vocabulary which informs the whole novel.

What concerns us here is more than the amazing manner in which all of these dichotomies are interrelated, creating a whole web of interactive meanings which is set in motion whenever one touches any individual point on it. But what turns a static column of oppositions into a dialectical process, is the discovery that, within each pair of oppositions in the entire network, boundaries are increasingly challenged, transgressed or effaced.

At the very beginning, the narrator indicates that Parmenides introduced a notion of values, an ethical evaluation, into his pairing of opposites: 'lightness is positive, weight negative' (p. 5), and so on. Consequently, a movement from the negative to the positive is implicit in every opposition. On the discursive level, the process is initiated on p. 33 when the concept of 'weight', initially associated with the earth, with the body, with physicality, is examined. At this stage the narrator extends the concept by introducing positive elements into it, through the linking of 'necessity, weight, and value', and the assertion that 'the greatness of man stems from the fact that he *bears* his fate as Atlas bore the heavens on his shoulders. Beethoven's hero is a lifter of metaphysical weights' (p. 33).

Very soon the argument enters the 'fabric of the story' (in the process of being 'fabricated'); this is particularly dramatic in Tereza's neurotic attempts to separate body and soul, to escape from the coarse physicality of her mother to the purity, the effervescence, the lightness of the soul – and the ironical manner in which she is constantly drawn back into the body. The very concept of Tereza as a character, the narrator confides on p. 39, derives 'from the rumbling of a stomach'. So Tereza enters the story as a marker of weight; her stomach rumbles the moment she arrives on Tomas's doorstep, and he reacts by making (physical) love to her (pp. 39–40); when she moves in she is literally weighed down by her 'enomously heavy' suitcase (pp. 10, 17, 28), as she is morally and spiritually weighed down by the memories of her mother (pp. 42ff), and later by jealousy (pp. 56, 143, 227); when she tries to respond to Tomas's easy-going ('light'-hearted) lovemaking to other women by embarking on an amorous adventure of her own (pp. 152–8), her mood is heavy and lugubrious, and her experience of sex makes her so disgustingly conscious of the *body* (p. 155) that she reacts by hurrying to the toilet to 'void her bowels' (p. 156). This links her with an episode imagined by Sabina in which Tomas seats her 'on the toilet in her bowler hat and [is] watching her void her bowels' (p. 247). More distressingly, it links her with the code of the 'onerous theological problem of shit' (p. 246).

It is indeed in the context of sexual relations that Tereza is most dismally marked by heaviness – that heaviness which the narrator ascribes to a particular literary tradition (which he never challenges): 'In the love poetry of every age, the woman longs to be weighed down by the man's body' (p. 5). This construction, which accepts the (weighty) authority of patriarchal literary discourse, leaves no room for female intervention or even for the possibility of a challenge from a position of female subjectivity. Thus a paradox is created in the text: Tereza's very weightiness is linked to an *absence*, a gap in her constitution as a human being – the absence of an own identity. Even if her 'weakness' might be construed as lightness, she is depicted as belonging 'among the weak, in the camp of the weak, in the country of the weak' (p. 73), that is, as one of a weighty multitude, lacking the lightness of an ephemeral, but exceptional, individual 'I'. And it is this weakness which arouses Tomas's male desire to begin with, the desire to invest – and to invade – her body with the burden of his maleness. This suggests an early, fatal, gendering of relations which will ripple throughout the language of the novel.

Yet, having been introduced within the context of 'weight', Tereza gradually shifts towards greater, and ever more unbearable, lightness; even in the midst of her love scene with the engineer, for the first time in her life the body is *not* the heavy common denominator she shares with all other (naked) women like her mother or Tomas's mistresses or the ladies of her dreams, but something unique, individual, ephemeral, *light*: 'the soul for the first time saw the body as something other than banal; for the first time it looked on the body with fascination: all the body's matchless, inimitable, unique qualities' (p. 155).[2]

And immediately after this episode she stops to rescue a dying crow buried in the dirt (p. 158): a totally 'meaningless' action within the grave historical context, an utterly 'light' action in the terminology of the discourse. (But note, too, that through the repetition of the incident in the text – pp. 158, 209, 219–20 – it acquires a different kind of *narrative* weight, now no longer negative but, like the Beethoven motif, positive.) Some time later she follows this up by her seemingly ludicrous, 'senseless' ministrations to her dying dog Karenin (p. 290). Through these a-historical actions she celebrates lightness, the 'unbearable' lightness of being, reminiscent of the lightness lived by Sabina (pp. 121–2).

What makes her move towards lightness infinitely more complex is the way in which she develops as a photographer; when she photographs the Russian tanks invading Prague, she enters history; she is, briefly, in control. In terms of the conventional role assigned to the camera, she fulfils a male function at this moment (in the more positive sense with which Kundera tends to invest maleness). But as she withdraws from history, she becomes more looked at than looking, as in the densely erotic scene with Sabina: the object of a gaze, the insignificant and unsignifying Other relegated more and more to the outside of language.

The Tomas diagonal in the narrative crosses that of Tereza, as he moves from 'lightness' to increasing 'weight': having turned his back on his parents and shed the burden of marriage and even the responsibility for his son, he lives the light, inconsequential life of a bachelor. Even when he assumes the burden of marriage to Tereza, he escapes into innumerable illicit affairs (p. 201). The only 'weight' in his life – an experience of fatefulness, of living *Es muss sein* to the full – is his career as a doctor; but even that is abandoned (albeit, admittedly, under duress). Gradually, however, heaviness invades his existence: as a 'déclassé intellectual' (p. 232), he becomes, not an exception to a rule, but one of a multitude, a type, a class, walking in a Great March of his own; more importantly, he grows to assume the full weight of responsibility for his conjugal love with Tereza (pp. 219, 239). And in the end, of course, he is literally crushed to death by the weight of the truck on him (p. 373).

Their history, their histories, promote a process through which the demarcations of the initial dichotomies are violated from outside, or dissolved under internal pressures. What is private is made public: Tereza's diary is read aloud by her mother when she is fourteen (p. 134); private conversations are broadcast by the security police (pp. 133, 222); when Franz informs his wife of his affair with Sabina, his mistress promptly leaves him, furious that the privacy of their love has been made public, and thereby has been transformed from lightness to heaviness (pp. 113, 115); Tomas's private language, in his Oedipus article, is not only made public, but edited and revised in the process (pp. 175–8). Photographs taken by Tereza and others to support the cause of the Czechs against the Russians are used by the invaders to identify dissidents (p. 142).

Through the devices of narrative, as *everything* is turned into a story, there is no longer any distinction between 'dream' and 'reality' (this is most evident in Tereza's dream of being executed on Petrin Hill: p. 147). If Oedipus assumes his guilt, even though he could not have known that he killed his father and married his mother, the frontiers between guilt and innocence are erased (p. 218). In Franz's farcical march to Cambodia the boundaries between the heaviness of 'act' and the lightness of 'gesture' disappear (p. 268). The most amusing example of the erasure of dividing boundaries is the dog Karenin: a female animal bearing a male name, 'a bitch whose body seemed reminiscent of the German shepherd and whose head belonged to its Saint Bernard mother' (p. 24), a canine that has a pig as its best friend; a creature in which lightness and heaviness themselves merge – the lightness of its ludicrous existence and the heaviness of routine; the lightness of joy and the heaviness of suffering; the lightness of an individual life and the heaviness of death.

The process is taken so far that opposites actually change places. Cowardice and courage displace each other as 'the norm of behaviour' (p. 181) when surgeons are instructed to collaborate with the security police. Stalin's son dislodges both God and shit from their established, polar positions ('no one felt more concretely than Yakov how interchangeable opposites are, how short the step from one pole of human existence to the other': p. 244). In Tereza strength and weakness change places (p. 310) as her very weakness turns Tomas into a victim. 'When the strong were too weak to hurt the weak, the weak had to be strong enough to leave' (p. 75).

Through these processes, fixed meanings, the fatum of the logocentric *Es muss sein* (which, in narrative terms, means that a story must run its ineluctable course; and means, also, that its meanings are fixed) are displaced by the more deconstructive approach of *Es könnte auch anders sein*, which releases limitless light possibilities. This is expressed, for example, in Tereza's choice of Tomas as a lover: '[I]t was only a matter of chance that Tereza loved him and not his friend Z. Apart from her consummated love for Tomas, there were, in the realm of possibilities, an infinite number of unconsummated loves for other men' (p. 34).

This is an eloquent demonstration of the Saussurian model of signification which is based on difference rather than essence. The same openness in terms of possibilities underlies the episode in which Tereza's mother chooses a husband from eight suitors (p. 42), and, more spectacularly, the many episodes in which a series of purely coincidental events constitute a fatum, a biography, a story – comparable to the way in which a haphazard collection of phonemes shape a word, an embryonic meaning, and a series of words a sentence, a series of sentences a chapter, a series of chapters a novel. Bearing in mind, always, that this is never a purely linear or metonymic process, but that it is continually complicated through metaphoric intervention and accretion.

4

What we have arrived at so far, is the discovery that there are no fixed meanings in the basic patterns of the text; there are not even stable opposites in the Parmenides paradigm which prompted the narrative investigation. Instead of 'opposing' each other (which would also mean 'defining each other from opposing poles') each term is used to *cover* the other; each contains its opposite within itself (specifically when it comes to lightness/weight), each hides and conceals the other without denying or excluding it. In fact, each term may be regarded as constituting a *disguise* for its ostensible opposite.

Disguise is, indeed, one of the most pervasive tropes in the text, whether it emerges as a country village where all the original Czech place-names have been 'disguised' with Russian ones (p. 165), or Tereza disguising her naked body in clothes, or the Russians disguising their violent invasion of the country as an act of friendship, or Tomas disguising, initially, his affair with Tereza by renting a separate room for her (p. 13). Tereza herself summarises this code on p. 166:

She was thinking how all things and people seemed to go about in disguise. An old Czech town was covered with Russian names. Czechs taking pictures of the invasion had unconciously

worked for the secret police. The man who sent her to die had
worn a mask of Tomas's face over his own. The spy played the
part of an engineer, and the engineer tried to play the part of the
man from Petrin. The emblem of the book in his flat proved a
sham designed to lead her astray.

All these processes of disguise find their ultimate expression in
those strategies of language which demonstrate two quite different,
yet complementary, functions: to cheat with speech; and to cheat
speech. These appear to coincide, at least broadly, with male and
female speech – because the ceaseless tension between the two
underlies almost everything that happens in *The Unbearable Lightness of Being*.

The novel may be said to be structured in the missionary position: male language is always on top, pressing down with its full
weight on the female silence below. Only in relation to the male
does the woman acquire language: 'Love begins at the point when
a woman enters her first word into our poetic memory' (p. 209).
Seldom does this word amount to more than 'an orgasmic shout'
(p. 247), which is pre-lingual. This is intensified by the novel's
designation of its readership as, to all intents and purposes, exclusively male; the narrator's 'We' invariably excludes women. In one
typical example of narratorial comment, the narrator discusses the
etymology of the word 'compassion': ' "To take pity on a woman"
means that *we* are better off than she, that *we* stoop to her level,
lower ourselves' (p. 20, my emphases). This percolates through all
the layers of the narrative.[4]

Even Tereza's dreams are controlled by Tomas (and ultimately,
of course, by the explicitly male narrator). This is evident from the
fear expressed in these dreams of other women who, because they
are all potential mistresses for him, inhabit her subconscious as
menacingly as they do her conscious mind (p. 18). Any woman
who does not fit Tomas's concept of femininity is relegated to one
of two destinies: either she becomes a monster like Tereza's mother
or Franz's wife Marie-Claude or Tomas's first wife, or she is
silenced in the text. This precludes the formation of any female
identity not formulated by men, that is, by male language.[5] In all
the crucial *political* scenes in the book, women are absent. (Tereza's
potentially significant political role as a news photographer is
rapidly dissipated.) Most of the sexual scenes rely on overt physical violence; even the seemingly rational, dispassionate description

of Tomas's pursuit of women is suffused with violence; they must always be 'conquered' (p. 199); 'with his mistresses he could never quite put down the imaginary scalpel. Since he needed to take possession of something deep inside them, he needed to slit them open' (p. 200). He feels compelled to dominate; literally and figuratively, he must always be 'on top', which becomes the metaphor for gender relations in the novel.

5

This gendering process, which *underlies* most of the discourse in the novel, implicitly informs most of the dualities brought to light more explicitly in the text, usually in the form of a meeting, or a collision, between different 'worlds' – whether in the form of discourses, or metaphors, or narrative 'lines' or 'layers'.

Most visibly this occurs in the confrontation between two different sign systems: writing and music. The 'quotation' from Beethoven's last quartet on p. 32 has the effect of allowing the reader to see, through a 'cut' or a 'gap' in the written text, another world of signification. On the narrative level this surfaces when Sabina mocks the half-dressed Tomas looking for his sock, so that from his love-making with her he can return to his wife as the dutiful husband: 'You seem to be turning into the theme of all my paintings [. . .] The meeting of two worlds. A double exposure' (p. 22). And the key to her paintings lies in the description of a scene of a steelworks construction, on which she accidentally dripped red paint:

> The trickle looked like a crack; it turned the building site into a battered old backdrop, a backdrop with a building site painted on it. I began playing with the crack, filling it out, wondering what might be visible behind it. And that's how I began my first cycle of paintings. I called it 'Behind the Scenes' ... On the surface, there was always an impeccably realistic world, but underneath, behind the backdrop's cracked canvas, lurked something different, something mysterious or abstract [. . .] *On the surface, an intelligible lie; underneath, the unintelligible truth.* (p. 63, my emphasis)

True to the style of the novel, Kundera is not content with evoking a dichotomy (the surface of the painting and the scene behind it); the canvases themselves have a dual existence – one for Sabina herself and her friends who are allowed to see them in private; another for the authorities and the public, who do not even know about their existence.

Another highly relevant sign in the scene is the short statement, 'I called it "Behind the Scenes" '. The dualism in the paintings, the meeting of two worlds, only acquires its full significance *when it is named, when it becomes language.* It is a small *mise-en-abyme* of the way in which, in the novel as a whole, a vast complex of thought and of experience is translated into language. It only 'makes' sense once it becomes language.

The discovery of what lies below the surface causes vertigo – that existential experience which has pervaded the modern novel since Kafka: 'Vertigo is something other than the fear of falling. It is the voice of the emptiness below us which tempts and lures us, it is the desire to fall, against which, terrified, we defend ourselves' (p. 60).

And this 'emptiness below' has another name in the text, to which words like 'tempts' and 'lures' and 'desire' alert the reader: it is *woman.*

6

The Sabina scene alerts the reader to the way in which the code of 'two worlds' is embedded throughout the course of the narrative. The conciliatory speech Dubcek delivers after his humiliation in Moscow, is offered as an interplay of speech and silence: the public reacts to the speech on the surface; those who know better 'read' the silences underneath (p. 72). Again, a whole paradigm of different worlds meet – and interact, and interchange – in the scene where Tereza and Sabina photograph one another: their worlds as wife and as mistress, as 'woman of the world' and 'peasant girl', as artist and model, subject and object; but also the worlds of clothing and nakedness; of three-dimensional 'reality' and the reflection in the mirror – all of them converging, again, in the bowler hat, which becomes 'a bed through which each time Sabina saw another river flow, another *semantic* river' (p. 88).

One is reminded of Kundera's pronouncement that 'writing means breaking through a wall behind which something immutable [...] lies hidden in darkness' (Kundera 1988:115).

In *The Unbearable Lightness of Being* Tomas registers the meeting of 'two worlds' whenever he performs an operation on a patient and cuts through the surface to reveal the inside of the body 'as if it were a piece of fabric – a coat, a skirt, a curtain' (p. 194). And it is precisely this experience he translates into his epic pursuit of women, to discover in each of them individually the glimpse of the 'unimaginable [...] the millionth part dissimilarity [which] becomes precious, because, not accessible in public, it must be conquered' (p. 200).

Above all, of course, the worlds of lightness and weight meet and intersect, as we have seen; and once again the wretched dog Karenin embodies this terrible and miraculous ambivalence: when Tereza and Tomas come together, after a heated quarrel, at the dog's death-bed, their very togetherness emphasises the isolation of their worlds (as Tomas and Tereza; as man and wife; as male and female; as heaviness and light; as bearers of different perceptions of the world): 'Each of them was alone. Tereza with her dog, Tomas with his' (p. 295).[6] As if the dog were a word in a dictionary, read and interpreted differently by two readers.

7

In the heart of the map of misreading presented by *The Unbearable Lightness of Being* lurks a dictionary. This should come as no surprise. 'A novel', says Kundera in his reflections on the art of the novel, 'is based primarily on certain fundamental words' (1988:84.) In Part Three, which bears the significant title 'Words Misunderstood', the relationship between Sabina and Franz is narrated, primarily, not as a conventional 'story' or a 'plot' with a beginning, a middle, and an end. We know, after all, that Kundera is constantly in search of methods of 'breaking out of the linear mode', of 'rifts that allow us to step outside the novel's linear pattern' (Kundera 1988:74). Instead, it is read as a dictionary, all of whose words are interpreted differently by the two lovers – whether it is 'woman', or 'fidelity and betrayal', 'light and darkness', 'strength', 'the old church in Amsterdam' or 'cemetery'.

The most significant discovery this section leads to is not, simply, that we assign different meanings to words because we approach them from different experiences, different biographies, different worlds, but the *opposite*: we live different kinds of lives *because we describe them in different words*. And here 'we' means, specifically, men and women.

This leads us back to that aspect of the novel's construction which is involved with the exploration of the meanings of words, Sabina's 'semantic river'.

The defining pair in the paradigm of oppositions the reader encounters from the moment he/she reads the title of the book is that of weight/lightness; and one of the entries into this opposition highlighted by the narrator is the dualism *Muss es sein?* (in which is already implied the possible escape of *'Es könnte auch anders sein* [It could just as well be otherwise]') and its opposite, *'Es muss sein* [It must be]'. On the one hand, the question, which is open, permitting of any conceivable number of answers; on the other, the reply, which is rigorously circumscribed, excluding all other possibilities. And the only difference between these two opposites, in the surface structure of the sentence, is the shift of one single word: *Muss es sein – Es muss sein*. Grammar, language, the word, indeed comes to provoke the world into being, just as, in the myth of our Beginning, light became light when a word – 'Let there be light' – made it so.

Hence, in the world of this novel, whole complicated narrative processes are set in motion, are made possible, by positing certain *words* or phrases ('eternal return', p. 3; 'Einmal ist keinmal', pp. 8, 39; 'Es muss sein', pp. 32–3, 195; 'compassion', pp. 19–21; 'lyrical' and 'epic', p. 201, and so on) and then exploring them. Not one of them 'has' any a priori meaning; language itself becomes *a search for meaning*, as it moves from 'lightness' (that is, the inconsequential: see pp. 179–80, 206 and elsewhere) towards the 'weight' of accumulated meaning, of values and value systems; as it moves from the uniqueness of a specific text – novel, poem, play – into the canon of literature and cultural heritage, or, if you wish, as it breaks through the surface lie into the submerged truth.[7]

This is activated on the narrative level when Tomas's whole life (his dismissal as a surgeon, his new career as window-cleaner, finally as farmer) is determined by an article he writes on Oedipus (pp. 175, 178), that is, a written text, a manipulation of language – and its further manipulation and distortion by the magazine editors and the authorities.

Even the seemingly 'straightforward' or 'simple' Tereza, as she is defined by the male language of the narrator, is complicated through other strategies of language; she arrives on her lover's doorstep carrying Tolstoy's *Anna Karenina* in her hand (at the end of the novel she and her husband will repeat, in their world, Anna

Karenina's death under the wheels of a train); literature, we are constantly reminded, defines and constitutes her life, 'For she had but a single weapon against the world of crudity surrounding her: the books she took out of the municipal library, and above all, novels' (p. 47).

When they make their final decisive move into the country, it is again prompted by language: 'Her image of it [the country] came entirely from what she had heard. Or read' (p. 168; also p. 282); and even while living there 'she was never without a book' (p. 284). Her very relationship with her dog becomes an experience of language, as she trains him 'to provide him with the elementary language that enabled them to communicate and live together' (p. 298).

Because speech is the key to humanity, Dubcek's *silence*, upon his return from Moscow, is the sign of his dehumanisation (pp. 26, 72). Nothing acquires meaning until it becomes language. Tomas fails to recognise an important person from his past before he is told the man's name ('Now I place you. It was the name that did it': p. 211); Sabina, as we have already seen, must give titles to her paintings; her relationship with Franz is unfolded in the terms of their private lexicon – and it ends when he *tells* his wife about her; even our consciousness of the void, in our state of vertigo created by the fusion and confusion of words and notions in the world, is expressed, as we have noted in a passage quoted earlier, as an awareness of 'the *voice* of the emptiness below us' (p. 60, my emphasis). Even – and perhaps especially – sexual love, that key experience in Kundera's novelistic world[8] has to be interpreted in language before it 'makes sense', as is most evident in the philosophical ruminations on 'epic' and 'lyrical' sex (p. 200). And the initial step on 'the steep and narrow path of sexual conquest' is said to be 'the first piece of verbal aggression' (p. 207).

8

But in the final analysis it is the novel itself – this novel, *The Unbearable Lightness of Being* – verbalised by the reader in the process of reading it, which spectacularly confirms the nature of the world we live in and its linguistic and narrative conditionings. The novel is, after all, a process of 'making language' out of 'life': it is the decisive demonstration of polarity and the breakdown of polarity, of the 'meeting of worlds'. This happens, not just in a general way (*all* novels, as we have seen in the previous chapters, turn the world into the word; all novels are verbal or verbalised experience), but through the specific self-consciousness with which it is assembled and pursued in front of the reader's eyes and with the reader's sanction and collusion.

The text opens like a philosophical discourse: 'The idea of eternal return is a mysterious one, and Nietzsche has often perplexed other philosophers with it' (p. 3). In the course of its presentation an unidentified voice offers a 'theme for discussion'; only in Chapter 3 is the discussion placed into the framework of narrative: 'I have been thinking about Tomas for many years. But only in the light of these reflections did I see him clearly' (p. 6). At this stage, Tomas (like Tereza) still functions as a personage who may conceivably exist outside the boundaries of this text; but, after a number of warnings and signals, the opening of Part Two makes explicit their existence as fictitious, and fictional, characters:

> It would be senseless for the author to try and convince the reader that his characters once actually lived. They were not born of a mother's womb; they were born of a stimulating phrase or two or from a basic situation. Tomas was born of the saying *'Einmal ist keinmal.'* Tereza was born of the rumbling of a stomach. (p. 39)

From this moment, the narrator continues to take the reader into his confidence; to take him/her aboard his vehicle, the novel, on the journey of exploration, the quest for meaning. He insists on making language visible, on the page; and, equally, on making visible the processes of the story – as play, as process of thought, as dream and as conquest and subversion of time.

Among many other results, this procedure instils in the reader an awareness of *how* the novel functions, and of *why* it functions in just this way. This random example is from p. 224: 'Several days later, he [Tomas] was struck by another thought, which I record here as an addendum to the preceding chapter.' This appears to highlight the dichotomy between 'world' and 'word': Tomas 'first' thinks his thought, which is alleged to be recorded, subsequently, by the narrator. But it is, of course, a *false* dichotomy, like all the others in the text, just as Tomas is himself a fabrication of the narrator, a fiction in which 'world' and 'word' coincide. But the implications of the strategy go far beyond this: it is a strategy of *repetition*, of *recurrence*, of Nietzschean 'eternal return', enhanced by the fact that the thought Tomas is reported to have had, also has 'eternal return' as its subject. If Tomas is alleged first to have reflected on something, and this reflection is afterwards reported in the novel, then its 'lightness' – *Einmal ist keinmal* – is cancelled. It acquires the weight of recurrence, the weight of 'history'.[9]

Often whole scenes or incidents are repeated: the meeting of Tomas and Tereza is reported more than once; their death occurs *no less than three* times, on pp. 122, 272, 276. This is different from the well-known strategy employed in, for example, Durrell's *Alexandria Quartet*, where the same story is told from different angles; in Kundera's text, Tomas and Teresa *die three times* and are inserted into history, into the theme of 'eternal return', through this process. For Chvatik (1995:159) the function of the repeated death scene is to strip it of literary tragedy and pathos in order to focus exclusively on the 'happy ending'. This seems to me a rather facile reading which goes against the grain of the text: that kind of lightness would be eminently bearable. What makes it *un*bearable is the awareness of *Einmal ist keinmal* which accompanies it, juxtaposed with the weight of the knowledge of the history – and the language – about to crush it.

Now history itself, as a record of the unique events constituting a country's memory, is regarded as 'light' and inconsequential: 'History is as light as individual human life, unbearably light, light as a feather, as dust swirling into the air, as whatever will no longer exist tomorrow' (p. 223).

But once history is *repeated* (in language, for example) it becomes heavy; the heaviness of accumulation, which may be unbearable and negative, like epic womanising, collecting 'trophies'; or the positive, valuable heaviness of meaning, like lyrical womanising, which provides access to the notion of a Whole, an Idea. Misurella (1993:108) phrases it differently, interpreting the desire for sex (linked to Eros) as lightness, the desire for love (linked to sleep and death, Thanatos) as weight.

This means that the novel is *both* lightness and weight, which goes beyond the union of 'the extreme gravity of the question "Does man deserve to live on this earth..." and the extreme lightness of the form' (Kundera 1988:95). Or, to approach it from a different angle, it is an opening, a space, a gap, through which lightness and weight are glimpsed, and within which they make contact and even exchange places. The 'trap' the world is depicted to be (p. 221) does not only manifest itself *as* language: the trap *is* language. But the miracle is that language simultaneously represents an attempt to escape from the trap.

Tomas, confronted with a clothed woman and imagining her naked body, is driven to test his idea of her nakedness against its reality, in order to discover what makes her different from others; he is aware of an entire process unleashed by the interstice between the two states: 'between the approximation of the idea and the precision of reality there was a small gap of the unimaginable, and it was this hiatus that gave him no rest' (p. 199).

Once again, this time most literally, we are returned to that much-quoted passage from Barthes (1976:9) about 'the most erotic portion of a body *where the garment gapes*'. Transposed to reading (he is, after all, discussing 'the pleasure of the text'), he notes that 'what "happens", what "goes away", the seam of the two edges, the interstice of bliss, occurs in the volume of the languages, in the uttering, not in the sequence of utterances' (p. 13). Not the one *or* the other creates meaning, pleasure, adventure, but the gap: the gap of the unimaginable, which is synonymous with Derrida's notion of the *hymen*:

> The hymen, the confusion between the present and the non-present [...] produces the effect of a medium [...] It is an operation that *both* sows confusion *between* opposites *and* stands *between* opposites 'at once'. What counts here is the *between*, the in-between-ness of the hymen. The hymen 'takes place' in the 'inter-', in the spacing between desire and fulfillment, between perpetration and its recollection. (Derrida 1981:212)

So this is what the long list of Parmedian binarities 'stands for' in *The Unbearable Lightness of Being*: not the exclusion of opposites, but the celebration of the gap or the hymen 'in between' – that gendered and gendering gap which both propels and contains the narrative.

'The novelist is neither historian nor prophet: he is an explorer of existence', says Kundera (1988:44). And that exploration of 'what the novel alone can discover' (p. 64) takes place, precisely, *inside the gap*, in the fluid moment in which meanings intersect and change places.

We know by now that it is no simple procedure. When Tereza arrives to photograph her husband's mistress, this is how the moment of transition is described: '[Sabina] came out in her bath-robe. Tereza picked up the camera and put it to her eye. Sabina threw open the robe' (p. 65). It is indeed the instant when 'the garment gapes'. Yet this is the consequence: 'The camera served Tereza as both a mechanical eye through which to observe Tomas's mistress and a veil by which to conceal her face from her' (p. 65).

The novel, too, obscures *and* reveals. It is in search of an 'I' ('All novels, of every age, are concerned with the enigma of the self': Kundera 1988:23): but the self is as elusive and inchoate as the attributes accumulated to describe or contain it. In the final analysis, it is a self accessible only through words. No, more: it is a self that *exists* only by virtue of language.

9

The end of the journey is also its beginning; at the end of the novel we are sent back to Chapter 1, where 'lightness' and 'weight' still seemed relatively unproblematic. This is, itself, a form of eternal return. Which means that the processes we have identified – both embedded in, and released by, the story of Tomas and Tereza, of Tomas and his mistresses or his son, of Tereza and her mother, of Tomas and Sabina, of Tereza and Sabina, of Sabina and Franz – the processes of constructing dichotomies and breaking them down, uniting them and pulverising them, have all been possible *only because those processes are part of language itself*. Language is neither heavy nor light, neither positive nor negative; it is always contextual, not simply textual; it is real, visible, audible, material, historical – and at the same time it is the imagination breaking through all barriers. It is serious thought; above all, it is play. It takes any gap it sees to subvert, to deconstruct, to destroy and reassemble, to make fun of, to lament, whatever we call 'reality'; whatever we conceive of as a 'self'.

It does not only 'take' a gap: as we have already noted about the 'trap', *language is the gap*.

It is the Black Hole, invisible in itself, perceived only through its effect on contiguous bodies, into which everything entering its sphere of gravity is sucked; existence collapsed into itself, dark and unfathomable, resplendent and miraculous. Language *is* both the unbearable lightness and the improbable heaviness of being.

14

Possessed by Language

A. S. Byatt: *Possession*

1

The Quest. The gendering of language. The reach of desire and the postponement of fulfilment. The interrogation of history, private and public. Language as translation, this time complicated by notions of the translation of poetry into prose, of past into present. In all these respects, and more, A. S. Byatt's *Possession* (first published in 1990), gathers threads from our previous readings into itself. But the particular *urgency* of the text derives from its exploration of language as a form of possession. And the peculiar shape it assumes is inspired by the way in which it inserts itself, as a Postmodernist novel, into a tradition of romance – romance as genre, romance in its relations with history and historiography, romance in its relations with Realism, romance as a strategy of gendering – which also foregrounds some of the intriguing links between some forms of Postmodernism and some forms of Feminism. As a result, as in so many of the novels we have explored, language becomes a demonstration of trickery; and the narrator plays the immemorial role of trickster.

2

In *Possession*, which Byatt herself conceived of as 'a nineteenth-century type novel about the nature of history and evidence' (quoted by Kenyon 1988:56), a group of academics are depicted in their passionate pursuit of historical and literary evidence about two fictitious Victorian poets, Randolph Henry Ash and Christabel LaMotte. As their poetry and their lives are discovered to develop into increasingly complex mutual entanglements, the two researchers at the heart of the quest, Roland Michell and Maud Bailey, find themselves replicating and extending the experience of their Victorian predecessors. Not only do they become more and more 'possessive' about their material and the objects of their pursuit (p. 91),[1] but more and more 'possessed' by them. The first time the hazardous nature of the undertaking is brought explicitly to the reader's attention is in Chapter 3, when Professor James Blackadder's obsession with the work of Randolph Henry Ash is noted, with the acknowledgement 'that all his thoughts would have been another man's thoughts, all his work another man's' (p. 29). In both the 'thoughts' and the 'work' language is implicated; and in both cases the mind is controlled, and invaded, by the language of *another*. If this extends Atwood's preoccupation in *Surfacing* it is at the same time very different. Certainly, the male/female gendering of language will play an enormous role in *Possession* – both in the differences between the poetry of LaMotte and Ash, and in their interaction with Roland and Maud – but the primary difference posited in the text is not that between male and female but between Self and Other. It is complicated by gender, as it is complicated by history (the interval between the Victorian age and that of Postmodernism).

This complication resides particularly in the novel's awareness of textuality, since both Roland and Maud (as well as the pack of academics surrounding them) realise that even history, in the form of the lives of LaMotte and Ash, is accessible only through texts, in language. This is how, and why, the 'possession' of the novel becomes primarily an obsession with language – not just the language of the contemporary and Victorian protagonists, but that of the larger English literary tradition. 'I speak to you', confesses Ash in an early letter to LaMotte, 'as I might speak to all those who most possess my thoughts – to Shakespeare, to Thomas Browne, to John Donne, to John Keats' (p. 177).

On the most practical level, possession in the novel, when it refers to the all-important letters of the two Victorian poets, becomes 'a complicated question of ownership and copyright' (p. 415), both of which keep the reader firmly within the space of written language. But of course the novel goes far beyond this in its exploration of the meanings and manifestations

of 'possession'. When Ash and LaMotte travel together in the train
to the resort where their love will be consummated, the man's
passion for the young woman is wholly 'literarised'. First of all,
the entire passage in Chapter 15 which describes the journey is cast
in the language of a Victorian novel. Then it is revealed that his
infatuation has been one of the imagination, informed by the literature of romance: 'For months he had been possessed by the
imagination of her. She had been distant and closed away, a princess in a tower' (pp. 276–7). His gaze, fixed upon the real woman
opposite him, is informed by the memory of another poetic love,
that of Wordsworth for 'his solitary Highland girl', and as he looks
at her he is 'voracious for information. He learned her', which
keeps the description strictly within the world of books and literature, even if he tries to persuade himself that 'he saw her clearly,
despite her possession of him' (p. 278). And he sets it as his aim to
'teach her that she was not his possession' (p. 279). Three times in
as many pages the word surfaces; and even the third reference,
which appears to be directed at a decision on the emotional or the
moral level, is immediately directed towards the processes of writing, of fabricating language: 'I have an idea for a poem about
necessity' (p. 279).

   Much later, Ash will confess his love of LaMotte to his wife: 'I
could say it was a sort of madness. A possession, as by daemons'
(p. 453). But even this experience of possession becomes such only
in the process of verbalising it. The reader knows at this stage that,
for Ash, life and love exist only in function of language: his love is
lived as if it were a poem; his poetry, in the fullest Derridean sense
of the word (and most especially according to the exegesis provided in J. Hillis Miller's 'The Critic as Host', 1979:217–32), is the
parasite of his life. This is why not only the story or stories of
Possession 'deal with' various experiences of obsession, but why the
language of the novel itself may be read as a demonstration, and as
the primary form, of possession.

   One of the most pertinent remarks of the novel is a quotation
from Balzac: '*Le dégoût, c'est voir juste. Après la possession, l'amour
voit juste chez les hommes* [Disgust means to see correctly. After
possession, men's love sees correctly]' (p. 282). The clarity of the
view becomes a clarity of language. Even if, as in this instance,
with exquisite irony, it is a foreign language. This play with language becomes the condition of the bag of tricks at the disposal of
the writer of romance.

3

Byatt herself conditions her reader by offering as her opening epigraph a passage from Nathaniel Hawthorne which claims for romance 'a certain latitude, both as to its fashion and material' that is not allowed the novel; specifically, Hawthorne locates it 'in the attempt to connect a bygone time with the very present that is flitting away from us' (Byatt 1991a:v). This would immediately conjure up visions of those medieval romances, either chivalric (like the tales of Amadis of Gaul) or philosophical (like the *Roman de la Rose*), which preceded the emergence of the novel in the *Don Quixote*: extravagant stories of quests and jousts, of noble knights fighting dragons and Saracens or rescuing beautiful damsels from fortified castles, of courtly love and the requirements of feudal *cortesia*. Even in its later developments, notably in the historical romances of Sir Walter Scott, it remained attached to that remote past, to the view of which distance lent its sometimes questionable enchantment.

As the novel, in the infinite variety produced by its irrepressible rise through the centuries, seemed in one way or another to pre-occupy itself with the 'real', romance appropriated more marginal territories where the imagination could run wild. Hence the hint of *excess* invariably associated with the genre. In Henry James's description, 'romance is essentially inessential, its only law the law of excess over itself' (Elam 1992:6). However, as the novel came to be regarded more and more seriously, romance, im-mensely popular as it has remained, came to be dismissed as 'mere' invention, and – in the worst and most chauvinistic senses of the word – fit only to be written by females for female consump-tion, reaching specific heights in the work of Mrs Gaskell, Mary Shelley, and Charlotte Brontë. All the more reason, Diane Elam argues, for 'postmodernism (to) turn to romance in order to dis-place notions of historical propriety and authenticity' (Elam 1992:24). In romance Postmodernism finds the kind of *space* it thrives on – a space which makes it possible to question assump-tions about history, and the place of women in it.

This becomes strikingly evident in the use of the Melusina myth (to which I shall return in due course); in her identification with Melusina, the story of Charlotte LaMotte conveys primarily the power of female desire, expressed both in sexuality and in writing. This is possible only in romance, a 'female' genre beyond the reach of history – that is, of history as a patriarchal system of knowledge in which the female figure is allowed to participate only inasmuch as she is predefined by the male gaze. And in writing, of course, the male gaze is translated into language. Once she transgresses the limits imposed on her identity by patriarchal control, Melusina indeed becomes terrifying. In this respect romance becomes, in Cixous's terminology, 'the laugh of the Medusa' (Cixous 1976).

This wild freedom underlies much of the impact of *Possession*. But in many other respects, too, the text manifests itself as a romance. There is first of all the Romantic orchestration of the plot as a *Quest*. In one of the stories-within-the-story, LaMotte's tale about the little tailor and the glass coffin, there is this crucial line, 'The key is the key to an adventure, if you will go in search of it' (p. 60); in another, 'The Threshold', the old woman warns the Childe 'to keep boldly on along the track, deviating neither to right nor left, though creatures might call and beckon him enticingly' (p. 150); on p. 238 Maud herself says, 'I want to – to – follow the – path [...] I want to *know* what happened [...] It isn't professional greed. It's something more primitive'; and on p. 328 she possessively affirms, 'It is our Quest.' Aspects of romance are also evident in many of the individual scenes within the encompassing Quest: the Gothic extravagance of churchyards and castles and midnight terrors, the trials and tribulations of lovers, or the magnificent melodramatic excess in the final reunion between father and daughter. Apart from this, there are several explicit references to the genre, characteristic of the self-consciousness of the Postmodernist text. In the *Journal Intime* by Sabine Kercoz, Christabel LaMotte is quoted as saying that,

> Romance is a land where women can be free to express their true natures [...] in Romance, women's two natures can be reconciled. I asked, which two natures, and she said, men saw women as double beings, enchantresses and demons or innocent angels. (p. 373)

Roland, who himself bears the name of an ancient hero of romance, sees himself – absolutely correctly – as existing 'in a Romance, a vulgar and a high Romance simultaneously, a Romance was one of the systems that controlled him, as the expectations of Romance control almost everyone in the Western world' (p. 425).

Upon hearing of Randolph Henry Ash's final illness, Christabel refers to her arrangements for their child as 'a lie more appropriate to a romance than to my previous quiet life' (p. 500). And in the final episode, the *tour de force* of the whole novel, Ash requests from Maia a lock of hair as a memento, 'Like a fairy story' (p. 510).

4

The splendid artificiality of the Postmodernist enterprise – the text of life as *story*, and as *performance* – is evoked in the very opening scene, set (like so many texts of this kind in Borges, Calvino, Eco and others) in a *library*, a world of Books and of Literature, the make-believe and self-constructions of language. All of this is visualised, in the description of the Lincoln Library, which is Maud's domain, as the London Library is Roland's, as a *fabrication* ('like a box of toys or a giant ConstructoKit' (p. 43), which amusingly recalls the end of Thackeray's *Vanity Fair*). It is a world of *reflections* and *repetitions*, 'like Tinkerbell's fairylights in her Never-Never-Land' (p. 43).

From this book-world emerges the full quest of the romance, the attempted reconstruction of the lives of the two nineteenth-century poets, the male Ash and the female LaMotte, primarily in terms of the only 'reality' available to the researchers: poetry, journals, letters, documents: *language*. And it is both amusing and revealing that one of the results of the quest is that Roland himself becomes a poet, gradually assembling, from washing-lists of disconnected words, a series of poems.

The names of the characters are themselves indicators of literariness (and on p. 418 we are informed specifically that 'names accrue meaning'). I have already referred to Roland, of medieval *Chanson* fame. His opposite and eventual ally is, of course, Maud of Tennysonian repute: an arch-Victorian name if ever there was one. She may also recall Arthur Conan Doyle's Lady Maude, the spirited young aristocrat who agrees to marry Alleyne after he has proved himself as a knight in the novel *The White Company*, set in the Middle Ages.[2] Among the most important other dramatis personae who may be read as variations of pre-existing literary models are Beatrice Nest, a Dantesque companion on a crucial part of the Quest; Fergus Wolff, whose paradigms haunt much of the text, whether as medieval wolves or as the huge beast that guards

Christabel, herself a nineteenth-century variant of the serpent-fairy-witch Melusina; and Professor Blackadder, a serpent in the Paradise Lost so much of the text attempts to restore. Most copiously, Randolph Henry Ash's name acquires a remarkable proliferation of associations in the course of the text, from the Tree of Life in the Garden of Proserpina (the 'World Ash' on pp. 194 and 464, 'rooted in the underworld and touching Heaven': p. 95) to the ashes of volcanic eruptions or of death (Blackadder's work place is known as the 'Ash Factory' or the 'Crematorium'), or of the apocalypse (p. 167) from which the phoenix is reborn (pp. 198, 502). We encounter 'mountain ash berries' (p. 46), the Ask and Embla ('ash' and 'alder') from which the first man and woman were created (p. 241), the 'sturdy ash-plant' the poet uses as a walking stick (pp. 247, 509), 'ash-saplings' in the poem *Melusina* (p. 266), '*Ash* volcanic' in another poem (p. 273), and many more.[3]

5

Behind each character seems to move the (almost spiritistic) shadow of a Predecessor. It marks one of the primary impulses this novel shares with texts as disparate as *Middlemarch*, *Death in Venice* or *If on a Winter's Night a Traveller*: a return to origins. This is as much Roland's obsession (in spite of his live-in companion Val's disparaging view of it: p. 19) as it is Maud's ('How strangely appropriate', says Blackadder, 'to have been exploring all along the myth of your own origins': p. 503), or LaMotte's (in her return to her father's Casaubonesque *Mythologies*: p. 31). But 'possession' by the notion of origins, of An Origin, affects more than just the characters: it is a *textual* obsession.

This is expressed metaphorically in images of the original Garden (whether the Garden of Proserpina (pp. 1–2), or Eden (pp. 262, 286)), as a kind of mythological sanction for the many references to *sources* real and literary, including something as seemingly innocent as an 'Eau de Source' on p. 269, which culminate in the orchard of the Rowan Tree Inn where the denouement is set (p. 487), and, of course, in the garden (or meadow) of the final encounter between Ash and his daughter (pp. 508–11).

It is conveyed even more strongly in the most persistent metaphor of the text, that of the fairy Melusina in all her many avatars (most completely on p. 33): essentially the story of a magic female creature, sometimes half-fish, sometimes half-dragon or half-serpent, who builds castles, fortresses, strongholds, and then marries the mortal knight Raimondin. As long as he respects her wish not to be looked at on Saturdays when she takes a bath – that is, when she returns to her female element, water – their love is prosperous and wholesome (even if they do have monstrous offspring); but when he disobeys it leads to destruction. Free from the gaze of men, immersed in her own self-sufficient sexuality, Melusina possesses an identity the male gaze cannot cope with. Aspects of her story, her existence beyond history, will be repeated throughout the text, not only literally, in a form of pastiche, when Roland – with the best of intentions – watches Maud through the keyhole of the bathroom door, but more subtly whenever someone in the text 'spies' on another, most notably when the twentieth-century researchers 'spy' on their nineteenth-century predecessors and 'models' (who themselves repeat more archetypal models).

This urge towards beginnings determines, on the most obvious level, the romantic quest of the novel: the attempts by Roland and Maud, as much as by Blackadder, Cropper, Leonora or even Beatrice, to find the 'real' origins and sources for the poetry of Ash and LaMotte. It means, also, that the drive towards beginnings involves many processes of *resurrection*.[4] Ash's 'Proserpina' is read as 'a meditation on the myths of Resurrection' (p. 3); his 'Ragnarök' is seen as a Christian 'resurrection' of a Norse myth (pp. 9, 163 and elsewhere). Most spectacularly there is the 'resurrection' of Ash and LaMotte as 'real people' from the grave of obscurity.[5]

Behind the urge lies, of course, the yearning towards a state of wholeness, of self-sufficient being, for example in the image of the 'self-sustaining ponds' and 'controlled environments' of Victorian experimentation (p. 16); in Ash's imagery of the three Ases wandering across the plains – 'They were themselves alone' (p. 239); and, strikingly, in the image of Narcissus, 'the unstable self, the fractured ego' (p. 251). This will be explored with intensified urgency in the quest for *female* self-sufficiency: 'The new feminists see Melusina in her bath as a symbol of self-sufficient female sexuality needing no poor males' (p. 34).

The problem of the enterprise lies in the constantly repeated discovery that *origins are illusory*. The reader is alerted to this as early as p. 2, when Roland, looking for sources of Ash's *Garden of Proserpina*, stumbles upon the book which triggers the whole ensuing search: Vico's *Principii di una Scienza Nuova*. Now in the mind of any twentieth-century reader after Joyce's *Finnegan's Wake*, Vico represents, not 'originality' but 'eternal recurrence'; in Vico's philosophy, replicated in the shape of Joyce's great novel, there *are* no beginnings or endings: everything exists as a continuum in which the same events are eternally repeated in different keys, on different scales. These range from the divine (represented here by the myths of Melusina and others) via the heroic (which may include Ash who was, after all, a contemporary of Carlyle), to the paltry (satirised in the ferocious competition among literary scholars in their search for more and more 'meaning'). Phrased differently (and different phrasings lie at the heart of *Possession*), all styles from the heroic to pastiche to satire are represented here. Instead of a controlled and logical motion towards a predefined target, the motion is here, in a word applied to Roland himself, 'haphazard' (p. 3). An image of this is provided by his dream on p. 149:

> In his dream he was hopelessly entwined and entangled with an apparently endless twisted rope of bright cloth and running water,[6] decorated with wreaths and garlands and tossed sprays of every kind of flower, real and artificial, embroidered or painted, under which something clutched or evaded, reached out or slid away. When he touched it, it was not there; when he tried to lift an arm or a leg it prevented him, gripping, coiling.

It is clear that Ellen Ash, in her journal, was not the only one who 'wrote [...] to baffle' (p. 220).

6

The urge towards a beginning is balanced by an equally strong urge towards an ending: it is the *given* of narrative that, once begun, it runs its course, then ends. 'We need the end of the story', says Maud on p. 498. And when Blackadder warns that, 'There is no guarantee that *that* is what we shall find', she retorts, 'But we must *look*.' Which repeats LaMotte's own earlier exclamation, in a letter to Ash, 'I cannot bear not to know the end of a tale', (p. 176).

Endings, limits, frontiers also provoke the urge to *transgress* them: 'We are defined by the lines we choose to cross or to be confined by' (p. 431).

This means that in *Possession* we should expect a constant play of stops and starts, interruptions and transgressions, and inasmuch as one can speak of 'presence', it will be, in Ash's words to Christabel, 'a threshold-presence' (p. 181): each episode, and each character, represents a *crossing* of endings and beginnings. 'How shall this be the end, that is in its very nature a *beginning*?' asks Ash (p. 193). And the consummation of the Roland/Maud love story itself emblematises the kind of *textual* experience to which 'there seemed to be no boundaries' (p. 507).

7

In this open-ended story world, where beginnings and endings are at most illusory, the reader, deprived of a master narrative, is left with a play – and an interplay – of endless variations and repetitions and versions. 'All old stories, my cousin', writes Sabine in a diary entry she knows the cousin will not read, 'will bear telling and retelling again in different ways' (p. 350). What matters is the telling: 'The stories', writes the same Sabine, 'come before the meanings' (p. 355). This is the only 'narrative shape' Byatt confesses she could conceive of 'which could expose the continuities and discontinuities between the forms of nineteenth- and twentieth-century art and thought' (Byatt 1991b:6).

The story opens, as we have noted, with Roland working through a *copy* of Vico; when he returns home to the flat he and Val share, he is confronted with different *pictures* of Ash (that is, copies of portraits of the poet), which ironically he finds 'somehow more real [...] because they were photographs. Less full of life, the life of the paint, but more realistic, in the modern sense, according to modern expectations' (p. 17).

Much later they are described with greater urgency: 'The light in Roland's hall caught the photographed painted light in the shiny thickness of the crystal ball. It illuminated the hints and traces of reflected light on the glass-contained jungle-ferns and watery sea-depth behind the head' (p. 466); and the two pictures are said to depict 'recognisably the same man and yet utterly different, years apart, visions apart' (p. 467).

This kind of play on the concept of *version* persists throughout: Fergus Wolff's hair is 'the 1980s version of the 1930s' (p. 32); the Stant Collection of Ash memorabilia is housed in a version of the

Cabinet of Treasures in Cropper's father's home (p. 103); Randolph Ash spent his honeymoon at the Fontaine de Vaucluse where the earlier poet Petrarch had lived amid scenery itself reminiscent of a Pre-Raphaelite painting (p. 109);[7] when Maud is in the bathroom in the Bailey mansion Roland imagines, not her nakedness, but her reflection in a mirror (p. 148); the present-day explorers visit a *restoration* of LaMotte's house (itself a 'copy' of the Biblical Bethany), commenting that 'It's a good restoration job [...] A simulacrum' (p. 210); Ash in his poetry is preoccupied with 'the persistent shapeshifting life of things long-dead but not vanished' (p. 256); all Ash's poems are copied out by his wife, just as Maud and Roland copy key passages from the old letters; when on his rhapsodic adulterous journey with Christabel they make love for the first time his thoughts are about:

> How many men have had that thought [...] in how many places, how many climates, how many rooms and cabins and caves, all supposing themselves swimmers in salt seas, with the waves rising, all supposing themselves – no, knowing themselves – unique. (p. 283)[8]

But these are only details of copying within the texture of the narrative. The text itself is constructed according to much larger 'repeating patterns' (the phrase is Maud's, when she comments on the way in which LaMotte's life echoed the fates of fictitious heroines like Gretchen, Hetty Sorrel, Wordsworth's Martha: p. 422).

It is Melusina who, once again, determines the most pervasive repeated pattern in the text. More than any other character in the novel, Christabel revives the passions and perversions of the creative and dangerous fairy woman. Not only does the poem *Melusina* represent the summum of her life's work – rewritten, we are told, at least eight times (p. 41) – but on page p. 501, in her last letter to the dying Ash she confesses, '*I have been Melusina* these thirty years.' But her cousin Sabine, in her 'castle' in Brittany, also rehearses the story of the fairy; and in the end we meet Christabel's own fairy child, Maia. But even before that moment is reached, we have also encountered Melusina in the warrior woman Leonora, and even in LaMotte's companion Blanche Glover, the pale harbinger of death. And in Ash's life she features as Proserpina: an extract from the poem appears *twice* in the text, on p. 1, and again on p. 464, and, significantly, *the two versions are not identical*. From both

LaMotte and Ash, Maud (who also *resembles* both) inherits the fairy's potential for either creation or destruction, especially after Roland enacts with her the fatal bathroom scene.[9]

The pattern which determines the course of the narrative concerns the repetition, by Roland and Maud, of the relationship between Ash and LaMotte. Roland himself, as a self-conscious textual construct, reflects – 'partly with precise postmodernist pleasure' (p. 421) – that,

> Coherence and closure are deep human desires that are presently unfashionable. But they are always both frightening and enchantingly desirable. 'Falling in love', characteristically, combs the appearances of the world [...] out of a random tangle and into a coherent plot. Roland was troubled by the idea that the opposite might be true. Finding themselves in a plot, they might suppose it appropriate to behave as though it was that sort of plot. And that would be to compromise some kind of integrity they had set out with. (p. 422)

Consequently, the pleasure of the text resides not simply in the way in which the two contemporary romantic characters follow the course modelled by their predecessors (who, in turn, replicated the story of Melusina and her human prince), but in the ways in which they reshape and even break the pattern in the process. The poetry of Ash and LaMotte 'followed' and 'mirrored' their lives, yet, as fictitious – or rather as *fictionalising* – accounts, they also *distorted* the 'originals'. And the same holds true for the equation Roland/Maud – Ash/LaMotte.

Yet it is all so relative. One of the most amusing and startling discoveries, for the reader, in the evolving relationship between Roland and Maud, comes when they deliberately decide to break the pattern: on their visit to the Midlands they take one day off to visit the Boggle Hole, convinced that this is a wholly original excursion; significantly, they do not even take books with them (p. 268), yet barely twenty pages later the reader finds out that Ash and LaMotte, too, had taken a day off to visit the Boggle Hole (p. 286). If, at first sight, it would seem that Roland and Maud are indeed so fully 'possessed' by their predecessors that even in their private, 'independent' actions they are predetermined by them, the Postmodernist feature of this discovery lies in the fact that the nineteenth-century episode is narrated *after* the account of the twentieth-century event. Chronology, historicity is not only suspended but inverted, and *Ash and LaMotte are determined as much by their successors as vice versa.*

This process is embedded within another functioning of intertextuality: initially, Roland works on Ash, Maud on LaMotte (see pp. 216, 218, 316); as the lives of the biographees begin to interact, Roland starts immersing himself more in the LaMotte text (pp. 246, 264), Maud in the Ash; both horizontally and vertically texts begin to interact, as the 'continuity and interdependence of all life' (p. 249: read 'all *texts*') becomes foregrounded. (Only Melusina appears to know the *whole*, both beginning and end (see p. 245), but Melusina herself is not so much an 'origin' as a 'construct' of the text: she is the *figure of intertextuality*.)

Similarly, when Maud buys a brooch for her female friend Leonora (p. 308), this is much more than a repetition of what LaMotte did, a century before, for *her* friend Blanche Glover (p. 308); the decisive factor here is not chronology, but narration, and LaMotte's action is as much the *result* of Maud's as the entire reconstituted love life of Ash and Christabel is the *result* of the investigation by Roland and Maud. This would illustrate Elam's argument that 'Postmodernism is not a perspectival view on history; it is the rethinking of history as an ironic coexistence of temporalities' (Elam 1992:3).

One crucial line of 'development' in the story concerns the way in which the *separate* biographies of LaMotte and Ash become inextricably linked in a *single* narrative: 'They belong together. It's not only that they need to be read consecutively to make any sense – they – they are part of each other' (p. 480). And another 'line' in the text concerns the gradual intertwining of nineteenth- and twentieth-century lives; the importance of this lies no longer in reading them 'consecutively' but in reading them as part of the same expanding story.

In the process, what remains of 'originals' is persistently interrupted, and *corrupted*. 'There was never an error-free text', Cropper remarks on p. 25. Later Roland will concur: 'All you can see is imperfections and reflections', (p. 142). And on p. 367 it is Christabel's turn: 'All that I touch [...] is damaged.'

Metaphorically, these strategies are encapsulated in the experience of *déjà vu* in spiritism (p. 166); in Ash's poetic 'ventriloquism' (pp. 104, 246); in the notions of charade (p. 457), parody (p. 422), and pastiche (p. 425); and most significantly in the notion of *meta-*

morphosis. 'Metamorphoses', says Ash on p. 280, 'are our way of showing, in riddles, that we know we are part of the animal world.' If this is very much a nineteenth-century view, the Postmodernist view would make use of metamorphosis to demonstrate the gliding movement from one text – and one *kind* of text – to another. It would encompass, too, what Blackadder describes as 'the *false* or *fictive* bringing to life of the dead' (p. 299), and Ash's acknowledgement, in the poem 'Mummy Possest', that 'Our small deceptions are a form of Art' (p. 408).

8

This brings us to the crucial enterprise, the quest to find an image for the past; in other words, the attempt to resurrect the nineteenth century as a twentieth-century text.

Possession can be compared in many respects to Julian Barnes's *Flaubert's Parrot.* Using the 'Realist concern with documentation and fact' (Lee 1990:11), Barnes's narrator, Dr Geoffrey Braithwaite, sets out in search of the 'truth' about Flaubert – only to discover what is inevitable to a Postmodernist: that only 'parrotings' exist, that originality is irrecoverable.

> All literary texts are woven out of other literary texts [...] in the more radical sense that every word, phrase or segment is a reworking of other writings which precede or surround the individual work. There is no such thing as literary 'originality' no such thing as the 'first' literary work: all literature is intertextual. (Eagleton 1983:183)

In *Flaubert's Parrot,* 'Gustave Flaubert is an historically verifiable entity, but we can only know him through the written evidence of words, letters, and reminiscences' (Lee 1990:39). But, like Nabokov in *Pale Fire,* Byatt goes beyond that, since Randolph Henry Ash and Christabel LaMotte are *not* 'historically verifiable entities' but *themselves* constructs of language. It becomes part of the novel's fake search for fake origins that *behind* Ash we see looming the familiar Victorian figure of Robert Browning (and to a lesser extent also Tennyson, even Swinburne, Rossetti and others), but there is no simple equation, and Ash does not 'equal', is not a 'reconstruction' of Browning. The situation becomes even more fascinating if we allow for the possibility that LaMotte, in her turn, is informed not only by Christina Rossetti or Elizabeth Barrett Browning (or even, occasionally, by Emily Dickinson), but *also* by the male Robert Browning[10] – which suggests that Browning is not a Freudian father figure at all, but features more as a spiritistic 'medium' *through* which the reader is allowed to reach even further back, into Browning's poetic 'world' where female figures and forces play a significant role.[11]

With the basic Realist distinction between ' "lying" literature and "true", "objective" history' (Lee 1990:29) removed, the text is set before the reader (as the Victorian Ash-LaMotte 'text' is set before the twentieth-century research team) as a *performance* to be enacted and entered into. What this entails is suggested in a passage by Richard Schechner in the essay 'News, Sex, and Performance Theory' reminiscent of the Elizondo epigraph in Llosa's *Aunt Julia and the Scriptwriter* quoted in the Introduction to this study:

> A person sees the event; he sees himself; he sees himself seeing the event; he sees himself seeing others who are seeing the event and who, maybe, see themselves seeing the event. Thus there is the performance, the performers, the spectators; and the spectator of spectators; and the self-seeing-self that can be performer or spectator or spectator of spectators. (quoted in Lee 1990:92)

As I have suggested before, the lives of Roland and Maud are as much *produced* by those of Ash and LaMotte as the latter are products of the research embarked on by the twentieth-century team.[12]

9

This kind of complication, encouraged by the genre, also influences our reading of gender in the text.

When Ash goes to Brittany in search of Christabel, in search of what with a characteristic demonstration of male possessiveness he terms 'my' child, his particular quest is informed by the anxious question (and 'quest' and 'question' are of course closely linked): 'Why did you turn away from me? Out of pride, out of fear, out of independence, out of sudden hatred, *at the injustice of the different fates of men and women*?' (p. 456, my emphasis).

But if this is very much a preoccupation of the nineteenth century (which does not suggest that it has lost its validity in our own), *Possession*, as a Romance, that is, as a 'female' form, written by a woman, also subverts the notion of predetermined, fixed gender roles.

To begin with, in the twentieth-century cast, the woman researcher Maud is the one with job security, with a clearly defined research project, living independently, confident of her identity and her sexuality (even if this has been shaken by the depredations of the wolf, Fergus), while Roland, wholly unlike his heroic predecessor, is timid, with doubts about his identity and his place in the academic world, with no secure job, no prospects for the future, no social skills, his only true desire the yearning for a virginal white bed. Professor Cropper's arrogance is more than matched by the aggressive and assertive presence of Leonora Stern; in the Bailey household the handicapped and dependent Lady turns out to be more decisive and influential than her vicious and suspicious husband. The most important 'guide' on the French leg of the quest (which, as the narrator points out, is turning more and more into 'Chase and Race': p. 425), is the woman Ariane Le Minier.[13]

But a simple reversal of roles would be suspiciously facile. What is much more rewarding is to read *Possession* as a Postmodernist attempt 'to revalue romance in the name of female desire and discourse' (Elam 1992:2), because, as the same critic argues,

> If realism can only deal with woman by relegating her to romance, if real history belongs to men, and women's history is merely the fantasy of historical romance, postmodern cultural analysis of history and the 'real' offers a way of revaluing female discourse [...This is possible because] within postmodern romance the figure of woman is what allows the work of remembering to be performed. (ibid.:3, 16)

In this respect, Christabel LaMotte is a key figure. The wholeness and self-sufficiency of the feminine space she has established with her companion Blanche Glover is challenged, and eventually invaded, by the prowler, the wolf, Randolph Henry Ash.[14] Ash, the male, becomes a determining influence in her work – notably in the shaping of her major poem, *Melusina*, which in many subtle and not-so-subtle ways he in fact tries to appropriate. But at the same time she becomes as vital a shaping influence in *his* poetry: a single illuminating example is the reference to 'A mermaid swam in a hermetic jar' in Ash's *Swammerdam* (p. 204). Their very styles, in verse as in letters, begin to converge, at last to merge in Browning. More importantly, if it is indeed LaMotte who writes, and 'lives' (in her own words), the fairy story, Melusina informs the lives of *both* LaMotte and Ash: in *her* their separate existences converge. This happens especially during their secret residence at the seaside resort (the sea is Melusina's sign) and it is confirmed in the birth of the girl-child, Maia, who re-activates a world of matriarchal mythology,[15] since we are reminded that 'Maia was the mother of Hermes, thief, artist and psychopomp' (p. 509). He is also, as will be noted in the chapter on Calvino, the guardian of all knowledge (hermeneutics is the science of Hermes). And *knowledge* – closely associated with *language* – is the aim of the quest which lies at the heart of narrative generally, and *Possession* in particular. In a vital passage of the novel Roland is described as 'being uselessly urged on by some violent emotion of curiosity – not greed, curiosity, more fundamental even than sex, the desire for knowledge' (p. 82). While, as we have seen before, Ash is described as 'voracious for information. He learned her' (p. 277).

That very Origin and Beginning which 'possesses' the searchers for knowledge is concerned with the notion of *autonomy*; and if males also aspire to it (Fergus Wolff wrote a paper on 'Gender and the Autonomous Text': pp. 56–7), their definition of it is a distortion of and a borrowing from *female* wholeness, of which the egg is the metaphor (see pp. 137, 502).

Of course Woman can assume dangerous and even destructive forms too. It is Leonora who, in a letter to Maud, refers to 'the undines and nixies and melusinas' as 'women perceived as dangerous' (p. 139), particularly in their functioning as witches. Christabel refers to herself living 'in a Turret like an old Witches' (p. 450, repeated on p. 500). Beatrice Nest appears in the graveyard scene 'with streaming white woolly hair [...] like some witch or prophetess' (p. 496). And in Ash's notorious *Mummy Possest* evil female power is viewed by a male who is, himself, of course, the creature of a female author (p. 410).

But since Woman is perceived as a witch only through male attempts to write her out of power as part of a programme of repression within patriarchy, *Possession* may also be read as attempting a measure of restitution and rewriting: Melusina is *restored* to her position of benign power through an act of historical correction. Also, the research undertaken by the male/female team of Roland and Maud (with Cropper, Blackadder, Stern and Nest looking over their shoulders) are aimed at reconciling the male and female lives and sensibilities of the Ash/LaMotte team. One of the most significant processes of the text is the one through which male and female are subsumed in one another, involving a merging of their value systems – including, as I have pointed out, an effacing of stylistic differences in the work of the two nineteenth-century poets. In the final analysis the ash tree, as the Tree of Life, *reconciles* male arrogance with the female forces of regeneration and growth.

Those characters in the narrative who cannot accept the necessary interaction of the genders, lose out: Fergus by being confirmed as wolf; Blanche by committing suicide. Those who do learn, assume the only power that matters, that of the imagination, of language, as Maud does when the banal fact of her inheriting – and thus coming into *possession* of – the letters of both LaMotte and Ash, even more than being the issue of their union, makes her the guardian of the accumulated knowledge of their lives, as well as the (female) key to *this* text.

10

We are returned to the facts of *textuality*, that is, of language.

In her essays, Byatt makes it clear that if one of the passions of her mind is lodged in the 'anxieties and interests in the relations between language and the world' (Byatt 1991b:5), she has reservations about the extreme Postmodernist view of language as the *only* reality. 'I do believe language has denotative as well as connotative powers', she affirms (Byatt 1991b:24). And much of *Possession* is constructed from, and on, her understanding of the relationship between what Foucault would call 'words' and 'things'. Language may even be seen to *threaten* the real, as Roland intimates when he asks, 'Do you never have the sense that our metaphors *eat up* our world?' (p. 253).

Early in the narrative, when Maud and Roland discuss the need to move beyond the poems of their subjects into their lives, she says (and he concurs), 'I even feel a sort of squeamishness about things she might have touched, or places she might have been – it's the *language* that matters, isn't it, it's what went on her mind' (p. 55).

But it is a distinction, we soon discover, which for them can never be absolute. And when they read a letter by Christabel in which she asserts that, 'I am a creature of my Pen, Mr Ash, my Pen is the best of me' (p. 87), the relation is beginning to become more complicated. In the case of the two nineteenth-century lives the *only* access is the written word – even if, as Maud says, 'you will always get a sense that there's something missing, something bio-graphers don't have access to, the real thing, the crucial thing, the thing that really mattered to the poet herself' (p. 89).

Yet even if the 'real world' exists, even if it *is there*, our under-standing of it, and our access to it, remains largely conditional upon language: 'It is possible', the narrator reminds us on p. 470, 'for a writer to make, *or remake at least*, for a reader, the primary pleasures of eating, or drinking, or looking on, or sex' (my empha-sis). Yet the supreme pleasure, she suggests, is that of reading itself, a *dangerous* pleasure, because of 'the regressive nature of the plea-sure, a *mise-en-abyme* even, where words draw attention to the power and delight of words, and so *ad infinitum*, thus making the imagination something papery and dry' (p. 470).

But it depends on the reader, and on the nature of the reading: there are 'dutiful readings', she says; and there are 'personal read-ings' ('I am full of love, or disgust, or fear, I scan for love, or disgust, or fear': p. 471); there are 'impersonal readings'. And then there are readings which totally involve, and engulf – *possess* – the reader; readings in which

a sense that the text has appeared to be wholly new, never before seen, is followed, almost immediately, by the sense that it was *always there*, that we the readers, knew it was always there, and have *always known* it was as it was, though we have now for the first time recognised, become fully cognisant of, our knowledge. (pp. 471–2)

This is why Sabine, in her journal, when after many false starts she finally has something 'real' to tell, reverts to language as story:

'So now. I have something to tell which is not to do with Gode's tale, though it was then that. Start again. Write it like a story, write it to *write* it – how wise I was to keep this journal for my eyes only. For now I can write to find out what I saw. And turn a

kind of pain into a kind of interest, a kind of curiosity, which is
to be my salvation'. (p. 356)

It is equally significant that at the end of her story she is forced also
to reflect – in words which Byatt herself might echo? – on the
inadequacy of her writing: 'No I have not told it like Gode. I have
missed out patterns of her voice and have put in a note of my own,
a literary note I was trying to avoid' (p. 362).

Nothing in *Possession* is so illuminating of the concept of language developed in the text, and so marks the text as Postmodernist, as its Postscript, dated 1868 (that is, nine years after the
relationship between Ash and Lamotte has been terminated, and
some twenty-one years before his death). At this stage, the story
seems to have reached a perfect closure: Christabel's final, unopened, letter from the desecrated grave has now been read, leaving the team of researchers with the ultimate piece of their jigsaw
puzzle, the ironical discovery that in this letter, withheld from Ash
by his wife, Christabel sought reconciliation, and divulged to him
the identity of their daughter (which also marks Maud as their heir
and descendant).

And then, out of the blue, comes this postscript to unsettle
everything, to undermine closure, to tease the reader with the
kind of *deus ex machina* intervention characteristic of romance: it
is a scene in a garden, in a meadow; a stranger, whom we soon
recognise as Randolph Henry Ash (bearing in his hand, as always,
his own emblem, his phallic walking-stick, his 'ashplant': p. 509)
accosts the little girl May, whom we identify as his lost daughter
Maia Thomasine, brought up by Christabel's sister. He offers her a
crown for a May Queen (crowning her, as it were, as the newest
Melusina), and gets in exchange a lock of her fair and fairy hair,
which we now identify as the plaited strands kept in his watch.
Like Maud, and Roland, and the other researchers, like Ash's own
wife, we, the readers, have assumed the lock to be Christabel's (see
pp. 452, 460, 498, 510). So we have all misread the text, and now
stand corrected.

The problem is that our reading has been informed by the text
itself: our clues have been those supplied in letters, poems, diaries,
journals and other writings unearthed and cited in the text. So in a
sense this final revelation, coming to us in a disclosure by a narratorial voice that has had no 'status' in the text constructed from
many interwoven voices, appears 'unfair'.

But is it? We may now turn back to other improbabilities: we have read Ash's last, unposted letter to Christabel (pp. 455–7) which, we know, his wife Ellen burned – to ashes – after Ash's death. So how *could* we have read it? It is 'non-existent'. And we have read an account, not gleaned from documents but in the form of 'straight narrative', about the holiday of Ash and LaMotte on the coast (pp. 273–88), and of Ellen Ash's mourning of her husband's death (pp. 446–62). Strictly speaking, this too was 'unfair' – though in the end we discover how cleverly the narrator has in fact prepared the final intervention.[16]

In one of her essays Byatt insisted that, 'Whilst it was once attractive (*séduisant?*) to think that whatever we say or see is our own construction, it now becomes necessary to reconsider the idea of truth, hard truth, and its possibility' (Byatt 1991b:24).

But the ending of *Possession* questions even the author's certainties. Through the narration of this scene we are brought back, with a jolt, to the *fact* of narrative, of fiction, of lies, and of language.

Through the rules of the conventional contract between narrator and reader we 'could not have known' this ending, yet we *do* know – because it has been *told*, because it has found its way, by hook or by crook, into language. We cannot but acknowledge, now, that the narrator might have told us *anything* else, might have spun us *any* yarn. It would have been neither less nor more valid than the choice of *this* romance. But as we are such stuff as tales are made on, we are returned from one fabrication to another, from a read story to a lived life, and we can say, with Thackeray, 'Come children, let us shut up the box and the puppets, for our play is played out.'

15

The Pranks of Hermes

Italo Calvino: *If on a Winter's Night a Traveller*

1

Reading *If on a Winter's Night a Traveller* at this point creates the curious impression that the text has been prefigured by almost all the others in this enquiry. Through the prestidigitations of Ermes Marana it presents a notion of language-as-translation which appears to continue from where the *Don Quixote* left off. (To translate, we are reminded by de Lauretis (1987:74), 'is to carry beyond, to convey, to transport elsewhere'.) In addition, the novel as a whole is constructed as much upon strategies of post-ponement, interruption and avoidance as Diderot's *Jacques the Fatalist and His Master*. But it also exploits the possibilities of language as infinite quotation, already anticipated by *Middlemarch*. It presents the conflict of different discourses we have encountered, in other guises, in Madame de Lafayette and Thomas Mann. In the games it plays we are reminded of an early predecessor like Jane Austen. Various aspects of the struggle of language against silence have already surfaced in George Eliot and in Kafka, whereas the unmasking of 'character' as a construct of language has already been noted in *Moll Flanders*. Startlingly different forms of 'death by language' have already been presented by *Madame Bovary* and *Le Voyeur*, whereas the experience of vertigo when confronted with the void behind – and within – language has also been discovered to permeate the fiction of Mann and Robbe-Grillet. Even the gen-dering of language, which characterised much of *La Princesse de Clèves* and all of *Surfacing*, returns in Calvino – in such an extreme demonstration of language as the embodiment of male desire that de Lauretis devoted one of her most brilliant essays to it ('Calvino and the Amazons: Reading the (Post)Modern Text': in de Lauretis 1987).

2

What is most radically subverted in this eminently Postmodernist text is the very notion of narrativity: the expectation of a story to unfold from a beginning, through a middle, to an end. But such a subversion cannot take place unless narrative, and the expectations aroused by it, are first posited. Most specifically it concerns the notion of narrative as quest, as we have encountered it, in one of its earliest and most glorious expressions, in the *Don Quixote*, and later in forms as diverse as the texts by Márquez, Atwood and Byatt.

If Calvino restores the genre (tongue in cheek, it must be said), to its phallocratic orientation in the male Reader's blatant domination of the female Other Reader, his target seems to me to be the logocentrism of patriarchy just as devastatingly as it was the target of *Surfacing*.

His starting point, inevitably, is that desire Julia Kristeva sees as driving one onward, 'not toward the absolute but toward a quest for a little more truth, an impossible truth, concerning the meaning of speech, concerning our condition as speaking beings' (Kristeva 1980: ix). As de Lauretis (1987:70) reminds us, Calvino specifically offers us 'the intimate connection of narrative with love, articulated in the necessary link of distance and desire'. This was already the driving force behind Calvino's early collection *Gli Amori Difficili* (*Difficult Loves*); but what she found densely satisfying in the early text, is debased in *If on a Winter's Night a Traveller* to mere 'spectacle, masquerade, and self-reflexive excess' (de Lauretis 1987: 70). It is constructed around the relationship between a Male Writer and a Woman Reader:

> In this book reading, like writing, is a function of desire, literally.
> The pursuit of the book's ending corresponds to the pursuit of
> the unattainable love object, narrative closure is impeded by
> *écriture*, the dispersal of meaning, writing as *différance*; and the
> pleasure of the text is infiltrated or undercut with the *jouissance*
> of the text. More simply put [...] the archetype of this fiction is
> the male sexual act. (ibid.:76)

But just as surely as Jacques and his master were denied consummation, male desire is frustrated and ultimately ridiculed and subverted in *Traveller*. This is possible because of the spectacular subversions perpetrated on language in the course of the novel.

3

In the opening words of the novel the reader is not only addressed directly but involved in the text: 'You are about to begin reading Italo Calvino's new novel, *If on a Winter's Night a Traveller*. Relax. Concentrate. Dispel every other thought. Let the world around you fade' (p. 3).[1] From this moment and until the last page of the novel, the reader becomes a conspirator in the text. This happens, first of all, through the use of the second person of the verb as if it were a variant of the third (a device also used by Butor in *La Modification*, and of course by Diderot in *Jacques the Fatalist*); even if, for the real reader of the book, this 'you' does *not* mean you (especially if the real reader is female), the *you* in this text necessarily becomes a *doppelgänger* of the reader outside. And this intradiegetic Reader (who will from now on be designated with a capital, as in the novel), functions not only as a sounding-board for the narrator's opinions, but, increasingly, as an actor within the action, as catalyst, and even as condition, for the evolving narration.

The Reader, who is explicitly constructed as a male, is reminded how he presumably bought this novel from among many others in a bookshop, with the implication that a primary and decisive act of choice was involved, and when, at a later stage, the Reader is confronted with the Non-Reader Irnero, one of the functions of their encounter is to warn the Reader that the continuation of the act of reading also depends upon repeated acts of choice. In other words, he becomes engaged in a constant struggle with the narrator who is trying to negate his freedom of choice by 'involving' him in the 'events' of the narrative. This determines the magnetic field of movement and counter-movement, which is the space within which the narration takes place, constantly liberating new possibilities of meaning.

After bringing the Reader face to face with the text in the opening chapter – that is, 'confronting something and not quite knowing yet what it is' (p. 9) – one turns the page to what is supposed to be the 'real' novel *If on a Winter's Night a Traveller*. The new chapter, after all, bears the same title as the book. The story, told in the first person, involves a secret agent arriving at some godforsaken station on a winter's night, in search of a stranger with whom he is supposed to exchange code words and suitcases. But the stranger never turns up and at last the narrator is warned by the local chief of police (who may be another agent) to escape while he can still do so, as his opposite number has been murdered. The chapter ends with the narrator hurrying towards the shop of a woman who has been mentioned earlier; she has recently been divorced from her doctor husband and there are indications that the latter may be capable of revenge on any new suitor.

A whole array of expectations has been raised, but the 'story' goes no further, and is never resumed – at least not within the presented world of the text – because in Chapter 2 the Reader is informed that he has accidentally got hold of a faulty copy of the novel which contains only that opening chapter. When he returns to the bookshop to exchange his copy, he meets a young woman on exactly the same errand, and through this confrontation of the (male) Reader and another (female) Reader,[2] a new story begins to take shape within the narration of the novel as such.

Apart from the 'novel to be read' another 'possible novel to be lived' (p. 32) is taking shape under the Reader's eyes – with the obvious implication that we, the 'real' readers of both those stories, may in a comparable manner be caught in (or drawn into) our *own* gradually evolving stories. This foregrounds both the differences and the similarities between so-called 'fictitious' and 'real' worlds. Similarly, both the narrator and the author are involved in the process; when the 'character' of the doctor's wife begins to emerge from a cluster of words, a signified from an accretion of signifiers, the narrator warns quite explicitly: 'and it is your expectation, reader, that drives the author towards her' (p. 20). One is reminded of Russell Hoban's inspired introduction to *Household Tales of the Brothers Grimm*; in which he points out that the original German, *Es lebte einmal ein Königin* ... should not be translated, as is customary, as *Once upon a time there lived an old queen* ... but, literally, as *Once upon a time it lived an old queen* ... It is as if she is lived into being by something both inside and outside the story:

> We take it for granted that there will always be fiction of one kind or another in the form of stories: forming, shaping. Why do we take that for granted? Why do we make fiction? Why do we say, 'What if ... ?' [...] We make fiction because we are fiction. Because there was a time when 'it lived' us into being [...] It lived us into being and it lives us still. We make stories because we are story [...] (Hoban 1977:11–13)

It is significant that Calvino uses an identical formulation to explore the possibilities of saying, 'not "I think" but "it thinks" as we say "it rains"', concluding that 'The universe will express itself as long as somebody will be able to say, "I read, therefore *it* writes"' (p. 176).[3]

4

What is involved here – what is, in fact, one of the novel's most fascinating achievements – is the construction of a philosophy of language. As the text unfolds, it manifests itself more and more dramatically as what Calvino himself elsewhere described as 'an itinerary toward silence' (quoted in de Lauretis 1987:71).[4]

One should begin by imagining the universe as *silence*: an enormous welter of wordless being, an uninterrogatable silence – uninterrogatable, because the problem of that silence is precisely that it cannot answer our questions. Yet language is an attempt, as doomed as it is indispensable, to do just that, to correct silence – even if it is known beforehand that silence is incorrigible. Language becomes a *supplement* to silence, which is why, on p. 153, the narrator asks,

> But how to establish the exact moment in which a story begins? Everything has already begun before, the first line of the first page of every novel refers to something that has already happened outside the book. Or else the real story is the one that begins ten or a hundred pages further on, and everything that precedes it is only a prologue.

Language is everything that is not silent, everything that challenges or provokes silence; silence is whatever is not language. And there is a relationship between the two, since 'the book should be the written counterpart of the unwritten world' (p. 172). And the starting point of Calvino's argument is that, 'I do not believe totality can be contained in language; my problem is what remains outside, the unwritten, the unwritable' (p. 181).

Somewhere in the ocean of silence, language now emerges like an island. But, like an island seen from afar, it is, as a whole, only a blob, a blur; it is, in relation to silence, a 'murmur', a 'susurrus', a 'hum', as Barthes points out in *Le Bruissement de la langue* ('The hum of language'). Barthes compares it to the sound of an engine functioning perfectly – which is a paradox, since what functions perfectly makes no sound. This, Barthes terms the paradox of 'ultimate noise, an impossible noise, the noise [...] without noise' (Barthes 1984:94, my translation); and what one aims at is 'the trembling of meaning which I interrogate in listening to the murmur of language' (p. 96, my translation).

This means that, in approaching language, as the reader approaches a story, the world 'fades', as happens on the first page of this novel (p. 3); it becomes 'vagueness, grayness, [...] a kind of no man's land of experience reduced to its lowest common denominator' (p. 12), in which the reader reads 'both the murmuring effect [it is revealing that Calvino himself also uses this word][5] and the effect of the hidden intention' (p. 8).

What is on the page – language – surfaces from a meaningless flux below: 'only a few elements surface on the written page' (p. 20); these are 'verbal lumps' as opposed to 'flowing narrative' (p. 53). But the surfacing is *arbitrary*, as a result of which the reader is placed 'at the mercy of the fortuitous, the aleatory, the random' (p. 27), and 'the world is reduced to a sheet of paper on which nothing can be written except abstract words' (p. 251). At the same time, however arbitrary or random its emergence may have been, it *assumes* meaning (p. 143): 'It is only through the confining act of writing that the immensity of the nonwritten becomes legible' (p. 183).

This explains why around every story the reader perceives 'a saturation of other stories' (p. 109); why every word is surrounded by others; every sentence by yet more; every book by the whole immensity of language, an endless 'fluctuation of time' (p. 25), creating in the writer a 'hovering of presentiments and suspicions to reach the person who reads me not as an accidental obstacle to understanding what I write, but as its very substance' (p. 61).

By the same token, the act of reading (that is, the attempt at understanding language) becomes simultaneously an act of *radical destabilisation of language*. Each of the Readers in Calvino's novel reads the 'same' novel, yet experiences it as a 'different' novel; the whole process of reading unsettles fixed meanings; even reader and writer change places in a space which 'dramatizes the unclosable distance between [them]' (Dipple 1988:109).[6]

A consequence of this approach, both in terms of Calvino's perception of language and of our reading of this novel, is that there is, in every sentence, in every story, in every chapter, a movement both forward and backward, both towards the future and towards the past. 'The thing I'd like most in the world', the traveller in the first story tells the woman in the bar, 'is to make clocks run backward' (p. 21); and Ludmilla, the Other Reader, who always reads several books at the same time, tends to move forward in her reading while trailing all her unfinished stories behind her (p. 147). It is not only a temporal movement, reaching towards past and future, but also a spatial movement that goes both inward and outward, on the one hand an 'expanding universe', on the other a zooming in towards the infinitely small (p. 26).

Ultimately, these contrary impulses in language reach both towards a Primal Beginning, ('the only thing we can do is to go to the source of all this confusion': p. 91) and an End, a Conclusion, a Final Meaning.

This simultaneous urge towards Origin and Closure is irredeemably male in inspiration: it is the urge which determines genealogies and quests, the primal urge of narrative – which is why, behind the many stories spun in *Traveller*, there is the suspicion of an Ur-Narrator, 'an old Indian known as the Father of Stories' (p. 117). At the same time we should remember that elsewhere in his work, in *Cosmicomics*, Calvino assigns exactly the same role to a 'Woman as Mother [who] is responsible for the beginning of symbolization' (Barr 1992:260). At the very least, this should serve as a reminder about the essentially *ludic* nature of the *Traveller*, and as a warning not to overlook the tongue in the narrator's cheek. It is, perhaps, precisely because the novel's quest is directed towards *male* origins and endings that neither can be achieved.

But I am running ahead of the novel's argument. All that needs to be noted at this stage is that both origin and end are denied by the narrative's theory of language, because surrounding the island of any text is only the immensity of other texts, the never-ending hum of language.

However, if Beginning and End cannot be discovered, the *impulse* remains: the impulse to transgress, to transcend, to break through barriers of time and space. There is a surge forward in language, in any sentence that reaches forward to its (provisional) syntactic conclusion, which suggests 'the drive to break away from it, to run toward the unknown' (p. 37), as surely as the Reader is driven by the sexual urge to follow Ludmilla on her wanderings (p. 47). There is a need, not only in this novel as it progresses from one beginning chapter to the next (p. 76), but in language itself, to 'continue in the beyond' (p. 71). 'The book I'm looking for', says an enigmatic figure in Chapter 10, 'is the one that gives the sense of the world after the end of the world, the sense that the world is the end of everything that there is in the world, that the only thing there is in the world is the end of the world' (p. 243).[7]

Beyond all reach of language, then, lies silence. But it exists as much 'in here' as 'out there'. In the very interstices of language lurks silence, just as much as 'empty and insensitive space' intervenes between the falling leaves in the 'Japanese' chapter (p. 209).

On the practical level, this means that the reading of this novel – and of *any* text – continues within the reader beyond the physical limits of the text; and on the level of language philosophy it means that meaning is constantly, and forever, deferred. Because this dual urge in language – both forward and backward in time, both outward and inward in space – is ultimately a reaching back towards the surrounding *silence* ('The void all around us is more and more void': p. 249).

The problem is that once language has emerged from silence, it cannot silence itself, it can only erase what has been said by continuing to say more and more. And so the motion towards *erasure* is simultaneously a process of accumulation:

> I would like to swim against the stream of time: I would like to erase the consequences of certain events and restore an initial condition. But every moment of my life [read: every new sentence I utter] brings with it an accumulation of new facts, and each of these new facts brings with it consequences; so the more I seek to return to the zero moment from which I set out, the further I move away from it. (p. 16)

The tragedy – or the farce, depending on how one looks at it – of this philosophy of language resides in the fact that not even that portion of 'the world' that breaks into language (our only means of apprehending it) can be trusted, for language itself, in its random and coincidental nature, is falsification and disguise and fraud. Just as we apprehend silence via the murmur of language, we apprehend truth only via the manifestations of falsification. 'Artifice is the true substance of everything' (p. 180), says the fraudulent translator Marana, whose activities determine the whole text; and the narrator himself insists that 'there is no certitude outside falsification' (p. 193), which is echoed by the girl who may or may not be called Corinna, when she asserts that, 'Once the process of falsification is set in motion, it won't stop' (p. 212).

On the narrative level we encounter this 'truth' in the presentation of the series of stories we are invited to read. They do not simply 'exist' in the text, as in an anthology of stories, but come to us with all the baggage, and all the wrappings, of the processes through which they are being told. In other words, we are never allowed even the illusion of direct access to these stories: they are all *mediated*, which is just another way of saying that they are fabricated, that is, falsified. The chapter entitled 'If on a winter's night a traveller' cannot be read 'innocently, because it has already been *retold* by the narrator: 'The novel begins in a railway station, a locomotive huffs, steam from a piston covers the opening of the chapter, a cloud of smoke hides part of the first paragraph' (p. 10). The same procedure introduces 'Outside the town of Malbork' (p. 34). At first sight, 'Leaning fom the steep slope' *appears* to be offered to us unmediated, but on the preceding (and following) pages we are explicitly reminded that this is the way in which the story is being *translated and read aloud* by Professor Uzzi-Tuzii, who is presented as a most untrustworthy translator (p. 53).

'Without fear of wind or vertigo', in turn, is a translation read aloud by Lotaria. And as a result of our immersion in these texts as *mediated* texts (that is, in language as, itself, a 'medium', a something-in-between), we are conditioned to read even the subsequent chapters, offered with an appearance of direct narration, as mediations, which of course they are, since they are all the fabrications of the notorious translator Ermes Marana, the archetypal *traduttore traditore*.

The whole intricate process of mediation – like observing through a telescope of which one segment after the other is pulled out – is illustrated on the narrative level by the dazzling series of focalisations in the 'Japanese' chapter: the professor looks at his daughter who is looking at the couple making love, who are reflected in the professor's pupil...(p. 208). This, Calvino conveys to his reader, is how *language* works.

5

Against this background, let us return to the *Traveller* text. In the bookshop to which the Reader and the Alternative Reader have both returned to demand new copies of the novel they had begun to read and which ended so abruptly in mere repetition, they learn that the reason for their confusion is the fact that an entirely different novel, *Outside the Town of Malbork*, by one Bazakbal, has accidentally been bound into the hard cover of the Calvino. So both return home with a copy of Bazakbal under the arm.

However, it turns out to be a totally different story. This one is set in what appears to be Poland, and is 'about' a man who brings home his son to save him from a feud with another family; the next day the father sets out for the site of the feud accompanied by a different boy, the narrator; the boys have exchanged places, each becoming a supplement of the other, that is, both a substitution and an excess. In fact, a kind of transformation takes place: the second son 'becomes' the first, a *mise-en-abyme* of a multiplicity of similar strategies on different levels of text.

This is the critical moment to which the second story-within-a-story takes us; the rest of the Bazakbal book, we learn in Chapter 3, consists of blank pages only – a premonition of the Void threatening the characters of the ensuing stories, as well as the reader behind the surface of the words which have stopped functioning as reliable *signs*. 'Beneath every word there is nothingness', we read on p. 83; on p. 210 a flight to South America is described as crossing 'a gap in space'; and on p. 239 none other than the great fraud Ermes Marana summarises the experience by saying that 'behind the written page is the void: the world exists only as artifice, pretense, misunderstanding, falsehood'.

Driven by the obsession to continue his reading, blinded by what Frank Kermode termed 'the sense of an ending', and, in the process, discounting his own freedom of choice, the Reader telephones the Alternative Reader only to learn that her copy of the Bazakbal has been as flawed as his. They end up at the university, in the Department of 'Bothno-Ugaric' languages where it seems the original text of their maimed novel exists in the dead Cimmerian language. A caricatural Professor Uzzi-Tuzii undertakes to read it to them, translating as he goes on, in his office in the heart of the labyrinthine university building (another demonstration of the language code, much like Eco's library in *The Name of the Rose*), surrounded by countless thousands of books – 'this world dense with writing that surrounds us on all sides' (p. 49):

Reading is always this: there is a thing that is there, a thing made of writing, a solid, material object, which cannot be changed, and through this thing we measure ourselves against something else that is not present, something else that belongs to the immaterial, invisible world, because it can only be thought imagined, or because it was once and is no longer, past, lost, unattainable, in the land of the dead [...] Or that is not present because it does not yet exist, something desired, feared, possible or impossible... Reading is going toward something that is about to be, and no one yet knows what it will be. (p. 72)

We either accept, with Professor Uzzi-Tuzii, the old logocentric argument which refers to 'original meaning', to the Word which in the beginning was with God, and was God – or we take the leap into deconstruction, through which meaning is generated in an endless series of possibilities, not as a bundle of clothes prepacked into a suitcase by some sender and unpacked, still intact, by a receiver at the other end. This is the option suggested by the Alternative Reader, who by now has a name in the text, Ludmilla. (Would it be far-fetched to discover, lurking inside her name, the Hebrew *mila* which means 'a word'?)

As the signifiers surrounding her become denser, the sexual subtext of the quest for meaning also intensifies – not, I submit, as a serious rehearsal of the immemorial male/hunter quest as de Lauretis proposes to read it, but as a spoof, a send-up, an outrageous parody. Certainly, in the relationship of desire that defines their trajectory through the text, one cannot misread the gendering of the different discourses[8] they 're-present' the phallogocentric male and the deconstructive female; the linear and the diffuse; the hierarchical and the text-ured. And it is the tension between these options, these world-views, these approaches to fiction and to language, which will be interrogated in Calvino's text as a whole.

In Chapter 3 this process has barely begun; and it comes as no surprise that the professor's Ur-text turns out to be no more than another story, the opening chapter of a new narrative leading nowhere – or leading, at most, to the discovery of still more fiction.

This new story, *Leaning from the Steep Slope*, told in the first person like all the others, presents a stranger in a Nordic resort who, tricked by a girl on the beach into procuring a length of rope which she wants to draw, becomes involved in an adventure in which a prisoner is helped to escape from gaol. His innocence –

like that of the reader who allows himself/herself to be 'drawn into' a story – exposes him to great danger and an awe-inspiring responsibility, but the narrative ends, once again, with a perception of the Void which opens when we discover that the chapter has no sequel. Still, the reader has begun to make a significant discovery: totally unrelated as these stories – or beginnings of stories – may be, they all function as variations or parodies of detective stories in which the risk of *arrest* is balanced by the possibility of liberation or *escape*. They all form part of a code which signifies the reader subjected to the totalitarian power of an invisible author who tricks him/her out of all certainties and freedom of choice, in direct proportion to the extent in which the reader gets enmeshed in the search for a story-behind-the-narration, or a meaning-behind-the-story, or behind language. But even this is no simple choice, since involvement in a story also implies 'escape' from the bondage of the here-and-now, that is, the reader's experience of 'reality'.

Both the male Reader and his female Alternative persist in their quest to find the 'original' novel, the 'complete' novel (a search which will become, more and more, a pre-text for the Reader's sexual pursuit of Ludmilla). Disillusioned by Professor Uzzi-Tuzii's 'wrong' variant, the Reader attends a seminar by another academic who is expected to discuss the 'correct' text. Needless to say, it turns into another cul-de-sac (for the Reader, that is; within the larger context of Calvino's text a whole set of new possibilities are triggered). This story, titled *Without Fear or Vertigo*, presents three young people in a besieged city: a situation of betrayal, narrated with such skill and subtlety that it is almost impossible to determine who betrays whom. 'What is behind all this?' the Reader wonders, totally intrigued. But the reply – if anything as simple as a reply can still be expected – should surprise no-one: 'The void, the void down below ... Help ... vertigo ...' (p. 92). Vertigo becomes the marker of an individual's discovery that language has no ultimate meaning and can only run out into silence.

6

From this point onwards the novel offers an increasingly dizzying experience of reading, with each chapter acting as supplement to what has gone before and as a preface to the next, a remarkable demonstration of Derrida's views on the subject: 'On the one hand', writes Derrida (1981:35),

> the preface is ruled out but it must be written: so that it can be integrated, so that the text can be erased in the logic of the concept which cannot *not* presuppose itself. On the other hand (almost the same) the preface is ruled out but it is still being written in that it is already made to function as a moment of the relaunched text, as something that belongs to a textual economy that no concept can anticipate or sublate.

In his futile attempts to find 'the source of all this confusion' (p. 91), the Reader visits the publishing firm where all the unfinished books have been compiled. From the factotum Cavedagna he learns that they are all the result of a great fraud perpetrated by one Ermes Marana. The name Ermes, of course, is slyly charged with several meanings, pointing towards the god Hermes: de Lauretis (1987:74) describes him as 'the Olympian trickster who deceives even Apollo with his song [...] the eternal gambler and the god of travelers, who takes mortals across the last frontier'. In addition, one should remember, he is also, in the form of Hermes Trismegistus, the god of all arcane knowledge.

This Ermes Marana, a translator by profession, has started fabricating pseudo-translations either from languages he does not even know, like Cimbrian (p. 99), or of apparently non-existent 'originals'. Cavedagna offers the reader a new novel, *Looks Down in the Gathering Shadow*, supposedly written by a francophone Belgian, one Bertrand Vandervelde, another story of a double or triple agent who, with the aid of his mistress, tries to shake off his shady past – which proves as impossible for him as it is impossible for the novel to shake off its own 'past', that is, the preceding four chapters.

Desperately trying to trace the 'real' elusive novel, the Reader begins to work his way through much of the publisher's correspondence with Marana, bringing to light a mosaic of countries and places and times, anecdotes and shreds and shards of philosophy. The correspondence leads the Reader to the discovery of an Irish writer Flannery, who lives in Switzerland. While the world is eagerly awaiting his next bestseller, he appears to be stumped because Marana has stolen the first chapter of the new book and is trying to use computers to finish it. But Flannery himself, it turns out, has plagiarised the Belgian writer's latest novel; and in the feverish hope that this may prove to be the long-lost text, the Reader takes up *In a Network of Lines that Enlace* only to find that it is yet another beginning: a jogger runs past an open window and hears a telephone ringing inside; he stops to answer it, and is dragged into a kidnapping. In other words, responding to a challenge from *inside* the house, a space different from the *exterior* where he finds himself, the jogger embarks on an adventure as hazardous as that undertaken by any reader who, from the outside of a book, responds to a call from inside. In an earlier story the narrator was described waiting for 'messages, signals, warnings' (p. 54) from *outside*, because it is a two-way process constantly involving *both* exterior and interior, 'text' and 'reality'. 'I pass through a series of places', the narrator of another opening chapter in the novel confesses, 'that ought to be more and more interior, whereas instead I find myself more and more out-side' (p. 225).

While our Reader is still engrossed in the fragment written by either the true or the false Flannery, his own telephone rings and he is summoned to Ludmilla's home. (In other words, the 'story' mirrors what has just happened in the 'story-within-the- story', and it is no coincidence that mirrors and kaleidoscopes feature so prominently in the text.) However, Ludmilla is not at home, and in his 'pursuit of the interrupted book' (p. 151) the Reader stumbles upon a whole secret collection of books – mostly Flannery's – amid undeniable signs of Marana's own presence. In the correspondence he was reading at the publisher's, the Reader has come across constant references to a woman resembling Ludmilla; now to dis-cover the opposite, namely signs of Marana in *her* house, is unner-ving indeed. Once again two worlds seem to be merging into one another from opposite directions.

When Ludmilla returns, all their pent-up frustrations are expressed in a scene of violent and ecstatic lovemaking. In the vein of Eco's famous passage on love in the age of Barbara Cartland,[9] Calvino ironicises the love scenes of Romance:

Ludmilla, now you are being read. Your body is being subjected to a systematic reading, through channels of tactile information, visual, olfactory, and not without some intervention of the taste buds [...] all codes, all the poor alphabets which one human being believes that he is reading in another human being. (p. 24)

But the description feeds on more (and 'erases' more) than the literature of love: it is, surely deliberately, infused with the sexual terminology with which writers like Barthes (1976, 1979) or Kristeva (1980) approach the act of reading. Barthes (1975:33): 'This is a vast commonplace of literature: The Woman copies the Book. In other words, every body is a citation: of the "already-written".'

The Reader believes that he has finally found the 'real' Flannery in Ludmilla's library, but of course he has misread the title. This one, called *In a Network of Lines that Intersect*, presents a tycoon obsessed with mirrors and kaleidoscopes ('It is my image I want to multiply': p. 164), who gets kidnapped – but whether it is done by his opponents or by his own people acting on his instructions, is left open.

Still caught in 'the spell of interrupted readings' (p. 241) the Reader goes in search of Flannery as a possible Primary Source. Chapter 8 offers us notes from Flannery's diary, jotted down in his efforts to find inspiration for his new book as he sits leering at a woman (who may be Ludmilla) reading in a deck-chair below his chalet. He imagines two writers (one of them his alter-ego Vandervelde whom he supposedly plagiarised) gazing at just such a woman and trying to write what each of them believes she wants to read. Dazzling possibilities are released, each of them a prismatic comment on what has gone before in the text. One of Flannery's most significant suggestions is formulated thus:

> between the book to be written and things that already exist there can be only one kind of complementary relationship: the book should be the written counterpart of the unwritten world; its subject should be what does not exist and cannot exist except when written, but whose absence is obscurely felt by that which exists, in its own incompleteness. (p. 172)

Once again we are brought back to the notion of the supplement; if it offers, as Flannery suggests, something complementary, deriving from an awareness of an 'incompleteness', a lack, it must necessarily involve, when approached from the other end, a notion of excess:

> Each narrative seems to have something excessive, a supplement which remains outside the closed form produced by the development of the plot. At the same time, and for this very reason,

this something-more, proper to narrative, is also something-less. (Todorov 1977:77)

And the meeting-place of these supplements, simultaneously insufficient and excessive, is the reader. Through his/her intervention, and only through that intervention, the relations are activated. In the Calvino text this is demonstrated by the function of the Reader within the narration: he is a 'character', a 'creature' of the narrator, but at the same time he acts, as we have noted, 'on behalf of' the real reader. His presence dramatizes the gaps in the text; he *becomes* 'the' gap in the text – as well as, through the act of reading, the plug that fills the gap.

In the conversation between the Reader and Flannery, which follows the reading from Flannery's diary, the Irish writer (and what else can he possibly be but an Irishman?) divulges that he knows the 'true' text behind the two fabrications the Reader has most recently unearthed. It is, he says, a Japanese novel titled *On the Carpet of Leaves Illuminated by the Moon* by one Takakumi Ikoka, which he offers (in English translation) to the Reader. The chapter ends with a meditation on the Reader:

> Perhaps his reading is so intense that it consumes all the substance of the novel at the start, so nothing remains for the rest. This happens to me in writing: for some time now, every novel I begin writing is exhausted shortly after the beginning. I have had the idea of writing a novel composed only of the beginnings of novels. (p. 197)

followed by a precise summary of the book we have been reading up to this point. This is Hutcheon's 'narcissistic narrative' at its most flagrant: a book writing itself, or at least looking at itself in the process of emergence, just as we are observed in the act of reading. As we read, we are being read; as we read, we are being written; as we read, we are writing. The movement outside has run into the flux inside, and once again the point of contact is the reader, you, I.

7

The new (Japanese) chapter we encounter is a *tour de force* in its exploration not of 'entities' but of 'relationships', which has been the essential preoccupation of the nascent novel itself, the subtle tracing of a Japanese student's academic and personal relationship with his professor – expressed but also countered by his growing erotic interest in the professor's daughter and the ironical way in which it leads to a situation where he makes love to her *mother*. Calvino employs a 'typically Japanese' device of oblique reference in describing falling leaves when he is 'really' concerned with his characters:

> The shower of little ginkgo leaves is characterized by the fact that in each moment each leaf that is falling is found at a different altitude from the others, whereby the empty and insensitive space in which the visual sensations are situated can be subdivided into a succession of levels in each of which we find only little leaf twirling and one alone. (p. 209)

This in itself replicates the key episode referred to earlier, in which the student, while making love to the mother, becomes aware of both the daughter and the father watching them: 'In his cold pupil, in the firm twist of his lips, was reflected Madame Miyagi's orgasm reflected in her daughter's gaze' (p. 208).

It is possible that this latest 'misreading', like its predecessors, can also be attributed to the elusive Ermes Marana who, we learn, has just been to Japan; so it is inevitable that our Reader must now go in search of this shady character. He sets off for South America where Marana has most recently been seen. A woman who looks suspiciously like Ludmilla's sister Lotaria but who insists that she is Corinna (also known as Gertrude, Ingrid, Sheila, Alfonsina, Alexandra and so on) joins him; and soon he lands in prison, although it is impossible to tell whether she is acting for or against him. This literal (or literary?) imprisonment is the logical outcome of all the arrests witnessed in earlier chapters; just as the South American dictator who imprisons our Reader is no more than the political counterpart of the many dictatorial authors who have crossed our path in the novel (beginning as early as p. 4, where the narrator presumes to 'know' everything about his explicit Reader and to predict all his reactions): 'Reader, what are you doing? Aren't you going to resist? Aren't you going to escape? Ah, you are participating...' (p. 219).

In prison, the Reader opens a book banned in the country itself, called *Around an Empty Grave* and clearly a pastiche of the work of

Jorge Luis Borges. In the new story the narrator goes in search of his mother and comes up with two equally plausible possibilities, each with a beautiful daughter with whom he would love to have an affair, if only he could be sure that she isn't his sister. It leads to a Borgesian confrontation with his alter ego Faustino Higueras who practically rises from the grave (just like so many of the earlier characters in the novel have been resuscitated from the graves of their prototypes) to face him with the possibility of his own death.

The government of the South American country in which the Reader has been imprisoned turns out to be 'on his side' – unless this, too, is a trap – and after his release he is sent on an official mission to another country, presumably behind the Iron Curtain. It transpires that Marana himself was recently imprisoned there, but has subsequently been set free: 'A fake escape, a fake clandestine expatriation, and his trial was lost again [...] Now he practises mystification for mystification's sake' (p. 240). We are discovering more and more the unsettling way in which this novel, as it peels layer after layer from its onion self, is actually turning inside out to be translated into the terms of 'our' reality: a world of politics and authoritarian regimes where the exercise of power is startlingly similar to the strategies of a writer within his/her own work.

8

In the new country the Reader gets hold of yet another manuscript, *What Story Down There Awaits Its End*? But because the secret police are hard on his heels he manages to read only the first chapter. In it, the narrator is approaching his beloved Franziska, literally writing all the obstacles between them out of his way – buildings, and their occupants, barracks and guard houses and police stations, also fires and garbage and mail and the economy: 'A layer of the earth's crust is all that has to remain, solid enough underfoot, and everywhere else, nothingness' (p. 247).

When the police try to intervene he obliterates them with his words and ends up, with Franziska, in a café whose walls are covered in mirrors, exactly as he has imagined it to be.

We are left, it seems, with nothing but the words in which the final story is told: as things are erased, words remain. In the process of allegedly annihilating 'things' the narrator has no choice but to *name* them.

In the end we are not even left with a story, only with the *telling* of a story. 'The text "rehearses" its irreducible structure of non-presence', writes Harari (1979:38), 'and, by way of its supplementary logic, it self-deconstructs in the very act of constituting itself.' But that 'telling of a story', that 'act of constituting itself' involves more than words: as each story ends in its own cul-de-sac, it also transgresses its own borders into the continuous peregrinations of the explicit Reader, and via him into the enquiry of the 'real' readers. In short, the word spills into the world.

9

The Reader and Ludmilla decide to get married. At the beginning of the last chapter the Reader and Ludmilla are in bed. This appears to be the satisfaction of the desire that drives both narrative and sex; it looks like the beginning of a happiness for ever after. If so, it would be a final bow to that convention which equates male desire with the telling of a story.

But is it?

When Ludmilla turns off her bedside light and invites her new husband to do the same, in what is clearly an invitation to make love, he prefers to finish his reading: 'You say, "Just a minute, I've almost finished *If on a Winter's Night* by Italo Calvino"' (p. 260). It may be argued that, having witnessed by now that the motions and processes of the novel, and of reading, are also the motions and processes of love and desire, the Reader's reading *equals* making love to Ludmilla. But that would still leave us with the unappetising spectacle of the *Traveller* as a celebration of phallocratic language. And it seems to me quite clear that the novel communicates the *opposite*; throughout the narrative the Reader has doggedly pursued the linear course towards the kind of meaning which is conceivable only within patriarchy, that is, a meaning driven by the male desire of conquest and fulfilment, confident of origins and of closure, bolstered by the structures of hierarchy, authority and presence, whereas the text has demonstrated, quite spectacularly, through its proliferation of words, words, words, that there is only silence and the void below. There *is* no final meaning. In pursuing the elusive Text, the Reader has found a woman, who is now in his bed; yet he still prefers his book to her. And Ludmilla represents the opposite to everything he cherishes: she never finishes a book;

she eschews the company of authors, publishers, all the purveyors and agents of dominant discourses. He may have married her, but he does not 'have' her. On the one occasion he made love to her, he got no farther than reading her like a book (which, like all the books encountered so far, can be nothing but an *incipit*).

In the only other sex scene in the book, the Reader was practically raped, in his cell in South America, by the woman-with-many-names who may, or may not, be Ludmilla's sister Lotaria: a no-nonsense woman who is as much inclined to play the 'masculine' role as any writer. Her 'assault' on him, which humorously, *and* darkly, demonstrates to the Reader what it means to have done unto you what you have done to others, has unmasked both the aggressiveness and the uncertainties which define his role within the patriarchal order. He failed that test. But he didn't really learn anything, except in future to focus his pathetic desires on the apparently much more compliant Ludmilla. And this bedroom scene, an end which offers no closure whatsoever, is a decisive and derisive laugh at the expense of the single-minded logocentric Reader.

10

An Ultimate Author, like a final meaning, has eluded the Reader. We know, from Barthes's 'Death of the Author', that 'to give a text an Author is to impose a limit on that text, to furnish it with a final signified, to close the writing', and that, 'once the Author is removed, the claim to decipher a text becomes quite futile' (in Lodge 1988:171). Yet, back from his voyages, burrowing in a library, once more 'saturated with literature', the Reader begins to apprehend something infinitely more significant which has come to light, not merely the accumulation of obstacles the text has set up against the quest for 'a' meaning, but the fact that the text itself has become both quest and obstruction, both the knife peeling the onion and the onion itself – because the text has first written itself into being through the intervention of the reader, and then 'erased' itself as part of the same process. 'No system is static', says Hoban (1977:13), 'it is always in the process of becoming what it is not. Any putting-together charges whatever is put together with the energy that will tear it apart.'

No Author has been found, but the Reader and his Alternative have found each other and in their sexual union another kind of union has been consummated between Reader and reader, creating in the process a whole new range of possibilities within the concept of intertextuality. All we can be more or less persuaded of, is that 'the ultimate meaning to which all stories refer has two faces: the continuity of life, the inevitability of death' (p. 259).

In the Library scene, where the Reader is frantically filling in one card after the other in search of all ten of the elusive books whose traces he has found across the face of the earth, he discovers that all ten titles strung together form a single sentence:

If on a winter's night a traveller, outside the town of Malbork, leaning from the steep slope without fear of wind or vertigo, looks down at the gathering shadows in a network of lines that enlace, a network of lines that intersect, on the carpet of leaves illuminated by the moon around an empty grave – what story down there awaits its end? (p. 258)

Syntactically, everything appears to be 'rounded off' in a complete sentence, which inevitably reminds one of Todorov's exploration of the sentence as a model for narrative, with which this enquiry began. But Calvino goes further than Todorov: a *sentence* may indeed have been completed, but the *sense* of the narrative sentence lies in the manner in which it has crossed syntactical and linguistic frontiers to merge with the full experience of the reader. Phrased differently, 'the' sentence emerging from Calvino's narrative amounts to no more than a loaded question to which the reader has to respond.

As Dipple (1988:113) puts it, 'This threading together of the ten titles of the tales, or reiteration of the fictions, once again begins the endless task of trying to write anew in the world of letters that outside world that longs insatiably for expression.'

It can be interpreted radically, and pessimistically: the 'sentence' constructed in the course of the novel is a nonsense sentence, a no-sense sentence, an interpellation of silence, *which cannot, ever, answer*. But a more positive reading is equally possible, by agreeing with Genette (1980:261): 'The work is ultimately only an optical instrument the author offers the reader to help him read within himself.' In such a reading, what Calvino 'really' effects is to provoke the reader into revolt against phallogocentric textual authority or finality in order to assume one's full responsibility as a human being.

Notes

Introduction: Languages of the Novel

1. In Chapter 7 below I shall try to demonstrate that MacCabe's notion of nineteenth-century 'metalanguage' is by no means so readily applicable to Eliot, and that where he sees firmness of purpose and positivist assurance in the narrator's stance, the language of *Middlemarch* (as, in fact, in Eliot's other novels) reveals much more self-doubting and much more self-awareness, than has generally been assumed.
2. To the question, 'Does Postmodernism exist?' Thiher (1984:227) replies at the end of *Words in Reflection*: 'If one means by this term a series of discriminating traits – identifiable fibres of an approximate length – that allows us to see ruptures as well as continuities, then I think the term is reasonably useful.' Thiher provides an illuminating exploration of twentieth-century fiction on its way towards Postmodernism, against the background of recent linguistic theory.
3. The word 'novel', derived from the Italian *novella*, literally meant 'a small new thing'. Or, as Dr Johnson so charmingly described it in his dictionary, 'a small tale, generally of love' (quoted in Day 1987:1).
4. This would hold true whether we assume that the novel began with Defoe, or with Aphra Behn or Madame de Lafayette, or with Cervantes or Rabelais, with *Njal's Saga* or *The Thousand and One Nights*, or with the long prose narratives of Antiquity written by Apollonius of Rhodes, or Chariton, or Longus or Apuleius.
5. In the transmission of a *message* from an *addresser* to an *addressee*, the Jakobson model requires that it be enclosed in a *code* in the form of speech, writing, dance, or whatever, and transmitted via some oral, visual or other *contact* between sender and receiver, with reference to a shared *context* from which it can be decoded.
6. In the original meaning of *fiction* as derived from *fingere*: to fabricate, to make up, to invent.
7. Derrida is of course not referring to physical writing on a page but to the *notion* of writing, that is, of language remote in time and space from the authority and presence of an author; in this sense it becomes a 'supplement' to the traditional notion of authoritative speech. See Derrida 1976:6ff.
8. Heidegger does not consider what to some of his successors, especially after the Holocaust, would become a most vexing problem and what to fiction writers and readers can become a matter of course: that the choice of a specific word may in fact *supplant* the experience or perception which prompted the choice of that word in the first place.
9. Traces are, as it were, signs in search of meaning: they may *appear* to reach out towards 'original signifieds', but the very notion of an origin is ruled out. So, at most, 'Traces [...] produce the space of their

330

inscription only by acceding to the period of their erasure': Derrida (1978:226). In other words, 'the trace is not only the disappearance of origin – within the discourse that we sustain [...] it means that the origin did not even disappear, that it was never constituted except reciprocally by an origin, the trace, which thus becomes the origin of the origin' (Derrida 1976:61).

10. The supplement, Derrida indicates, is *both* that which 'seems to be added as a plenitude to a plenitude, [and] equally that which compensates for a lack' (Derrida 1978:212). Elsewhere he clarifies it even further: 'The supplement supplements. It adds only to replace. It intervenes or insinuates itself *in-the-place-of*' (Derrida 1976:145).

11. Derrida links iterability to the functioning of the parasite, which is never merely external to its host: '*L'itérabilité altère, elle parasite et contamine ce qu'elle identifie et permet de répéter; elle fait qu'on veut dire (déjà, toujours, aussi) autre chose que ce qu'on veut dire, on dit autre chose que ce qu'on dit et voudrait dire, comprend autre chose que... etc*: Iterability alters, it parasites and contaminates what it identifies and allows itself to repeat; it makes one want to say (already, always, also) something different from what one wants to say, one says something different from what one says *and* would like to say, one understands something different from... etc.' (Derrida 1977:33, my translation).

12. The Symbolic Order is discussed, *inter alia*, in Lacan 1977:65, around the statement that, 'Man speaks [...] but it is because the symbol has made him man.'

13. At first sight it may seem inconsistent that I do, however, discuss Diderot and Flaubert, both of them famous for their foregrounding of language and/or narrative technique. But Diderot was selected because he is less familiar to the English reader than Sterne; and Flaubert because, although his use of language has been the subject of innumerable studies, my focus falls more on the *implications* of that usage for our reading of the narrative – an approach already central to many discussions of Sterne and Joyce.

1 The Wrong Side of the Tapestry

1. All references are to J. M. Cohen's excellent translation in the Penguin Classics (1950). References to the original Spanish are to the 1958 edition published by Emecé in Madrid.

2. There is a wonderfully revealing moment in this scene when Don Quixote, mounted on the wooden horse, is described as looking 'like nothing so much as a figure in a Flemish tapestry, painted or woven, riding in some Roman triumph' (p. 729). Given that, on p. 877, the image of a Flemish tapestry will recur, this time as an illustration of the coarseness and unreliability of translation, this may be read as a particularly subtle instance of narratorial intervention, once again to alert the reader to the dubious quality of *everything* related in the story.

3. Riley (1962:179–99) devotes a whole chapter to a discussion of 'Verisimilitude and the Marvellous'. It is a useful starting point for such an

enquiry, even if it lacks Kundera's inspired vision. Compare, from *The Art of the Novel*: 'At the time [of Cervantes] novels and readers had not yet signed the verisimilitude pact. They were not looking to simulate reality; they were looking to amuse, amaze, astonish, enchant. They were *playful*, and therein lay their virtuosity' (Kundera 1988:94–5).

4. And in *The Art of the Novel* he says, 'To take, with Cervantes, the world as ambiguity, to be obliged to face not a single absolute truth but a welter of contradictory truths (truths embodied in *imaginary selves* called characters), to have as one's only certainty the *wisdom of uncertainty*, requires [...] courage' (Kundera 1988:6–7). In our present context it is necessary, once again, to insist that this whole 'wisdom of uncertainty' depends on the novel's presentation of language.

5. In recent years more and more critics have suggested that this 'debunking' of chivalric romance was not nearly so straightforward a project as it might have appeared for so long, but that the text of the *Don Quixote* reveals in many ways a nostalgia for the genre in Cervantes. As Riley (1962:180) phrases it, 'The difference between his use of the extraordinary and that in the romances he condemned is *the difference between controlled and uncontrolled fantasy*' (my emphasis).

6. In I:xxv Sancho extemporises on the same theme: 'I know her well [...] and I can tell you that she pitches a bar as well as the strongest lad in the village. Praise be to God! She's a brawny girl, well built and tall and sturdy, and she will know how to keep her chin out of the mud with any knight errant who ever has her for his mistress. O the wench, what muscles she's got, and what a pair of lungs ...' (p. 209).

7. Centuries later, in Kafka's *The Trial*, a situation will obtain in which, as Kundera (1995:208) puts it, 'K. is guilty not because he has committed a crime but because he has been accused.'

8. Riley (1962:65) suggests that Dulcinea is no more than a pretext for this penance: 'The real motive cause is the desire to carry out a famous exploit in imitation of Amadis of Gaul, who, spurned by his lady Oriana, changed his name to Beltenebros and retired to live the life of a hermit on Peña Pobre.'

9. This is but one instance among many where the *Don Quixote* anticipates Márquez's *One Hundred Years of Solitude*.

2   Courtly Love, Private Anguish

1. All references to the English translation of *La Princesse de Clèves* are to the Penguin Classics edition (1992); references to the French (made only where differences of nuance appear) are to the edition of Le Livre de Poche (1983).

2. In French: '*Une sorte d'agitation sans désordre*' (p. 23).

3. In French: '*Cet air de mystère et de confidence*' (p. 153).

4. In his Introduction to the English translation Robin Buss argues that, 'in seventeenth-century French, the word was both more specific and less: a standard modern dictionary of classical French defines a "lover" as any man who *declares* his love to a woman, regardless of whether or not he

may be sincere; and this emphasis on the act of speech, with none on the act of sex, entirely displaces the relationship from the private to the social sphere, where it acquires an element of play' (p. 6). But Buss does not consider that *amant* need not *always* designate only a suitor: there are indeed instances when it denotes a sexual relationship. What makes *La Princesse de Clèves* so intriguing, is that one can never be entirely sure about its usage in any given context: the ambiguity of the word itself becomes significant once one begins to explore the language in which the narrative is – almost literally – clothed.

5. It is part of the strict code of behaviour which determines the narrative that we are never even told her first name: she is introduced simply as 'a beauty who attracted every eye' (p. 29) and the reader is informed of her family connections; after that, when she is not referred to as 'the daughter of Mme de Chartres', she is, at most, 'Mlle de Chartres'; and after her marriage 'Mme de Clèves' or 'the princess'. Neither are we told the first name of her lover, the Duc de Nemours. This may be partly explained by the fact that in the midst of so many characters taken from history, these two are (more or less) fictitious. But the main reason seems to be that even at moments of dramatic monologue or intimate description the *language code* imposes this external formality on the narrative. This will be dealt with extensively later in the chapter.

6. The use of parentheses in the sentence suggests the *conscious* control of different layers of language by the narrator.

7. ' "Do not oblige me", she said, "to admit something to you that I do not have the strength to admit, though I have many times intended to do so. Only consider that it is unwise for a woman of my age, who is mistress of her own conduct, to remain exposed in the midst of the court" ' (p. 113). The impact of the scene as a whole derives, of course, not only from the force of her passionate sincerity, but from the fact that it is overheard by Nemours, *and that the reader is aware of it.*

8. The Prince de Clèves's immediate reaction to the Princesse's first moving confession about her innocence in the face of temptation, is, 'Oh, madame! [...] I cannot believe you' (p. 115). Following the scene in the Dauphine's bedroom she confronts her husband with the discovery that their private conversation has become common knowledge and suggests that he is the only person who could have spread the news. In a rage, he turns the tables on her: 'It is rather for you, madame, to consider to whom you have been speaking: it is more likely that the secret was revealed by you than by me' (p. 129). When she passionately protests her innocence and denies the accusation, he is shaken: 'He did not know what to think' (p. 129) – evidently because he is not used to language as a vehicle of truth. And in the final crisis of his life, when the vague report of the footman he has sent to spy on her and Nemours is refuted by her frank account of what really happened, he cannot refrain from the most vicious and destructive remarks (pp. 155–7), revealing the total confusion brought about by his conditioning through the false language of the court: ' "Do not continue", M. de Clèves interrupted, "False oaths or a true confession would perhaps cause me equal distress" ' (p. 157).

9. Significantly, on another occasion of great linguistic confusion, the Prince tells his wife: 'I am being unjust. Refuse me whenever I ask you such things, but do not be offended if I ask them' (p. 116). And during one of their most tempestuous scenes he asks: 'How could you hope that I should be reasonable?' (p. 143).

10. The only occasions when males become secretive are those in which personal feelings become too unruly for expression within the conventions of court language; and even then, more often than not, in moments of great distress, they make use of confidants to speak their mind. This is what Sancerre does when he turns to the Prince de Clèves with his story about Mme de Tournon's deceptions (pp. 62 and following); or the Vidame when the intrigue surrounding his lost letter gets out of hand (pp. 93ff); or the Duc de Nemours to the Vidame when he cannot contain his excitement about what he has overheard in the pavilion (pp. 118ff). They all concur that 'it was necessary in life, to have someone to whom one could talk' (p. 95). It is pointedly illustrated by the Prince's reaction to the news about Mme de Tournon: 'As soon as M. d'Anville had finished telling me this news, I went over to Sancerre to pass it on to him, as a secret that had just been imparted to me, forbidding him to speak about it' (p. 63). There is an extension of this narrative strategy (which both extends the network of intrigue, and *de-authorises* language, by allowing it to be invaded by more and more 'readings' along the way) in the constant recourse to messengers and intermediaries. This leads to the mordant irony of the last scene between the Princesse and the Duc de Nemours, after her husband's death, when she finally, and in utter frankness, confesses all her feelings to him – and then breaks off the relationship, while at the same time encouraging him to spread the news: 'This conversation shames me: I permit you, and even beg you, to report it to M. le Vidame' (p. 170).

11. Women, too, are allowed access to confidantes, presumably because that restricts language to the private sphere where (if all goes as it should, which, as we have seen, is not always the case) it cannot interfere with the web of language spun in court society. While Mme de Chartres is still alive, the Princesse has ready access to her mother. Her real dilemma occurs when this important guide and confidante is taken from her. This explains, to a large extent, her subsequent attempt to place the Prince in the role, not of husband but of confidant, which is partially responsible for the resulting confusion, since husbands inevitably belong, at least in part, to the society of intrigue. (She is reminded by the Dauphine, after all, that 'it is your fault for giving him the letter: there is not a woman in the world except you who confides all that she knows to her husband': p. 107.)

12. The Princesse's final withdrawal into silence follows a long series of moments in the narrative where the inadequacy of language is unmasked, prompting characters to fall, or remain, silent when speech is called for. When two fast friends, the Prince and the Duc de Guise, discover that they are in love with the same woman, 'this aspiring to the same hand had put a barrier between them, so that they could not

discuss their feelings' (p. 33); when Nemours and the Princesse find themselves alone for the first time, 'he could say nothing. Mme de Clèves was equally speechless' (p. 74); in the emotional pavilion scene where the Princesse first confides in her husband, the confession is preceded by 'a deep silence' (p. 113); even the final, and crucial, meeting between the two lovers opens in silence: 'For some while they remained without saying anything' (p. 164). Without this accumulation of pointers towards the *limits* of language the end could not be as dense with meaning as it is. But, of course, the problem with silence, as with alternative sign-systems, is that it can so easily be misinterpreted, which happens constantly in the narrative. And this adds to the burden of the narrator who has to use all her skill to correct both silence and the distortions of language.

13. She is referring to an episode earlier that day when she witnessed the Duc de Nemours suffering an accident on horseback, which upset her so much that she involuntarily betrayed, by her manner, feelings she would never have dared express in words.

14. This last example is particularly telling, as it precedes the final confession scene in which the Princesse *herself* defines her feelings at such length and with such clarity.

3 'The Woman's Snare'

1. Even if only male authors were considered, this has now been proven to be inaccurate, as Salzman, among others, has demonstrated in *English Prose Fiction 1558–1700* (1986). By the time Defoe turned to the novel at the age of almost sixty, he had a rich tradition of English rogue novels and criminal biographies to draw on (apart from the Spanish picaresque genre to which he felt particularly attracted). These influences included the tendency towards 'questioning society' (Salzman 1986:113), the 'mixing of modes' (ibid.:202), 'the ambivalent moral stance of the author' (p. 206), 'the breach between reflection and action, morality and pragmatism, as a product of the harsh world in which the picaro must survive' (p. 209), even 'the expanding world of travel narratives' (p. 218). For a discussion of early women novelists, see Dale Spender's illuminating if occasionally overstated *Mothers of the Novel*, 1986.

2. All references to *Moll Flanders* are to the Penguin Popular Classics edition, 1994.

3. According to a note at the end of the text Moll's autobiography dates from 1683; but critics are agreed that the society depicted in it is based extensively on the London in which Defoe lived at the time of writing and publishing his novel (1722).

4. In this chapter 'history' and 'story' are used with the meanings Defoe assigns to them, 'history' designating a written (narrative) text that purports to refer to a signified with an alleged independent existence which may also be evoked through other signifiers in other texts, and 'story' designating a written narrative text in which the signifieds,

constantly deferred, can in no way be evoked through signifiers beyond the borders of the given text.

5. In the Preface to *Roxana* the Editor also refers to the intervention of a ghost writer 'dressing up the story in worse clothes than the lady whose words he speaks'.

6. An editorial hand seems to be at work in the obvious censoring of lewd passages, as promised in the Preface: but these may just as well have been suppressed by a later, more prudent Moll reviewing the excesses of her life. By acknowledging a *double* narratorial voice, a greater richness of textured meaning may emerge from a number of episodes. These would include the account of an amorous encounter with her first lover, which is interrupted by a reference to 'some other follies which I cannot name' (pp. 126–7), or the way a veil is drawn over the details of the night she spends with a drunken gentleman she has seduced for the sake of robbing him, as these are alleged 'not so proper for a woman to write' (p. 256). When a second meeting between them also results in sex, the description is once again curtailed with the brief remark that 'it went on to what I expected, and to what will not bear relating' (p. 259). The double voice speaking in these episodes suggests an extension of the notion of dialogic language.

7. The actantial structure of the narrative is informed by contemporary socio-politico-economic factors discussed at length by Novak (1962), Richetti (1975), Thompson (1975), Earle (1976), Alkon (1979), and others: the development of laissez-faire and free trade, the situation of women and the conditions of marriage and divorce, poverty and the structure of wages, population and emigration, development of the colonies, a redefinition of the notion of criminality in the wake of the breakdown of feudalism, and so on. As Richetti (1975:17) suggests, in opposition to Watt (1963:98), 'Defoe's novels are not [...] naïve celebrations of individual possibility. They are most accurately described as what can be called the individualistic dilemma. They communicate by their arrangements and strategies an implicit grasp of the tangled relationships between the free self and the social and ideological realities which that self seems to require.'

8. 'These were they that gave me the name of Moll Flanders' (p. 234). The significance of the name in Moll's material and mercantile world is discussed, inter alia, by Blewett (1979:56–60).

9. Only James Cole (whose name she bends to 'Jemmy': p. 168) is identified by name – and even he is simply called, more often than not, 'my Lancashire husband' (p. 324) or, later, 'my fellow prisoner' (p. 340).

10. Her real concern, of course, is not the gentleman, but herself and what *she* is going to do; and the passage continues with the resolve: 'Well, if I must be his wife, if it please God to give me grace, I'll be a true wife to him ... I will make him amends if possible, by what he shall see, for the cheats and abuses I put upon him, which he does not see.'

11. For Moll, as a woman, the situation is further complicated by the discovery that her physical being, her body, is itself perceived in terms of economics: in the final analysis it is her *female body* which becomes the object of barter and exchange. In a revealing moment just

after the elder brother in the Colchester household has begun to show an interest in her, one of his sisters remarks, 'Betty wants but one thing, but she had as good want everything, for the market is against our sex just now; and if a young woman have beauty, birth, breeding, wit, sense, manners, modesty, and all these to an extreme, yet if she have not money, she's nobody [...] for nothing but money now recommends a woman; the men play the game all into their own hands' (p. 21). In Defoe's original text this is highlighted even more by a slight turn in the phrase, '*if she have not Money, she's no Body*'. As the substance of the (female) body in the novel is predicated on the *language* men use, first to describe it and then to possess it, the identification of money and language becomes even more nefarious.

12. In one of many comparable episodes, Moll reflects on Jemmy's departure: 'his manner of parting with that large share which he gave me of his little stock left – all these had joined to make such impressions on me, that I really loved him most tenderly' (p. 170).

13. 'I had the terrible prospect of poverty and starving, which lay on me as a frightful spectre, so that there was no looking behind me', she confesses on p. 131 when she decides to accept the rich married gentleman from Bath as a lover. 'But as poverty brought me into it, so fear of poverty kept me in it.' When he fades as a prospect, she reiterates that 'the terror of approaching poverty lay hard upon my spirits' (p. 141), because 'with money in the pocket one is at home anywhere' (p. 195). Through such remarks the reader comes to understand Moll's desperate preoccupation with one thing above all, 'the preservation of my own life' (p. 244). Indeed, 'to dismiss (Defoe's) characters as rogues is to disregard the seriousness of their lives and problems [...] For Defoe's heroes and heroines survival is a genuine, and indeed the most important, problem they must face' (Novak 1962:67).

4 The Dialogic Pact

1. Alter indeed quotes with approval Mayoux's characterisation of Sterne's text as 'a portrait of the mind as it runs' (Mayoux 1936:524), which is a preoccupation of Modernism from Proust to Faulkner, and from Kafka to Durrell (cf. Alter 1978:71).

2. Kundera also notes the wonderful paradoxes at the heart of *Jacques the Fatalist*: 'Is this magnificent disorder the effect of admirable construction, subtly calculated, or is it due to the euphoria of pure improvisation? [...] [T]he question I spontaneously asked showed me that a prodigious architectural potential exists within such intoxicated improvisation, the potential for a complex, rich structure that would also be [...] perfectly calculated, calibrated and premeditated' (Kundera 1995:19–20). A propos of his own theatre adaptation of *Jacques the Fatalist*, he also makes the important observation that for all the dazzling 'modern' features of his text, Diderot remains a writer of the eighteenth century, not one of the twentieth. Most particularly, 'the eighteenth century was optimistic, my time is not' (ibid.:80).

3. All references to the English text are to Michael Henry's translation, *Jacques the Fatalist and His Master* in the Penguin Modern Classics (1986). Where French texts by Diderot are cited, the reference is to the Collected Works in Diderot: *Oeuvres* (Paris: Gallimard, Bibliothèque de la Pléiade, 1951).

4. See Hegel 1977:111: 'Self-consciousness exists in and for itself when, and by the fact that, it so exists for another; that is, it exists only in being acknowledged.'

5. The simultaneity of the two writings is underscored in the French text by the use of the imperfect *étaient*, with its strong suggestion of duration and continuity in time.

6. In an easy extension of the notion of the Scroll, the Narrator sometimes substitutes references to the 'source' of his story, to an 'original text' he has consulted and in which, for example, the word 'ventriloquist' is used for the term 'engastrimyth' employed by Jacques (p. 203), or 'hydrophobic' for a less erudite word which would have found a more credible place in Jacques's vocabulary (p. 239). Most specifically, one of the three endings of the novel, the one which appears to bring us closest to 'the story of Jacques's loves', is derived explicitly from *Tristram Shandy* (pp. 251, etc.). But *Tristram Shandy* is not quoted verbatim; and it is evident that these other alleged sources (as distinct from the numerous sources identified in the narrative, through which a dense weave of intertext is established) have no independent existence at all, which once again opens the debate about a death of the Author. As a result, 'there is no other time than that of the enunciation and every text is eternally written *here* and *now*' (Barthes 1988:170).

7. On another level in the narrative, the Narrator confesses during a break in the narrative at the inn, 'I don't know whether these reflections were made by Jacques, his master, or by me' (p. 114). Here, practically in front of the reader's eyes, the Auctor abdicates from his position of authority.

8. The term *Erwartungshorizont*, a key concept in Reception Theory, was appropriated by Hans Robert Jauss (1970:9) from German phenomenology, with specific reference, *inter alia*, to *Jacques the Fatalist*.

9. Kermode (1966) uses the phrase more specifically with reference to apocalyptic fiction.

10. Alter (1978:58–61) discusses at some length the difference in approach between Sterne's and Diderot's versions of the episode (Diderot's interest, he argues, 'lies in transmitting it deftly and elegantly as a narrated event, not in recreating it as an experience to be felt on our pulses'), but without adequately considering what I regard as the conclusive point of difference: the fact that Sterne stops the narration before the climax, leaving Uncle Toby to bring it to a 'decent' end, while Diderot's scene debouches in the ambiguity of a *word*, and a crucial word indeed, the French 'baiser'.

11. Among Kristeva's most influential texts are *Histoires d'Amour* and, in English, *Desire in Language*; one of Barthes's *A Lover's Discourse*.

12. The French *quiproquo* (p. 518) is more illuminating, suggesting as it does the substitution of one perception for another.

5 Charades

1. A good example is McMaster's exploration of 'the beautifully symmetrical pattern of the precept laid down and discussed in theory, the practical test, and the access of knowledge with experience' (McMaster 1975:82). Other critics focus on Austen's orchestration of marriages within a social or class framework (Kettle 1951); the interaction of 'the social world and the moral world' (Bradbury 1962:217); or Austen's remarkable ability to work within severe constraints (Bayley 1968; Auerbach 1986).

2. Mudrick's *Irony as Defense and Discovery* is probably the most extensive analysis in this regard; particularly useful is his analysis of 'the primary large irony of [...] the deceptions of surface'. He argues that, in *Emma*, 'the brilliant façades of Emma and Frank Churchill have no door' (Mudrick 1968:201).

3. Foremost among these are Johnson (1988) and Gilbert and Gubar (1979), to which I shall be referring later.

4. All references are to the Penguin Classics edition, 1985.

5. Greimas conceives of the overall structure of a narrative in terms of actantial patterns within which the characters are clustered as 'actants', according to whether in any given sequence they are senders, objects or receivers, with a secondary category of helpers, subjects or opponents.

6. In her essay 'Properties and Possessions in Jane Austen's Novels', Juliet McMaster explores aspects of the relationship between people and objects, but without interrogating the way in which some (classes of) characters are themselves relegated to the status of 'properties and possessions' (in McMaster 1976:79–105).

7. This should be qualified, of course: in much of the novel the narrator's concern, as I am trying to argue in this chapter, is *precisely* the confusions and muddling caused by language – but Austen's achievement resides in the way she manipulates language in order to convey, lucidly, the obfuscations on which it rests.

8. Yet it is significant that even Knightley at times misleads Emma about his 'real' intentions; and perhaps even more significant that he misreads *her*: 'He had misinterpreted the feelings which had kept her face averted, her tongue motionless' (p. 368).

9. This is repeated on p. 287 where, in the face of all the evidence, Emma again resolves that, 'She must be under some sort of penance [...] There is great fear, great caution, great resolution somewhere [...] But why must she consent to be with the Eltons? Here is quite a different puzzle.'

10. In this respect, one is reminded of the fact that Jane Austen herself in 1802 rejected a particularly good offer of marriage (see Kaplan 1992:109).

11. This would be somewhat at odds with the reading by Fleishman (1983:255), who compares Emma's perception of the real and the ideal in one vision with the practice of writers like Cervantes: 'Though Emma is no artist, lacking the control of her own language, she sees as they see.'

6   The Language of Scandal

1. References to Flaubert's work in French, including *Madame Bovary*, are to the collected edition of La Pléiade (1983). For reasons of accessibility, my references to the English version are to the translation by Alan Russell in the Penguin Classics which was first published in 1950; but it is in many ways an unfortunate text, which loses most of the rhythmic consciousness that informed Flaubert's writing. As for the writer's celebrated agonising over *le mot juste*, very little of this is reflected in a translation characterised more by its chattiness and a Mills-and-Boon tendency towards the pink and the purple than by precision and metaphoric felicity. Often the very sense of a passage is lost. A single example: when Flaubert's narrator describes Lheureux as working like 'cinq cents diables', Mr Russell offers 'a million niggers' as his equivalent (p. 264). One wonders not only at the kind of racial consciousness underlying the equation of one devil = 2000 'niggers' (even in 1950 this should have raised the odd eyebrow; and by the 1980s the text had still not been amended), but at the staggering lack of perceptiveness the passage demonstrates. And this coarseness pervades the translation as a whole.

2. A century later, when scandalised citizens in South Africa agitated for the banning of *Seven Days at the Silbersteins'* (1962) by Etienne Leroux, one much-repeated argument advanced by theologians was that the book was immoral 'not so much because of what is described in the text as because of what readers can imagine happening *between* the chapters'.

3. This phrase is the premise of a particularly revealing reading of language in *Madame Bovary* by de Lattre (1980:94): '*La phrase [...] se met où Dieu seul aurait pu se placer* [The sentence puts itself in the place only God could have occupied]'. He sees Flaubert's entire realism as vested in language: not, as the traditional view has it, in the *object*, but in the *sentence*, '*qui fait et qui produit. Qui annule ce qu'elle dit parce que, dans le fait, il n'en est plus besoin* [which establishes and which produces. Which cancels what it says, because in the act there is no longer any need for it]' (p. 68; see also p. 89).

4. How significant that Rodolphe, of all people, should express this, since he does it as part of a rhetoric of seduction, which already demonstrates the devaluation of language.

5. The only alternative is a language-beyond-language, a pure sign-language of the kind we shall encounter in Atwood's *Surfacing*, when the narrator leaves the world of speech to learn the semiotic systems of trees and water. In *Madame Bovary*, in the very scene where Emma first 'becomes a part of her own imaginings', she is significantly described in a natural context of 'shivering leaves' and 'whistling grasses' (p. 175).

6. It works the other way as well: a character designed to make a negative impression, like Madame Homais, is revealed as having a limited capacity for speech. She is 'so slow-moving, so wearisome to listen to, so common in appearance and *so limited in her conversation*' (p. 109).

7. It is striking how most of the exceptions work with images of natural force, and are developed much more elaborately than the similes: 'Love, she believed, must come suddenly, with thunder and lightning, a hurricane from on high that swoops down into your life and turns it topsy-turvy [...] She did not know how on the terrace of a house the rain collects in pools when the gutters are choked; and she would have continued to feel quite safe had she not suddenly discovered a crack in the wall' (p. 113); or: 'Her remembrance of Léon became the centre of her discontent; it crackled there more fiercely than a fire left burning in the snow by travellers in the Russian steppes. She ran to it, huddled herself against it, carefully stirred it when it flagged, and cast about for fresh fuel to revive it' (p. 136) – and from there it is developed through two long paragraphs.
8. 'même il parlait argot pour éblouir [...] les bourgeois, disant *turne, bazar, chicard, chicandard, Breda-Street,* et *Je me la casse,* pour: Je m'en vais' (Pléiade, p. 545).
9. Flaubert also uses, to great effect, ideolects in the presentation of his characters, and many critics have commented on the remarkably subtle inflexions of French used to distinguish one character's speech from another's. Homais is probably the most viciously amusing instance, but the finely tuned ear, or the observant eye, can detect it in each of the many characters, from the opening scene when Charles Bovary distinguishes himself through the jumbled pronunciation of his own name. No wonder that when Emma goes to that ball which will change her life she first registers her outsidership in the course of 'listening to a conversation full of words she didn't understand' (p. 64).
10. On only one occasion, as I have indicated, is Emma actually described as naked (Part III, Chapter 6), and in that episode the description of her physical appearance stops at the moment she sheds her clothes in order to shift to her emotional state.
11. 'This scene', writes Valency (1966:285–7), 'marks the very zenith of Chekhov's art [...] The sound of the breaking string remains mysterious, but it has finality. The symbol is broad; it would be folly to try to assign to it a more precise meaning than the author chose to give it. But its quality is not equivocal. Whatever of sadness remains unexpressed in *The Cherry Orchard,* this sound expresses.'
12. Among the most emblematic of these is the ball scene already referred to: 'Here she was, at the ball. Outside, over everything else, hung a dark veil' (p. 65). In fact, the very first time Charles meets Emma, he finds her 'standing with her forehead against the window, looking out into the garden, where the bean- sticks had been blown down by the wind' (p. 29). Later, on a market day in Yonville, Emma again looks out, and a significant comparison is made: 'in the country the window takes the place of theatres and park parades' (p. 139). In yet another crucial scene, just after she has received Rodolphe's letter of farewell, she tries to hide indoors ('"Oh, in here", she thought, "I'll be safe"') but is driven inexorably to the window: 'the dazzling sunlight flooded in' (pp. 216–17): and it is, of course, this dazzle from the space beyond her strictly confined existence which will eventually blind and destroy her.

13. It is significant that the old beggar, who turns out to be, in appearance, actions and language, *offensive* in the most original sense of the word, is finally destroyed by language – i.e. by Homais's vicious little letters to the newspaper (p. 355).
14. As may be expected, numerous critics have explored the functioning of this 'mysterious *we*' (Llosa 1978:194) in particular, and the 'extremely mobile' narrative voice in general (see Butor 1984:80), as well as the narrator's versatile use of the free indirect mode, in which both private and public voices meet and mingle, dissolving all sense of hierarchy (see for example Gengembre 1990:72 and Llosa 1978:195). But precisely because this aspect of language usage has been so extensively commented on, I have preferred in this essay to focus on other aspects.

7 Quoted in Slang

1. All references are to the Penguin Classics edition, 1965, edited by W. J. Harvey.
2. MacCabe does add a measure of qualification: 'Within her novels there are always images which counter the flat and univocal process which is the showing forth of the real' (1991:162); and, 'Classic realism can never be absolute; the materiality of language ensures there will always be fissures which disturb the even surface of the text' (p. 167), but as I shall try to demonstrate, the usage of language in *Middlemarch* offers much more than merely incidental or accidental deviations from a norm of transparency and 'flatness'. My reading is more closely related to that of J. Hillis Miller, who acknowledges Eliot's 'recognition of the deconstructive powers of figurative language' (Miller 1975:144).
3. Such a view already challenges all ready-made notions of 'realism'.
4. Gilbert and Gubar (1984:505) demonstrate that 'the book is Casaubon's child, and the writing of it is his marriage, or so Dorothea believes as she realizes how completely textuality has been substituted for sexuality in her married life'. But the image and the argument invites completion by indicating the significance of the fact that, after Casaubon's death, Dorothea on several occasions chooses precisely the library as the site of very intense, if mostly suppressed, sexual negotiation with either Lydgate or Ladislaw, through which female sexuality once again dares to confront – and eventually to vanquish – male textuality.
5. It is also significant, as Gilbert and Gubar (1984) point out, that gossip is one of the only ways in which women are allowed to play a decisive role in the weaving of the social fabric. One is also struck by the similarities between Eliot's approach in this regard and the view expressed by her contemporary Engels in a letter to Marx: 'History makes itself in such a way that the final result always arises from conflicts between many individual wills, of which each again has been made what it is by a host of particular conditions of life [...] What each individual wills is obstructed by everyone else, and what emerges is something that no one willed [...Yet] each contributes to the resultant and is to this degree involved in it.'

6. D. M. Miller (1991:191) provides a particularly incisive reading of this scene.

7. As a consequence, Rosamond's quite remarkable rebellion against her husband in particular and patriarchy in general, as illuminated by Gilbert and Gubar (1984:514 etc.), may also be approached as a revolt against narratorial manipulation.

8. The same viciousness informs the narrator's conclusive image of Rosamond: In fact there was but one person in Rosamond's world whom she did not regard as blameworthy, and that was the graceful creature with blond plaits and with little hands crossed before her, who had never expressed herself unbecomingly, and had always acted for the best – the best naturally being what she best liked (p. 716).

9. Not only the contents of the *Cours*, but to a very important extent the very concept of a great architectural construction, links Comte with Eliot and, within *Middlemarch* itself, with Casaubon and Lydgate. 'Like Lydgate or Casaubon, this narrator is searching for the hidden structure that gives coherence and meaning to the whole' (Gilbert & Gubar 1984:523). It is also a ticklish thought that James Frazer's *Golden Bough* was published a mere decade after *Middlemarch*.

10. That this is, at best, an ambiguous image, in view of the fact that the narrative does *not* allow Dorothea, or even someone like Mrs Cadwallader, to rest in an unvisited tomb, has been abundantly commented on over the years.

11. Aspects of this interval are also discussed in Gilbert and Gubar 1984:491 and following.

12. Nina Auerbach (1986:265 and following) focuses more specifically on Laure as *actress* rather than as *murderer*, exploring Eliot's handling of 'that fine point between honesty and dissimulation'.

8   The Tiger's Revenge

1. References to the English text are to H. T. Lowe-Porter's version, first published in 1929 and used in the Penguin Modern Classics since 1955, resulting in the unfortunate perpetuation of a fluent and ambitious but extremely unreliable translation which more often than not, even in its most felicitous passages, does little justice to the subtleties of Mann's original. It misses, as Heller (1958:102) points out, 'the ironical elegance ... subtly ridiculing the habitual posturing of the German language'. Even if one grants the notorious difficulty of rendering Mann into English, surely there can be no justification for the survival of such a particularly untrustworthy translation. References to the German text are to *Der Tod in Venedig*, in the paperback edition of Fischer Bücherei (1954).

2. Many commentators have examined the relationship between narrator and protagonist in *Death in Venice*, but usually within the context of irony: see notably Heller (1958). Cohn (1978:26–30) offers a particularly perceptive reading of the relationship as one of 'dissonance and consonance', in a form of 'psycho-narration': 'In the early sections, when

Aschenbach is still in full control of his rational faculties, his self-image very nearly coincides with his narrator's image of him, whereas in the later sections there is a marked ironic gap' (Cohn 1978:27). However, as I try to show, the 'gap' is *always* there, and is articulated most dramatically on the level of narrative language.

3. It adds an interesting dimension of meaning to the text to read this figure as an allusion to a famous image of Folly in Erasmus, namely the description of hideous old men on the verge of death who are so desperate to appear young 'that one dyes his white hair, another covers up his baldness with a wig [...] while another is crazy about a girl and outdoes any young man in his amorous silliness' (Erasmus 1971:109).

4. Nicklas (1968) explores several forms of irony in the text: direct, tragic, compositional, and attitudinal.

5. It is also important to bear in mind that in one of his manifestations Apollo himself is the god of pestilence and of epidemics. As far as Dionysus is concerned, there is a revealing comment by Apter (1978:51): 'Mann's model of total suppression and then violent release has more in common with Euripides's portrayal of Pentheus's struggle against Dionysus...his punishment is to be torn apart by the Maenads, the representatives of impulse in its crude, orgiastic state.' The involvement of a female force in the shape of the Maenads is particularly significant.

6. It is illuminating to note that all the works by Aschenbach referred to in the text were projects on which Mann himself had been working during the years 1900–1911, i.e. just prior to the writing of *Death in Venice* (Scherrer & Wysling 1967:23; also Heller 1958:98). But this does not mean that in the text of *Death in Venice* Aschenbach 'stands for' or 'equals' Mann: as a writer, Mann goes beyond his protagonist inasmuch as he writes the narrator who writes Aschenbach.

7. Lehnert (1968:99ff) points out that Aschenbach's exquisite little essay appears to be identical with Mann's own 'Ueber die Kunst Richard Wagners', written during the author's stay at the Lido, but never published during his lifetime.

8. The German text is much stronger, and much more subtle: '[...] *flüsterte er die stehende Formel der Sehnsucht, – unmöglich hier, absurd, verworfen, lächerlich und heilig doch, ehrwürdig auch hier noch: "Ich liebe dich!"*' (Mann 1954:47).

9. In German this passage with its strong Homeric echoes reads: '*Aber der Tag, der so feurig-festlich begann, war im ganzen seltsam gehoben und mythisch verwandelt. Woher kam und stammte der Hauch, der auf einmal so sanft und bedeutend, höherer Einflüsterung gleich, Schläfe und Ohr umspielte? Weisse Federwölkchen standen in verbreiteten Scharen am Himmel gleich weidenden Herden der Götter. Stärkerer Wind erhob sich, und die Rosse Poseidons liefen, sich bäumend, daher, Stiere auch wohl, dem Bläulichgelockten gehörig, welche mit Brüllen anrennend die Hörner senkten. Zwischen dem Felsen geröll des entfernteren Strandes jedoch hüpften die Wellen empor als springende Ziegen. Eine heilig entstellte Welt vol panischen Lebens schloss den Berückten ein, und sein Herz träumte zarte Fabeln*' (Mann 1954:45).

10. The deft introduction of a female element in the form of the goddess Eos cannot pass unnoticed. In the relationship between Aschenbach and Tadzio the *youth* represents virginal femininity, but in this passage the participants in the equation change roles. And in the decisive passsage from the *Phaedrus* quoted at the end, Aschenbach clearly identifies himself with the poets who 'are all like women' (p. 89).

9   A Room without a View

1. All references to the English text are to Idris Parry's commendable translation in the Penguin Twentieth-Century Classics edition (1994); references to the German text are to the edition based on the manuscript and prepared by Malcolm Pasley for S. Fischer Verlag (1990).
2. The German title, *Der Prozess*, indeed captures more amply than 'trial' the impression of the vast machinery in which K is caught.
3. This is more than can be said of *The Castle*, which breaks off in the middle of Chapter 18, with a further two and a half chapters added later, and tentatively, from a jumble of notes and papers collated by Max Brod.
4. According to Max Brod, the novel is '*nach Ansicht des Dichters freilich unvollendet, unvollendbar, unpublizierbar* [in the author's view, utterly incomplete, incompletable, unpublishable]' (quoted in Kafka 1990:360).
5. One is reminded of later attempts to subvert temporality in the novel. One of the most famous examples is *The Unfortunates* by B. S. Johnson (1969), which is presented as an assortment of loose sections in a box; before reading the text, the reader is requested to shuffle the sections like a deck of cards.
6. This scene derives its particular force from, *inter alia*, the fact that on only two other occasions in the novel a moonlight scene is featured – K's furtive visit to Fräulein Bürstner's room (p. 17), and his first love-making with Leni in the advocate's house (p. 84) – both of which are heavily charged with sexuality.
7. Kundera (1995:226) argues beguilingly that throughout the text there are moments that 'briefly open onto a landscape far away from K's trial [...] onto a world where, even at the harshest moments, characters retain a freedom of decision which gives life the happy incalculability that is the source of poetry'. I am not sure that this accords entirely with the many references to windows where a view is specifically denied or restricted; but even if one grants the occasional glimpse of 'another' (Tolstoyan) world, as in Kundera's example, from p. 28 of the novel, in which a girl at a water pump stares at K while she fills her jug, this would ultimately *reinforce* the claustrophobia of being trapped indoors.
8. This is echoed in the scene in Titorelli's room where a canvas on the easel is obscured by a shirt draped over it (p. 114); on several occasions, especially in Titorelli's studio and the house of the advocate, pictures and windows tend to fulfil the same function.
9. It is even stronger in German with its suggestion of physical encroachment: '*wenn mir jetzt der Process, förmlich im Geheimen, immer näher an den Leib rückt*' (Kafka 1990:154).

10. Derrida 1981:212: 'The hymen [...] produces the effect of a medium [...] It is an operation that *both* sows confusion *between* opposites *and* stands *between* the opposites "at once". What counts here is the *between*, the in-between-ness of the hymen. The hymen "takes place" in the "inter-", in the spacing between desire and fulfilment, between perpetration and its recollection. But this medium of the *entre* has nothing to do with a center.'

11. See, for example, the *Letters to Milena* (Kafka 1967). In the present context it is particularly revealing that Kafka's natural affinity with women was threatened by the aggressive male chauvinism of his father (see Gray 1973:41) who is replicated in many of the male functionaries of the judicial system in *The Trial*.

12. The German word *Verworfenheit* even bears a theological connotation of 'damnation'.

13. It is interesting that the merchant Block (who may or may not have a liaison with Leni concurrently with Josef K) later intimates that 'the outcome of a case can be seen in the accused man's face *and particularly in the line of his lips*. And these people say said that, *judging by* your lips, *you are sure to be convicted*' (p. 136, my emphasis). Once again the metonymic relationship between lips and language is highlighted.

14. Derrida 1976:145: 'The sign is always the supplement of the thing itself [...] But their common function is shown in this: whether it adds or substitutes itself, the supplement is *exterior*, outside of the positivity to which it is super-added, alien to that which, in order to be replaced by it, must be other than it.'

15. Nicolai (1986:176) points out that the term *Fratzen* (translated in Parry's text as 'rascals': pp. 112ff) denotes more than 'young rogues' with smirking or grimacing faces and that Kafka often uses it 'as a sign of immoderate behaviour, of sexuality and of an animal nature persisting in man [*als Zeichen des Unbeherrschtseins, der Sexualität und des sich noch manifestierende Tierischen*]'. In addition, it suggests something of a 'freak of nature'. All of this lends the girls a very ominous air of viciousness, even of evil. As a result, they collectively come to represent all the females in the text.

16. One should bear in mind, however, that among the uncompleted chapters of Kafka's manuscript omitted from most translations, there is one entitled 'Zu Elsa'.

10   The Perfect Crime

1. Although there appear to be certain objects, like his collection of strings in a shoebox and the drawing of the seagull, which he remembers in remarkable detail, there are frequent references to his defective memory – concerning childhood friends, the topography of the town or the island, or even the location of the house of his birth. This constitutes another significant, and signifying, gap in the text.

2. All references to the English text are to *The Voyeur*, translated by Richard Howard, first published by Grove Press, Inc. in 1958. It happens

to be, still, the only available English translation; but it is a most unreliable piece of work and can only be read with great circumspection. Most glaringly, it plays havoc with Robbe-Grillet's meticulously controlled shifts between tenses. It loses a network of subtle verbal correspondences (if the links between *voyageur* and *voyeur* or *ficelle* and *fillette* must have been, admittedly, difficult to establish in English, others appear to be lost through sheer carelessness). It misses significant variations in repeated passages while introducing random echoes of its own. Important nuances are sacrificed to mere glibness: on p. 17 Robbe-Grillet's *représentations* becomes *memories*; on p. 143 a straightforward *fût* ('was') becomes *represented*. By brutally anglicising the names of some characters the vital connotations of *Violette* (*viol, violée*) are lost; mercifully, but illogically, Mathias does not become Matthew. In a text where everything depends on the specificities of grammar, semantics, choice of words, or the rhythms of prose, this is simply untenable. For this reason quite extensive referencing to the original French text has been necessary. Such references are to *Le Voyeur*, first published by Les Editions du Minuit in 1955.

3. The term 'scene' appears to me justified in the circumstances, as Robbe-Grillet's cinematic approach is evident throughout his *oeuvre*.
4. Blanchot (1959:196) speaks of '*ce point obscur qui nous permet de voir* [this dark point which allows us to see]'. And Robbe-Grillet himself refers to 'an organising void' (quoted in Jefferson 1980:142).
5. In the English text it becomes a 'whistle' (p. 3), which quite literally obliterates the first warning signal in the text. As Sturrock (1969:182) and others have pointed out, Mathias's response to the sound of a *siren* suggests important erotic connotations.
6. In the French text, the present tense suddenly pops up here, in mid-sentence, with startling effect (Robbe-Grillet 1955:117). In English, not only the surprise, but the reminder of the *textuality* of the scene, is lost.
7. The same kind of grammatical breakdown occurs at several other points in the narrative. Among the most revealing examples is the scene in *A L'Espérance* just after Mathias has missed the return boat, when he overhears a discussion on Jacqueline's disappearance: 'Tonight, when Mathias would climb upstairs to his room [...] he would see, a few steps higher, showing him the way up the dark staircase, so slender in her little black peasant's dress, Violette as a child ... Violette! Violette! Violette!' (p. 146). Another is the confrontation with Julien, during which 'He didn't even know this was the place she had fallen ... fallen ... fallen ... He stopped. Julien was looking at him. Julien was going to say: "She didn't fall either." But the boy did not open his mouth' (p. 185). (In these quotes, as in all others, I have restored the anglicised names to their original French form.)
8. Admittedly, there are other parallel descriptions which do come close to verbatim repetition, but almost invariably small differences do occur.
9. The crossroads itself, a single and constant signified, is referred to, in the French text, by three different signifiers, *croisement, bifurcation* and *tournant*; when all three of them recur in a single sentence (Robbe Grillet 1955:197) it has a tremendous effect, largely lost in the English

translation which sticks more or less doggedly, with some idiosyncratic exceptions, to *crossroads*.

10. This is a wrong quotation of the words on p. 122, which may seem to
add another layer of misreading whereas in fact it is only another
sloppy translation. In French Mathias's original remark and the one
later ascribed to 'Pierre' are identical: 'Elle ne viendra plus, mainte-
nant' (Robbe-Grillet 1955: 142 and 183).

11. This becomes even more likely if, purely on the level of narrative, one
starts interrogating the meeting on the clifftop. In other words, *if* the
narrative is taken seriously (a very big 'if' indeed), does this scene 'take
place' at all, or is it, like so many other scenes where Mathias *imagines*
damning words coming from somebody's mouth, a form of hallucination? When he first conjures up an image of a visit to the Leduc house,
in which he would use the sailor's description of the family as a pretext,
Mathias imagines a reply: 'I have no brother' – but realises immediately
that these are 'words too brief to correspond to the movement the lips
had made a moment before' (p. 30). Sitting on the rocks before he sets
out on his round, Mathias remembers the earlier scene (which may or
may not have happened) between the brutish café owner and the
timorous girl, hearing again the words, 'Are you asleep?' (p. 62). Then
the scene is repeated once again, 'in the same low voice but muffled and
almost hoarse this time: unintelligible' (p. 63). After his long, convoluted explanation to the fat woman in the café near the lighthouse,
about his comings and goings during the morning, Mathias 'doubted
whether he had spoken aloud at all' (p. 96). Surely these scenes should,
at the very least, cast doubt on the reliability of the entire encounter
with Julien on the clifftop? In which case it would be another trick of
language employed by Robbe-Grillet to warn the reader against conventional narrative expectations in the reading of *this* text.

12. We know that his memory is notoriously bad (see note 1 above): like
the language of the text, it is characterised more by its gaps and holes
than by the threads that keep these together. But even so, if (and only
if) the narrative were to be taken at face value, then, given Mathias's
predisposition towards some kind of sexual psychosis involving sadis-
tic practices performed on barely nubile girls, it would be highly
unlikely that he should have forgotten such a legend. It can only be
absent from his mind if its existence is dependent, exclusively, on the
language in which it is being invented *at this moment*.

13. Soon afterwards, when Mathias is prevailed on to accompany his
unknown friend, Jean or Pierre or whomever, to lunch, it is indeed
served in soup plates (p. 115).

14. The other marker of mechanical precision, the bicycle, also turns out
to be malfunctioning – but only *after* Mathias has first lied about this.
His verbal construct of malfunctioning turns out to produce 'actual'
malfunctioning.

15. Vareille (1981:121) points out that, '*Chez Alain Robbe-Grillet il n'y a pas
de début; seule existe la reprise. Rien ne commence, tout re-commence* [With
Alain Robbe-Grillet there is no *beginning*; only repetition exists. Nothing begins, everything *recommences*]'.

16. On one occasion, p. 198, there is even a typographical break *without* a concomitant break in chronology.
17. The difference between Jacqueline and Violette in this scene is stated explicitly: 'It was not Violette, of course, but someone who looked very much like her...' (p. 67).
18. 'Young Violette' is another mistranslation. It should be an exact echo of the phrase 'Violette as a young girl' used with reference to the photograph on p. 67 (see Robbe-Grillet 1955:83 and 87).
19. If this scene in the present (and, possibly, the whole scene in the cottage) is read as a fiction, the encounter with the girl on the cliff the next day would also have to be read as imaginary, since the watch is then returned. Such a reading would be in keeping with an *imagining* of the encounter with young Julien: in both cases Mathias would then be projecting possible obstacles in the way of his alibis. But once again such scenes appear to be manipulated, not to establish any kind of difference between 'levels of reality' in the novel, but to demonstrate the untenability of *any* notion of 'reality' between the pages of a book.
20. Bernal (1974:194) argues that, *'Le regard est un acte comme c'est la voix et il peut l'être dans un sens moral, métaphysique et psychologique* [The gaze, like the voice, is an act, and can be such in a moral, metaphysical and psychological sense]' – concluding that in *Le Voyeur* observation becomes 'un acte de non-engagement' (p. 189), representing 'un abstinence moral' (p. 206).
21. There is a particularly eloquent scene in *A l'Espérance*: 'The barmaid looked at the floor in front of her feet. The proprietor looked at the barmaid. Mathias watched the proprietor looking at her. The three sailors looked at their glasses' (p. 45).
22. Among these: the cord looped like a figure 8, the mark on the side of the pier, the iron rings, the wood-knots on the front door of the (imagined) Leduc house, spectacles, handcuffs, the lighthouse with its stunning new lenses – all of which stare at Mathias in their unsettling silence.
23. The two may occasionally coincide, as Janvier (1964:138) indicates in referring, by implication, to Sartre: *'Voir c'est violer* [To see is to violate]'.
24. In fairness to such critics it should be remembered that Robbe-Grillet himself commented that *'l'acte principal, le meurtre, est un creux dans Le Voyeur* [the main action, the murder, is a gap in *Le Voyeur*]' (quoted by Bernal 1974:119). Closer consideration of the remark reveals that, for whatever it may be worth, the author does not actually commit himself one way or the other about *Mathias's* role in the event.
25. We should bear in mind that Julien, himself, never claims to have witnessed the murder. At most, he adduces evidence about the bicycle, the lie Mathias has told about visiting the farm, a cigarette and a sweet wrapper he has allegedly found on the scene. All this evidence put together indeed appears coherent and damning. But Julien never attempts to tell 'his story': in fact, he even subverts the story his own evidence appears to establish. It is as impossible for the reader or anyone else to 'prove' that he has seen anything. All he does is to

consent quite passively to the whole of Mathias's account, which leaves the hole at the heart of *Le Voyeur* intact.

26. In the most literal sense, as de Lauretis (1984:129) makes clear, narrative desire, impelled by authority, is implicated in the male enterprise of appropriation and conquest. De Lauretis's essays, in the same volume, dealing with cinema and the eye of the camera (another passion of Robbe-Grillet's) pursue the argument.

27. Bernal (1974:196) is even more emphatic: '*Le mot, comme l'objet littéraire, est toujours choisi. En littérature, il n'y a pas de déscriptions "littérales", elles sont toujours intentionnelles* [The word, as literary object, is always chosen. There are no "literal" descriptions in literature, they are always *intentional*]'.

28. This is reminiscent of Josef K's experience in the bank, where the flogging scene in the closed room appears to depend exclusively on his presence as an observer.

29. Vareille (1981:59) takes this kind of argument to a somewhat excessive conclusion in insisting that the novel as a whole should be read as a production from '*[la] matrice sexuelle et agressive* [the matrix, simultaneously sexual and aggressive]' of a single, specific letter, the V (as in either Voyeur or Voyageur): '*rappelant à la fois les jambes écartés de la victime et le sexe féminin* [recalling both the spread legs of the victim and the female sex]'.

11   Making and Unmaking

1. All references to the English text are to the felicitous if flawed translation by Gregory Rabassa in the Picador edition (London, 1978). Reference to the original Spanish text are to the Mondadori edition (Madrid, 1987).

2. 'The ancient Indo-European Sanskrit would seem to represent language in general and thus an appropriate vehicle for recording universal human experiences', writes McMurray (1977:85), but this appears to me to impose an easy symbolism on the novel, in line with McMurray's endeavour to enforce a reading of a 'rounded whole' and of closure.

3. The acts of speech and sex are first associated when in José Arcadio's early encounters with Pilar Ternera 'they reached such a state of intimacy that later, without realizing it, they were whispering to each other' (p. 31). This is confirmed, and emphasised, in his encounter with the gypsy girl where his transport 'burst forth with an outpouring of tender obscenities that entered the girl through her ears and came out of her mouth translated into her language' (p. 35). Later in the novel the language of sex and that of social intercourse significantly tend towards mutual exclusion: on Rebeca's wedding night with José Arcadio she is bitten by a scorpion on the foot, as a result of which 'her tongue went to sleep, but that did not stop them from spending a scandalous honeymoon' (p. 83) – an event repeated to some extent when in her early episodes of lovemaking with Aureliano junior Ursula Amaranta is obliged to gag herself 'so that she would not let out the cat howls that were already tearing at her insides' (p. 321).

4. The somewhat crude active voice of the English translation is more muted in the original, which refers to 'su impermeabilidad a la palabra de los hombres' (Márquez 1987:263). But the link between language and sex remains obvious.

5. It is curious to note how Macondo retains its sense of isolation through more than a hundred years of narrated time, even though from its earliest days it is visited from abroad: first by the gypsies, then by emissaries from the government, later increasingly by troops and the representatives of commerce. Even after a regular mail service is introduced and a railway link established, it remains strangely intact.

6. See Williamson (1987:59): '*One Hundred Years of Solitude* sets forth two distinct modes of reading history [...] Each mode is predicated upon a certain type of consciousness. Aureliano's reading might be termed "incestuous"; it is devoid of objectivity, of reference to external reality and to linear time [...] If Aureliano is an internal reader of the Buendía history, who witnesses his own fate in Melquíades's "speaking mirror", the ordinary reader remains outside the narrated events and is therefore capable of an objective, distanced view of that history.' But since the writer of the second narrative, Gabriel Márquez, is also implicated in the first, as a character, 'he can look back on his experience and write a history of Macondo to rival the interpretation of Melquíades [...H]e must construct his account in such a way as to reflect Macondo's history without himself falling prey to the siren-song of nostalgia' (ibid.:61).

7. This is also the ideal envisaged by Beckett's narrator in *Malone Dies*.

8. In this respect Márquez perhaps comes closer than anywhere else to Cervantes who, in the *Don Quixote*, also makes use of a 'fictitious foreign historian' (Bell 1993:61), in the form of Cide Hamete Benengeli, to write his story (see also, *inter alia*, Martin 1987:112). And Cide Hamete in some respects becomes a 'character' in his own story by the time Don Quixote, in Book II, looks back on the first volume of his written adventures.

9. These letters are as 'empty' as her husband's correspondence with his 'partners' in Brussels, about consignments of planes which never arrive (pp. 310, 317).

10. At the appointed hour she awaits their arrival, covered in a sheet and with her head pointing north, and when she wakes up the next morning she discovers 'a barbarous stitch in the shape of an arc that began at her crotch and ended at her sternum' (p. 281). What amounts to a form of crude writing – in which language and sex are once again closely linked – is, in every sense of the word, a *non sequitur*. And then a letter from the invisible doctors arrives, as 'real' or as 'imaginary' as anything else in the narrative, to complain that they could not find anything corresponding to her complaints. This is blamed on 'her pernicious habit of not calling things by their names', and it leads to a diagnosis of a dropped uterus for which pessaries are prescribed. (Fernanda's most common confusion, in writing as in speech, has been that between rectum and vagina.) Another implication of 'barbarous'

may also be relevant here, as the term evokes a form of distinction between Self and Other (that is, the Barbarian) which often creeps into descriptions of Macondo and its Others. And in this connection it is amusing to observe that when José Arcadio's penis, that very organ later to be tattooed in foreign tongues, is first observed by Pilar Ternero, she exclaims, '*Qué barbaro!*' (Márquez 1987:37) – a nuance sadly lost, like a number of others, by the limp English 'Lordy!' (p. 28). It is picked up again near the end when Amaranta Ursula meets Aureliano Babilonia again, once more using the exclamation, '*Qué barbaro!*' (Márquez 1987:306) – this time translated as 'My, my!' (p. 306). It is meant to recall, importantly, the first great virile member of the family; but at the same time it brands *him* as the 'stranger', whereas *she* is the one newly arrived from foreign climes.

11. It is very unfortunate that the key phrase of the novel, *había de* should be translated (correctly) as 'was to' in the first instance and (incorrectly) as 'would' in the second. Many invaluable nuances of the original have been sacrificed by such carelessness. Here it loses the whole notion of a *reprise*, a new cyclic beginning in the narrative.

12. It is another feature of the text, and another 'trick of language', that days of the week or month should be very precisely specified, but without reference to any year, so that the very specificity becomes a marker of vagueness. In *appearing* to signify, language does the opposite; and upon inspection the apparently confident signifier turns out to be empty.

13. The final deft comic touch is added with the subsequent reference to 'the inconsiderate Fernanda [who] was going about mumbling to herself because her sheets had been carried off' (p. 205).

14. Throughout the text the notion of the 'real' is problematised, as innumerable commentators have pointed out. Which makes it piquant, to say the least, to note how persistently characters are described as feeling that 'reality is slipping away' from them: the community as a whole experience it during the sleeping sickness (p. 46); José Arcadio Buendía experiences it when he is tied to the tree (p. 93) – whereas, surely, he of all people has reason to doubt reality from the first visits of the gypsies with their magnifying glasses and their ice and their flying carpets; Colonel Aureliano experiences it during his wars (p. 165); Ursula feels it in her dotage (pp. 201, 266); Amaranta Ursula and Aureliano Babilonia break through the final barriers of the real in their lovemaking (p. 326)...

15. The 'emptiness' of language as such is illustrated by many episodes in the novel, ranging from the capon story to the endless ramblings and rantings of Fernanda (pp. 262–5), by an acknowledgement of 'hate' which turns out to be 'love' (pp. 222, 228), by Aureliano's disembodied voice giving senseless messages on the telephone (pp. 136, 140), by Ursula's conversations with the ancestors (p. 266), or by Aureliano Babilonia's (admittedly short-lasting) discovery that all the languages he has learned 'were as useless as the box of genuine jewellery that his wife owned' (p. 329).

12 Withdrawal and Return

1. All references to *Surfacing* are to the Virago edition, 1995 (1972).
2. One is reminded of Eco's conviction that language is any system that can be used for lying. In *Surfacing*, the reader has to negotiate the narrator's lie about the 'drowning' of her brother (p. 26) and the whole nexus of imagery that springs from it, and her compulsive lying about her 'marriage' (pp. 41, 137–8).
3. In this lies the point of her creating her own life-story in 'their' language (see especially pp. 23, 81–2), which works like a 'motto, the words printed on a scroll like a fortune cookie' (p. 82). Which is why she so urgently reminds herself (an early warning to the reader about the 'revelation' to follow much later): 'I have to be more careful about my memories, I have to be sure they're my own and not the memories of other people telling me what I felt, how I acted, what I said: if the events are wrong the feelings I remember about them will be wrong too, I'll start inventing them and there will be no way of correcting it [...] I run quickly over my version of it, my life, checking it like an alibi' (p. 67).
4. The blight of victimhood has preoccupied Atwood both in her novels and her theoretical writings, starting with *Survival*, published in the same year as *Surfacing*: in that study she approaches Canada itself as 'a collective victim' (Atwood 1972:36) and much of her argument goes into defining 'basic victim positions' and the possibility of escape from it. But the density of *Surfacing*, in which language becomes both signifier and signified of victimhood *and* of processes of liberation from it, goes much further than any argument in *Survival*.
5. Even the male body is said to be as 'insistent as one side of an argument' (p. 141).
6. In the power to kill resides, perhaps, also the knowledge of the male's own impending death: 'a species once dominant, now threatened with extinction' (p. 2).
7. It is significant to remember that the narrator herself divides her narration into parts and chapters.
8. The remark is all the more poignant in view of the fact that the very word 'polite' is itself derived from 'polis'.
9. The narrator, of course, enjoys subverting their seriousness by insisting on the fallibility of their male authors: 'Burns was an alcoholic, Cowper was a madman, Doctor Johnson a manic-depressive and Goldsmith a pauper' (p. 32).
10. It is significant that, at the same time, she assumes more and more of her *father's* role, in acting as guide and mentor to the visitors.
11. This is part of the process of (symbolic or real) maiming and dismemberment inflicted by patriarchy on women to brand them as victims: woman without names abound in the narrative; the woman in the grocery shop has an arm missing; an emblematic image, applied to the narrator herself, is that of the 'woman sawn apart in a wooden crate' (p. 102).

13   Taking the Gap

1. All referenes are to Michael Henry Heim's fluent and sensitive English translation, Faber & Faber 1984.
2. Here she resembles Tomas in his 'epic' – that is, eclectic – search for female beauty, 'an originality that demonstrates its own irrelevance' (p. 200).
3. 'Tereza', says her mother on p. 45, 'can't reconcile herself to the idea that the human body pisses and farts': an attitude which links her with that of kitsch, which finds its *raison d'être* in the exclusion of 'shit' – except that Tereza also embodies the *rejection* of kitsch. In this sense, as in others, she becomes her own opposite.
4. For some aspects of the discussion about gendering in *The Unbearable Lightness of Being* I am indebted to an unpublished postgraduate essay by Natasha Distiller (1994).
5. It is true that in the 'dictionary' at the heart of the novel words are defined by both Franz and Sabina. But as a male, his definitions have *narrative* power, while hers are mainly *descriptive*. A single eloquent example of the functioning of male language: Franz thinks of Sabina, who has walked out on him, as his 'love'; the new woman in his life, who loves him, is identified as his 'mistress'. Their respective places in his life, and in the narrative, are wholly dependent on his definition of them. For him, 'not every woman was worthy of being called a woman' (p. 89).
6. It is both touching and revealing that on p. 294 Tereza should think that 'her home was Karenin, not Tomas': this female creature, turned into a male by language when a bitch was given the name of a man, defines much of Tereza's own status as outsider to Tomas's life, and as alien in the text. She can assume her femininity only by living into Tomas's language, that is, his definition of 'woman'.
7. All the more damning, then, that Kundera should insert the 'lightness' of his treatment of women in *this* text within the whole weighty tradition of Western literature.
8. In an interview, Kundera stated that, 'When my characters make love, they grasp, suddenly, the truth of this life or their relationship' (McEwan 1984:30). In *Testaments Betrayed*, he elaborates apropos of Kafka on 'sex in conflict with love; the strangeness of the other as a condition, a requirement, of sex; the ambiguous nature of sex: those aspects that are exciting and simultaneously repugnant; its terrible triviality, which in no way lessens its frightening power' (Kundera 1995:46).
9. The strategy of repetition functions on several different levels in the novel. Apart from the repetition of scenes, the text also presents forms of visual 'repetition' of parents in their children (Tereza and her mother, p. 42; Tomas and his son, p. 216). Most noticeably, there is a constant recurrence, like musical motifs, of certain phrases, words, or images.

14   Possessed by Language

1. All references are to the Vintage edition of the novel: London, 1991.

2. Another significant parallel with classic romance is that of the relationship between the poor young man (Alleyne, Tennyson's narrator and
Roland) and the aristocratic rich young woman (Lady Maude, Tennyson's Maud and Byatt's Maud).
3. In the light of Christabel's identification with Melusina, the crude
implications of Christabel's surname in French ('*la motte*' signifies the
female genitalia) may also be intentional.
4. Apropos of *The Virgin in the Garden* Byatt commented: 'In the *Virgin* I
wanted to substitute a female mythology for a male one. The male
mythology is the Dying God and Resurrection. The female one is birth
and Renaissance [...] I'm interested in Renaissance because things go
on being born' (quoted by Kenyon 1988:60).
5. The preoccupation with spirits and spiritism is an extension of the urge
towards beginnings – to such an extent, in fact, that the narrator herself
may be said to function as a *medium*, an 'instrument' through which
the characters may speak to us. Compare p. 395, where Ash, speaking
as writer, remarks, 'They speak to me too, through the medium of
language.'
6. Compare the persistent water imagery in descriptions of Melusina;
also of Maud's *hair*, on pp. 272 and 296.
7. The interplay of the 'real' and the 'artificial' is also a feature of the text.
Two random and revealing examples: on p. 83 Maud's face resembles
a painting by Latour; on p. 133 'the stained glass worked to defami-
liarise her'.
8. In an interview quoted by Kenyon (1988:55) Byatt commented that,
'When I'm describing love-making I'm not just interested in that couple, but in the genetic order of love-making.'
9. Other structuring repetitions/variations in the narrative concern
LaMotte's yearning for innocence, expressed in the image of clean
sheets, which recurs in both Roland's and Maud's minds; the strands
of hair interwoven in a brooch; the recurrent description of flowing
hair, and other images.
10. See Byatt's seminal essay 'Robert Browning: Fact, Fiction, Lies, Incar-
nation and Art' in which she expresses admiration for his ability, *inter
alia*, to see women 'as complex human beings, with their own minds
and desires, and hopes for dialogue' (Byatt 1991:30–1). Even more
relevant is her comment that Browning's work as a whole is 'a sustained attempt to embody and contemplate the problems which cen-
trally occupied the nineteenth-century European mind: the problems
of the relation of time to history, of science to religion, of fact in science
or history to fiction, of lies, in both, and of art to all of these' (p. 30).
11. It is significant, too, that in the spiritualist scene in *Possession*, both Ash
and LaMotte are reaching out, not towards a *father*, but towards a *child*:
and of course their 'real' offspring, in the text, is the twentieth-century
Maud.
12. The outcome of this performative interaction is *story*. One of the stories
by which Ash is most possessed is that of Balder, and of Hermodur's
journey to the Underworld to seek his release, 'an account of the
human mind imagining and inventing a human story to account for

the great and beautiful and terrible *limiting facts* of – existence' (p. 461). More than anything else, it is this perception of life, of reality itself, as story, which invites us to read *Possession* as a Postmodernist romance.

13. Once again, the name invites – if not demands – literalised reading. She is Ariadne who provides the thread with which to escape from the labyrinth; she is also the (male!) 'miner' (Le Minier) who brings hidden meanings to the surface.

14. Later, Roland will be depicted, in relation to Blanche Glover, Christabel LaMotte and Maud Bailey, and even Beatrice Nest, as 'an intruder into their female fastnesses' (p. 58).

15. One is reminded of the Queen of the Drowned City, who is closely associated with Melusina (p. 419).

16. This organising narrator has announced his/her presence on many occasions, and in many ways: in describing the reading sessions in the mansion, yet informing us that 'what they read will be discovered later' (p. 142); in presenting Sabine's journal while informing us that 'What they thought will be told later' (p. 335); or in choosing, throughout, *when* to divulge *what* information to the reader. In *Mummy Possest* we have been prepared to 'read' the narrator as *trickster* (p. 405).

15 The Pranks of Hermes

1. All references to the English version are to William Weaver's brilliant translation published by Secker & Warburg, London in 1981. References to the Italian text are to *Se una Notte d'Inverno un Viaggiatore*, Turin, Einaudi, 1979.

2. The felicities of the Italian language make it possible for Calvino to speak of *Il Lettore* and *La Lettrice*, which Weaver solves by using the terms *Reader* and *Other Reader*. Highlighting alterity is something of a gain, but it is a pity that the markers of gendering have to be sacrificed.

3. Unfortunately the translation misses an early opportunity of conveying this. On p. 9, just before the first chapter opens, the Reader is told that, even if he should hesitate, 'you go on and you realize *that the book is readable* nevertheless, independently of what you expected of the author' (my emphasis). In Italian, the crucial phrase is '*il libro si fa leggere*' (literally, 'the book lets itself be read'): Calvino 1979:9.

4. De Lauretis, on the other hand, argues that Calvino defeats the purpose of this 'itinerary toward silence' by presenting the reader with, 'not the impossibility of expression, the absence, the traces, the shredding and dissolution of language into silence, but instead the massive presence, the concrete materiality, the pressure, the multiplication of words and meanings' (de Lauretis 1987:81). But as I shall try to show later in this chapter, the accumulating materiality of language becomes, precisely, a sign of the urgency to cover up the void below: it is a sound and fury, signifying nothing.

5. In Italian, *un brusio di voci indistinte* (Calvino 1979:18), which is a perfect equivalent of Barthes's '*bruissement*'.

6. This happens in spite of Calvino's often stated wish for writer and reader to merge, to become one: 'It is true an ideal literature for each one of us: the end being that every one of us must be, that the writer and reader become one, or One' (quoted by Dipple 1988:98).

7. This is balanced by the opposite impulse: 'the first line of the first page of every novel refers to something that has already happened outside the book' (p. 153) – a remark just as applicable to Robbe-Grillet as to Calvino.

8. Each 'character' in the text (inasmuch as conventional terminology still applies) finds her/himself at an intersection of a number of discourses: this is why not one of them can ever be 'fixed' in a single identity.

9. 'I think of the postmodern attitude as that of a man who loves a very cultivated woman and knows he cannot say to her, "I love you madly", because he knows that she knows (and that she knows that he knows) that these words have already been written by Barbara Cartland. Still, there is a solution. He can say, "As Barbara Cartland would put it, I love you madly." At this point, having avoided false innocence, having said clearly that it is no longer possible to speak innocently, he will never-theless have said what he wanted to say to the woman: that he loves her, but he loves her in an age of lost innocence. If the woman goes along with this, she will have received a declaration of love all the same. Neither of the two speakers will feel innocent, both will have accepted the challenge of the past, of the already said, which cannot be elimi-nated; both will consciously and with pleasure play the game of irony [...] But both will have succeeded, once again, in speaking of love.' (Eco 1985b:68)

References

Alkon, Paul K. 1979: *Defoe and Fictional Time*. Athens: University of Georgia Press.

Alter, Jean 1966: *La Vision du monde d'Alain Robbe-Grillet*. Geneva: Librairie Droz.

Alter, Robert 1978 (1975): *Partial Magic*. Berkeley, Calif.: University of California Press.

Alter, Robert 1989: *The Pleasures of Reading in an Ideological Age*. New York: Touchstone (Simon & Schuster).

Apter, T. E. 1978: *Thomas Mann. The Devil's Advocate*. London: Macmillan.

Armstrong, Nancy & Tennenhouse, Leonard (eds) 1989: *The Violence of Representation*. London and New York: Routledge.

Ashcroft, Bill; Griffiths, Gareth & Tiffin, Helen 1989: *The Empire Writes Back*. London and New York: Routledge.

Atwood, Margaret 1972: *Survival. A Thematic Guide to Canadian Literature*. Toronto: Anansi.

Atwood, Margaret 1995 (1972): *Surfacing*. London: Virago.

Auerbach, Eric 1974 (1946): *Mimesis*. Princeton, New Jersey: Princeton University Press.

Auerbach, Nina 1986: *Romantic Imprisonment*. New York: Columbia University Press.

Austin, J. L. 1962: *How to do Things with Words*. New York: Oxford University Press.

Bachelard, Gaston 1957: *La Poétique de l'espace*. Paris: Presses Universitaires de France.

Bakhtin, M. M. (ed. Michael Holquist) 1981. *The Dialogic Imagination*. Austin: University of Texas Press.

Barnes, Julian 1985 (1984): *Flaubert's Parrot*. London: Jonathan Cape.

Barr, Marleen S. 1992: *Feminist Fabulation. Space/Postmodern Fiction*. Iowa City: University of Iowa Press.

Barthes, Roland (trans. Richard Howard) 1972 (1964): *Critical Essays*. Evanston: Northwestern University Press.

Barthes, Roland (trans. Richard Miller) 1975 (1970): *S/Z*. London: Jonathan Cape.

Barthes, Roland (trans. Richard Miller) 1976 (1975): *The Pleasure of the Text*. London: Jonathan Cape.

Barthes, Roland (trans. Richard Howard) 1979: *A Lover's Discourse*. London: Jonathan Cape.

Barthes, Roland 1982: Structural Analysis of Narratives. In: Sontag, Susan (ed.) 1982.

Barthes, Roland 1984: *Le Bruissement de la langue*. Paris: Seuil.

Barthes, Roland 1988: The Death of the Author. In: Lodge, David (ed.) 1988.

Bayley, John 1968: The 'Irresponsibility' of Jane Austen. In: Southam, B. C. (ed.) 1968.

Bell, Michael 1993: *Gabriel García Márquez. Solitude and Solidarity.* London: Macmillan.

Bernal, Olga 1974: *Alain Robbe-Grillet: le roman de l'absence.* Paris: Gallimard.

Blanchot, Maurice 1959: *Le Livre à venir.* Paris: Gallimard.

Blewett, David 1979. *Defoe's Art of Fiction.* Toronto: University of Toronto Press.

Bloom, Harold (ed.) 1979: *Deconstruction and Criticism.* London: Routledge & Kegan Paul.

Boardman, Michael 1983: *Defoe and the Uses of Narrative.* New Brunswick: Rutgers University Press.

Bollème, Geneviève 1979: L'Ecriture comme expérience-limite chez Rousseau et Flaubert. In: Carlut, Charles (ed.) 1979.

Booth, Wayne 1961: *The Rhetoric of Fiction.* Chicago and London: University of Chicago Press.

Borges, Jorge Luis 1972 (1964): *Labyrinths.* Harmondsworth: Penguin.

Bradbury, Malcolm 1962: Jane Austen's *Emma.* In: Lodge, David (ed.) 1968.

Bradbury, Malcolm & Palmer, David (eds) 1979: *The Contemporary English Novel.* London: Edward Arnold.

Brown, Lloyd W. 1976: The Business of Marrying and Mothering. In: McMaster, Juliet (ed.) 1976.

Buckley, Jerome H. (ed.) 1975: *The Worlds of Victorian Fiction.* Cambridge, Mass.: Harvard University Press.

Burden, Robert 1979: The Novel Interrogates Itself: Parody as Self-Consciousness in Contemporary English Fiction. In: Bradbury, Malcolm & Palmer, David (eds) 1979.

Butler, Marilyn 1976: *Jane Austen and the War of Ideas.* Oxford: Clarendon Press.

Butor, Michel 1984: *Improvisations sur Flaubert.* Paris: Editions de la Différence.

Byatt, A. S. 1979: People in Paper Houses: Attitudes to 'Realism' and 'Experiment' in English Postwar Fiction. In: Bradbury, Malcolm & Palmer, David (eds) 1979.

Byatt, A. S. 1991a (1990): *Possession. A Romance.* London: Chatto & Windus.

Byatt, A. S. 1991b: *Passions of the Mind.* London: Chatto & Windus.

Calvino, Italo 1979: *Se una notte d'inverno un viaggatore.* Turin: Einaudi.

Calvino, Italo (trans. William Weaver) 1981: *If on a Winter's Night a Traveller.* London: Secker & Warburg.

Campbell, Josie P. 1988: The Woman as Hero in Margaret Atwood's *Surfacing.* In: McCombs, Judith (ed.) 1988.

Carlut, Charles (ed.) 1979: *Essais sur Flaubert.* Paris: Editions A.-G. Nizet.

Cervantes de Saavedra, Miguel de (trans. J. M. Cohen) 1950 (1605, 1615): *The Adventures of Don Quixote de la Mancha.* Harmondsworth: Penguin.

Cervantes de Saavedra, Miguel de 1958 (1605, 1615): *El ingenioso hidalgo Don Quijote de la Mancha.* Madrid: Emecé.

Chabrol, Claude (ed.) 1973: *Sémiotique narrative et textuelle*. Paris: Larousse.

Chvatik, Kvetoslav 1995 (1994): *Le Monde romanesque de Milan Kundera*. Paris: Gallimard.

Cigada, Sergio 1989: Le Chapitre des comices et la structure de la double opposition dans *Madame Bovary*. In: Lecercle, F. & Messina, S. (eds) 1989.

Cixous, Hélène (trans. Keith and Paula Cohen) 1976 (1975): *The Laugh of the Medusa*. In: *Signs* I, Summer (pp. 875–99).

Close, A. J. 1990: *Miguel de Cervantes. Don Quixote*. Cambridge: Cambridge University Press.

Cluett, Robert 1983: Surface Structures: The Syntactic Profile of *Surfacing*. In: Grace, Sherrill & Weir, Lorraine (eds) 1983.

Cohn, Dorrit 1978: *Transparent Minds. Narrative Modes for Presenting Consciousness in Fiction*. Princeton, New Jersey: Princeton University Press.

Craik, W. A. 1979 (1965). *Jane Austen. The Six Novels*. London and New York: Methuen.

Day, Geoffrey 1987. *From Fiction to the Novel*. London and New York: Routledge & Kegan Paul.

Defoe, Daniel 1994 (1722): *Moll Flanders*. Harmondsworth: Penguin.

de Lattre, Alain 1980: *La Bêtise d'Emma Bovary*. Paris: Librairie José Corti.

de Lauretis, Teresa 1984: Desire in Narrative. In: *Alice Doesn't. Feminism Semiotics Cinema*. London: Macmillan.

de Lauretis, Theresa 1987: Calvino and the Amazons: Reading the (Post)-Modern Text. In: *Technologies of Gender*. Bloomington and Indianapolis: Indiana University Press.

Derrida, Jacques (trans. David B. Allison) 1973 (1967): *Speech and Phenomena, and Other Essays on Husserl's Theory of Signs*. Evanston: Northwestern University Press.

Derrida, Jacques (trans. Gayatri Chakravorty Spivak) 1976 (1967): *Of Grammatology*. Baltimore and London: Johns Hopkins University Press.

Derrida, Jacques 1977: *Limited Inc*. Baltimore and London: Johns Hopkins University Press.

Derrida, Jacques (trans. Alan Bass) 1978: *Writing and Difference*. London: Routledge & Kegan Paul.

Derrida, Jacques (trans. Barbara Johnson) 1981: *Dissemination*. London: Athlone Press.

Derrida, Jacques 1982: *L'Oreille de l'autre*. Montreal: VLB Editeur.

de Toro, Alfonso (ed.) 1987: *Gustave Flaubert. Procédés narratifs et fondements epistémologiques*. Tübingen: Gunter Narr Verlag.

Diamond, Arlyn & Edwards, Lee R. (eds) 1988 (1977): *The Authority of Experience. Essays in Feminist Literature*. Amherst: University of Massachusetts Press.

Diderot, Denis 1952: *Oeuvres*. Paris: Gallimard.

Diderot, Denis 1986 (1796): *Jacques the Fatalist and His Master*. Harmondsworth: Penguin.

Dipple, Elizabeth 1988: *The Unresolvable Plot*. New York and London: Routledge.

Donovan, Robert Alan 1969 (1966). The Two Heroines of *Moll Flanders*. In: Kelly, Edward (ed.) 1973.

Drechsel Tobin, Patricia 1978: *Time and the Novel. The Genealogical Imperative*. Princeton, New Jersey: Princeton University Press.

Duchet, Claude 1976: Discours social en texte italique dans *Madame Bovary*. In: Issacharoff, M. (ed.) 1976.

DuPlessis, Rachel Blau 1985: *Writing beyond the Ending*. Bloomington: Indiana University Press.

du Preez, P. 1991: Polyphonic Beings. In: *A Science of Mind*. London and San Diego: Academic Press.

During, Simon 1992: Madness. In: *Foucault and Literature*. London and New York: Routledge.

Eagleton, Terry 1983: *Literary Theory*. Minneapolis: University of Minnesota Press.

Earle, Peter 1976. *The World of Defoe*. London: Weidenfeld & Nicolson.

Eco, Umberto 1979 (1976): *A Theory of Semiotics*. Bloomington: Indiana University Press.

Eco, Umberto 1985a: Innovation and Repetition: Between Modern and Postmodern Aesthetics. In: *Daedalus* vol. 114:4 (pp.161–84)

Eco, Umberto 1985b: *Reflections on* The Name of the Rose. London: Secker & Warburg.

Elam, Diane 1992: *Romancing the Postmodern*. London and New York: Routledge.

Eliot, George 1965. *Middlemarch*. Harmondsworth: Penguin.

Erasmus of Rotterdam (trans. Betty Radice) 1971 (1511): *The Praise of Folly*. Harmondsworth: Penguin.

Farrar, Janet & Stewart 1987: *The Witches' Goddess*. London: Robert Hale.

Fish, Stanley 1976: How to do Things with Austin and Searle: Speech Act Theory and Literary Criticism. In: *Modern Language Notes* vol. 91 (pp. 983–1025).

Flaubert, Gustave 1983 (1857): *Madame Bovary*. In: *Oeuvres* (ed. A. Thibaudet & R. Dumesnil). Paris: Gallimard.

Flaubert, Gustave (trans. Alan Russell) 1983 (1950): *Madame Bovary*. Harmondsworth: Penguin.

Fleishman, Arrom 1983: Two Faces of Emma. In: Todd, Janet (ed.) 1983.

Fokkema, Douwe 1984: *Literary History, Modernism and Postmodernism*. Amsterdam and Philadelphia: John Benjemans.

Fokkema, Douwe & Ibsch, Elrud 1988: *Modernist Conjectures. A Mainstream in European Literature 1910–1940*. New York: St Martin's Press.

Foucault, Michel 1977 (1966): *The Order of Things*. London: Tavistock.

Foucault, Michel (ed. P. Rabinow) 1984: *The Foucault Reader*. Harmondsworth: Penguin.

Foucault, Michel (trans. Richard Howard) 1985 (1961): *Madness and Civilisation. A History of Insanity in the Age of Reason*. London: Tavistock.

Fowler, Roger 1977: *Linguistics and the Novel*. London: Methuen.

Freud, Sigmund (trans. James Strachey) 1974: *The Standard Edition of the Complete Psychological Works of Sigmund Freud* vol. 24. London: Hogarth.

Frey, Gerhard Walter 1987: Héloïse Dubuc – une interprétation de *Madame Bovary* dans la perspective de l'histoire des mentalités. In: de Toro, Alfonso (ed.) 1987.

Fuentes, Carlos 1990 (1988): *Myself with Others*. New York: Noonday Press (Farrar, Strauss & Giroux).

Garnham, B. G. 1982: London: Grant & Cutler Ltd.

Genette, Gérard (trans. Jane E. Lewin) 1980: *Narrative Discourse*. Oxford: Blackwell.

Gengembre, Gérard 1990: *Gustave Flaubert*. Madame Bovary. Paris: Presses Universitaires de France.

Gilbert, Sandra M. & Gubar, Susan 1984 (1979): *The Madwoman in the Attic*. New Haven and London: Yale University Press.

González, Aníbal 1987: Translation and Genealogy: *One Hundred Years of Solitude*. In: McGuirk, Bernard & Cardwell, Richard 1987.

Grace, Sherrill and Weir, Lorraine (eds) 1983: *Margaret Atwood. Language, Text and System*. Vancouver: University of British Columbia Press.

Gray, Ronald (ed.) 1962: *Kafka. (Twentieth-Century Views)*. Englewood Cliffs: Prentice-Hall.

Gray, Ronald 1973: *Franz Kafka*. Cambridge: Cambridge University Press.

Greimas, A. J. 1973: Les Actants, les acteurs et les figures. In: Chabrol, Claude (ed.) 1973.

Gribbin, John 1984: *In Search of Schrödinger's Cat. The Startling World of Quantum Physics Explained*. London: Wildwood House.

Griffith, Margaret 1979: Verbal Terrain in the Novels of Margaret Atwood. In: *Critique. Studies in Modern Fiction* vol. XXI:3 (pp 85–93).

Hägg, Thomas 1983 (1980): *The Novel in Antiquity*. Oxford: Blackwell.

Harari, Josué V. (ed.) 1979: *Textual Strategies. Perspectives in Post-structuralist Criticism*. London: Methuen.

Hardy, Barbara 1975: *Tellers and Listeners*. London Athlone Press.

Hardy, Barbara 1976: Properties and Possessions in Jane Austen's Novels. In: McMaster, Juliet (ed.) 1976.

Hassan, Ihab 1987: *The Postmodern Turn. Essays in Postmodern Theory and Culture*. Michigan: Ohio State University Press.

Hatfield, Henry (ed.) 1964: *Thomas Mann. A Collection of Critical Essays*. Englewood Cliffs: Prentice-Hall.

Hazlitt, William 1973 (1830). Meddling with the Unclean Thing. In: Kelly, Edward (ed.) 1973.

Hegel, G. W. F. (trans. A. V. Miller) 1977: Lordship and Bondage. In: *Phenomenology of Spirit*. Oxford: Clarendon Press.

Heidegger, Martin (trans. Albert Hofstadter) 1971: *Poetry, Language, Thought*. New York: Harper & Row.

Heiserman, Arthur 1980 (1977): *The Novel before the Novel*. Chicago and London: University of Chicago Press.

Heller, Erich 1958: *The Ironic German*. London: Secker & Warburg.

Hermans, Hubert J. M., Kempen, Harry J.G. & van Loon, Rens J. P. 1992: The Dialogical Self. Beyond Individualism and Rationalism. In: *American Psychologist* vol 47:1, January (pp. 23–33).

Hoban, Russell 1977: Introduction to *Household Tales of the Brothers Grimm.* London: Picador.

Hofstadter, Douglas R. 1980: *Gödel, Escher, Bach: An Eternal Golden Braid.* Harmondsworth: Penguin.

Hulme, Peter 1986: *Colonial Encounters. Europe and the Native Caribbean 1492–1797.* London and New York: Routledge.

Hutcheon, Linda 1980: *Narcissistic Narrative.* New York and London: Methuen.

Hutcheon, Linda 1988: *The Canadian Postmodern.* Toronto: Oxford University Press.

Issacharoff, M. (ed.) 1976: *Langages de Flaubert.* Paris: Minard.

Jakobson, Roman 1960: Closing Statement: Linguistics and Poetics. In: Sebeok, Thomas A. (ed.) 1960.

Janvier, Ludovic 1964: *Une Parole exigeante.* Paris: Editions du Minuit.

Jauss, Hans Robert 1970: *Literaturgeschichte als Provokation.* Frankfurt: Suhrkamp.

Jefferson, Ann 1980: *The Nouveau Roman and the Poetics of Fiction.* Cambridge: Cambridge University Press.

Johnson, Claudia L. 1988: *Jane Austen. Women, Politics and the Novel.* Chicago and London: Chicago University Press.

Jones, Ann Rosalind 1981: Writing the Body: Toward an Understanding of l'Ecriture Feminine. In: *Feminist Studies* vol. 7:1, Summer.

Josipovici, Gabriel 1971: *The World and the Book. A Study of Modern Fiction.* London: Macmillan.

Kafka, Franz (trans. Willa and Edwin Muir) 1962 (1926): *The Castle.* Harmondsworth: Penguin Modern Classics.

Kafka, Franz (ed. Willy Haas) 1967 (1953): *Letters to Milena.* London: Corgi Books.

Kafka, Franz 1990: *Der Prozess.* Frankfurt: S. Fischer.

Kafka, Franz (trans. Idris Parry) 1976 (1925): *The Trial.* Harmondsworth: Penguin.

Kaplan, Deborah 1992: *Jane Austen among Women.* Baltimore and London: Johns Hopkins University Press.

Kelly, Edward (ed.) 1973: *Daniel Defoe: Moll Flanders.* New York: Norton and Company.

Kelly, Kristine 1993: *The Responsibility of Re-form: Robbe-Grillet's* Le Voyeur. Unpublished seminar paper in the MA Literary Studies Programme: University of Cape Town.

Kenyon, Olga 1988: *Women Novelists Today.* Brighton: Harvester Press.

Kermode, Frank 1966: *The Sense of an Ending.* London: Oxford University Press.

Kettle, Arnold 1951: Emma. In: Lodge, David (ed.) 1968.

Kettle, Arnold 1969 (1964). In Defence of *Moll Flanders.* In: Kelly, Edward (ed.) 1973.

Kristeva, Julia (ed. Léon S. Roudiez) 1980: *Desire in Language.* New York Columbia University Press.

Kristeva, Julia 1986: Women's Time. In: Moi, Toril (ed.) 1986.

Kroeber, Karl 1975: Subverting a Hypocrite Lecteur. In: Weinsheimer, Joel (ed.) 1975.

Kroetsch, Robert 1989: *The Lovely Treachery of Words*. Toronto: Oxford University Press.

Kundera, Milan (trans. Michael Henry Heim) 1984: *The Unbearable Lightness of Being*. London and Boston: Faber & Faber.

Kundera, Milan (trans. Linda Asher) 1988 (1986): *The Art of the Novel*. London and Boston: Faber & Faber.

Kundera, Milan (trans. Linda Asher) 1995 (1993): *Testaments Betrayed*. London and Boston: Faber & Faber.

Lacan, Jacques (trans. Alan Sheridan) 1977: *Écrits. A Selection*. London: Tavistock.

Lacan, Jacques (trans. Sylvana Tomaselli; ed. Jacques-Alain Miller) 1991a and 1991b: *The Seminar of Jacques Lacan*. Book I and Book II. New York and London: Norton and Company.

Lafayette, Madame de 1983 (1678): *La Princesse de Clèves*. Paris: Le Livre de Poche.

Lafayette, Madame de (trans. Robin Buss) 1992 (1678): *The Princesse de Clèves*. Harmondsworth: Penguin.

Lecercle, F. & Messina, S. (eds) 1989: *Flaubert, l'autre*. Lyon: Presses Universitaires.

Lee, Alison 1990: *Realism and Power. Postmodern British Fiction*. London and New York: Routledge.

Lehnert, Herbert 1968: *Thomas Mann – Fiktion, Mythos, Religion*. Stuttgart: W. Kohlhammer Verlag.

Lerenbaum, Miriam 1977. Moll Flanders: 'A Woman on her Own Account'. In: Diamond, Arlyn & Edwards, Lee R. (eds) 1988.

Lerner, Laurence 1967: *The Truthtellers. Jane Austen. George Eliot. D.H. Lawrence*. New York: Schocken Books.

Llosa, Mario Vargas (trans. Albert Bensoussan) 1978 (1975): *L'Orgie perpétuelle. Flaubert et* Madame Bovary. Paris: Gallimard.

Llosa, Mario Vargas (trans. Heler R. Lane) 1983 (1977): *Aunt Julia and the Scriptwriter*. London: Faber & Faber.

Lodge, David 1966: *Language of Fiction*. London: Routledge & Kegan Paul.

Lodge, David (ed.) 1968: *Jane Austen:* Emma. *A Casebook*. London Macmillan.

Lodge, David (ed.) 1988: *Modern Criticism and Theory*. London: Longman.

Lodge, David 1990: *After Bakhtin*. London and New York: Routledge.

Lodge, David 1991: *Middlemarch* and the Idea of the Classic Realist Text. In: Newton, K. M. (ed.) 1991.

Loftus, Elizabeth & Ketcham, Katherine 1994: *The Myth of Repressed Memory*. New York: St Martin's Press.

MacCabe, Colin 1978: *James Joyce and the Revolution of the Word*. London: Macmillan.

MacCabe, Colin 1991: The End of a Metalanguage: From George Eliot to *Dubliners*. In: Newton, K. M. (ed.) 1991.

Macherey, Pierre (trans. Geoffrey Wall) 1978 (1966): *A Theory of Literary Production*. London: Routledge & Kegan Paul.

Mann, Thomas 1954 (1912): *Der Tod in Venedig*. Frankfurt and Hamburg: Fischer Bücherei.

Mann, Thomas (trans. H. T. Lowe-Porter) 1980 (1912): *Death in Venice*. Harmondsworth: Penguin.

Mariscal, George 1989: The Other Quixote. In: Armstrong, Nancy and Tennenhouse, Leonard (eds) 1989.

Márquez, Gabriel García 1978 (1967): *Cien años de soledad*. Madrid: Mondadori.

Márquez, Gabriel García (trans. Gregory Rabassa) 1978 (1967): *One Hundred Years of Solitude*. London: Picador.

Martin, Gerald 1987: On 'Magical' and Social Realism in García Márquez. In: McGuirk, Bernard and Cardwell, Richard 1987.

Mayoux, Jean-Jacques 1936: Diderot and the Techniques of Modern Literature. In: *Modern Language Review* vol. 31:4 (pp. 518–31)

McCombs, Judith (ed.) 1988: *Critical Essays on Margaret Atwood*. Boston: G. K. Hall and Co.

McEwan, Ian 1984: An Interview with Milan Kundera. In: *Granta* 11.

McGee, Patrick 1988: *Paperspace. Style as Ideology in Joyce's* Ulysses. Lincoln and London: University of Nebraska Press.

McGuirk, Bernard and Cardwell, Richard 1987: *Gabriel García Márquez. New Readings*. Cambridge: Cambridge University Press.

McKeon, Michael 1987: Cervantes and the Disenchantment of the World. In: *Origins of the English Novel 1600–1740*. Baltimore and London: Johns Hopkins University Press.

McMaster, Juliet 1975: Love and Pedagogy. In: Weinsheimer, Joel (ed.) 1975.

McMaster, Juliet (ed.) 1976: *Jane Austen's Achievement*. London: Macmillan.

McMurray, George R. 1977: *Gabriel García Márquez*. New York: Frederick Ungar Publishing Co.

Miller, D. A. 1991: George Eliot: 'The Wisdom of Balancing Claims' (*Middlemarch*). In: Newton, K. M. (ed.) 1991.

Miller, Henry 1957: *Tropic of Capricorn*. Paris: Olympia Press.

Miller, J. Hillis 1975: Optic and Semiotic in *Middlemarch*. In: Buckley, Jerome H. (ed.) 1975.

Miller, J. Hillis 1979: The Critic as Host. In: Bloom, Harold (ed.) 1979.

Miller, Nancy K. 1950: *The Heroine's Text. Readings in the French and English Novel, 1722–1782*. New York: Columbia University Press.

Mills, Sara et al. 1989: *Feminist Readings/Feminists Reading*. Charlottesville: University Press of Virginia.

Minta, Stephen 1987: *Gabriel García Márquez: Writer of Colombia*. London: Jonathan Cape.

Misurella, Fred 1993: *Understanding Milan Kundera*. Columbia: University of South Carolina Press.

Moi, Toril 1985: *Sexual/Textual Politics*. London and New York: Routledge.

Moi, Toril (ed.) 1986: *The Kristeva Reader*. Oxford: Blackwell.

Monod, Jacques (trans. Austryn Wainhouse) 1979 (1970): *Chance and Necessity. An Essay on the Natural Philosophy of Modern Biology.* Glasgow: Collins.

Morrissette, Bruce 1963: *Les Romans de Robbe-Grillet.* Paris: Editions du Minuit.

Mudrick, Marvin 1952: Irony as Form: *Emma.* In: Lodge, David (ed.) 1968.

Mudrick, Marvin 1968: *Jane Austen. Irony as Defense and Discovery.* Berkeley and Los Angeles: University of California Press.

Musil, Robert 1952: *Der Mann ohne Eigenschaften.* Hamburg: Rowohlt.

Nelson, Lowry (ed.) 1969: *Cervantes. A Collection of Critical Essays.* Englewood Cliffs: Prentice-Hall.

Newton, K. M. 1981: *George Eliot: Romantic Humanist. A Study of the Philosophical Structure of her Novels.* London: Macmillan.

Newton, K. M. (ed.) 1991: *George Eliot.* London and New York: Longman.

Ngugi wa Thiong'o 1986: *Decolonising the Mind.* London: James Currey.

Nicklas, Hans W. 1968: *Thomas Mann's Novelle 'Der Tod in Venedig': Analyse des Motivzusammenhangs und der Erzählstruktur.* Marburg: Elwert.

Nicolai, Ralf R. 1986: *Kafka's 'Prozess'. Motive und Gestalten.* Würzburg: Künigshausen & Neumann.

Novak, Maximilian E. 1962. *Economics and the Fiction of Daniel Defoe.* Berkeley and Los Angeles: University of California Press.

Ohmann, R. 1971: Speech Acts and the Definition of Literature. In *Philosophy and Rhetoric* vol. 4 (pp. 1–19).

Pascal, Roy 1982: *Kafka's Narrators.* Cambridge: Cambridge University Press.

Pearce, Lynne & Mills, Sara 1989: Marxist-Feminism. In: Mills, Sara et al. 1989.

Piercy, Marge 1988: Margaret Atwood: Beyond Victimhood. In: McCombs, Judith (ed.) 1988.

Poovey, Mary 1984: *The Proper Lady and the Woman Writer. Ideology as Style in the Works of Mary Wollstonecraft, Mary Shelley and Jane Austen.* Chicago and London: University of Chicago Press.

Pratt, Marie-Louise 1977: *Towards a Speech Act Theory of Literary Discourse.* Bloomington: University of Indiana Press.

Prince, Gerald 1982: *Narratology. The Form and Functioning of Narrative.* Berlin: Mouton Publishers.

Rault, E. 1975: *Théorie et expérience romanesque chez Robbe-Grillet:* Le Voyeur. Paris: La Pensée Universelle.

Ray, William 1990. *Story and History.* Oxford: Blackwell.

Richetti, John 1975. *Defoe's Narratives. Situations and Structures.* Oxford: Clarendon Press.

Rigney, Barbara Hill 1987: *Margaret Atwood.* London: Macmillan.

Riley, E. C. 1962: *Cervantes's Theory of the Novel.* Oxford: Clarendon Press.

Robbe-Grillet, Alain 1955: *Le Voyeur.* Paris: Editions du Minuit.

Robbe-Grillet, Alain (trans. Richard Howard) 1958: *The Voyeur.* New York: Grove Press.

Robbe-Grillet, Alain 1961: *L'Année dernière à Marienbad*. Paris: Editions du Minuit.

Robbe-Grillet, Alain 1963: *Pour un nouveau roman*. Paris: Editions du Minuit.

Robert, Marthe 1980 (1972): *Origins of the Novel*. Brighton: Harvester Press.

Rolleston, James (ed.) 1976: *Twentieth Century Interpretations of* The Trial. Englewood Cliffs: Prentice-Hall.

Salzman, Paul 1986: *English Prose Fiction 1558–1700*. Oxford: Clarendon Press.

Saussure, Ferdinand de (trans. Wade Baskin) 1959: *Course in General Linguistics*. New York: McGraw-Hill.

Schechner, Richard 1983: News, Sex and and Performance Theory. In: Lee, Alison 1990.

Scherrer, Paul & Wysling, Hans 1967: *Quellenkritische Studien zum Werk Thomas Manns*. Bern and Munich: Francke Verlag.

Searle, J.R. 1969: *Speech Acts: An Essay in the Philosophy of Language*. Cambridge: Cambridge University Press.

Searle, J.R. 1974: The Logical Status of Fictional Discourse. In: *New Literary History* vol. 6:2 (pp. 319–32).

Sebeok, Thomas A. (ed.) 1960: *Style in Language*. Cambridge, Mass.: M.I.T. Press.

Shukman, Ann (ed.) 1983: *Bakhtin School Papers. Russian Poetics in Translation No. 10*. Oxford: Holdan Books.

Shuttleworth, Sally 1984: *Middlemarch*: An Experiment in Time. In: *George Eliot and Nineteenth-Century Science*. Cambridge: Cambridge University Press.

Sontag, Susan (ed.) 1982: *A Barthes Reader*. London: Jonathan Cape.

Southam, B. C. (ed.) 1968: *Critical Essays on Jane Austen*. London: Routledge & Kegan Paul.

Spaull, Sue 1989: Gynocriticism. In: Mills, Sara et al. 1989.

Spender, Dale 1986: *Mothers of the Novel*. London and New York: Pandora.

Starr, G. A. 1971. *Defoe and Casuistry*. Princeton, New Jersey: Princeton University Press.

Stokes, Myra 1991: *The Language of Jane Austen*. London: Macmillan.

Stoltzfus, Ben F. 1964: *Alain Robbe-Grillet and the New French Novel*. Carbondale: Southern Illinois University Press.

Sturrock, John 1969: *The French New Novel*. London: Oxford University Press.

Thibaudet, A. 1935: *Gustave Flaubert*. Paris: Gallimard.

Thiher, Allen 1984. *Words in Reflection. Modern Language Theory and Postmodern Fiction*. Chicago and London, University of Chicago Press.

Thompson, E. P. 1975. *Whigs and Hunters*. London: Allen Lane.

Todd, Janet (ed.) 1983: *Jane Austen. New Perspectives*. New York and London: Holmes & Meier.

Todorov, Tzvetan 1977. *The Poetics of Prose*. Oxford: Blackwell.

Tong, Rosemarie 1989: *Feminist Thought*. Boulder and San Francisco: Westview Press.

Valency, Maurice 1966: *The Breaking String. The Plays of Anton Chekhov*. New York: Oxford University Press.

Van Ghent, Dorothy 1961 (1953). *The English Novel. Form and Function*. New York: Harper & Row.

Vareille, Jean Claude 1981: *Alain Robbe-Grillet l'étrange*. Paris: A.-G. Nizet.

von Gronicka, André 1964: Myth Plus Psychology: A Stylistic Analysis of *Death in Venice*. In: Hatfield, Henry (ed.) 1964.

Watt, Ian 1963 (1957). *The Rise of the Novel*. Harmondsworth: Penguin.

Weil-Malherbe, R. 1965: '*Le Voyeur* de Robbe-Grillet: un cas d'epilepsie psycho-moteur'. In: *French Review* vol. XXXVIII:4 (pp. 469–76).

Weiner, S. S. 1962: A Look at Techniques and Meanings in Robbe-Grillet's *Voyeur*. In: *Modern Language Quarterly* vol. XXIII (pp. 217–24).

Weinsheimer, Joel (ed.) 1975: *Jane Austen Today*. Athens: The University of Georgia Press.

Williamson, Edwin 1987: Magical Realism and the Theme of Incest in *One Hundred Years of Solitude*. In: McGuirk, Bernard & Cardwell, Richard 1987.

Wittgenstein, Ludwig (trans. C. G. Ogden) 1983 (1921): *Tractatus Logico-Philosophicus*. London: Routledge & Kegan Paul.

Wood, Michael 1990: Gabriel García Márquez: *One Hundred Years of Solitude*. Cambridge: Cambridge University Press.

Woolf, Virginia 1919: Defoe. In: Kelly, Edward (ed.) 1973.

Index